Praise for Ira Berkow

"Ira Berkow is one of the great American writers, without limitation to the field of sports. His writing is agile, clever, and sparked by observation of perfect details."—Scott Turow

"With the keen eye of a reporter, the literary touch of a highly skilled writer, and above all a feel for the humanity in every story, Ira takes his readers to a place beyond and above what even competent sports writing generally delivers."—Bob Costas

"I follow Ira Berkow in the *Times* with unfailing interest."—Saul Bellow

"Ira Berkow over the years has regularly given us sports writing of the most elegant kind—his work glistens with intelligence and sensitivity." —David Halberstam

"Sports at its best is a kind of music and sports writing is a kind of libretto. Ira Berkow is among the best—a Sondheim of the sports page."—George Will

"Ira Berkow belongs to that rare breed personified by the late Red Smith: a writer who specializes in sports but whose subjects represent a broad range in human aspiration and challenges."—Gay Talese

"Ira Berkow is a master of his craft."—Studs Terkel

"If there is anyone doing sports who is even close, I haven't read him."
—Mike Royko

Praise for *How Life Imitates Sports*

"Berkow is a clear-eyed observer with a great ear and a stylish way with words. That is why he is one of the rare sportswriters who attracted the praise and admiration of *literary* writers."—Rick Kogan, *Chicago Tribune*

"What Berkow offers is a smorgasbord of sports' greatest entertainers. Each page is a consistency of excitement and enlightenment."—Don Laible, WBIX-AM contributing sportswriter

Praise for *Beyond the Dream: Occasional Heroes of Sports Occasional*

"Ira Berkow gets inside people. It can be stated as a law that the sports writer whose horizons are no wider than the outfield fences is a bad sports writer because he has no sense of proportion and no awareness of the real world around him. Ira Berkow knows that what is important about a game is not the score but the people who play it."
—Red Smith, from the foreword to *Beyond the Dream*

"Wrapped together in this neat package, (these pieces) show Berkow as an astute observer of the national scene. . . . The best of these stories are as good as any ever written."—Rick Kogan, *Chicago Sun-Times*

"Atypcal sports stories—pithy human interest vignettes with the focus on the athlete rather than his performance."—*Kirkus Reviews*

Praise for *Rockin' Steady: A Guide to Basketball and Cool* (by Walt Frazier and Ira Berkow)

"I read *Rockin' Steady* with my date—Diane Keaton—in a Chinese restaurant. We laughed all the way through. It was brilliant and charming and very funny. We had a great time with it."—Woody Allen

"*Rockin' Steady* has kept me steady for several days and I have been enjoying it, particularly since I had never heard of Clyde (I live a sheltered life)."—E. B. White

"I bought the book when I was twelve years old. I loved all the fashion stuff and how to catch flies with your bare hands."—President Barack Obama (as told to Ira Berkow)

"This is a departure from the standard book by the standard sports hero. Walt Frazier, generally known as Clyde, is a different sports hero, and with the writing help of Ira Berkow, he has put together a sparkling and delightful book."—*The Sporting News*

"*Rockin' Steady* isn't just pretty good. It's fantastic. . . . I've never read anything like it."—Eric Neel, ESPN.com

Praise for *The Corporal Was a Pitcher*

"Gripping and inspiring."—*Sports Illustrated*

"A fantastic book—great reporting, great writing."—Mel Antonen, *USA Today*

"Whether you are interested in military history, baseball history or simply the story of a man who conquered great odds to achieve more than could be normally expected, you must read this book."—Gary Bedingfield, *World War II Baseball Book Reviews*

Praise for *It Happens Every Spring: DiMaggio, Mays, The Splendid Splinter, and a Lifetime at the Ballpark*

"(As much as portraits of the major personalities) it's the little moments Berkow recounts . . . that make the book sing."—*Sports Illustrated*

Praise for *Maxwell Street: Survival in a Bazaar*

"The book is a grand portrait gallery, and in its way a historical treasure . . . There are as well pocket manuals of the hard-sell and terrific picaresque stories and scenes."—Richard Stern, *New York Times Sunday Book Review*

"An urban classic."—William Braden, *Chicago Sun-Times*

Praise for *Red: A Biography of Red Smith*

"Red Smith (is) . . . the subject of Ira Berkow's skillful biography." —Wilfred Sheed, the *New York Times Book Review*

"*Red* is a terrific book, and a fine tribute to one of the best writers of our time."—Peter Delacorte, *San Francisco Chronicle Sunday Book Review*

"A warm and revealing portrait."—*Publishers Weekly*

Praise for *Court Vision: Unexpected Views on the Lure of Basketball*

"Wonderful reading."—*Booklist*

"Each of the contributors (from Saul Bellow to Julia Child to Secretary of Defense William Cohen to Donald Trump to Walter Matthau to Sharon Stone) gives a different, nuanced, and intriguing look at the game."—*Library Journal*

Praise for *Pitchers Do Get Lonely: And Other Sports Stories*

"Ira Berkow is simply one of America's best writers, sports or otherwise."—Jim Bouton

"Ira Berkow goes where the story is, and when thre isn't one clearly visible on any given day, he digs all that much deeper."—Daniel Okrent, *USA Today*

Praise for *To the Hoop: The Seasons of a Basketball Life*

"An extraordinary look into the art of pickup basketball. Who would have guess that, along with his writing talents, Ira knows how to play the game!"—Bill Bradley

"A fine book by a fine writer and a wise man."—*Booklist*

"Ira Berkow is one of the best sportswriters around, so it is no surprise that his basketball odyssey is one of the best sports books of this or any other year. . . . Very few sports columnists have the genius to produce a timely piece that is also timeless. Ira Berkow has that ability in spades."—George Plimpton

"It is rare for a sportswriter to illuminate more than scores and statistics and stadiums, and that is what makes Ira Berkow such a pleasant anomaly. More than anything he wants to know how the cultural environment . . . influences particular sports and athletes, and what the effect is."—*Street and Smith's* magazine.

Praise for *The Man Who Robbed the Pierre: The Story of Bobby Comfort and the Greatest Hotel Robbert Ever*

"Ira Berkow has written a delectable book about a thief that's full of drama and tension, more exciting than most fictional thrillers."—David Holahan, *Chicago Tribune*

"Ira Berkow has thoroughly documented the 'inside' story of this robbery and its mastermind . . . Berkow recounts in plain but sturdy prose how Comfort grew up. . . . The narrative retains its dramatic edge in the final third of the book as Berkow tracks the all-out police and FBI investigations."—Stuart Rohrer, *Washington Post*

"A fast-paced rump through the life of an engaging yegg."—*Kirkus Reviews*

Nominated Best Fact Crime, Edgar Allan Poe Awards, Mystery Writers of America, 1988.

Praise for *Giants Among Men: Y.A., L.T., the Big Tuna and Other New York Giants Stories*

"Berkow is a stylish and often lyrical writer, and he's an even better observer."—*Booklist* (starred review)

Praise for *The DunSable Panthers: The Greatest, Blackest, Saddest Team from the Meansest Meanest Streets in Chicago*

" . . . Guided by black coach Jim Brown, [the all-black team] broke down a color barrier in reaching the Illinois state basketball finals. . . . Berkow captures, through excellent play-by-play descriptions, the tense excitement of the final clash. A vividly written, pointed sports replay . . ."—*Booklist*

"A 'brilliant book.'"—Barry Temkin, *Chicago Tribune*

"Ira Berkow's *DuSable Panthers*, Rick Telander's *Heaven is a Playground*, and Marty Ralbovsky's *Destiny's Darlings* stand as superior studies of the impact of sports on the lives of young persons."—*Journal of Sports History*, Vol. 5 No. 3, Winter 1978

Praise for *Counterpunch: Ali, Tyson, The Brown Bomber and Other Stories of the Boxing Ring*

Winner, the A. J. Liebling Award for Outstanding Boxing Writing, the Boxing Writers Association of America.

". . . Boxing was a perfect subject for Ira Berkow's gifts. No other sport offers so many characters, so much color, so much drama, so few scruples, so many tragic endings. This is the raw material that Berkow so ingeniously molded into classics. . . . Nobody covered the fight game with more artistry and insight, with more compassion and humor, than he did."—Jeremy Schaap, from the foreword.

BASEBALL'S BEST EVER

BASEBALL'S BEST EVER

A HALF CENTURY OF COVERING HALL OF FAMERS

IRA BERKOW

SPORTS
PUBLISHING

Sports Publishing books may be purchased in bulk at special discounts for sales promotion, corporate gifts, fund-raising, or educational purposes. Special editions can also be created to specifications. For details, contact the Special Sales Department, Sports Publishing, 307 West 36th Street, 11th Floor, New York, NY 10018 or sportspubbooks@skyhorsepublishing.com.

Sports Publishing® is a registered trademark of Skyhorse Publishing, Inc.®, a Delaware corporation.

Visit our website at www.sportspubbooks.com.

10 9 8 7 6 5 4 3 2 1

Library of Congress Cataloging-in-Publication Data is available on file.

Jacket design by Kai Texel
Jacket photographs: Getty Images

Print ISBN: 978-1-68358-445-2
Ebook ISBN: 978-1-68358-446-9

Printed in the United States of America

For Dakota

Table of Contents

Foreword:
On Visits to the Hall

As both a sports reporter and sports columnist, first for the national feature syndicate Newspaper Enterprise Association, and later the *New York Times*, I traveled to Cooperstown on numerous occasions to cover the weekend Induction Ceremonies at the National Baseball Hall of Fame and Museum for recently elected retired players.

The setting, in the pastoral village in central New York State, and near the sparkling Lake Otsego, gave one a chance to intermingle with the players, the new Hall of Famers as well as the several dozen who had been previously elected, in a relaxed and invariably upbeat circumstance.

They gather in twos or threes or more whether in the antebellum, white-columned Otesaga Hotel where the players are domiciled, or on the quaint, broad five-block-long Main Street, scattered with baseball memorabilia stores and lined with elm and horse chestnut trees (no fast-food chains allowed) or in the Hall itself, particularly on the Friday night when only the Hall of Famers and family and reporters are allowed in, and in which they may cruise the three floors of artifacts and the first-floor area where the plaques honoring the players are hung.

I was in the hotel lobby when a reporter came up to Yogi Berra and asked him to sign a baseball, but with his full name, "Lawrence Peter Berra." Yogi took the ball and pen from the man and paused. He looked up and said, "I haven't signed 'Lawrence Peter Berra' in such a long time, I've forgotten how to spell it."

I was walking down Main Street with pitching great Bob Feller one day and talking baseball. But at that time, the biggest news of the day was the mystery surrounding O. J. Simpson and the murders of his former wife and a male friend. As we were about to cross the street, and following perhaps discussions on hurling against a Williams or a DiMaggio, I said out of the blue, "Bob, what do you think? Did O. J. do it?" He was slightly taken aback at the abrupt change in topics, and momentarily paused. "Well," he said, emphatically, "if he didn't do it, who did?!"

The gray-haired DiMaggio, in tailored suit and natty tie, ever elegant even when munching on a cluster of grapes from the food table in the cathedral-like Plaque Gallery of the Hall on a Friday night, was seated not far from his bronze plaque. The plaque highlighted his still-existing record of hitting in 56 straight games. I asked him about that record. The streak was stopped in Cleveland, he recalled, in the summer of 1941, some forty years previous. The one-time Joltin' Joe said that the strangest encounter occurred a few years ago in Cleveland with a man who said he once was a taxi driver in town. It had often been written that on the day DiMaggio's streak ended, the cabbie driving him to the game in Cleveland that morning predicted he would go hitless.

Yankees pitcher Lefty Gomez, Joe's roommate, immediately gave the cabbie hell, Joe said, and then pulled DiMaggio out of the taxi. The two walked the rest of the way to Municipal Stadium. "Now, this happened over thirty years ago when I ran into the man in front of the hotel I was staying in in Cleveland.

"And the guy is very serious. He apologized. Well, my God, I felt awful. I mean, he thought he might have been spending his life thinking he had jinxed me. But I told him he hadn't. My number was up, was all."

One Friday night I was looking at the exhibits on the third floor and came across a life-sized cardboard cutout of New York Giants center fielder Willie Mays making that famous, amazing over-the-shoulder catch on Vic Wertz's drive in the 1954 World Series. When I walked back down to the second floor, there in a business suit was, of all people, the real Willie Mays, looking at the exhibits. I said to him, "What are you doing here, Willie? I just saw you upstairs making a great catch." Mays laughed. "I'm upstairs, too?" he said, in his familiar squeaky voice. "Yes," I said. Mays continued looking at the exhibits, but a few minutes later I overheard him say softly to his companion, "Why don't we take a look upstairs?"

This book encompasses a selection of some 150 columns and feature stories (approximately 150,000 words) I wrote over a fifty-plus-year sportswriting career—the book covers pieces I wrote from 1967 to 2022. It is not all-inclusive of Hall members, but centers on Hall of Famers as well as others who crossed my journalistic path and who had an important hand in the evolution and popularity to what is still called, "The National Pastime." I had the good fortune to write about them in a variety of ways, and for national publications.

I'd like to believe that this book is an historic view of America as seen in the strivings of a wide swath of our greatest American sports heroes. They reflect our life and times and aspirations from world wars to race issues to significant changes in our workplace economy. The time line extends from the turn of the twentieth century to the turn of the twenty-first. All of the subjects, including managers and executives and writers, have made a mark on the game, some made an indelible mark on our culture, from Babe Ruth to Jackie Robinson to Marvin Miller to Ring Lardner.

I had learned that the best writers strive to capture a person in the truest light, often seeing that person in a setting in which they are comfortable and/or unsuspecting. That is, in the best of all possible worlds the writer is the fly on the wall, sometimes the clubhouse or dugout wall. I hope that if I hadn't altogether succeeded in getting "inside" these Hall of Famers, I gave it what for me, a onetime Sullivan high school pitcher and first baseman in the Chicago Public League in the mid-'50s, was a full swing, and of course not just with interviews and covering the induction speeches at the Hall, but seeing my subjects in their homes or in some dugouts, or at games, or doing research (I never did meet Babe Ruth, say, but I indeed wrote about him, from an interviewee's having known the Bambino firsthand—from pitcher and teammate Waite Hoyt to the inimitable Casey Stengel—or from other forms of reporting).

There were insights into what made them special, and how they may have dealt with tragedies, and became, as the saying goes, mere mortals, on numerous levels. And, from Satchel Paige (throwing his "bow tie pitch" close to where a batter's bow tie if he wore one would be, to keep him off balance), to Phil Rizzuto to Casey Stengel, there is humor, which is the flip side of perspective. There is Carl Yastrzemski, a rookie in a slump for the Red Sox, and having Ted Williams upon request of management fly up to Boston from his fishing lodge in the Florida Keys to give him tips. They helped propel him to the Hall.

There was Reggie Jackson, emotional in his induction speech, saying how important his father, a former Negro League infielder, was in giving him the overview he needed to succeed.

There is Ferguson Jenkins confronting the murder and suicide of his live-in girlfriend and his baby daughter.

There is Babe Ruth, in the rain at a Yale-Harvard football game, and befriending a Yale freshman by using a strip of linoleum as a kind of overhead shelter, and sharing a jug of whiskey sours as the game progressed. The student, now an English professor, relates the story.

There is a retired Ernie Banks, trying a variety of civilian occupations, even as a bank official, but lost and confused without baseball.

And there is Greg Maddux, unfamiliar with Picasso, but a mesmerizing artist on the mound.

As mentioned earlier, this book doesn't include all of the Hall of Famers, just those that I had some journalistic contact with, or interest in.

While the title of this book is *Baseball's Best Ever*—a strict inclusion of those voted into the Hall of Fame—there are, in my estimation, a handful of players who have not been so elevated and ought to be, from Shoeless Joe Jackson to Barry Bonds and Roger Clemens. But the most controversial omission for entry to the Hall in recent times has been Pete Rose.

Rose had been handed in 1989 (his last year as a manager of the Reds, and three years after he retired as a player) a lifetime ban from participation in Organized Baseball for gambling on major-league ball games (this stems from the major-league taboo on gambling due to the 1919 "Black Sox" World Series scandal). The Hall, which is supposed to be independent of Organized Baseball, has chosen to never have included Rose on its annual ballot, so writers, unlike in most other instances, have never had a chance to decide for themselves whether Rose deserves a Cooperstown plaque.

There has been no evidence that Rose bet on baseball games other than on his own team to win during his 24-year playing career. As a player, he was known as "Charlie Hustle" and holds numerous records, the most impressive, in my view, are most hits in a career (4,256, breaking Ty Cobb's record that stood for fifty-seven years) and having been named as a starter in an unequaled five positions in his 17 All-Star Game appearances (first base, second base, third base, left field, right field). Both of those records may never be broken. What he did as a player on the field, as long as he didn't throw games, ought to be the only consideration made for Hall acceptance.

The pieces in this book are arranged in the decades in which the subject either began his big-league career or at the height or at the end, or beyond his playing days, depending on the context of the article and the insight—sometimes seemingly offbeat (see, for example,

Tommy Lasorda's recipe for his favorite pasta dish)—that I had hoped to attain.

It was a pleasure and an education (and some sweat, to be sure) to dig deeper into who these people were, and how they came to accomplish the feats that they did. I had endeavored when in the throes of gathering the material and then converting it from idea to print, that each piece may be, in some instances, a kind of short story, in others, a revelatory vignette. I hope the reader finds it to his or her satisfaction, and perhaps even edification.

Introduction:
The Smell of the Ball

B ig-league baseball is subtle; cloaked in summer languor, moving with the slow, supple grace of a ballerina practicing backstage, yet taut and technical in its skills. To view a baseball game and appreciate it takes concentration.

The setting is dramatic. This is especially so in the evening. Bright lights cut through the dew and illuminate the infield and outfield. Deep, brown dirt circles the bases and trims the outfield edge, in sharp contrast to the green. Slim, simple white foul lines slide along until they crawl up and over the outfield wall.

White-and-gray-flanneled figures dart and dive, swoop and slide, loop and leap; and sometimes they just stand, gloved hand on hip, dreamily watching the spike marks in the dirt as though waiting for them to crawl away.

There is much to see in a baseball game if one is not overly preoccupied with chasing down vendors or foul balls. The superior thing about baseball watching is that the maneuverings on the field are so easy to see (so easy to carry around in memory, too), as opposed to observing the baroque entanglements in football and the surrealistic postures in basketball.

Bowie Kuhn, commissioner of baseball, has said that he likes to take his wife and daughters to a game and point out how outfielders watch the way the wind is affecting the Rags in center field, consider the power and precedence of the batter, take into account their own speed afoot and strength of arm, then step some steps this way or that. Computations worked out, they then wait.

There is no greater drama than the confrontation of pitcher and batter, this small white sphere being hurled at great speeds to a man who must have reflexes honed to decide in the split of a second whether to swing and, of primary interest, when to jackknife to keep his health.

A difficult aspect to cage in concentration is the strategy of the pitcher: a high inside fast ball, a low outside curve, another fast ball up, a slow breaking pitch that will twist a batter into a pretzel.

Reggie Jackson, slugger, said he revels in watching Joe DiMaggio in Old-Timers' games still able to stroke those "frozen ropes": line drives that come screaming of the bat and which can an infielder into the outfield.

And the catcher clanking like a fat knight after a foul pop; an outfielder smoothly moving at the crack of the bat, back, back to the wall, as the ball visits among the stars, then descends apace and culminates in a leather plop; and a runner tipping the edge of the first-base bag and barreling into second with a neat hook slide that stirs just a tuft of dust.

Of course, the double play with a pirouette by the second baseman, a split by the first baseman and, by the straining runner to first, an arabesque.

And the excellence of the athlete, who has spent uncountable hours getting the snap in his swing, tracking down a ball that has just fallen out of the sun, developing his throw to display before the deep-throated, insatiable world of the stadium.

"I have tremendous respect," essayist E. B. White has said, "for anyone who does something extremely well, no matter what." It is thrilling to see excellence, whether it be Brooks Robinson or Rembrandt or a plumber.

Baseball retains its appeal because it is not frenetically and self-consciously modern. Baseball is a link for the country in a way that no other sport is. Baseball was here with stiff collars and bustles, before the motor car, after man's landing on the moon. No other spectator sport in America has meant so much to so many for so long. Though baseball officials have tried to "modernize" the sport—with artificial turf and artificial cleats—the game is still timeless. In fact, it is played without a clock. Unlike football and basketball, there is no timepiece in baseball ticking silently, hands pacing in relentless monotony, ending where it finished and informing the fans not to forget that they were in some vague rush.

Baseball has been in disrepute in some circles as a remnant of the past for its so-called slow pace. Yet former Senator Eugene McCarthy, who played first base long ago in Minnesota's semipro Sioux League, predicted that baseball will revive in popularity now that the Vietnam War has come to a close for us. The country, he said, is dog-tired of violence. Baseball, in contrast to football, represents sanity in a world gone haywire.

Strange how tight a grip baseball has on one's gentle boyhood. For a large slice of the male population in America, baseball is a very big deal in early years, is eclipsed in young manhood by other concerns such as young ladies and acne, and then slowly seeps back into interest as one grows toward senility.

One spring morning in 1971, when I was thirty-one, I stood behind the batting cage at Wrigley Field in my official capacity as sportswriter. I was faking it, for really I was eleven years old and I knew that at any minute an usher would escort me out of there by the scruff of the collar.

A ball rolled under the cage and I picked it up. It was still white but discolored by a bruise of brown and a stain of green. The red stitching stood out. For some unaccountable reason I smelled it. Pungent to the core. There is a distinct, unforgettable muskiness—to the tanned horsehide of a baseball. Smell being one of the greatest memory devices, it was so easy to be transported several yards and twenty years away to the moment I got my first big-league baseball.

The day before, my friends and I had fought in the autograph jungle under the cool stands as the Cubs of those days, Andy Pafko, Roy Smalley, Hal Jeffcoat, and Hank Sauer, emerged like gods from the clubhouse after the game, big and leathery-tanned and hair-slicked.

Roy Johnson, whom everyone called "Hardrock," came out. He was a tough-looking coach, but pigeon-toed, which gave away the humor under his gruff veneer. He was in a hurry, he said, and had no time to sign. I continued in hot pursuit. No, no, he persisted. In desperation he said, "Come to the park tomorrow, kid, and I'll give you a ball," slamming his car door a millimeter from my finger.

I believed him. My friends were much too sophisticated. He was just givin' you the slip, dope. It was not all that easy to fall asleep that night.

Armed with my lunch—with the usual soft fruit my mother packed carving a soggy hole in the bottom of the brown bag—I was off to Wrigley Field with my friends. They poked little jokes, even up to the time I left them in the grandstands. I ran down through the shadowy stands as the park began to fill, past vendors hawking pea-guts, past the steamy hotdogs on portable grills.

I had come down to the short, red-brick wall along the first-base line. Straight out was No. 42, Hardrock Johnson, cracking fungoes into the bright sky. I watched a ball drop through the clouds, down past the Baby Ruth billboard on the building across the street, get lost momentarily in the scattering of white shirts in the sunny bleachers, and finally disappear silently into the outstretched glove of a fielder against the ivy-covered wall.

"Mr. Hardrock, sir," I called through cupped hands. No answer. I called again. "You promised me a ball yesterday, Mr. Hardrock, sir."

Nothing, but the crack of his bat. "Just a dirty old ball, Mr. Hardrock." The few adults seated nearby tittered.

I'm not certain how long I kept this up, several minutes, surely. Soon, there was that predictable yank at the collar. I was explaining the situation to the grim usher when there came this great, throaty rumble, "Hey kid!" Hardrock Johnson tossed me a ball in a long' underhand toss. Up the stairs I flew.

They all wanted to see the ball, and I showed it to my friends. One by one—with me holding it. The ball created an uncomfortable but wholly welcome bulge in the right front pocket of my jeans. Home, I fondled the hard ball with the upraised stitching. I inspected the dirt and grass smudges closely, the Spalding trademark in a small baseball, the stars alongside "Official Ball, National League." The signature of Ford C. Frick, then League president. I smelled that tanned-horsehide smell that has not changed in twenty years, that has not changed in a hundred years.

Many suggestions were offered to get the ball as clean as new. The one that sold me was to put it in milk. I immersed the ball in a large bowl of milk for two days, periodically coming by and rolling it around with my finger to make sure no patch was left un-milked.

When I finally removed it, the ball had turned a sick yellow. I mounted the ball on a shelf in my room, for a while. But somehow it got out into the streets. Soon, one end was unstitched and became a flappy tongue and, shortly, the ball was reduced to a sphere of string.

At the batting cage now, I felt the red ridges against the smooth, off-white horsehide. I slowly tossed the ball in the air a couple of times. I smelled it. Then I casually squeezed the ball into my suit-pants' pocket.

As a sports columnist syndicated in seven hundred newspapers, I have had a chance to indulge my childhood fantasies. I have sat and talked with the heroes of my youth, such as Joe DiMaggio, Ted Williams, Casey Stengel. As a man, you see them now as men—warts and all, their ill-humors, their petty conceits (Williams wears a warm-up jacket on the hottest days to conceal his bay window)—yet they remain special in a romantic and probably foolish way.

But, as Roy Campanella has said, "To be good, you've gotta have a lot of little boy in you. When you see Willie Mays and Ted Williams jumping and hopping around the bases after hitting a home run, and kissing and hugging that goes on at home plate, you realize they have to be little boys."

I believed that to be true, and not just for athletes. Picasso is a prankster, Hemingway was a ham. Perhaps the most honest artists, in any field, see things with the fresh enthusiasm of their youth.

I once asked Tom Seaver, the great Mets pitcher, about Campanella's remark. "I think the good professional athlete must have the love of a little boy. And the good players feel the kind of love for the game that they did when they were Little Leaguers." Seaver said he never tires of the game. "Baseball is so challenging and complex that the more you learn the more there is to learn.

"But what in life isn't a game? Look, when a bank president puts over a big deal, isn't that a game of sorts? He doesn't jump up and down like a ball player who has hit a homer, but that's only because of the difference of environments. If he were wearing a jock strap: and sweat pants, he'd be clapping his hands and hopping on his desk, too."

Being a sports columnist has permitted me entree into ball parks in a way I had been totally unaccustomed to as a kid. In the past, I would scale a fence, jump over a turnstile, or fade angelically into a church group getting off a bus, Or, when workers' eyes were elsewhere, slide down the ice chute that stuck out like a long tongue from a beer truck through a ground-floor window of Wrigley Field. It was a chilling experience if you slid down on your fanny instead of on your heels.

And once my job permitted me to bat against a big-league pitcher. I went down to Lakeland, Florida, in June of 1970, to do a story on

Denny McLain. McLain had been suspended from baseball for the first half of the season, and was now preparing to return in July.

Every evening around suppertime, with the warm sun down, but still a couple hours left before nightfall, McLain pitched a nine-inning "Piggy Moveup" game to a ragtag of local high school and college players. His catcher was Jim Handley, the local high school baseball coach who had caught in the New York Met and Detroit Tiger farm systems.

The seven fielding positions were taken by the kids; Handley was permanently behind the plate. McLain stayed on the mound, throwing about three-quarters speed as the rotation continued.

That afternoon, when I had learned of the games, I asked McLain if I might play. "Why not?" he said with a shrug.

I confess I was rather excited about the prospect because I hadn't faced a big-league pitcher in some 20 years. It had been something like the 1951 World Series, Yankees versus Giants, played against the wall of the Bryant Elementary School on the West Side of Chicago. Jerry was Vic Raschi, and Allie Reynolds, too. And I, crouched with a bat and the rectangle of strike zone chalked on the dark wall behind me, waiting for Raschi to serve up that pink Spalding rubber ball, I was Willie Mays.

So now I stood, batting helmet and gym shoes and soft knees, facing the real McLain. As McLain, in Bermuda shorts, stooped in that classic pose, gloved hand on left knee to get the sign, I waggled my bat. Mostly for effect, for I was nervous. I gripped the bat tightly. McLain appears chunky, from 60-feet-6-inches away, but becomes formidable as he kicks and whirls and comes around in that graceful, smooth, grooved delivery and the ball popped into Handley's mitt. Strike one.

A breaking ball broke low and outside. I tried to watch the ball all the way, as I had read to do years before in *The Way to Better Baseball* by Tommy Henrich, the "Old Reliable" of the Yanks. But how magnificently McLain hid the ball. You never saw the white of it until it was traveling plateward.

I fouled off a ball to the right that bounced down and almost into the hazy lake, fringed by mossy pine trees. The count went to 3-and-2 and then, staring and frozen, I struck out on an outside fast ball. I trotted head down to right field.

Next time up, on the second pitch, I hit it up the middle, past McLain's right, and I ran like hell. I knew I shouldn't watch where the ball was going, but I had to. The shortstop charged over but threw late. I had beaten out a hit!

The inning ended with me stranded on first. But I had another turn at bat. I was up second in the inning. And I was concerned. McLain's pride might be hurt. He told me once that he wants to win at everything, that he'd even whip his mother at Monopoly. (Later, he said with a smile when I bragged a bit, "That hit? It took 13 bounces.") His competitive fires burn bright.

At bat again in the darkening evening, the fielders seemed far away, while McLain loomed close. His tanned face and arms were dark with sweat, and so was his gray T-shirt with "Detroit Tigers" lettered across the chest.

Quickly, the count came to 2-and-2. A high, medium fast ball pushed me back. "Oh gee," said McLain, with feigned anxiety, "I wouldn't want to hit him." Meaning a sports writer. Handley echoed a laugh from behind his mask. I swallowed. (At the time, I was only faintly aware that I had just experienced an authentic brushback pitch.) A 3-and-2 count. McLain wound up and—my God!—he was coming in sidearm. "Where are you going?" asked Handley, as I strode into the bucket.

The ball came in and, as I swung awkwardly, creakingly, the ball kept coming in. A change-up! By the time it had reached the plate, I had crumpled to one knee.

McLain's smiling white teeth looked very bright against the dark of his face. Yes, I had struck out ignobly, but as I trotted out to right field in the warm haze of the Florida evening, I was absorbed in the already fading details of my hit. I was batting .333 against Denny McLain. I still am, and will be, forever.

There is, however, no evidence of my feat in Baseball's Hall of Fame, in Cooperstown, New York, I suspect there never will be. Though not long ago I drove the five hours to Cooperstown from New York City. I went up there because, well, because I hadn't been there since I was twelve years old.

The town itself is a harmless little hoax. Streets are broad and lined with shading elms and horse-chestnut trees and the homes are tidy and there is a most pure, placid lake. There are no Vietnams here. No race wars. Hardly even inflation. It is still the nineteenth century here and one fully expects that, to get out of town, you still go eight miles by steamboat across Lake Otsego and then seven miles to Richfield Springs by tally-ho.

To sports fans, the town is best known for the Hall of Fame and Museum, and, until recently, was generally accepted as "the birthplace of baseball," as it says on local oompah signs.

But the claim has been dispelled, even by Hall director Ken Smith, who said that "They made a mountain out of a molehill." Baseball, tradition has it, was supposed to have been invented in Cooperstown by Abner Doubleday in 1839. Actually, no one knows baseball's origin. Some historians have marked the beginnings in Pharaoh's Egypt. But even in the museum there is a painting of youngsters playing "rounders" in 1802.

Yet Doubleday, a Civil War general from Cooperstown, has his army footlocker laid to posterity in the museum alongside Lou Gehrig's historical vertical locker. A reluctance to disavow the past, no matter how patently apocryphal, is integral to baseball love and lore.

A letter I received about my column on the Hall-of-Fame visit brought this home to me. I wrote that baseball, though a dream world, has been corrupted by big business and bigotry. The arrogance of owners—which has resulted in players often being treated like serfs, and the economic fear of owners which resulted in the despicable delay in breaking the color line for players and still holds for blacks on a managerial level—has helped rend fans' interest to a degree. As a youth, one rarely sees this side or cares. And as a youth, one only sees heroes through the glow of the halo. Then I wrote: "The Hall of Fame with its revered plaques is set in an impressively austere, columned corridor, and how the great men of the game have changed for the man who was last here as a boy. You know now that Grover Cleveland Alexander was an alcoholic, that Babe Ruth's famous 'bellyache' was actually a case of social disease, that Cap Anson was a racist. Yet you are touched by the old favorites, by the memories of the effortless DiMaggio, the electric Williams, the daring Jackie Robinson. . . ."

The letter was from an army sergeant in Wichita Falls: "You might take a look into your own past prior to slandering a giant like The Babe. I won't mention the things you failed to mention in your article, for these things would mean nothing to an individual who never participated in so much as a marble shooters game. . . . If you want some constructive advice as a sports writer—you stink. And you might try something more in line with Ann Landers's column. The girls would love it. With a name like Ira it's questionable to which gender you belong."

This cut me to the quick. My manhood was impugned. Not only had I shot marbles in my time, but just a month before that letter I had belted (well, more or less) a base hit off Denny McLain, 31-game winner.

Like the sergeant, I am both male and a longtime baseball lover. And like those enshrined in the Hall of Fame, I have wanted to play baseball well, and have admired those who look good in the field.

In this regard, I will always respect a Willie Mays, a Tom Seaver, a (yes) Babe Ruth, and a certain outfielder who played on a high school team against my team. I don't remember his name, but I will never forget him. A long high fly was hit his way. He wheeled back for it, ran, and his cap flew off. He halted in his tracks, picked up the cap, put it back on his head and, dapper again, resumed the chase for the ball that he would not catch.

* * *

Published 1973 in *Popular Sports* magazine reprinted in the *Best Sports Stories* annual, 1974.

Part I: From 1903 to the 1920s—The Babe and Beyond

This period is known as the "Modern Era," in which, among other moments, the first World Series was held, and shortly thereafter came the transforming figure of George Herman "Babe" Ruth.

Babe Ruth and a Jug of Whiskey Sours

November 23, 1985

For the 102nd annual Harvard-Yale game at the Yale Bowl in New Haven this afternoon, the weatherman said there was a chance of rain, but not necessarily a torrent. It seems unlikely that it would be anything like the 1932 Harvard-Yale game, which was played in one of the worst rainstorms in New Haven history. It rained so hard for so long that even Babe Ruth left the game early.

The *New York Times* of November 20, 1932, reported the details of the game, a 19–0 victory for Yale, highlighted by Walter Levering's touchdown runs of 45 and 55 yards. Following the account of the game, there appeared a small item, which read: "Babe Ruth sat in the downpour with Mrs. Ruth until even his massive physique could not stand it

1

any longer. He left in the fourth quarter totally unnoticed. He was just another bedraggled figure heading for the exits."

Someone who will never forget that game, and keeps that clipping among his Yale memorabilia is Milton White, professor emeritus of English at Miami University in Oxford, Ohio. He was a seventeen-year-old freshman at Yale in 1932.

He remembers the days leading up to the big game, and the excitement. "I wasn't a great sports fan, but, after all, this was the Harvard-Yale game, and there would only be two that I could go to as an undergraduate," he said. "I didn't think I could attend the two at Harvard. I mean, it was the Depression, and I was very poor—destitute, I guess you'd say—and my father, who was a merchant-tailor in Springfield, Massachusetts, had saved hard to send me to Yale. I thought I'd never be able to afford to go to Boston for the game."

Freshman White was supposed to have a date for the game. A girl he knew in Springfield was going to come down for it, and earlier in the week he had arranged with a woman who worked in a local florist to buy a white chrysanthemum for 35 cents. "But my date conked out at the last minute," said White. He had also planned a double-date at the game with his roommate and his date, but they decided to stay indoors because of the rain.

He gave the chrysanthemum to his roommate for his girl, and young White went off to the game alone. He had never known it to rain so hard. Wearing a yellow slicker and a yellow rain hat to match, he waited in the rain for a trolley, and dodged the spray of taxicabs. Finally, the trolley clanged into view and he boarded it to the Yale Bowl.

On the way, he saw parties going on in the warmth of rooms in dormitories and apartments. Those people were simply not going out in this rain. But Milton White was determined to attend the game.

When he arrived at the Yale Bowl, he trudged through puddles and sloshed down the aisle to a seat near the 30-yard line.

"I remember that the stadium looked pretty empty," he said.

He sat down on the soaking bench. The rain had dripped from the collar of his slicker down the wool jacket he wore underneath and made him uncomfortable.

"I've always hated the smell of wet wool," he said.

Most of the people at the game were huddled around the 50-yard line. "I was too shy to go there at first, but after a while I said, 'Oh, why not?'"

So he moved down and took a seat closer to the 50-yard-line, a solitary figure in the pouring rain. He had been sitting there only a moment or so when he felt someone tapping him on the shoulder.

"You don't want to sit alone," the man behind him said. "Come sit with us."

The man was with a woman and they were sitting "sort of off to the side," recalled White. The couple held a large strip of linoleum to protect them from the rain. White, even through rain-streaked glasses, recognized him immediately. He looked like all the pictures he'd ever seen of him. "I know you, you're Babe Ruth!" he said.

"He had a wonderful smile," White recalled, "and he introduced me to his wife. I was aghast. She said, 'Come on under, you don't want to get wet.'" The couple shifted the linoleum in order to extend a piece of it for White. At about this time, the Yale and the Harvard teams came sloshing onto the field and the small crowd cheered. The Yale Band struck up "Boola Boola."

"The game was just about to begin, and Babe Ruth lifted a gallon jug from under the bench," said White. "He poured something into a paper cup for himself and he poured one for me. They looked like whiskey sours. "He handed me a cup." 'To Eli Yale,' he said. "My hand was shaking. 'Eli Yale,' I said. Babe Ruth grinned at me. We raised our cups and drank."

"I remember that he seemed somehow to understand my loneliness, and I wondered if he was lonely, too, even being so famous. But I never dared asked him anything like that. In fact, I don't really remember anything else about the game, except that Yale won."

He said he didn't even recall when he left, but it was probably when his companions departed in the fourth quarter with their strip of linoleum that had protected the three of them against the rain.

How Good Was Babe Ruth?

How good was Babe Ruth? Example: When Ruth hit 60 homers in 1927, his total represented nearly one-seventh of all homers hit in the entire American League that year. Ruth was such a Colossus that a league-leader today would have to hit about 200 homers to bestride the field as Ruth did.

For decades, Ruth's record of 714 career regular-season home runs appeared untouchable; it was nearly 200 more than the 524 hit by the second-place man, Jimmie Foxx. The National League record was a paltry 511, by Mel Ott.

Ruth could also hit for average and has a .342 career mark. With customary braggadocio he once replied to someone who suggested he might have been able to hit .500: "Hell, I coulda hit .600 easy, if I had gone for them singles. But the people were payin' to see me hit them home runs."

He was also a marvel as a pitcher. He won 23 games in 1916 and 24 in 1917. He compiled a 94–46 record over four years, with a 2.28 earned run average. He was 3–0 with an 0.87 ERA in World Series play. His World Series record of 29 and two-thirds scoreless innings pitched stood for forty years. Eight times he pitched head-to-head against Walter Johnson, one of the all-time great pitchers, and Ruth won six, three by 1–0.

Ruth told people that his greatest thrill in baseball was when, in a key ninth-inning situation, he struck out the feared Tigers threesome: Bobby Veach, Sam Crawford, and Ty Cobb.

4

Cobb, in fact, always had trouble hitting Ruth. And when Ruth became a hitter to rival—or surpass—Cobb, it was easy to see why the frenetically competitive Cobb would enjoy getting Ruth's eminently easy goat. Cobb would jibe Ruth that he looked like a beer barrel on two straws. Ruth grew enraged.

Rube Bressler, a fine outfielder of those days, recalls Ruth: "lie went on the ball field like he was playing in a cow pasture, and before cows. He was never nervous. He played by instinct, sheer instinct. He wasn't smart, he didn't have any education, but he never made a wrong move on the baseball field . . .

"He became a great judge of a fly ball, never threw to the wrong base when he was playing the outfield, terrific arm, good base runner, could hit the ball twice as far as any other human being. He was like a damn animal. He had that instinct. They know when it's going to rain, things like that. Nature. that was Ruth!"

It was his hitting. though, that in the end created and perpetuated the epic hero Ruth, a man who became worldly famous. One legendary story concerns Japanese troops during World War II. They shouted to American soldiers what they considered the supreme insult: "To hell with Babe Ruth." Some eight years after Ruth had retired.

Even today, ask a young British taxi driver which American athletes he is familiar with and he'll start with "Babe Ruth." And maybe end there, too.

All because Ruth could propel a spheroid great distances by flailing a piece of lumber. But how he did it!

In *Baseball: The Golden Age*, historian Harold Seymour describes the magic: "In a 'closed stance' he gripped a heavy (42-ounce) bat at the end of the handle and moved it back and forth slowly and easily, the way a cat lashes its tail, as he peered over his shoulder awaiting the pitch.

"He swung the bat from his shoestrings, quick and rhythmic, with a little upward arc. When he hit one over the fence he jogged around the bases with little mincing steps, his arms bent, elbows close to the body, and tipped his cap as he crossed home plate.

"He was awesome even in failure . . . The crowd shuddered and buzzed: 'What if he had connected?'"

Ruth said he copied his swing after Shoeless Joe Jackson's. "His was the perfectest," Ruth once told Grantland Rice. At bat. he once told a *Sport* magazine writer: "I don't try to outguess the pitcher. I think about the pork chops I had the night before and if there shoulda been more salt in the barbecue sauce . . . Or if I look good in a tux . . . But the second the pitcher rears back, everything goes out of mind but the ball."

His wayward ways off the field and wondrous ways on the field amazed even Cobb. Cobb wrote: "I've never seen such an appetite. Ruth would start shoveling down the victuals in the morning and never stop. I've seen him at midnight propped up in bed, order six huge club sandwiches and put them away along with a platter of pigs knuckles and a pitcher of beer. And all the time he'd be smoking a big black cigar. Next day he'd hit two or three home runs and trot around the bases, complaining all the way of gas pains and a bellyache."

In 1925, Ruth almost died. The public story circulated around the world was that he had a stomachache after having eaten twelve hot dogs and drunk twelve bottles of soda pop. Others, though, said it was from a Gargantuan drunk. While some whispered he had been struck by a social disease.

Ruth's unbridled appetites were matched by his cavalier misbehavior, which included run-ins with Commissioner Judge Landis and Yankee owners and managers. He also had fist fights with opponents as well as teammates.

His ambition was to manage a big-league team. He never did. Owners asked: "How could he manage a team if he couldn't manage himself?" He became an embittered man, believing baseball had forsaken him and died of throat cancer in 1948 at the relatively young age of fifty-three.

In the end, this wildly improbable and beloved public figure was a mere mortal. As mortal as the man who will break Ruth's career home run record, Henry Aaron. As mortal as the man who held that record before Ruth, someone named Cactus Cravath.

Ruth and Gehrig in a Classic Home-Run Race

September 6, 1998

It had turned into a two-man race for the major league home run lead, and a dramatic pursuit by both players of the single-season home run record. Sound familiar?

Two men neck and neck as the season wound into the home stretch, two men not only playing in the same league, but also, in this case, on the same team. The year was 1927, the men were Babe Ruth and Lou Gehrig, batting third and fourth in the Yankee lineup. And the record they were pursuing was that held by the Bambino himself, who had crashed 59 homers in 1921.

Roger Maris and Mickey Mantle would be an identical Yankee tandem on an identical quest 34 years later, and Mark McGwire—who hit his 60th home run yesterday—and Sammy Sosa are linked by league, if not by team. But the convivial Ruth and the reticent Gehrig were the historical prototypes for the two-man pursuit of one of the most revered records in sports.

"Oh, it was the big sports story of the year," recalled Irwin Rosee, now eighty-nine years old, but a student at James Madison High School in Brooklyn in 1927. "There were no radios in those days, and so you had to wait for the late edition of the afternoon papers to get the news. Everybody used to huddle around the newsstands waiting for the papers to arrive. There was a lot of excitement. It was like Lindbergh flying over the ocean. It was the same year."

From April to the middle of August in 1927, Gehrig not only matched Ruth homer for homer, but by August 10, he also led Ruth, 38 to 35. Since Ruth had switched over from being a full-time pitcher to an everyday outfielder, in 1919, no one until now had seriously challenged him as the home run king of his day. He had led the league in homers in seven of the previous nine years (missing titles only because he had been out of action for nearly two months in each of the other two seasons). But now Gehrig, at age twenty-four, eight years younger than Ruth and in only his third full season in the big leagues, had suddenly found the home run range.

In the end, Ruth fought off the challenge with a charge that began in mid-August and lasted to the end of September and left him with the record of 60 homers that would stand for 34 years, or until Maris did him one better in, as has been widely known and discussed, a schedule that consisted of 162 games, eight more than Ruth's.

During his late-season surge, Ruth caught Gehrig at the end of August, moved two home runs ahead on September 1, but then lost the lead. On September 6, at the beginning of a doubleheader against the Red Sox, the two sluggers were tied at 44 home runs each. On that day, Gehrig hit one home run, and Ruth hit three—two in the first game and one in the second—to take a 47–45 lead.

Ruth hit two more the next day. Four days later, he hit No. 50.

"When he hit his 50th he talked of breaking his record, but it seemed all but impossible; there were only 17 games left to play," wrote Robert W. Creamer in the Ruth biography, *Babe: The Legend Comes to Life*. But Ruth continued slugging homers, while Gehrig slowed down, seemingly worn out. Ruth appeared to be relishing the competition.

"On No. 56," wrote Creamer, Ruth "carried his bat around the bases with him to frustrate souvenir-seekers. As he passed third base a boy came out of the stands, pounded him joyfully on the back and grabbed the bat. Babe dragged the boy and bat all the way across home plate."

He went two games without hitting a homer, and there were just four games left. But in the next three games he hit three homers—the 59th a grand slam against the Washington Senators.

It was now September 30, the next-to-last day of the season (the Yankees ended up playing 155 games because of a tie). Ruth, facing Tom Zachary with a man on base, hit a shot down the right-field line and into the seats for a home run. Zachary yelled "Foul ball! Foul ball!" and argued with the umpire, to no avail.

"While the crowd cheered and the Yankee players roared their greeting," reported the *New York Times*, "the Babe made his triumphant, almost regal, tour of the paths. He jogged around slowly, touched each base firmly and carefully, and when he imbedded his spikes into the rubber dish . . . hats were tossed liberally and the spirit of celebration permeated the place."

"In those days," Creamer said by telephone recently, "the number 60 had a magical ring to it. People used to say, 'Going like 60,' which probably came from racing a car at what was an incredible speed back then."

After the game, Ruth was exuberant about his feat. "Sixty, count 'em, 60!" he shouted in the clubhouse.

Gehrig managed 47 homers for the season—he had just three in September, while Ruth had walloped 17. (The National League leader was Cy Williams of Philadelphia with 30.) That season, though, Gehrig hit for a higher average than Ruth, .373 to .356, and led both leagues in runs batted in, 175 to Ruth's 164.

As for challenging Ruth's home run record, Jimmie Foxx in 1932 and Hank Greenberg in 1938 could get as far as 58. And then came Maris—and now McGwire.

The Yankees of 1927 were a tremendous team, setting an American League record for victories in a season, with 110 (that stood until Cleveland won 111 in 1954), and then sweeping the Pirates in the World

9

Series. As for Ruth, there was one more regular-season game for him to play after he hit his 60th. He went 0-for-3.

But no matter, for he belted two more homers in the World Series while Gehrig had none. The Sultan of Swat had prevailed again.

* * *

In 2001, Barry Bonds of the San Francisco Giants hit 73 home runs to establish the single-season home-run record, though it came with a controversy of his contested use of steroids.

Waite Hoyt in the Rain

August 28, 1984

On Saturday, the Brooklyn Schoolboy died. Waite Charles Hoyt was just two weeks shy of his eighty-fifth birthday, but during his 21-year major-league career and for much of his life, the Hall of Fame pitcher bore that fledgling's nickname.

It derived from his being signed to a contract with the New York Giants in 1915, when he was a fifteen-year-old student at Erasmus Hall High School in Brooklyn, though he didn't get into a big-league game with the Giants until 1918, and then for just one inning. The next year he was traded to the Boston Red Sox, and there his outstanding career took flight.

Though he pitched for seven clubs, his finest days were with the powerful Yankee teams from 1921 to 1930. Two years ago he was in New York from Cincinnati to attend a Yankee Old-Timers' Day, and the next week this reporter interviewed him for a television documentary.

"Years have flown," he said, "years have flown. The other day, when they called our names at the Stadium, I went out and stood on the mound just to see how it felt, once more. Oh, Jesus, it made you—well, I got teary, just standing there, oh, gee, did I."

He was a man of what might be average size today—6-feet and 180 pounds—but fairly large for his day. He was an old man now, white hair combed neatly straight back, tie just right and sparkle in his eyes. They had obviously never lost the effervescence of his school days. That, and his large, strong hands, with which he punctuated, prodded, and shaped his sentences, were memorable.

His playing days ended in 1938, and four years later he became a radio announcer for the Cincinnati Reds games. His reputation as a raconteur grew. Fans looked forward to rain delays so they could listen to the stories he spun, the best of which were captured in a record album called *Waite Hoyt in the Rain*.

His favorites were about his teammate Babe Ruth. His tales of that grand American folk hero helped to illuminate not only Ruth but Waite Hoyt as well.

"The first time that I ever saw Babe Ruth was in the Boston Red Sox clubhouse," he once said. "I walked in to report to the Red Sox, and they took me around and introduced me to everybody on the team, and when they got to him—you know, he couldn't remember anybody's name, he'd call you 'Happy Jack,' 'Pete,' 'Charlie,' 'Stud,' anything that came up in his mind—and he said, 'Hello, keed.' And he's sitting there, and he didn't look like a monster or anything, but he had black curly hair that dripped down over his forehead like ink, like there was spilled ink on his forehead, and he was utterly unbelievable.

"There is nothing like Ruth ever existed in this game of baseball. I remember we were playing the White Sox in Boston in 1919, and he hit a home run off Lefty Williams over the left-field fence in the ninth inning and won the game. It was majestic. It soared. We watched it and wondered, 'How can a guy hit a ball like that?' It was to the opposite field and off a left-handed pitcher, and it was an incredible feat.

11

"That was the dead-ball days, remember; the ball normally didn't carry. We were playing a doubleheader, and that was the first game, and the White Sox did not go into the clubhouse between games. They stood out there and sat on our bench and talked about the magnificence of that home run." Ruth was a man of prodigious appetites, including drink, though "he was not a drunk," Hoyt emphasized.

"And he liked the ladies. He was good in that sport, too. But he was popular with everybody, and everybody forgave him. In Chicago, we used to go to church with Ruth. I'm Protestant, and he was Catholic, and the Protestants wanted to go with Ruth to watch him. And when the fella came for the contribution, why, Babe would put a fifty-dollar bill in the plate, and the guy's eyes would pop open. The Babe was paying for his sins, and we always got a kick out of that."

Another time in Chicago, an attractive "bon ton" woman was walking down the steps of the hotel where the Yankees were staying. Ruth and a group of teammates were about to take a taxi to the ball park.

"The girl said to Babe, 'You're Mr. Ruth, aren't you?' He said, 'Yeah, that's me.' She said, 'Mr. Ruth, we're going to the ball park. Would you like to ride with us?' He said, 'Gee, swell.' So he's waiting for the car, and finally two little old ladies join the girl and Ruth, and drive off. The car was one of those old electric things without a steering wheel! It's going about eight miles an hour. Ruth is in the back seat, and we pass him on Michigan Boulevard. We called out, 'Ho, Babe! Hello, Babe!' Babe looked kind of ugly in that big moon face, and he had an expression that would have killed a mule."

In 1948, when Ruth was dying of cancer, Hoyt and his wife were moved by a visit to the old slugger in his Manhattan hotel. The visit, which Bob Creamer described in the book *Babe*, was short, because Ruth was tired and in great pain. But before the Hoyts left, Ruth stood up and went to the refrigerator. He took a small vase with an orchid in it and brought it back to the living room. "Here," he said to Mrs. Hoyt, "I never gave you anything." Shortly afterward, in August 1948, Hoyt was one of the honorary pallbearers at Ruth's funeral.

"For some reason," said Hoyt, "there was a reverence connected with the funeral, a reverence, an amazement, a joke, everything that could possibly be incorporated in a man's character and disposition and personality. Joe Dugan, who was my roommate on the Yankees, was an honorary pallbearer, too. He was standing next to me as they were carrying the Babe down the steps of St. Patrick's Cathedral here in New York. There must have been five thousand people standing around on the sides of the street, and it was tremendous.

"It was a hot day, oh, a sinful day, about 98 degrees, and St. Pat's didn't have air conditioning, and the sweat was running down our faces and dripping down our chins.

And just as they were carrying the Babe down the steps of St. Pat's, Dugan, who used to talk out of the side of his mouth, whispered to me, 'Gee, I'd like to have a beer.' Just then the casket with the professional pallbearers went by. 'Well,' I said, 'so would the Babe.'"

The Son of Ty Cobb

July 1969 / Washington, DC

James Cobb sat at lunch and he had a book of baseball players' records and he was saying that his hobby was statistics.

"Here," he said, his fingers crooked into two parts of the book, "take a look at the totals, just take a look."

This was after Babe Ruth had been selected the Greatest Player of All Time by the baseball writers, and Ty Cobb, James Cobb's father, was presumably second to Ruth. The two pages James Cobb had under scrutiny were the lifetime records of Babe Ruth and Ty Cobb.

"Look at the number of hits," he said. It read: Cobb 4,191, Ruth 2,873. "And the batting averages." Cobb .367, Ruth .342. "And runs scored." Cobb 1,938, Ruth 2,213. Cobb also had more doubles, 724 to 506, and more triples, 297 to 136. But Ruth, of course, was several thousand light years ahead of Cobb in home runs, 714 to 117 and had more runs batted in, 2,209 to 1,954.

"I was only seven years old," said James Cobb, "when dad retired in 1928 and I don't remember him playing. But his record is the best, and people tell me the things he did were fantastic, like going from first to third on an infield out."

James Cobb's involvement with baseball is limited to working with youngsters in Santa Maria, California, his home town, and with representing his father—who died eight years ago—at awards ceremonies. He works as an expediter at Lockheed.

"I think there's a jinx with sons of famous athletes," he said. "None of them ever topped their fathers. Look at Dick Sisler and Big Ed Walsh's son. They never did make it real big. And I understand Stan Musial's son was a very good baseball player. But he gave it up."

Ty Cobb never pressed his three sons (Hershel and Ty Jr., died in early manhood) to be athletes. But James Cobb remembers the pride his father took in James's achievements. James is 5-foot-7, some five inches shorter than his father, and he feels that was one reason he amounted to little as an athlete.

"But I remember once playing junior high school touch football and the coach was about to substitute for me," he said. "But just then he saw dad arrive at the field and he decided to leave me in. Well, I blocked a punt and recovered it. I looked over at dad and he put up a fist, as if to say, 'Thataway to go, son.' I was on top of the world. The next day a local newspaper headline read: 'Son Blocks Punt as Father Watches.'"

James would also pitch to his father in their back yard. "I got so," said James Cobb, "where dad had to put a handkerchief in his glove to keep the swelling down."

Though Ty Cobb, a strict disciplinarian, rarely complimented his boys on their athletic feats, James recalled an incident when he was "playing possum," pretending to be asleep on the living room couch and he overheard his dad say to a friend, "Little Jimmy's got a pretty good ol' curve ball."

James said that he feels it unfair when people say his father had no friends and was a morose man. "He was nice to people and he had a good sense of humor," said James. "I remember Gabby Street coming to the house often and he and dad reminiscing—sometimes I'd be awakened at three in the morning by their laughter."

Ty Cobb rarely talked to his sons about his days as a player, except for one thing. James said his father was proudest of being the first man selected for the Hall of Fame. "He used to show me the clippings," said James, "where he got 211 out of a possible 214 votes."

One point Cobb did emphasize to his children (he had two daughters, also) was good grades. "He read a lot, like the news magazines and books," said James, "and he always wanted us to do well in school. He would deprive us of things if our grades didn't meet his approval. He always wanted us to work as hard as we could at anything we did. Just as he did.

"I remember in 1942 he was to play three golf matches against Babe Ruth as part of a war bond drive. About three months before the first match dad began practicing. Every day, putting, driving, chipping. Hour after hour.

"And during the matches he would do everything he could to win and to upset the Babe—he would come late, cough when the Babe was lining up a putt, walk around him this way, then that. Dad beat Babe two out of three."

"Stained-Glass" Casey Stengel

August 2, 1968

Casey Stengel said he recently celebrated his seventy-eighth birthday. The baseball record book says it oughta be seventy-nine. No matter. Casey is one of those rare birds who never grows old. That's because he's never been young.

For proof, note the following account by Damon Runyon of how Casey Stengel, then thirty-three (or thirty-four), hit an inside-the-park home run in the ninth inning to win the first game of the 1923 World Series, 5–4, for the Giants over the Yankees:

This is the way old Casey Stengel ran yesterday afternoon, running his home run home....

His mouth wide open.

His warped old legs bending beneath him at every stride.

His arms flying back and forth like those of a man swimming with a crawl stroke.

His flanks heaving, bis breath whistling,

His head far back.

Yankee infielders passed by old Casey Stengel as he was running his home run home, adjuring himself to greater speeds as a jockey mutters to his horse in a race, swore that he was saying 'Go on Casey! Go on!'"

Runyon added that Stengel's "warped old legs . . . just barely held out" until he reached the plate, running his home run home. "Then they collapsed," wrote Runyon.

16

Three thousand miles away in California, Edna Lawson, Stengel's fiancée, proudly showed newspaper clippings of Casey's game-winning blow to her father. "What do you think of my Casey?" she asked.

Her father shook his head. "I hope," he said, "that your Casey lives until the wedding." Edna and Casey were married the following August, and Casey's warped old legs even made it up the aisle. ("For the bridegroom," Casey said at the time, "it is the best catch he ever made in his career.")

Casey Stengel sat in the New York Met dugout at Shea Stadium prior to the recent old-timer game there. If accounts by Runyon and others of his day even border on accuracy, then Casey has not changed appreciably. If he could run a home run home then, he could probably do it now, too.

His white hair is sun-tinged in spots. A wave flaps over the side of his face, which is wrinkled like a rutted road. His blue eyes water now and then and he wipes them with a handkerchief as big as a flag. His tasteful blue suit is specked with light brown, and looks almost natty on him.

And his legs. Of course, his warped old legs. He crosses them at the knee and one works nervously under black executive socks. On his feet are black slippers. A young man wonders if old Casey Stengel wasn't shod in them when he ran his home run nearly half a century ago.

Old friends greeted Casey. Younger fellows introduced themselves to a legend in the parchment flesh. Some players that played for Casey when he managed the Amazin' Mets dropped by to chat briefly. And Casey talked. Someone has described Everett Dirksen as having a "stained-glass voice." If that is so, then Casey's voice is cracked stained-glass. And his syntax is as cloudy as rubbings from time-worn church-yard tombstones.

About the lack of hitting in the majors this year, Casey said: "They ask you, you ask yourself, I ask you, it's them good young pitchers between eighteen and twenty-four years of age that can throw the ball over the plate and don't kill the manager, isn't it?"

About the St. Louis Cardinals: "St. Louis can execute and do more for ya. I thought Baltimore was going to be something but I quit on 'em and then I thought Pittsburgh would excel but I quit on them, too.

"But you gotta admit they can run, St. Louis I mean. Yeah, we'll say they can run. And they got two left-handers who'll shock ya and now the right-hander is commencing to be like Derringer or some of the others was. And a three-gamer, too. Can pitch every third day. The center fielder is a helluva good player and the left fielder is doin' an amazin' job. The fella at third they always worry about but he's doin' everything anyone could want. The first baseman got lotsa power and the catcher's now throwin' out people."

An old sportswriter friend came by and said he had just seen Edna in the stands and she's looking as great as always.

Old Casey Stengel, who ran a home run home nearly half a century ago, jumped up on those warped old legs in black slippers and grabbed the old friend's hand.

Stengel's gnarled face beamed. "You got it, kid," he said, pumping the man's hand. "You sure do."

Casey Stengel the Vaudevillian

February 1, 1974

"Even though Babe Ruth ran me out of vaudeville," said Casey Stengel, "I still can't knock him."

"Now this fellow in Atlanta is amazing. He hits the ball the best for a man of his size. But I can't say he hits the ball better than Ruth. Ruth could hit the ball so far nobody could field it. And that's even with the medicinal improvements today. They come along now with the aluminum cup and it improves players who only used to wear a belt and it's better for catching ground balls."

Stengel jumped up on his bowed, lumpy, but still spunky eighty-four-year-old legs and hounded down an imaginary ground ball that bounded under the coffee table.

"I got an offer from Van and Skank, the biggest names in vaudeville—they were from Brooklyn—to go on the stage after the 1923 World Series.

"I hit two home runs to win two games in that Series. I hit one in the first game and one in the third game. And this was when I was with the Giants and the Yankees were already the Yankees with Babe Ruth.

"Now, I remember Ruth when he was a young pitcher with the Red Sox. I batted against him, and this was before he grew the barrel on his belly but he always had those skinny legs. Well, they figured they could make more money with him in the lineup every day instead of every fourth day so they moved him first to first base but they had a good fella there so they moved him to outfield.

"In that series I hit an inside-the-park homer to win the first game. I was thirty-three years old. And I had a bad heel so I wore a cup in my shoe. The cup started comin' out when I was roundin' the bases. All the pictures show my like this"—head with hunk of white hair thrust back—"and like this"—head flung forward, rheumy blue eyes wide, tongue thrust out from his deeply stratified face—"and puffin'."

"So then the vaudeville guys asked me, could I sing. Sure I can sing"—for this voice sounds like cracked stained glass—"and can I dance? Sure. They wanted to pay me a thousand dollars for a week. And I wasn't making but five thousand—maybe six thousand—for a season playing ball.

"I was riding high. But the Yankees and Ruth said, 'Better watch out,' after I got the home run. It was a threat to brush me back. In the third game I hit a homer over the fence to win the game. And I ran around the bases and I made like a bee or a fly had got on the end of my nose and was bothering me. I kept rubbing it with my thumb, and sticking my five fingers in the direction of the Yankee bench . . . Commissioner Landis fined me for that.

"So I began to practice my dancing and I thought I'd be the new Fred Astaire. But then Ruth hit three home runs in the last game and the Yankees won the Series and vaudeville forgot about me and nobody heard from me again for ten years.

"So now Ruth, he could have gone on vaudeville. Hell, he could have gone to Europe. It was near the end of my career and pretty soon I commenced managing. Ruth kept on hitting homers. Aaron is going to break his record, and so the National Broadcasting people asked me to talk for three minutes about Aaron being better then Ruth. I couldn't say that.

"It's a livelier ball today, and Aaron was up more times, And they use the fake fields, and the balls whoosh through faster. But Aaron is amazing the way he can hit 'em with his wrists.

"Now, Ruth struck out a lot. But any damn fool knows that nobody pays to see the world's greatest singles hitter. Or the world's greatest doubles hitter. Ruth was the world's greatest home run hitter and that's what everybody wanted. And that's what he gave 'em.

"It worked out okay for me, too. Because I'm still in baseball—vice-president of the New York Mets ballclub and in the Hall of Fame—and who knows what my future in vaudeville would have been. Just like I started out to be a dentist. The dean of my school said, 'Why don't you be an orthodontist?' That way I could have got a lot of rich kids and put a black filling in their mouth.

"The dean said, 'Always try to be a little different.' And today I make speeches all over. People ask me, Casey, how can you speak so much when you don't talk English too good? Well, I've been invited to Europe and I say, they don't speak English over there too good, either.

"So you can see why I can't knock Babe Ruth, even though he drove me out of the vaudeville business, can't you?"

The Great Honus Wagner Outplayed at Shortstop by Freddie Parent in First World Series (1903)

October 5, 1970

Freddy Parent Sr. is the last man alive who played in the first modern World Series, in 1903. He played shortstop for the Boston Red Sox—who beat the Pittsburgh Pirates five games to four—and outhit his rival shortstop, Honus Wagner, .281 to .222. Freddy Parent Sr. lives now in the Hillcrest Manor Nursing Home in Sanford, Maine. He will be ninety years old in a month, on November 25.

It is difficult for Freddy Parent Sr. to hear on the telephone. So questions were posed to his nurse, Mrs. Wood—some, who kindly spoke them to Freddy, who then answered the questions himself on the phone. His voice is firm and his words come quickly.

Do you still enjoy baseball, Mr. Parent?

"You're damn right," he said. "I don't miss anything on television. But I am bothered with the football programs and also the basketball programs. I'm bothered a lot on that account."

What do you remember most about that first World Series?

"I can remember the most when we was in Pittsburgh and they had us three to one in games and we finished it up in Boston. And, yes, we won five out of eight then."

Was interest as great for the World Series then as it is now?

"It must have been. They had to make special ground rules for a two-base hit that went into the crowd because the crowd broke down the fences and the gates in Boston. They didn't do as bad as that in Pittsburgh because they were losing.

"People in those days, they liked the Series because it was something new. Of course, it wasn't run like it is today, more of a business today. The people enjoyed it very good then."

You outplayed Honus Wagner in the Series, didn't you? "He wasn't in very good shape for the Series and he didn't do too good, which I enjoyed myself," said Parent. "But he was one of the great players."

(In the Series, Wagner, who had led the National League in batting with a .355 average—one of eight times leading the league in batting—hit only .222 in the Series, to Parent's .281—Parent batted .304 during the season. Wagner had no extra base hits in the '03 Series, Parent had three triples. Parent made three errors, Wagner six. It was believed that Wagner had injured his right leg late in the season, and was not quite himself throughout the Series. Wagner also struck out in the ninth inning to end the game and the Series.)

What is the difference, I asked Parent, between the players then and now? "We felt more nervous then. They seem to be more—well, they look at it to get more money fast." (The individual winner's share of the 1903 Series was $1,182.) "And we were pretty hard losers in those days. We tried to win harder than they do today. Don't know why. Maybe the lively ball and the short fields to hit on."

Who is the best player today?

"That fella plays first base for the Red Sox [Carl Yastrzemski]. All you got to do is get one hit in three times and you're going to win that title."

In 1911, at age thirty-five, Freddy Parent Sr. retired as an active player and became a coach under Jack Dunn for the old Baltimore Orioles. They had a rookie pitcher named Babe Ruth. Freddy Parent Sr. recalled that.

"I coached Babe more than anybody else at that time," he said. "I remember he was pitching in the late innings of a close game and there was two outs and the bases loaded and a dangerous left-handed hitter was up. He got two strikes on him. I ran out and told Babe to waste a pitch.

"The next pitch he throws right down the middle. Oh gee, a triple. Babe comes in and I said, 'What happened?' He said, 'I threw it waist high, didn't I?' I talked to him later when he was in the big leagues and I asked him how his 'waist' pitch was. He didn't like that very much."

Mrs. Woodsome says Mr. Parent "gets around just fine and looks wonderful. He reads and he walks around with the help of a little cane—when he feels like it."

"He wears glasses and he is white-headed, but has lots of hair. He shaves himself every day and dresses himself every day, with a nice shirt open at the collar and pressed pants. He's very proud of how he looks. He wears a felt hat when he takes little walks. And he's a gentleman. He certainly is.

"He talks to everybody about baseball. He is very pleased to talk about it. He is very alert and he watches all the baseball games on television. When the game is on, the set is Freddy's. Because of him everybody here has gotten interested in baseball. He sits on the edge of his chair and he makes comments and when something very interesting happens he taps his cane on the floor."

Tony Lazzeri Faces Grover Cleveland Alexander Again

March 4, 1991

There were things Tony Lazzeri, who was recently and unexpectedly named to the Baseball Hall of Fame after having been dead for forty-five years, never, or rarely, talked about when he was a star for the Yankees in the 1920s and 1930s. Those were the glory years when he was the important second baseman and clutch hitter on great pennant-winning

23

teams with Ruth and Gehrig and Meusel and Jumpin' Joe Dugan and Waite Hoyt and Red Ruffing.

Perhaps Lazzeri spoke little because he was naturally reserved. "Interviewing that guy," a sportswriter complained, "is like mining coal with a nail file."

Or perhaps Lazzeri was quiet because he hid a secret: he suffered with an illness, epilepsy, and in those days particularly epilepsy was considered a taboo subject. As far as can be determined, Lazzeri never had a seizure on the ball field. "I never knew until after his death that he was an epileptic," Red Barber, the longtime baseball broadcaster, said recently. "I didn't find out until he finished playing, and not until after he died did knowledge of his illness become widespread."

Those who have epilepsy can be anxious and even terrified that they could have a seizure at any moment, according to Reina Berner, the director of the Epilepsy Institute of New York. "There is an episodic sudden loss of control of bodily movement, with sometimes a loss of consciousness," she said. "And the epileptic worries: 'When will it happen? What will they think of me? Will I be able to keep my job?' And epileptics were often considered dangerous, or incompetent, and were unable to handle stress. It's not true, though sometimes stress can trigger a seizure, but much less so today because of modern medicine. But, my God, think of a ballplayer in front of all those people, and in those times. I can't believe he played."

Play Lazzeri did, from 1926 to 1939, and to the tune of a lifetime batting average of .292—one year he hit .354—and whacking out 178 home runs and driving in 1,191 runs. And at second base, Lazzeri, who stood nearly 6-feet and had long, graceful movements, was considered one of the smartest of players. Among his teammates, he was a respected leader, as well as a practical joker. Once when Babe Ruth showed up late for a game and tried to pull his spiked shoes out of the locker, he found them nailed to the floor. It was, the players knew, typical Lazzeri handiwork.

Something else Lazzeri didn't seem to discuss much was his importance to Italian Americans, the pride he infused in a community whose immigration to America was still a relatively new thing, and whose striving for assimilation, like that of other immigrant groups, was subject to discrimination and racial stereotyping.

Anthony Michael Lazzeri, a native of San Francisco and the son of a boilermaker who had been born in Italy, became the first player of Italian descent to star in the major leagues. (Joe DiMaggio broke in ten years after Lazzeri did.) Italian Americans began to crowd into Yankee Stadium and cry, "Poosh 'em up, Tony!"

"And now," wrote Frank Graham, in his history, *The New York Yankees*, "a new type of fan was coming to the stadium. A fan who didn't know where first base was. He came, and what he saw brought him back again and again until he not only knew where first base was, but second base as well."

Even before he was chosen for the Baseball Hall of Fame last week by the Veterans Committee—a group that meets annually to right possible old oversights—Tony Lazzeri's name was on a plaque in Cooperstown, in a melancholy context for him. It has been inscribed there since 1938 when Grover Cleveland Alexander was elected to the Hall. Part of Alexander's plaque reads: "He won 1926 World Championship for Cardinals by striking out Lazzeri with bases full in final crisis at Yankee Stadium." It is, by chance, the only negative reference to an opposing player on any plaque in the Hall of Fame.

Lazzeri, a twenty-two-year-old rookie for the Yankees in 1926, came to bat in the seventh inning of the seventh game of the World Series, with the bases loaded and two outs, and the Cardinals ahead, 3–2. Alexander, an old man now by baseball standards, was summoned in relief of Jess Haines.

Alexander got one strike and one ball on Lazzeri and then Lazzeri smashed a fast ball to left field that looked like a home run, until it curved just foul. On the next pitch, Lazzeri struck out. It was one of the most dramatic, and enduring, moments in baseball history.

For a few years after his playing days, Lazzeri managed in the minor leagues, then returned home to San Francisco, and became a partner in a bar there. On August 6, 1946, Lazzeri, while his wife and son were away on vacation, fell down the stairs at home, hit his head on the banister, and died. Some thought he might have suffered an epileptic seizure, but the coroner determined he had had a heart attack. Lazzeri was forty-two years old.

About a year before he died, Lazzeri spoke with a reporter about his career, which included seven World Series. "Funny thing," he said, "but nobody seems to remember much about my ball playing, except that strikeout. There isn't a night goes by what some guy leans across the bar, or comes up behind me at a table in this joint, and brings up the old question. Never a night."

Alexander's plaque in the Hall of Fame will not change. What's different in Cooperstown, though, is that Tony Lazzeri now has a plaque of his own.

When Joe Sewell Replaced Ray Chapman Who Was Killed by a Pitch

October 13, 1989

On the eve of the World Series, Joe Sewell vividly remembers the first one he ever saw, sixty-nine years ago. He remembers it so well because he played in it. Joe Sewell is the last living member of the 1920 Cleveland Indians team, which beat the Brooklyn Dodgers in seven games in the Series. And it is a curious slice of history that in the fifth game he actually assisted in the only unassisted triple play in a World Series game.

With no outs and men on first and second, Bill Wambsganss, the Indian second baseman, speared a line drive, and stepped on second base, doubling that runner. The man on first, Otto Miller, steaming for second, halted. Sewell shouted to Wambsganss:

"Tag him! Tag him!" Wambsganss did, for the third out.

While he probably didn't need the rookie's help, it still is not quite true that, as Ring Lardner wrote, "It was the first time in world serious history that a man named Wambsganss had ever made a triple play assisted by consonants only."

Another curious twist of history is that the last living member of that championship team got his chance because he replaced at shortstop "the only fella," as he described it, "that's ever died in a big-league game."

Shortly after Ray Chapman was hit in the head and killed by a Carl Mays submarine pitch, Sewell was called up from the New Orleans Pelicans. It was September 7, 1920. Sewell was young twenty-one years old—and small, at 5-foot-6 and 155 pounds, and scared. Scared not because of the Mays beaning—"I'd ducked plenty of pitches," Sewell said—but he felt he wasn't good enough, despite never having seen a major league game. "I thought big-leaguers were superhuman," he recalled. In a new book, *The Pitch that Killed*, the author, Mike Sowell, recounts that period and quotes Sewell when he learned he was being called up:

"I was more frightened than pleased, but as I traveled north I made up my mind that when I took the field in a Cleveland uniform I would forget that I was Joe Sewell and imagine I was Chapman, fighting to bring honor and glory to Cleveland."

Joe Sewell turned ninety-one years old on Monday. He lives in Mobile, Alabama, in the home of his son, Dr. James Sewell. Joe Sewell, by telephone recently, said he's convalescing from a broken hip though insists he's still in good health. "But I've shrunk up a little bit," he said, "humped over with the arthritis."

27

And he still has, in a glass case, the one and only bat that he used during his entire 14-year playing career, a bat that saw a lot of action because Sewell, who was elected to the Baseball Hall of Fame in 1977, compiled a .312 career batting average, with 2,226 hits, and, remarkably, struck out only 113 times in 7,132 official times at bat, a record for fewest strikeouts in an extended career.

The bat, a Ty Cobb model Louisville slugger, 40 ounces, 35 inches, is now nearly black, with age, and with the constant "boning" that Sewell applied to it, smoothing it with a Coke bottle, rubbing it with chewed tobacco "to keep the wood moist" and wrapping the handle with adhesive tape.

He says that he struck out so little because he saw the pitch so well, could see "the seams on the ball," and that he had developed his talent by spending hours as a boy hitting a rock or piece of coal with a broom stick, "and never missed."

When Sewell arrived in Cleveland in 1920, in felt hat and high-button shoes, the terrible sound heard throughout the park of the baseball crushing Chapman's skull, and the sight of blood rushing from the collapsed player's left ear, were still in the minds of players and fans. But the Indians talked little about it. "They were determined to win the pennant," Sewell said. And they did, with Sewell batting .329 in 22 games.

The manager, Tris Speaker, was, said Sewell, "like a second father to me."

"I made a lot of mistakes, but he calmed me down, and never gave me a cussin," Sewell said.

Through the years, Sewell faced Carl Mays many times. "He hit me, too, but never in the head," Sewell said. And though Mays was considered a tough guy by many, Sewell liked him. "We were later scouts with Cleveland," Sewell said, "and we talked about Chapman. He said he didn't intend to hit him. He said he had nothing against Chapman, that he was just trying to win a ball game. I think it's true."

As for modern-day batters, Sewell said, "They use these batting gloves and have valets—no wonder they can't hit." And the pitchers: "Some of 'em couldn't knock the hat off your head. They make a million dollars and I wouldn't give you 25 cents for 'em."

And how's the famed Sewell eyesight? "Good. I wear glasses only for reading." Could he still hit a rock with a broom stick? "Yeah, but I haven't been in the yard in a month. Too hot. I sit in the shade on the porch."

The Day Rookie Bob Berman Caught Walter Johnson

January 26, 1988

Bob Berman was a nineteen-year-old rookie for the Washington Senators when he was sent into the game in the bottom of the ninth to catch Walter Johnson. It was June 12, 1918, seventy years ago this summer, in Sportsman's Park, St. Louis.

Johnson, who would win 23 games that season and was possibly the best pitcher in baseball, was summoned in relief in the last inning against the Browns to try to protect a 6–4 lead. The Senators had rallied in the late innings and had used up their other two catchers—one was pinch-hit for, the other pinch-hit.

No one was left to catch Johnson except the third-string catcher, Robert Leon Berman. Berman had played in only one other game, as a pinch-runner. He was "a cocky kid," he said, but now, "I was nervous." Johnson, he later recalled, was "my prince in those days. Always had a pleasant smile. Oh, whatta guy!" Just before entering the game, said Berman, Johnson "wrapped his arm around me and said, 'Bobby boy, just remember, we're down in the bullpen, that's all.'"

And that's all that Berman remembers of that inning, his last appearance in a big-league game, and his only full inning.

"My memory," he said one day early last week, "she ain't what it used to be." He was in the home of his daughter, Barbara Cassidy, where he now lives. He walked into the living room, a little bent over, neatly dressed in a shirt and pants, and with sneakers cut open and no socks, for arthritis has been troubling him, particularly in his feet.

He had a birthday coming up very soon—it was on Sunday.

"How old are you going to be, Daddy?" asked his daughter.

"I'll be an old man, I know that," said Berman, with a shrug and a smile. "I shall be, let's see, I was born in 1899. . . ." He shook his head.

"C'mon, Daddy," his daughter gently urged.

"Haven't had my breakfast yet," he said, hoping this would get him off the hook.

"Eighty-nine," she said. "That's all?" he said. And they both laughed.

Bob Berman was born on the lower East Side to immigrant Russian-Jewish parents and graduated from P.S. 42 and Evander Childs High School.

"It was amazing for me, this kid from the sidewalks of New York, who grew up in cold-water flats—we had no hot water—and jumping to the big leagues," he said. "They paid me $150 a month, but I'd have played for nothing. My dad enjoyed my doing it, but not my mother. She wanted me to be a Latin teacher."

He did become a teacher after baseball, but in health and physical education and in ballroom dancing, for forty-three years in New York public schools.

For the last thirty-one of those years he was at Franklin K. Lane High School, until he retired in 1968, where he coached the baseball team. One of his prize pupils was Bob Grim, who became a 20-game winner for the Yankees.

From his days in the big leagues, Berman has kept two photographs in old, peeling frames.

One shows him posed on the sidelines in a slight crouch with his catcher's mitt, but without the rest of his equipment. His Senators cap with the "W" is tilted a little rakishly to the side, and the pinstriped uniform has long sleeves, like pajama tops.

The other photograph is a team picture. There are 18 players and the manager, in hat and coat and tie, is Clark Griffith.

Berman's daughter handed him the team photograph, in which he is kneeling, second from the right, in the first row.

"Ah, and there's old Walter," said Berman, pointing to a man standing second from the left in the second row, his arms folded.

"I was a young kid and Walter Johnson was like a god to me. People used to say, 'Where Johnson goes, Berman is sure to follow.' And I did, but he never seemed to mind.

"He threw three-quarters side-arm and I remember that his fastball rose. I had never experienced anything like that before. And he was fast. Sometimes your fingers would swell up on you if you didn't catch the ball in the proper place. Oh, brother!"

Berman looked again at the photograph.

"That's Joe Judge, and that's Nick Altrock, and there's Eddie Ainsmith; he was the first-string catcher, strong as a bull. Nobody fooled with Eddie." He paused. "None of the other faces look familiar anymore.

"But I know I'm the sole survivor of that team. My, my."

Berman didn't last the full season. "About two-thirds of it," he said.

The baseball season of 1918 was itself curtailed because of World War I, and Berman went into the Army for a few months, until the war ended in November of that year. He played the next few years in the minor leagues, but he never returned to the majors.

"I'm grateful for the little I enjoyed," he said. "Baseball was life to me."

Records revealed that Berman pinch-ran on June 6 after a pitcher named Jim Shaw had tripled and sprained his ankle. The inning ended with Berman still on third.

In the box score from that day in the files of the Baseball Hall of Fame, Berman was listed as "Beiman." When he caught Johnson six days later, that box score read "Bergman."

Berman was told that in the inning he caught Johnson, he was credited with two putouts, as Johnson struck out two batters, and retired the Browns without a run.

Berman had no errors, no passed balls. It was a virtual perfect inning for him.

"Sounds interesting," he said, "very interesting."

Did that jog his memory of details about when he caught Walter Johnson?

"Sorry," he said. "I can't remember anything about it. But it was the happiest day of my life. You couldn't talk to me."

Christy Mathewson: Blending Myth and Reality
June 25, 1983

Peter Berczeller, a Manhattan physician and ardent recreational tennis player, recently took note of Bjorn Borg, a fellow recreational tennis player.

"It came as kind of a shock to see Borg doing tennis commentary on television recently," said Dr. Berczeller. "I mean, he seemed declawed. Remember him playing? He had his beard and this end-of-the-world look, and even if he was down two sets to nothing you knew he'd fight back to win. And yet he was remote, like a Norse god. I guess that was the myth that was built up—that I built up, anyway.

"And now you see him on television in a blue button-down shirt, and clean-shaven, and suddenly he's not the same. He's now a socialized human being. He's tamed. And the impact that makes is strong, and you realize that there comes a time when you must separate myth from reality. But you do it—I did it—with a certain wistfulness."

The doctor's views brought to mind a stirring, beautifully written novel, recently published, that deals with the subject of myth and reality in sports. It is *The Celebrant*, by Eric Rolfe Greenberg.

It begins at the turn of the century with the introduction of a young European immigrant to the world of baseball in America. The baseball people and the games in the novel are historically accurate, but the off-the-field activities and conversations are imaginary.

Jackie Kapp is drawn to the sandlots of New York, shows talent as a pitcher, then hurts his arm and goes into the family jewelry business, where he will design rings for baseball players.

He becomes a Giant fan, once and always. "In the matter of rooting, a boy's first team is his team forever," writes Greenberg. At a game, Jackie Kapp sees a young pitcher who captivates his imagination: Christy Mathewson, "young as an April morning in that sweltering July." He is big and smooth, with "startling power."

"He bent for his sign, rolled into his motion, and threw." It is 1901, and Mathewson pitches a no-hitter against St. Louis. If, as Prof. Paul Weiss once wrote, "athletes are excellence in the guise of man," then Mathewson was in the first rank of excellence. He was one of this country's first national sports heroes, a handsome, dignified, superb athlete and one of the first professional baseball stars to have gone to college (Bucknell).

He was the model for the fictional e'er-do-well, Frank Merriwell. Jackie Kapp becomes a devoted Mathewson "celebrant": "I watched Mathewson and he became my youth; it was my fastball burning by Burkett, it was my curve that little Jess lifted to the outfield, and after the ball came back and around the infield I felt it was my glove closing around it, my arm that launched the fastball at Donovan's knees and the next that cut the black of the plate on the outside. . . . and I had the game and the no-hitter in my hand."

Kapp's brother, Eli, has a deal to sell rings to the players, and Jackie has an opportunity to meet Mathewson, but declines. He senses a wide gulf that he feels he must not cross.

"What, then?" asks Eli. "A worshiper from afar?" "Isn't that the proper distance for worship?" replies Jackie. Jackie designs a special ring for Mathewson to commemorate the no-hitter, however, and there grows in a curious fashion a mutual respect, for Mathewson believes Jackie is an artist in his own right.

And then Jackie draws closer to the pitcher, and in fact meets him, and has dinner with him and others one night. Mathewson says thoughtfully: "I stand on the pitcher's mound, the batter at home plate. We are surrounded by every manifestation of civilization: the manicured field, the rising grandstand, the railway beyond the outfield, the buildings on the bluff. Yet my action in throwing and his in swinging are the echoes of the most primitive brutality.

"Did Cartwright say that his endeavor was to balance the arithmetic of the game against its geometry? All of sport, from bushkazi (a Central Asian sport with horse-mounted players) to baseball, is man's endeavor to balance his animal instinct against his civilizing intellect. On the sporting field. . . . we are both ape and angel."

Jackie Kapp follows closely the career of Mathewson, through his triumphs—the unparalleled achievement of pitching three World Series shutouts, in 1905—to his disappointments: the 1908 pennant loss on Fred Merkle's "bonehead" play, the decline of the great Giant teams, the aging of Mathewson and then the betting scandals.

Mathewson became the manager of the Cincinnati Reds, and the Sir Galahad of baseball couldn't believe that one of his players, Hal Chase, might be throwing games, and took no action. For Mathewson, in his way, was also a celebrant of the game.

Christy, says a character in the novel, is either the most credulous man in America or, like his namesake, the greatest model of Christian forgiveness. "Perhaps both."

Mathewson left baseball to serve in the First World War, and shortly after landing in Belgium he was hit with poisonous gas. (Jackie Kapp is later stunned to see a photograph in which Mathewson looks grievously old. Mathewson is, in fact, dying.)

Upon his return, Mathewson was asked by a Chicago sportswriter, Hugh Fullerton, to monitor the 1919 World Series, between the Reds and the White Sox. Rumors of a scandal abounded. And, with sickening awareness, Matty saw that several of the Chicago players were throwing the games.

The Black Sox scandal shattered the innocence of many. "I prefer the memory," Jackie Kapp says to his father-in-law. "Illusion," says the old man. "It's our capacity to see complexity that increases, not complexity itself. We have a name for that capacity. We call it 'wisdom.'"

Connie Mack: Correspondence with a Promising Pitching Prospect and Wounded War Hero

2009

Tall, lean, soft-spoken and one of the most respected men in baseball—almost everyone called him "Mr. Mack"—Cornelius Alexander Mack (born McGillicuddy) was, at age seventy-eight, in 1941, nearing his 60th year in professional baseball as a player and manager. As manager on the Philadelphia A's bench he still wore a dark suit, the high, starched collar in turn-of-the-century fashion, and a straw hat. He rarely left the dugout during games, wigwagged signals with his scorecard to move his fielders into position, and always sent one of his baseball-suited coaches to the mound when making a pitching change.

He was impressed with a sixteen-year-old high-school South Car-
olinian left-handed pitcher who was a sensation in the competitive tex-
tile leagues in the state. At seventeen, he was invited by Mack to the
A's home ball field, Shibe Park, and remained impressed with Brissie's
crackling fastball and sharp breaking pitches, and his poise. Mack was
prepared to give the lad a contract. Brissie's father insisted that Lou not
go into professional ball at that time but go to college instead. Mack
agreed to pay Brissie's college expenses.

But in December 1942, following the Japanese attack on Pearl Harbor on the 7th, Brissie, brimming with patriotism, enlisted in the US
Army.

Brissie eventually was a corporal on the front lines in the Apennine
Mountains of northern Italy, but carried with him a letter that Mack
had written to "Brissie Sr." on letterhead that read, "American Base Ball
Club of Philadelphia, Office of the President."

Aug 24 1944

Dear Mr Brissie Sr. . . . As things are looking so good at present time
our hopes are that our club can have your son with us next season. It
looks also at this time that our club will be greatly improved over this
season. . . .

With kind regards, Sincerely yours, Connie Mack, president.
In the spring of 1944 Brissie wrote Mack that the war "looked like it
could be over this year."

Mack responded: "Our club is still in need of a left-handed pitcher
[and] only hope tht when you join our club the fans will forget such
pitchers as Rube Waddell, Eddie Plank and [Lefty] Grove. . . .[all
great former A's pitchers]. . .[and] hope that the Infantry unit you are

connected with will all survive the war in as good condition as you are now. . . ."

In November, Brissie wrote Mack the forlorn news: "Looks like we won't be getting home all that soon."

But on December 7, 1944, Brissie's unit met with German mortar fire that killed 11 of the 12 soldiers that Brissie was then on a patrol mission with. The lone survivor was Brissie, barely. He was left for dead in a snow-covered ditch, lying there for eight hours, but was finally rescued by a US Red Cross unit. In a surgery tent he was told that his left leg was so mangled by the grenade explosions that his left leg would have to be amputated up to the knee. He said, "No, you can't. I'm a baseball pitcher. I can't play on one leg." His leg indeed was saved—he became the first recipient of the "wonder drug," the antibiotic penicillin, in the Mediterranean theater—and would eventually go through twenty-three surgeries to save the leg.

On a letter dated December 12, 1944, Mack wrote the following before having learned of Brissie's travails:

Dear Lefty:
Was pleased to receive your letter of November 7th.

Attended the World Series at St. Louis, the games were well played and the best club [Cardinals] won although they had to work hard in every game played [versus the Browns]. [Marty] Marion was the real star of both teams. The newspapers are now classifying him with Honus Wagner, as a matter of fact, some feel that he is even [a] better [short-stop], however, I doubt this, due to Wagner being a great batsman as well as base runner . . . Will be pleased to hear from you whenever you can find time to write. . . .

Letter from Mack (to Brissie then in the American Military hospital in Naples, Italy) dated January. 16, 1945:

Dear Lefty:

Pleased to receive your letters of December 23rd and 28th, however, regret to hear that you met with such as serious injury and am glad that you are getting along so well.

Am in hopes you will be ready, if necessary, to continue your baseball and basketball playing this summer. The doctors can do great things today as they have already proven by their work in helping some of our boys.

Have heard from [pitcher] Bob Savage who was wounded a second time. He is expected to be able to leave the hospital by Christmas.

It was mighty nice of you to remember me on my birthday after all you have been through. Would like to have you keep me posted on your condition, however, do not overtax yourself by doing too much writing. . . .

Fifteen days later, Mack wrote again to his wounded pitching prospect . . . and the familiarity of the salutation "Lefty" gave way to the respect-ful "Corporal Brissie" (perhaps in respect and admiration for the battle he was waging in the hospitals).

January 31, 1945 (to Cpl. L. V. Brissie):

Was pleased to hear of your improvement and from what your doctor states, you recovery is going along satisfactorily. Am always pleased to hear from you, more so now than ever, so please keep on writing as I am interested in your condition.

Can understand your longing to play baseball, just keep up this feeling as it will go a long way in helping your present condition. . . .

Am expecting Earl Brucker [the A's pitching coach] to call most any day and will inform him that you intend to do some real pitching for the club in the near future. From all account [former A's pitcher

Phil] Marchildon is going all right although he is in a German camp. . . . With best wishes, Sincerely, CONNIE MACK, President."

"The idea that I would have the 'opportunity' to be a major league pitcher with the A's really lifted my spirits," Brissie would recall. "What more could anyone ask for than the opportunity."

On a letter dated June 18, 1945, Mack wrote to Brissie in rehabilitation at Finney General Army Hospital in Thomasville, Georgia:

"Dear Cpl. Brissie: Was pleased to receive your letter and to know that you are making such splendid progress. From what the doctors say it will not be long before you will be able to play baseball again.

"One of my pitchers, Phil Marchildon, has reported to our club and will be discharged from the Army July 23rd. As he has not done any pitching for the past three years (recall, some of that time was spent in a "German camp"), it will take sometime to get back his pitching form. Am in hopes he will be ready for next season.

Will be pleased to hear from you when it is convenient to write. . . .

On September 5, 1945, Mack wrote to Cpl. L. V. Brissie, Ward D-5 Northington Gen. Hosp. Tuscaloosa, Alabama:

Dear Lefty (Mack returned to his informal salutation for no apparent reason): Was pleased to hear from you, and to know that you are doing a little limbering up. No doubt, you will be able to throw the ball by the batt4ers in due time. . . .

Have heard from quite a few of the boys who are being discharged from the army . . . . A number of the boys want to be remembered to you, especially Earl Brucker.

Hope to hear from you often. Please remember me to your father. . . ."

On April 26, 1946, Mack wrote to Brisssie: "Note what you say at this time that you are not in the very best of condition that is as far as your running is concerned. Our club will be home for sometime starting July 21st and am going to suggest that you come up here at that time. Sincerely hope you will be able to join our club at least in another year. . . ."

On September 26, 1946, Mack wrote: "Was pleased to hear from you, thou (sic) sorry to hear that you lost your dear Father. You will get the contract at close of next season. . . ." The contract called for $200 a month.

On February 6, Mack wrote: "Dear Leland (Lou's given first name): Have been thinking of you and would like to know how your leg feels after the winter. Would like you to answer just as soon as you receive this short letter. Also, how is your family? (Brissie was now married and the father of a daughter.) The weather here [in Philadelphia] the past ten days makes one feel that they would like the baseball season to start. Hope you are in the best of health. . . ."

This ended their correspondence. Brissie, who had played one year in the high minors with Savannah in 1947, and was playing with a huge brace to protect his ever-painful left leg, was called up to the A's in late September and pitched in a starting role against the Yankees and, though performing adequately, lost the game. Brissie would go on to pitch for seven seasons in the big leagues with the A's until 1951 when he was traded to the Cleveland Indians, finishing his baseball career with them in 1953. A highlight of his career was making the 1949 American League All-Star team, pitching three creditable innings in relief in that game, and finishing the season with a 16–11 record. The season before, he was 14–10 and led the American League in strikeouts per nine innings, at 5.9.

Connie Mack retired as a manager following the 1950 season, at age eighty-seven, after fifty years as the A's manager, the longest-serving major-league manager in history. He was elected to the Baseball Hall of Fame in 1937. He died at age ninety-three, on February 8, 1956.

Brissie, now relegated almost exclusively to the use of crutches, was then the president of American Legion baseball and was in Arizona for regional meetings when he heard of Mack's passing.

"Even though he was an old man," Brissie said, "his passing came as a blow to me. Mr. Mack meant so much to me, had changed my life. He'd given me hope when his letters were about the only hope I had. And he looked past any infirmity I had and saw the abilities I had. He was a second father to me, and I wish I could have helped him win a pennant. It is one of the regrets I have in my life. Mr. Mack could have a temper, he could be very careful how he spent a dollar, but he was a kind, generous, thoughtful, smart, fine human being. Mr. Mack and my father were two of the best men I've ever known."

(Originally published in *The Corporal Was a Pitcher: The Courage of Lou Brissie* by Ira Berkow, Triumph Books, 2009.)

The Hand of Ojeda and Three Finger Brown

November 17, 1988

When last seen, Bobby Ojeda was roaming the Mets dugout during the recent and, for the New Yorkers, ultimately glum playoff series against the Dodgers. And he sat or paced or cheered in full uniform and with a white cast big as a boxing glove covering his pitching hand.

There remained great concern whether the thirty-year-old Ojeda, who had nearly cut off part of a finger in a freakish accident, would ever pitch again. Robert Smith, the esteemed baseball historian, recalled recently that at least two pitchers have come back from mangled pitching hands and succeeded handsomely in the major leagues.

The best known was Three Finger Brown, who as a boy lost the first joint of the index finger on his throwing hand in a corn-chopping machine.

The other pitcher was the more obscure Toad Ramsey, a nineteenth-century lefty. Toad had been a bricklayer and severed the tendon in the index finger of his pitching hand with a trowel. As a result, Ramsey pitched a natural knuckleball (unknown in his day) with a fastball motion, holding the ball with his index finger retracted since he could not straighten it out, and with just his finger tip on the ball. The pitch would drop suddenly as it reached the batter, and Toad had such control he could drop the ball right on the plate time after time.

All this might interest Ojeda because on Monday the Mets team physician, James Parkes, predicted that he would be back in the Mets rotation next season. Ojeda is scheduled to throw tomorrow at Shea Stadium in what is perceived as the first step of his comeback.

"I'm very happy to say that things look absolutely outstanding," Parkes told Steve Marcus of *Newsday*. "When you look at the finger it's hard to believe that anything happened. He's really moving it well. I'm very happy. I'm very optimistic."

Only about two weeks before the playoffs, Ojeda, one of the Mets' most dependable pitchers, nearly severed the upper part of his left middle finger with an electric hedge clipper as he trimmed the honeysuckle bushes at his home in Port Washington, Long Island (New York).

He immediately underwent five hours of microsurgery and his finger was saved. "The joint," Parkes said after the operation, "was stabilized."

42

As for Brown, his nickname Three Finger was so famous that many baseball followers are unaware of the pitcher's full name. It was Mordecai Peter Centennial (he was born in 1876) Brown, and that he also went under another nickname, Miner, for he was a coal miner in Coxville, Ind., before he was a "salaried pitcher," as he referred to his status in professional baseball.

Nor should he be confused with such other major leaguers as Boardwalk Brown, Buster Brown, Charlie Brown, Glass Arm Brown, Skinny Brown, Jumbo Brown, Gimpy Brown, Stub Brown, Downtown Brown or, even, Snitz Browne.

Three Finger Brown had been a third baseman in amateur ball, but because of his strong arm was once called in to pitch when the regular hurler was injured. Brown won 20 games six times for the Cubs from 1906 to 1911, and was voted into the Hall of Fame in 1949.

"Brown's pitch was a wide curve of the type that was called an out-drop in that day," said Robert Smith. "But Brown's 'drop' was a sudden dive that drove batters crazy. He was able to throw a natural sinker with his fastball motion, so that batters continually topped the pitch and rolled it out to be gobbled up, if not by Brown himself, who was one of the best fielding pitchers of his time, then by one of his noted stonewall infield—Tinker or Evers or Chance or Harry Steinfeldt at third base."

Smith added that Brown was a "true Ironman." Brown, said Smith, "could walk into a game without a warm-up and get all the batters out in the final two or three innings and then pitch nine innings the next day.

"Brown pitched 10 games in 22 days during the pennant drive of September 1908, and won both ends of a doubleheader in that stretch." The Cubs won the pennant by one game over the Giants with help not only from Brown but also from Fred Merkle of New York, who made the historic bonehead play.

Brown also accepted 108 fielding chances on the mound that season and, recalled Smith, "never made an error."

Not a great deal is known about Toad Ramsey, whose mother and the tax called Thomas A. Ramsey. The reason for the name Toad is not immediately available, but it's known that he once played for an amateur team in his hometown, Indianapolis, known as the Whens. Though it sounds like part of an Abbott and Costello routine, the team was really named for the local When Clothing Company.

Ramsey went on to pitch six years in the American Association when it was one of the major leagues. Ramsey's two best years were with Louisville, when he was 38–27 in 1886, and 37–27 the next season, when he struck out 17 batters in one game and led the league in strike-outs with 355.

"What made those feats especially noteworthy," said Smith, "is that 1887 was the year the rulemakers decided to allow a batter four strikes."

As for Ojeda, Smith said, "Inasmuch as the middle finger, which Bobby injured, is the one a pitcher lifts from the ball when he throws a sinker, I have a notion that Bobby's best days may lie ahead of him."

From Tinker to Evers to Chance

April 2014

A segment of the baseball world, and beyond, continues to consider the Chicago Cubs turn-of-the-century double-play combination of Tinker to Evers to Chance particularly wondrous, and the three—shortstop Joe Tinker, second baseman Johnny Evers and first baseman Frank Chance—indeed all entered the Baseball Hall of Fame together in 1946.

The reason for the uncommon fame of the double-play combination is a melodic triplet written by Franklin P. Adams in his column in the *New York Evening Mail* on July 10, 1910. Adams, who was from Chicago, was on his way to see a Cubs-Giants game in the Polo Grounds.

The poem is seen through a rueful Giants fan suffering because of the Cubs magical double-play trio. It is titled "Baseball's Sad Lexicon." These are the saddest of all possible words:

Tinker to Evers to Chance.

Trio of Bear cubs, and fleeter than birds,
 Tinker to Evers to Chance.
Ruthlessly pricking our gonfalon bubble,
 Making a Giant hit into a double—
Words that are heavy with nothing but trouble:
 Tinker to Evers to Chance.

While that double-play combo never led the league in double plays in any of the eleven seasons the trio played together (1902–12), and in only six if those seasons did they each play a full schedule, the three remain in popular culture to the present day. The Adams poem has apparently had a long-lived rhythmic resonance.

 The rock band Rush, for instance, listed in the liner notes of its 1993 album *Counterparts* such counterparts as Larry, Curly, and Moe—the Three Stooges—lock, stock, and barrel, as well as Tinker to Evers to Chance. They've also been referenced in novels, sitcoms, and films, inspiring, among others, the 1949 Frank Sinatra-Gene Kelly movie *Take Me Out to the Ball Game*, which included the song "O'Brien to Ryan to Goldberg."

 A 1949 poem by Ogden Nash titled "Line-up for Yesterday" pays homage to the three Cub infielders:

 E is for Evers
His jaw in advance;

Never afraid
To Tinker with Chance.

The Cubs were a dominant team in the first decade of the twentieth century, invariably in contention for the pennant, and won four National League pennants and two World Series in that time. Their player-manager was Frank Chance, husky, no-nonsense individual who was nicknamed "The Peerless Leader" by then *Chicago Tribune* sports columnist Ring Lardner, later to become a national figure for his short stories. . . . He wrote in the *Tribune* following a rainout in 1910: "Some of the boys [Cub players] went over to the racetrack to do a little donating. In the bunch [was] Frank Chance. . . ."

While Frank Chance was at one end of the storied double-play infield that Adams memorialized, at the other end, at third base in those glory years from 1905 to 1910, was Harry Steinfeldt. Steinfeldt is essentially lost in history because, although he started several double plays, "Steinfeldt to Evers to Chance" apparently didn't have the ring for Adams that the Tinker-initiated double play did, and Steinfeldt may have missed out on election to the Baseball Hall of Fame because of it.

Steinfeldt, however, ranks above Tinker in career batting average, .268 to Tinker's .263, only somewhat below Evers's .278. Chance, at .296, had the most formidable bat in that infield, though only Steinfeldt ever led the league in any batting category, driving in 83 runs in 1906. Chance gets his due, having led the NL twice in stolen bases.

In an intriguing sidelight, Tinker and Evers had stopped speaking to each other because of a dispute in September 1905—some five years before the Adams poem. The pair had a fistfight on the field because Evers, who bore the nickname Crab in part because of his less-than-sunny disposition, had taken a cab and left his teammates behind in the hotel lobby. Tinker and Evers did not speak to each other for thirty-three years, until they were asked to participate in a radio broadcast of the 1938 World Series—between the Yankees and the Cubs—where they were united in a tearful embrace. (Chance, being the manager during those standout playing years, spoke to the men together only when necessary.)

Addendum: Chance had moved on in 1913 as player-manager of the Yankees, and finished with a brief appearance at first base the year after, registering one putout in his only fielding chance. Tinker became the Cubs manager in 1916, at the very end of his playing career. He put himself into seven games, batting 10 times and had one single for his plate efforts. Evers also managed the Cubs, twice, both for one year. In 1922 he became manager of the Chicago White Sox, and at age forty-one put himself into the lineup at second base for one game and went hitless in three at-bats.

While Tinker and Evers lived to appear at their induction ceremony into the Baseball Hall of Fame in 1946—with Evers dying the year after, and Tinker the year after that—Chance did not. He died of respiratory complications, including influenza and asthma, in 1924, at age forty-eight. Oddly, Chance, the first baseman of the vaunted trio, was the first to depart, Evers, the second baseman, was second, and Tinker last.

(Originally published in *Wrigley Field: An Oral and Narrative History of the Home of the Chicago Cubs* by Ira Berkow, by Stewart, Tabori and Chang, 2014.)

Part II: 1930s—The Splendid Splinter and Joltin' Joe Head a Memorable Lineup

An Evening with The Kid, or Teddy Ballgame

November 12, 1988/Boston, MA

He was once called The Kid. He also had other nicknames: The Splendid Splinter, The Thumper, Teddy Ballgame. None of them quite apply anymore for Ted Williams, who recently turned seventy years old, except "The Kid."

No longer is he a splinter, splendid or otherwise, and he thumps no baseballs as in days of yore, nor plays any ball games, and hasn't for nearly thirty years.

But there is still the en-thoos-iasm, as he says the word, the stubbornness, perhaps, the dream of striving to be the best and striving for the best that marked him as a boy, surely, and as a young man, certainly, and as a senior citizen, absolutely.

On Thursday night in the Wang Center here, Theodore Samuel Williams, the last of the .400 hitters, The Kid, returned for kids. It was a benefit in his honor, "An Evening with 9, and Friends," for the Jimmy

Fund, a fund-raising arm of the Dana-Farber Cancer Institute, with a special interest in children's cancer.

For forty years Williams, who, no Red Sox fan need be told, wore the red No. 9 of their team, has been closely associated with the Jimmy Fund. He has visited ailing children, usually without photographers, attended affairs for the fund, and always lent his name to the cause. Never, though, until now, would he consent to be honored at a fund-raiser.

"It took an awful, awful, lot to get me here," he said before the evening's program. "I just thought there were millions and millions of people who've done a lot more for this than I have."

Friends finally prevailed, and Williams arrived even wearing a tie; he rarely submits to such a silly social convention. It was a black string tie held at the neck by a silver oval clasp with an embossed gold salmon, for, as the world knows, Williams is as avid about catching a fish as he was about clubbing a baseball.

For the evening with Williams, 4,200 people filled the ornate old theater and paid a total of $250,000 that went to the Jimmy Fund.

The friends of Williams, introduced one by one and "interviewed" by David Hartman on a stage set like a fishing cabin, included former teammates like Dom DiMaggio and Bobby Doerr, rivals like Joe Di-Maggio and Bob Feller; Tommy Lasorda and Reggie Jackson; John Glenn, who was Williams's squadron commander as a fighter pilot in the war in Korea; Tip O'Neill, the former Speaker of the House from Boston; Bud Leavitt, a Maine sportswriter and longtime fishing pal of Williams, and Stephen King, the writer and a New Englander, who represented baseball fandom and Williams fandom.

King spoke of our greatest baseball heroes as having "a resonance that others don't have," such as rock stars or movie stars. Their careers become the stuff of legends. And Williams perhaps resonated more than most, not only because of his extraordinary baseball prowess, but because of his dedication and his humanity, even his vulnerability: he might be quick to anger, would hold a grudge, he stubbornly refused to hit to left when teams packed the right side of the field in the notorious "Williams shift."

And there was in Williams that core of boyish delight in playing the game. When he first came up to the Red Sox in the spring of 1939, he informed the veterans with callow forthrightness about left field: "Hey, this job is mine!"

He cared so much about doing so well. Doerr recalled that Williams, the perfectionist, once stepped out of the batter's box and waited for a cloud to go by because the shadow it created was distracting to him. A film clip at one point showed Williams hitting a homer and nearly galloping with glee around the bases. The audience laughed with appreciation.

Lasorda came out and said: "He was electrifying with a bat in his hands, like a beautiful painting. Enough about Joe DiMaggio." More laughs.

But both Williams and DiMaggio were electrifying at the plate.

"Dom, who was the best hitter you ever saw?" asked Hartman, of the bespectacled Dom DiMaggio often known as "The Little Professor."

The audience hushed. "Well," said Dom DiMaggio, "the best right-handed hitter"—the audience roared at the unexpected but perfect cop-out—"was Joe. But the best left-handed hitter by far was Ted Williams."

Feller recalled how he could never get his famous fastball by Williams. Joe DiMaggio, his hair now all white, spoke of his admiration for "the best hitter I ever saw." And Reggie Jackson told of the encouragement Williams gave him as a rookie: "Never let anybody change your swing." Jackson called him "a real nice American natural resource."

Williams's son, John Henry, a young man, brought out a five-year-old boy named Joey Raymundo, who was wearing a tuxedo. Joey has leukemia and is being treated at the clinic. He presented Williams with a gift from the fund, an oil painting—the frame was as big as the boy—of Williams in baseball action.

Then Williams sat down and pulled out some notes—along with a pair of glasses. "Not a lot of people have seen these," said the man who was known for having remarkable eyesight.

He spoke of how lucky his life had been, and, to a question from Hartman, said, "You're not gonna make this old guy cry."

Finally, Williams looked around at his friends seated nearby on the stage and out to the audience.

"This has been an honor," he said, "and I'm thrilled and a little embarrassed." He paused. "And I wanna thank you."

And despite his resistance, there was a slight catch in his throat and, it seemed, a little moisture in The Kid's eye.

Ted Williams: The Slugging Professor

March 23, 1985/Winter Haven, Florida

In his open-air classroom here among the swaying palms and noisy bats, Prof. Theodore Samuel Williams was expounding on the virtues of getting your bellybutton out in front of the ball.

"It's that little magic move at the plate," he was saying recently, beside the batting cage on a field behind Chain O'Lakes Stadium. He wore a Red Sox uniform and a blue windbreaker with little red stockings embossed at the heart and stood on ripple-soled baseball shoes. It was late morning, cool but sunny as he spoke to a couple of young players. "Hips ahead of hands," he said in a deep, ardent baritone, "hips ahead of hands."

And the one-time Splendid Splinter—he is a Splinter no longer—demonstrated with an imaginary bat and an exaggerated thrust of his abdomen. "We're talking about optimum performance, and the optimum is to hit the ball into your pull field with authority. And getting your body into the ball before it reaches the plate—so you're not swinging with all arms—that's the classic swing. But a lot of batters just can't learn it, or won't."

Dr. Williams—and if he isn't a bona fide Ph.D. in slugging, who is?—is author of the authoritative textbook *The Science of Hitting*. He also is the last professor or hitter or anyone else to bat .400 in the major leagues (he hit .406 in 1941) and had a scholarly career average of .344. This spring, he is serving the Red Sox as batting instructor with minor league players.

Ted Williams on hitting is Lindbergh on flying, Picasso on painting and Little Richard on Tutti Frutti.

Williams is now sixty-seven years old and drives around the Red Sox complex in a golf cart, stopping now at this field, now at that. And though he says he's "running out of gas," it hardly seems so to the casual visitor, and there are many who come just to see him in the leathery flesh. He arrives before 9 a.m. at the training site and spends a long, full day under the Florida sun observing the young players.

He knows that there are as many theories on hitting as there are stars in the sky. "Like I've heard some where they tell a batter to keep his head down," he said. "No way you can open your body and carry through with your head down that way." He says that he may not be right for all the players, but he urges them to "listen—you can always throw away what you don't want, and keep what works for you."

And, like the good teacher, he listens, too. An image returns of him in the clubhouse, sitting on a storage trunk and nodding in understanding while a minor-leaguer quietly talks to him.

In the batting cage now was the third baseman Steve Lyons, a 6-foot-3, 190-pound left-handed batter who bears a physical resemblance to the young Ted Williams. Lyons, after four seasons in the minor leagues, has a chance to make the parent club.

Williams watched him swing. "He's improvin' good," said Williams, "improvin' good. Has good power and good contact."

Last season, Lyons's batting average jumped to .268 in Triple A ball, 22 points higher than the previous year in Double A. He credits some of that improvement to Williams.

"He's not quick to criticize or change you immediately," Lyons said. "He watches, and then when he talks, people listen. He tries to be positive in his approach. He'll say, 'You've got a good swing, but there's not enough action into the ball. Cock your bat back farther.'"

When Williams was young, he sought advice. Before his rookie year with the Red Sox in 1939, he met Rogers Hornsby and asked, "What do I have to do to be a good hitter?"

Hornsby said, "Get a good ball to hit."

"That's not as easy as it sounds," said Williams. "If the pitcher throws a good pitch, low and outside or high and inside—in the strike zone but not in the batter's groove—you let it go with less than two strikes. With two strikes, you move up a little bit on the knob of the bat. But too many hitters aren't hitters from the head up, and never become as good as they can be."

Sometimes the best advice is no advice at all. "When I was comin' up," said Williams, "Lefty O'Doul said to me, 'Don't let anybody change you.' And when I saw Carl Yastrzemski, I thought pretty much the same thing. He had a big swing, and I thought he should cut down his swing just a little. But I never came right out and said it. I'd say, 'Gotta be quicker, a little quicker.' And I think it took him longer than it should've to get his average up. Look at his record. He batted under .300 his first two years in the big leagues. Then he hit .321. Same guy, same swing, same everything. But he got a little quicker, got a little quicker."

It was Paul Waner who told Williams about getting the bellybutton out in front of the ball.

"And I saw the best hitters doing it. Cronin did it, and Greenberg did it, and York and DiMaggio," he said. Of current-day players, Pete Rose and Rod Carew hit that way.

"Reggie Jackson doesn't, but he's so strong that he can get away with that arm action.

Now, Al Oliver isn't the classic hitter—a swishy, inside-out hitter—but he's gonna get 3,000 hits because he makes such good contact.

"Guys like Mantle and Mays—great, classic hitters—could have been even better if they had thought more at the plate. They struck out too much—and they'll tell you that, too.

You got to concede a little to the pitcher, even the greatest hitters have to. Look at DiMaggio, he struck out only a half or a third as many times as he walked. It meant he was looking for his pitch—he was in control, not the pitcher."

Williams no longer teaches by example, and said that the last time he stood in the batter's box was in last year's old-timer's game in Fenway Park.

"I hit two little ground balls to the pitcher," he said. "I was so anxious up there, I couldn't wait for the ball, and hit them at the end of the bat."

Was he embarrassed? "Was I?" said the professor. "I didn't want to run to first base."

The Two Loves of Ted Williams

August 10, 1982/Lakeville, Massachusetts

"Just got a call from the people up at my cabin and they tell me the salmon are jumping in front of the door—jumping!" said Ted Williams. "I'm leaving for there this afternoon."

Ted Williams, the Hall of Fame hitter, would be heading, as previously scheduled, for his camp site on the Miramichi River in the province of New Brunswick. Now, though, he was at another camp, the Ted Williams Baseball Camp, which draws boys eighteen and younger. His remains a tale of two passions - baseball and fishing.

In *Ted Williams Fishing,* "The Big Three"— the big three being tarpon, bonefish, and Atlantic salmon—to be published in September by Simon and Schuster, he describes his singular techniques of angling with the same kind of rich and joyous detail with which he illuminated the classic, *The Science of Hitting.*

"Is fishing as challenging as hitting a baseball?" he said, walking around the numerous diamonds filled with kids and baseballs here. "I've always said that hitting a baseball is the hardest thing to do in sports. The hardest thing—a round ball, round bat, curves, sliders, knuckleballs, upside down and a ball coming in at 90 miles to 100 miles an hour, it's a pretty lethal thing.

"But fishing takes a lot, too—learning the habits of the fish, what kind of flies to use, how to rig 'em just right, when to apply tension to the rod, all that. And patience, patience, patience."

It was the same kind of enthusiasm, the same kind of electricity and vitality one felt watching him, the last of the .400 hitters, at the left side of the plate—his hands working at the bat handle, his shoulders and long neck bobbing at the pitcher, a little jiggle of his hips, and his right leg dipping back as he prepared to rip into the pitch. It was all in rhythm, like a be-bop two-step.

No longer the Splendid Splinter, he has grown comfortably with age—he will be sixty-four on August 30. He still appears fit and walks with that jaunty grace familiar to baseball fans from when he first came up to the Boston Red Sox in 1939 until he retired in 1960, with a career average of .344 and 521 home runs.

He spends most of his days in retirement fishing, in spring and summer in New Brunswick, the rest of the year at his home in Islamorada in the Florida Keys. He maintains an active interest in baseball, however, as a paid batting instructor for the Red Sox during spring training, and he still spends some time at his baseball camp, which he has had for nearly a quarter of a century.

He also follows the standings and listens to some Red Sox games that get through on radio to New Brunswick. "I wanted to be recognized as great a hitter as ever walked down the pike, and I played to that end, too," Williams said. "I remember when they pulled the Williams Shift on me in 1946—I was a pull hitter and they started putting three guys on the right side of the infield. I was having trouble with the shift—I was hard-headed and I tried to hit through it. Well, one day after a game in Yankee Stadium I met with Ty Cobb.

"I'll never forget that look in his face when he said, 'If they ever pulled that shift on me, I'd hit .800.' Not .500—but .800! Geez, probably would've, too, because he could hit the ball into left field so beautifully."

Another old-time player he remembers with admiration was Satchel Paige, the outstanding Negro League pitcher who made it to the major leagues as a rookie at age forty-two.

"I had heard all these stories about Paige," said Williams, "and I remember I'd be facing him and he'd have pretty good stuff, but I'd think—'Oh boy, this old guy must've really been great when he was younger.' Yeah, must've really been something. And before I knew it I was 0-for-5 against him that day."

Williams is critical of many of the players today. He thinks they lack dedication: "Maybe it's the big money, maybe it's all the extra luxuries, they don't have the obsession that some guys did when I was playing. They act like they've got it made."

An exception is Pete Rose, the Philadelphia Phillies first baseman. "People want to know how I like his hitting," Williams said. "I say, 'I don't like the way he hits particularly, but I want him on my team.'"

As his career wound down, Williams said he stepped up his own concentration: "I used to say, 'I got to be quick, this guy's faster than he looks.' I had to hang in there. It's like saying, 'Nothing is going to disturb me as far as my intensity to go into the ball.'"

In 1958, at age forty, he batted .328 and was the oldest man ever to win a big league title. After 1960, with a home run in his last time at bat, he retired. "I remember one day in September when I was on second base and I looked at third and I looked at home, and I said, 'But, that's a long ways.' And I knew it was time to go."

Now, he was on his way to New Brunswick, where, he said again, the salmon were jumping in front of his door. "Bring a net," it was suggested to him. "Oh, no," he said, the curl of his upper lip indicating that there's no challenge in that. "Oh, no."

For Ted Williams, A Joy Found In the Debate

July 6, 2002

Ted Williams was managing the Washington Senators in the spring of 1969, and I was a dewy-eyed young sports reporter given the assignment of following up on a thought that was growing more widespread around the country. That is: Is baseball doomed?

Why, even the media theorist Marshall McLuhan had said exactly that, that baseball wasn't a "hot" sport—too slow for modern times, and unsuited for television. It was at a time when defense was suffocating offense. Deadly dull, it was reasoned.

Ted Williams, with his team in spring training in Pompano Beach, Florida, was one of those I was to interview about whether baseball was on the verge of joining the pterodactyl in extinction.

I did not know, nor had I ever met, Williams, but of course I had followed his remarkable career. The first time I ever saw him, I was struck by him. I was a boy in the early 1950s, and he was a player with the Red Sox, and playing the Chicago White Sox, my hometown team, in Comiskey Park.

You couldn't take your eyes off him. And this was when he was on the on-deck circle.

Crouched on one knee, waggling the bat, he studied the moves of the pitcher with such intensity, such ferocity, it resembled a tiger in the bushes about to pounce on his unsuspecting lunch. I don't remember how Williams did in that game; it doesn't matter.

What he brought to that moment matters.

All this came back to me when I learned that William had died yesterday, in Florida, at age eighty-three, of cardiac arrest.

I had followed him in the box scores as a player, marveling at his batting feats. I was impressed with his military record in World War II and Korea—and his honesty. He had landed a burning plane during the Korean War, which exploded shortly after he fled it, and he had said, "Hell, yes, I was scared." Many said that Williams was a real-life hero. It was said that he was of the stature, and his voice sounded like, John Wayne. No, John Wayne sounded like Ted Williams. And John Wayne was a hero in celluloid.

Williams was flesh and blood.

And so when I went back to the small locker room of the Senators in their training camp, and found my way into the modest manager's office, I found Williams, tugging out of his uniform—he was no longer, at 6-foot-3, the Splendid Splinter, and had gained some weight, sometimes wearing a jacket to hide the paunch.

I introduced myself, and told him the story I was working on. A small, elderly clubhouse man was handing Williams a towel. When he heard about "Is baseball doomed?" the clubhouse man began to berate me: "Do you know who you're talking to? This is Ted Williams. He's baseball. What nerve to come in here and ask him such a stupid question."

I said nothing, taken aback. I turned to Williams for a reply. I had read about his occasional temper outbursts.

"It's OK," he said to the clubhouse man. Then he turned to me. "When I come out of the shower, I'll answer your questions."

The thing about Williams that I learned was that he was as challenged by a good question as he was by a good fastball. He was thoughtful, direct and candid. He liked an intellectual test, from figuring what Bob Feller's next pitch would be, to landing a salmon, to flying a plane, to a discussion that could lead to a dialectic. He loved a good argument.

When he emerged from the shower in Pompano, he did answer my questions. And the one answer I recall regarding my quest was: "Everything goes in cycles. Baseball will return to the popularity it has enjoyed in the past." He may have used several expletives to punctuate those brief sentences, for that was his style, and that was, as I perceived it, his grace. He made you feel comfortable in his presence.

Over the last three decades or so, I've had the pleasure of being in his company.

I once came across a newspaper story titled "Your Child's Creativity" that began: "What do Henry Ford, John F. Kennedy and Ted Williams have in common?" The answer: The burning drive for achievement.

I asked Williams about that. "I can't speak for those other guys, but to succeed I believe it starts with enthusiasm," he said. "And certainly no one ever worked at hitting a baseball harder than I did."

The last time I saw him was two years ago, and at one point we talked about death. "I don't know what's going to happen, if anything, when I'm dead," he said. "I'll tell you this, though, I'm not afraid to die."

For many of us, Ted Williams never will.

Joe DiMaggio and Marilyn Monroe

November 25, 1998

In the press room of Yankee Stadium not long ago I saw Joe DiMaggio sitting at a table with a few friends. Even in repose he looked elegant, still trim in his dark suit, hair graying and thin but neatly coiffed. I was reminded of a remark by Henry Kissinger when he sat near DiMaggio in the owner's box in Yankee Stadium. The Yankees had lost a playoff game and Kissinger, on the way out, had said, "Joe, put on a uniform—they can use you." In the mind's eye, Joe still could lope after a fly ball.

When I saw DiMaggio now I related to him an unfortunate incident that happened to him some forty-five years ago and which he didn't know about.

I was a small boy growing up in Chicago in the 1950s, I told him, and aware of the DiMaggio legend, as was anyone else who followed baseball in America. I had written to the Yankees for a photograph of him, was sent a glossy head shot with him in his baseball cap, and nailed the picture to my bedroom wall. The unfortunate part, I told DiMaggio, was that I hammered the nail right through his forehead.

"You did?" he said, wincing.

"Looks like it's OK now," I said.

"Oh yeah," he said. "I heal fast."

Today, which marks DiMaggio's eighty-fourth birthday, one wonders if he can heal as he lies in a hospital in Hollywood, Florida, amid reports that he has been battling lung cancer as well as pneumonia. He is fighting for his life. One wonders whether the man who once hit in 56-straight big-league games, a record that has stood for fifty-seven years, can summon the energy and, perhaps, the requisite miracle to regain health.

Even before his admission to the hospital on October 12, DiMaggio's name was in the news, in an indirect fashion. The Yankees sterling center fielder, Bernie Williams, the American League's leading hitter and Gold Glove fly-chaser, heir to DiMaggio and Mickey Mantle, and a free agent, has been in controversial negotiations with the Yankees. Williams is as distinguished a ballplayer, if not as iconic, as his famous predecessors.

It is difficult for fans to imagine that their athletic heroes are vulnerable to everything human. The youth of the ballplayer, or, sometimes, even the coach, is eternal, if only in photographs and film—DiMaggio in his baggy pinstripes is still rapping out hits in his familiar long stride and sweeping stroke of the bat—and in our memory.

Red Holzman can still be seen in that fashion in the huddle, instructing Bradley and Frazier, and Weeb Ewbank may be forever visualized discussing strategy with a mud-splattered Joe Namath on the sidelines. In that sense, Coach Holzman of the Knicks and Coach Ewbank of the Jets, who died recently, remain vital to us.

And Catfish Hunter, because of the Lou Gehrig's disease he has, may soon lose such control in his muscles that he will be unable to even grip a baseball. Such thoughts seem to fall off the radar screen of our comprehension.

And so it is with Joe D., that intensely proud man, that sometimes impatient and unforgiving man, who, the Yankee management knew, would be insulted if, at Old-Timers' Day, he should not be the last announced.

On the day I apologized for pounding that nail into his head, I gave DiMaggio a photograph of him and Marilyn Monroe taken by Richard

Sanborn, who is now a judicial magistrate living in Maryland. Sanborn had been a sergeant in the Army stationed in Tokyo in 1954 when DiMaggio and Monroe went on their honeymoon to Japan. I had done a column on DiMaggio and Sanborn sent it to me to give to DiMaggio, saying he had always wanted Joe to have it and didn't know how to get it to him. Would I do it? I did.

As most people know, bringing up his former wife to DiMaggio would end any conversation with him. It was too personal. But I handed DiMaggio the photograph. He thought it was great. "And this guy was just an amateur photographer?" DiMaggio said.

"I've got to send him a note and thank him."

Shortly after, alone with DiMaggio, I said, "Marilyn looked beautiful in the picture."

"She was beautiful," DiMaggio said, as though relating an insight.

I said, "Joe, there's a question I've always wanted to ask you, if you don't mind." He nodded, knitting his brow. "There's that great anecdote first written by Gay Talese," I went on, "about when you were in Japan and Marilyn was asked by the brass to entertain the troops in Korea. When she returned to your hotel room, you asked how it went and she said, 'Oh, Joe, you never heard such cheering!' And you said quietly, 'Yes I have.'

"Did it happen?"

"Yes," DiMaggio said, "it did."

Joe DiMaggio, a Neighbor, the Quake

October 10, 1989/San Francisco, California

Joe DiMaggio is her neighbor. She has lived for about ten years just a few doors down the block from the old Yankee ballplayer in the Marina District here, the lovely, snug area that took so terrible a jolt from last week's earthquake.

"I'd see Mr. DiMaggio in the grocery store, or just walking down the street, but I never spoke to him," said Sherra Cox. "He's a quiet man, seems like a nice man, but I never felt right just walking up and talking to him, or getting his autograph. I suppose it's OK for kids to do."

Cox, a middle-aged woman, smiled with some difficulty because of the stitches under her lip. She sat Sunday afternoon in a chair beside her bed in San Francisco General Hospital. Above her on a small television screen was the 49ers–Patriots football game.

She's a sports fan. A week ago today, she hurried home to her second-floor apartment from her job as manager in an accounting firm to watch the third game of the World Series. Suddenly, at 5:04 p.m., the earth shook violently, the floor she stood on opened like a trapdoor and she tumbled down, the rest of the building crashing around her.

She lay trapped under a door and doorjamb for some time. How long she doesn't know. She smelled fire, felt the creaking of the wood and stone around her, and thought she might be burned or crushed to death. She told herself, "Don't panic." She prayed.

A firefighter named Jerry Shannon would crawl in, spend the next two and a half hours struggling to dig her out.

"He was so reassuring," Cox recalled. "He said, 'Don't worry, when this is over I'll buy you a cup of coffee.'"

Shannon went through two chain saws, used two jacks to prop up the wood around Cox, and finally resorted to a hatchet. He thought they might not make it, but told himself not to think about it, just to "stay busy."

When Shannon discovered her, he told Cox he had to get equipment. "Don't leave me; I don't want to die in here," she pleaded. He promised to return.

"You're my hero," she told him later, on the stretcher, in the night lighted by flames, and she kissed him.

Now, a visitor said he'd seen in the newspaper a picture of her neighbor, DiMaggio, a seventy-four-year-old man in sports jacket and open-collared shirt, waiting in a long line at a shelter with other neighbors to learn whether his house would have to be demolished.

He'd been at the ball game the night of the quake, and escaped injury. Three doors down from his two-story home—and directly across the street from Sherra Cox's—three people perished. DiMaggio's house suffered some damage, but was saved.

Curious, said the visitor, that one of America's most celebrated men, one who has been raised to hero status, now elderly and white-haired, was in the end, like everyone else, simply trying to survive. Meanwhile, all around, courageous acts by unsung firefighters, rescue workers and everyday citizens were being performed in the aftermath of the earthquake.

"I wonder what the definition of hero is?" Cox said. "I suppose it has to do with saving lives."

There are people like Jerry Shannon, and those who crawled through the wreckage to find bodies in cars flattened to the size of license plates, who will never do a television commercial or be pictured on a bubble-gum card. This is no knock at those upon whom we confer the title of model or hero. It says more about the values of a nation that so prizes entertainers, including ballplayers, even those as fine and decent and elegant as Joe DiMaggio.

"I've thought for a long time," Rick Reuschel, the Giants pitcher, said the other day, "that ballplayers are elevated way too high. And when a disaster like this happens, we see how unimportant our job is in comparison to so many others."

Sherra Cox, meanwhile, feels that the Series should continue in the Bay Area.

"Life goes on," she said. "We pick up the pieces. And I'm rooting for the Giants!" The visitor had brought something for her. He had been to the rubble and debris that was once Cox's home and noticed a book among the shards. He picked it up—the only book he saw—just before a bulldozer could scoop it up. The book, with a purple dust jacket, was a little torn and charred but in otherwise good shape. He handed it to Sherra Cox.

"I had that book," she said. "I had hundreds of books, and records, and I bought that one but I hadn't got around to reading it."

Reflectively, she ran her fingers over the title. The book is by Truman Capote. It is called *Answered Prayers*.

"My goodness," Sherra Cox said. Her eyes were moist. "I think I'll have to read it now."

DiMaggio, 80 Today, Still Stars

November 25, 1994

The elderly man and his companion had driven off the New Jersey highway on a recent afternoon in order to use the facility of a restaurant. Once inside, the elderly man, not uncommonly, ignited a commotion among the patrons.

His familiar face is long and lined, his eyes rheumy, his hair now snow white. He is slightly stooped from an arthritic condition—his aching knees and arm, remnants of his former occupation. He wears a pacemaker to juice his heart, and fairly recently underwent stomach surgery for a long-suffered ulcer.

When the proprietor learned who had entered his establishment, he elbowed his way through the crowd.

"Follow me," he said. And led the man and his friend through the kitchen to the back door.

"Do you know how many kitchens I've had to go through in my life?" the man, offhandedly, said to his friend.

This was Joe DiMaggio, who turns eighty years old today. This was Joe DiMaggio who still, remarkably, cannot go out in public without heads turning and grown men and women reverting to the children inside them, and children pursuing someone as seemingly aged but fabled as Odysseus.

This was Joe DiMaggio who still, forty-three years after he played his last baseball game, remains a national symbol, a reigning star, a living and breathing legend.

"Who else is there who has his aura?" a friend was saying. "Ali? Sinatra? Who else?"

Few, to be sure. A baseball bat signed by him sells for $4,000, twice as much as any other living ballplayer past or present; his baseball for $400, also tops. When Paul Simon sought a line in a song about longing for another day, he wrote, "Where have you gone, Joe DiMaggio?"

The son of an Italian immigrant who was a San Francisco fisherman, DiMaggio carries himself with the dignity and grace of old, when, it was said, he never made a difficult catch in center field. That is, he never made a catch look difficult. He understood positioning, understood the hitters, was smoothly off with the crack of the bat.

When Hank Greenberg asked for advice on playing the outfield, DiMaggio instinctively instructed, "Float in for the ball."

DiMaggio has withstood the test of time, the world of coffee and banking commercials and the paparazzi, nine-month marriage to a woman who, on their honeymoon in the Far East in 1954, entertained the troops in Korea and signed her official Department of Defense ID "Norma Jeane DiMaggio."

Joe DiMaggio, trim and still impeccably dressed with suit and tie, manicured, hair cut regularly, ever conscious of his image, remains the acme of elegance in sports, and the prototype of a time past, a time glorious in some memories but not necessarily in fact. He was a baseball star during the Depression, when Jim Crow was rife, when World War II erupted, when the McCarthy era was burgeoning.

But during those years, he led the Yankees to the World Series 10 times in 13 seasons, socking 361 home runs over his career and, in 1941, hitting in 56 straight games, still a major league record. Dr. Bobby Brown, a Yankee teammate, remembers that DiMaggio could always be counted on. "Whenever there was a clutch situation, you knew that Joe was going to come through," he said, "and, even when he was sick or hurt, he almost always did."

He did it quietly, too, letting his actions speak for him, a quality that seems almost Victorian today. He carried much of the pressures inside him, however. He endured stomach problems, and developed ulcers during his famed hitting streak. He was immortalized by Hemingway when his Old Man in the sea daydreamed about taking "the great DiMaggio fishing."

DiMaggio himself is an old man now, sometimes cranky, sometimes forgetful, sometimes needing help in ways he never did before. But he too may go back in time, listening to the Big Band music on tape, or, even, one of the songs about him, like "Joltin' Joe."

On occasion, he will attend a game. Last season, said his friend Morris Engelberg, the two went to a Miami Marlins' game, not far from DiMaggio's condominium near Fort Lauderdale. "After watching the outfielders run back and forth and sideways chasing fly balls," Engelberg said, "Joe turned to me and asked, 'Can't anybody make an easy catch anymore?'"

For much of the nation, Joe DiMaggio, eighty years old today, still does.

Lefty Gomez Was Hard to Beat

February 20, 1989

In a 1931 photograph in the book *The American League: An Illustrated History* by Donald Honig, three strapping young ballplayers, three Yankees, are smiling into the camera. In the middle is Lefty Gomez, his glove, looking as big as a cushion (baseball gloves were puffier in those days), is thrown over the right shoulder of Bill Dickey, and Gomez's left hand—the one that won all those games—rests on the left shoulder of Lou Gehrig.

And there, halted blissfully for all time, are Dickey the catcher, Gomez the hurler, Gehrig the slugger: "Three future Hall of Famers," reads the caption. Three Yankee teammates, presumably after another winning game, in slightly undone pinstripes with T-shirts exposed and wearing flattened baseball caps (baseball caps were flatter in those days).

Ten years later, Gehrig, the Iron Horse, would be dead at age thirty-seven. Last Friday, at age eighty, a second in that sunny picture, Lefty Gomez, nicknamed El Goofy, and the Gay Castillion, for he was part Spanish and part Irish and part zany, died of congestive heart failure and pneumonia in Larkspur, California.

On Saturday morning, in his home on Choctaw Road in Little Rock, Arkansas, Bill Dickey, the third and last in that photograph, now eighty-one and recovering from a broken back, recalled Lefty, whom he caught for 13 of Gomez's 14 big-league seasons. "He was a great guy, a gentleman, and we were good friends," said Dickey. "I didn't sleep well last night, I guarantee ya."

Dickey remembered the first time he saw Gomez. "It was in spring training in St. Petersburg, in 1930, when he was a rookie," he said. "He was tall, about 6-foot-2, and very, very skinny, like a beanpole. And I saw him whizzin' that ball out there. He had the livest fastball I ever saw."

Dickey recalled that one batter Gomez had particular trouble with was Jimmie Foxx, the great power hitter. Gomez once said about Foxx, "He's got muscles in his hair." One time, with Foxx at bat, Dickey gave one signal after the other and Lefty shook them all off. Finally Dickey ran out to the mound. "What do you want to throw him?" "I don't wanna throw him nothin'," said Gomez. "Maybe he'll just get tired of waitin' and leave." Dickey laughed when telling the story. "Actually, Lefty was always in good humor except when he was in trouble," he said. "Then he'd be so nervous he'd shake. His hand used to shake real bad. I'd go out to the mound to try to relax him. He'd say, 'Give me the ball, give me the ball!'

"But then he'd reach back and give you that extra stuff. He did it in so many games. He was awfully hard to beat." Vernon Louis Gomez won 189 games and lost 102 and is ranked 13th on the career list for winning percentage. Four times he won 20 or more games in a season; his best year was 1934, when he was 26–5 with a 2.33 earned run average and led the league in victories, winning percentage, ERA, strikeouts, shutouts, complete games, and innings pitched. He had a 6–0 record in five World Series, and was the winning pitcher in four of the five All-Star games he started, including the first All-Star Game ever, in 1933.

Gomez, despite his pitching exploits, may be better known for his quips. When, for example, he was asked the secret of his success, he replied, "Clean living and a fast outfield." Another time, asked about an inning in which three hard-hit balls were caught by his outfielders, he said, "I'd rather be lucky than good." There were other sides to Lefty, as well. When a dispirited Gehrig, after playing 2,130 straight games, finally had to take himself out of the lineup because of the disease that would soon claim his life, Gomez sat down beside him on the dugout bench. "Hell, Lou," he said, "it took fifteen years to get you out of a game. Sometimes I'm out in fifteen minutes."

When Jimmie DeShong heard that Gomez had died, he called June O'Dea Gomez, Lefty's widow, to offer condolences, and tell her what

Lefty had meant to him. DeShong was a rookie pitcher with the Yankees in 1934 and was assigned to room with Gomez.

"In those days, veterans usually wouldn't give rookies the time of day," DeShong would recall. "But not Lefty. He made me feel a part of the team. Once I had a run-in with one of our veteran players, and Lefty told me, 'Don't bother with him, he's just a jerk.' I'll always be grateful to Lefty."

In 1932, Gomez fell in love and started "going with" June O'Dea, then the leading lady of the Broadway hit *Of Thee I Sing*. He recalled "hanging around the theater" and seeing "the show so often I could act myself."

"February 26," said June O'Dea Gomez, "would have made 56 years that Lefty and I were married." In newspaper clips, there were reports early on of a stormy marriage, and possible divorce—"He could be kind of high-strung in those days," she said—but they held on, and had four children and seven grandchildren.

Over the telephone now June O'Dea Gomez at home in Novato, in northern California, related a few of Lefty's stories that she loved, her voice sometimes cracking with emotion, then she would pause, gathering herself and chuckling again.

"We had such a good time, all that laughter," she said, "even up to the end. In the hospital about a week ago, the doctor leaned over his bed and said, 'Lefty, picture yourself on the mound, and rate the pain from 1 to 10.' And Lefty looked at him and said, 'Who's hitting, Doc?'"

Hack Wilson's Lesson Still Valid

September 5, 1998

When he died, in Baltimore on November 23, 1948, he was forty-eight years old, penniless, an alcoholic. He was also one of baseball's great players, who would later be voted into the Hall of Fame. This was Hack Wilson, whose National League record of 56 home runs in one season stood for sixty-eight years, or until Mark McGwire drew even and passed him with two homers Tuesday night.

In 1931, Wilson's salary was $33,000, the highest in the National League. He was said to have made more than a quarter of a million dollars in his 12-year major league career. Yet some of the expenses for Wilson's funeral were paid after some men in the bars he frequented passed the hat. The gray suit he wore in his coffin was donated by the undertaker.

A week before his death, Wilson said his life should serve for youngsters as an example of which road not to travel. "There are many kids in and out of baseball who think that just because they have some natural talent, they have the world by the tail," Wilson said on a *We the People* radio program over the Columbia Broadcasting System. "It isn't so. In life you need many more things besides talent. Things like good advice and common sense."

His remarks on that radio show were printed and are framed in a prominent place on a wall in the Chicago Cubs clubhouse at Wrigley Field, as a reminder to the players of today just how far a star may fall.

Wilson's heart-wrenching story, which has been replayed by many other athletes through the years, right up to this very moment, began when he was a young, oddly shaped sensation playing for the Martinsburg, Virginia Blue Sox in the minor leagues.

While he also played for the Giants, the Dodgers, and the Phillies in the majors, his best years were with the Cubs, from 1926 to 1931.

"My own idol was always Hack Wilson," the baseball team owner Bill Veeck wrote in his book, *The Hustler's Handbook*. Veeck added, "Having said that, I now have to admit that if any player of exceptional ability ever drank himself out of baseball long before his time, it was my boyhood idol."

Lewis Robert Wilson—he was called Hack because he was said to resemble a champion wrestler of his day named George Hackenschmidt—was built like a beer keg, on two thin sticks: he stood 5-foot-6, weighed 200 pounds, had an 18-inch neck, a powerful chest, short arms, short legs and child-size 5 1/2 feet. In batting practice, he would pick up a handful of dirt and wipe the sides of his pants. "By the time the game started," Veeck wrote, "Hack would always look as if had just delivered a ton of coal."

Despite his size, the power he generated was stupendous. He led the majors in home runs four out of five years. And in 1930 he not only hit those 56 homers, he also drove in 190 runs—a major league record that hasn't been threatened in decades. Yet four years later, he was out of baseball.

Perhaps the low point of his career came when, playing center field for the Cubs in the 1929 World Series against Philadelphia, he lost two fly balls in the sun in the seventh inning of Game 4. The Cubs entered the inning with an 8–0 lead, and they left losing by 10–8. Wilson came to the dugout after the inning with tears in his eyes. But he rebounded for his remarkable 1930 season, in which he also had a .356 batting average.

That winter, Wilson recalled in his radio broadcast: "I drank more heavily than ever, and I argued with my manager"—Rogers Hornsby—"and with my teammates. I spent most of that off season in tap rooms and I was in terrible condition the next spring, twenty pounds overweight, and I had a terrible year. They were expecting me to break Babe Ruth's record, but I hit only 13."

In his short career with the Dodgers, Wilson played for manager Casey Stengel. In a game against the Phillies in the compact Baker Bowl in Philadelphia, Stengel had come to the mound to remove pitcher Walter "Boom Boom" Beck. Wilson was in right field, his hands on his knees, his head down, exhausted from chasing baseballs hit off Beck.

It was hot, and maybe Wilson had been out late the night before. Beck didn't want to leave the game, argued with Stengel and then flung the baseball that hit the tin fence behind Wilson. Startled, Wilson leaped into action, raced to the fence, picked up the ball and made a perfect throw to second base.

"It was the best play Hack made all year," Stengel said.

And soon after, Hack Wilson was gone. His seasons in the sun ended quicker than he had ever imagined.

Edd Roush: The Original Holdout Makes a "Comeback"—and John J. McGraw

July 7, 1969

Edd Roush is seventy-six years old, but still appears in such fine fettle that few baseball veterans would have been surprised had he held out before the recent Old-Timers' game at Shea Stadium.

Of course, nowadays a holdout or sports retirement is about as common as a campus riot. It's Joe Namath one day, Richie Allen the next, Bill Russell the day after.

Doesn't anybody here want to play the game anymore?

But Roush was holding out and retiring long before it was fashionable. He rarely made it to spring training for more than a week before the season, opener. Once he waited until three days before the start of the season. And once, 1930, he just waited—and waited and waited and waited. By the time he got off his front porch, it was football season.

The Hall of Fame outfielder who played in three leagues, the Federal, American, and National, 1913 to 1931, and had a lifetime batting average of .312, did play in the Old-Timers' game, for fun if not for finances.

74

"The players now have troubles over something else, not salary, the way I did," said Roush. "I always stood up for what I was worth.

"I was twenty-two years old when I came up with the White Sox in 1913. I was making $125 a month, and only for five one-half months. So when the Indianapolis ball club in the Federal League got in touch with me and offered me $2,000, I went.

"In 1915 I made $4,000 in the Federal League and it would have taken me nearly 10 years to make that with the White Sox. The Federal League folded after 1915, for financial reasons."

In 1917, Roush—then with Cincinnati—led the league with a .341 batting average. The next year he lost. the batting championship by two points to Zack Wheat, who hit .335.

"And do you know what happened after that season?" he asked. "They wanted to cut my salary $500. Cut it! I was making $5,000 then, I held out until three days before the season began. To this day I still don't know what they could have been thinking about."

By 1919, however, Roush was earning $15,000 a year. That season the Reds beat the White Sox in the World Series. However, some Chicago players were not trying too hard. It resulted in the Black Sox scandal.

"You just can't mess around with gamblers if you're in front of the public," said Roush. "And you can't have gamblers frequenting your place of business like Joe Namath does.

"'We had some players on the Cincinnati ball club wouldn't stop going to places where gamblers were. This was about nineteen and twenty-one. We got rid of them.

In 1930, Roush again felt he was being underpaid. So he decided to quit.

"I figured that if I couldn't make anything out of it, I might as well stay home," he said. I was thirty-seven then. You gotta quit sometime. I felt that was as good a time as any. But the next year the team was hurt by the Depression and had to sell a lot of players. The owner asked me to come back to help draw crowds. So I went back for one more year."

Looking back, Roush almost quit after the 1926, when he was traded to the New York Giants and manager John J. McGraw for whom he played for in 1916.

"I didn't enjoy playing for McGraw," said Roush. "You make a bad play and he would use every swear word imaginable on you. I was going to quit and wrote him a letter telling him I would not play for any kind of money. He kept writing me letters offering me more money. But I was busy hunting quail in Oakland City, Indiana. Finally, he asked to see me in Chattanooga, where the team was coming north.

"I was supposed to be in his room at eight in the morning. But I lolled around with the players in the hotel. Finally, we met in his room at 12:30. After a little hassle, he offered me $70,000 for three years. I said okay, but I told him that if he ever cussed me out, he was damn liable to get hurt.

"I got in uniform and played six innings that day, got in two base hits in three times at bat. And I think Mr. John J. McGraw was hoping I'd break a leg."

Dizzy Dean Still Had Enough in the Tank

April 2014

To attempt to add beauty to Wrigley Field, the owner, P. K. Wrigley, had his general manager Bill Veeck install hundreds of ivy and bittersweet plants on the outfield walls in the 1937–38 offseason. The plants were part of the renovations that also added the massive steel scoreboard and expanded the bleachers.

Another part of the "renovation," it was hoped, was Jay Hanna "Dizzy" Dean, of all people. The Chicago Cubs paid the St. Louis Cardinals the lordly sum of $185,000 plus two pitchers and an outfielder to take Dean off their hands. Dean had been a 30-game winner four years earlier and had remained one of baseball's great stars and characters, but in the 1937 All-Star Game, he was hit by a line drive on the big toe of his right foot. When Dean was told the toe was fractured, he said, "Fractured hell, it's broken." Either way, he resumed pitching for the Cardinals but, unfortunately, it was too soon after the injury.

When he could pitch again it became clear that changing his motion because of his ailing toe had changed him as a pitcher. Yet the Cubs hoped that he still had some magic left—and, it happened, he indeed would prove to have just enough.

Dean came through with a 7–1 record and a sparkling 1.81 earned run average but admitted, "I never had nothin'. I couldn't break a pane of glass and I knew it." Dean, who had four times led the National League in strikeouts with 190 or more each season, now recorded just 22 of them. But he was a wily pitcher, throwing slow curves and even slower changeups with such great control that he walked only eight batters in 74 innings, And he helped pitch the Cubs into the '38 World Series.

"I ain't what I used to be," he said, "but who the hell is."

He started Game 2 against the Yankees and, with "nothin'," held the Bronx Bombers to five hits and two runs in seven innings. But in the eighth Frankie Crosetti batted in the tying and winning runs with an eighth-inning homer off Dean. The Yankees took that game 6–3 and the Series in four straight games.

Dean hung on for a few more years, though rarely rising beyond an average pitcher, and retired in 1941 at age thirty-one, his arm having finally given out. His 12-year record of 150 wins and only 83 losses justifiably landed him, in 1953, in the Hall of Fame.

(Originally published in *Wrigley Field: An Oral and Narrative History of the Home of the Chicago Cubs* by Ira Berkow, by Stewart, Tabori and Chang, 2014.)

Gabby Hartnett and Al Capone

The notorious crime boss Al "Scarface" Capone went to games at the Cubs park on Chicago's North Side (an area run by his rival Bugs Moran) even though Capone's office was on the South Side, a territory that he ran, and where he may have favored the South Side White Sox. However, on September 9, 1931, a widely distributed Associated Press photo was taken of the stout, balding Capone in suit and tie and his son in the front row of the box seats before a game at Wrigley Field. In the photo the Cubs star catcher Gabby Hartnett is seen smiling and autographing a baseball for Scarface's twelve-year-old son Al "Sonny" Capone Jr., also in suit and tie. Two of Capone's bodyguards, Frank Pacelli (aka Frank "Cowboy" Digiovanni), and Jack "Machine Gun Jack" McGurn, in fedora and suits, were seated directly behind the Capones.

When baseball commissioner Judge Kenesaw Mountain Landis saw the photograph, he reprimanded Hartnett for associating with a known hoodlum. Bad for baseball's image, Landis admonished.

"Judge," said Hartnett, "if you don't want anybody talking to the Big Guy, you tell him." In 1938, Cubs management believed that the team led by manager Charley Grimm, despite a winning record in the first half of the season, needed a lift to contend and it was hoped that a new manager could provide it. The Cubs didn't have to go far to find that man. He was behind the plate, in the form of Gabby Hartnett. . . . Besides leading the team with a great second-half surge, Hartnett also provided the push that would send the Cubs into the World Series.

On September 27, the first-place Pirates came into Wrigley Field for a season-ending three-game series, leading the Cubs by 1 1/2 games. Dizzy Dean beat the Pirates in the first game, 2–1. The Cubs were now a half game behind Pittsburgh.

The second game was tied 5–5 going into the ninth inning. It was getting dark, and there were no lights to illuminate the field. The Pirates went down in order, and the Cubs were told that the game would be halted after their at-bats. Mace Brown, the Pirates top reliever, retired the first two Cubs batters. Then Hartnett, the thirty-seven-year-old Cubs rookie manager, came to the plate. Brown got two strikes on him.

"Brown wound up and let fly," recalled Hartnett. "I swing with everything I had and then I got that feeling—the kind of feeling you get when the blood rushes to your head and you get dizzy."

The ball soared over the left-field wall, and the Cubs were in first place by half a game and, as it happened, in first place to stay. The blow has come down in history as "the Homer in the Gloamin." While the fans erupted with frenzied delight, the manager was mobbed at home plate by his Cub underlings.

The miracle ended, though, when Hartnett and his Cubs were swept by the Lou Gehrig-led Yankees (Babe Ruth had retired three years before) in the World Series in four straight games.

Hartnett was inducted into the Baseball Hall of Fame in 1955. In the 2007 yearbook published by the Hall, Hartnett is described thusly: "Charles 'Gabby' Hartnett, excelled both as a catcher and a hitter, becoming the first backstop in history to slug 200 home runs and drive in 1,000 runs. His catching prowess prompted his teammate Dizzy Dean to proclaim, 'If I had that guy to pitch to all the time, I'd never lose a game.'" Hartnett, who played 19 seasons with the Cubs, including four pennant winners, was the starting National League catcher in the All-Star Game the first five years the contest was held (beginning in 1933). He also won the NL Most Valuable Player Award in 1935, and finished second in 1937. He retired in 1941 with a lifetime batting average of .297.

(Originally published in *Wrigley Field: An Oral and Narrative History of the Home of the Chicago Cubs* by Ira Berkow, by Stewart, Tabori and Chang, 2014.)

Part III: 1940s—The War Ends and a Loathsome Barrier Falls

Jackie Robinson's Place in History

April 10, 1968

Last summer, a black shoeshine boy, in his early teens, was buffing the shoes of a white man in Chicago's Loop, not far from where the recent fires and killings and lootings took place.

The white man asked the boy who his favorite baseball players were.

"Ernie Banks," said the boy, above the rhythmic slap of the shoeshine rag. "Willie Mays, too. Yeah, I dig Willie Mays a whole lot. I wanna be a ballplayer too. Like him."

The white man asked if he would like to be a ballplayer like Jackie Robinson, too.

"Who?" asked the kid, looking up.

"Jackie Robinson."

"Never heard of' him," replied the bootblack, applying more polish.

And boys the age of the bootblack have thwarted dreams and frustrated ambitions and bursting bitterness toward American society.

They have "cry little knowledge of the history and achievements of the black man in this country. They were responsible for the bulk of the multimillion- dollar damage—resulting in the loss of lives and property—that ravaged the ghettos of Washington, DC, Chicago, Baltimore, Pittsburgh, Memphis. It was also boys of the age of that bootblack who were responsible for the relative calm in Harlem, Watts. Philadelphia, Detroit.

"There is no question about it," said Jackie Robinson, at lunch. "The kids were responsible for the riots and for the calm. The ones who rioted were releasing their frustrations and bitterness on a world that has ignored them. It was an expression of their desire to get a piece of the action of the affluent society around them. "Those who did not riot showed respect for the memory of Dr. Martin Luther King and his ideals of nonviolence."

Robinson broke the color line in organized baseball. In 1946, he joined the Brooklyn Dodgers and became the first Negro to play in the major leagues, From then on, the barriers for Negroes in baseball, as well as m almost all other sports, crumbled. Robinson is currently an assistant to New York Governor Nelson Rockefeller. He speaks often in ghetto neighborhoods.

"I don't try to influence," he said. "I just try to explain the problems and the position of the black man in America, And it's true, many of those kids have never heard of me. As Roy Wilkins, head of the NAACP, said recently, most of the kids rioting know very little about the black movement and have never even heard of the Montgomery bus boycott in 1956, which Dr. King led. That was the beginning of his nonviolent movement.

"That's the fault of the white society. That's what the Negro leaders are trying to 'change. The kids want this history, of what the black man has done in America, and they want it in their school books.

"If rioting is to be stopped, there has to be a willingness by the power structure of this country to understand the frustrations of these kids.

"And no amount of talking and promising is going to change their attitude. There has to be action. No one single person could have prevented those riots, not me. not Willie Mays, not Mayor Lindsay of New York, not President Johnson. Not even Martin Luther King. Dr. King's death was not the reason for the outbreaks; it was just an agent." Is there any way that black athletes can help?

"Black athletes can show their concern for other members of their race," said Robinson. "That's about all. Many don't do very much, like some of the San Francisco Giants, Mays and Jim Hart and Willie McCovey. Of course, some other athletes do. Bill White of the Phillies, Bill Russell of the Celtics and Arthur Ashe, the tennis player. have shown great concern. But some don't involve themselves enough. I know I didn't when I was a player. That was wrong.

"I have been out of baseball for 12 years. And the kids look at me like I'm just an old-timer. The guys playing today, though, carry prestige. They can be very significant in explaining the problems and encouraging the kids.

"When kids see the stands athletes like Tommie Smith and Lew Alcindor and Muhammad Ali take, this is important to them. These athletes are really projecting themselves. This doesn't mean that athletes can be great race leaders. They can't because they don't have the following. You know, Negro kids don't look at Negro athletes with the awe that white kids—and white adults—look at athletes.

"The Negro kid admires the black athlete, but he doesn't honor him in the way whites do. Blacks have more important problems than seeking autographs. This is something white people don't seem to understand. For example, black kids are proud of Ali and admire his skills as probably the greatest fighter of all time, but that does not mean they agree with or want to follow his racial views."

The black kids in the ghetto the age of that Chicago shoeshine boy, march to the tune of their own drummer.

Jackie Robinson: Hope by Example

November 27, 1972

Days after Jackie Robinson's death, I was still thinking of a lunch I had with him about four years ago . . . I had walked into his midtown Manhattan office to pick him up. He was on the phone, legs up on his desk, talking to some friend about a celebrity golf event to which, this year, he had not been invited. Robinson had gone to several previous tournaments in the series.

He wanted the friend to find out why there was no invitation. Did it have anything to do with some of his recent controversial remarks about "racism in America." "We'll give it a good fight," Robinson said, smiling. He had the shaft of his glasses in his teeth.

Jackie Robinson, it seemed to me, enjoyed the fight. Even then, at age forty-nine, suffering from diabetes, failing eyesight that would render him virtually blind before his death, high blood pressure, heart trouble, and the drug addiction of his son, Jackie Jr., he was still combative.

"Look at Jackie now," wrinkled Satchel Paige told me a couple years ago, "and his hair's white and you'd think he was my grandfather."

He didn't sound old, though speaking in that dynamic falsetto he sounded more like Liberace than you'd expect of this rough ex-ballplayer, who was so menacing on the bases, who suffered so many pitchers trying to stuff baseballs in his ear, who broke the color barrier in a white elitist game and had to live with "black bastard" echoing through the dugouts and the caverns of his mind.

At Jackie's funeral, however, the Rev. Jesse Jackson's eulogy rang through the great vaulted Riverside Church, and the phrase for Jackie Robinson had changed from "black bastard" to "black knight."

Robinson had become a Hall of Farrier, but his place in history does not stop at Cooperstown. Baseball provided the setting for a milestone in

84

the American human rights struggle. Robinson helped open the doors of opportunity not only in sports but also in many other areas of America.

Jesse Jackson compared Robinson to Louis Pasteur and Gandhi and Martin Luther King and Jesus, as a man who gave others hope by example. This may seem a wild exaggeration. But if you were a thirteen-year-old black boy like Ed Charles living in Florida—where blacks were still being lynched—it was not so wild.

"I owe so much to Jackie Robinson," said Charles, an ex-major-league infielder. "All black players do. We tend to forget. I never will. When Jackie Robinson came through my home town with the Dodgers in 1947, it was the biggest day of my life. It was the biggest day of all our lives.

"I realized then I could play in the major leagues. They pushed the old people to the ballpark in wheelchairs and some came on crutches and a few blind people were led to the park.

"When it was over, we chased the Dodger train as far as we could with Robinson waving to us from the back. We ran until we couldn't hear the sound any more. We were exhausted but we were never so happy."

I told Robinson at lunch that day that I had recently been in Chicago and had talked casually with a black shoeshine boy in his early teens. I asked who his favorite baseball player was.

"Ernie Banks," the bootblack said. "Willie Mays, too . . . Yeah, I wanna be a ball player, too. Like him."

I asked the fellow if he wanted to be a ball player like Jackie Robinson, too?

"Who?" he asked. "Never heard of him."

This was neither sad nor surprising to Robinson. He dealt in realities.

"It's true that many black kids have never heard of me," he said. "But they haven't heard of the Montgomery bus boycott in '56, either. And that was the beginning of Dr. King's nonviolent movement.

They don't get any kind of black history in their school books. They want it. They read only about white society. They're made to feel like nonpersons. This is frustrating. It's up to the power structure of this country to understand these kids. Then the burnings, the muggings, the dope, the despair, much of what plagues this country will be greatly lessened.

"Black athletes playing today carry prestige. They can be very significant in explaining the problems and encouraging the kids. But I've been out of baseball for 12 years. The kids look at me like I'm just an old-timer."

The "old-timer" fought until he died. He fought for better housing, he fought for better schooling, he fought for greater say for blacks in government, he fought for a black manager in baseball.

While he angered the mossbacks who thought he wanted too much too fast, he continued to inspire others with the courage of his fight that would encompass freedom for all men.

"No grave can hold his body down," said Jesse Jackson, "it belongs to the ages. His spirit is perpetual. And we are all better because a man with a mission passed our way."

How Pee Wee Reese Helped Change Baseball

March 31, 1997

The white boy was thirteen or fourteen years old, and his brother was about sixteen, when, with dusk descending on that summer day in Louisville, Kentucky, in the early 1930s, the older boy shouted a racial slur at six black kids, telling them, "Get off this street!" With that, the six black kids took chase after the white boys, and the two white kids ran with everything they had and made it safely home.

86

How did he feel about his older brother's action, the now seventy-eight-year-old man named Harold "Pee Wee" Reese, was asked recently.

Reese, recuperating from surgery for lung cancer a few weeks ago, rubbed a graying eyebrow in the living room of his winter home here as he thought about the incident involving him and his brother, Carl Jr. "I thought it was stupid," he said. "I mean, to throw out a threat like that when there were six against two!"

Reese, the former star shortstop for the Brooklyn Dodgers, and a member of baseball's Hall of Fame, smiled, for of course there was much more to it than the numerical equation.

Some fifteen years after that childhood incident, Pee Wee Reese became a pivotal figure in the acceptance and support of a rookie team-mate, Jackie Robinson, who broke the color barrier in the major leagues in 1947.

Looking back now, fifty years after Robinson's historic break-through into the so-called national pastime, two moments in particular stand out between Reese and Robinson.

Reese, in a cream-colored short-sleeve shirt, green pants and tan buck shoes, his hair gray, his arms creased with age and the flesh not as tight as in his Dodger days, and a slightly tired look in his eyes from a radiation treatment in the morning, thought back upon those years.

The first of the two incidents occurred at the beginning of spring training in 1947, when Robinson had been called up to the Dodgers from Montreal, Brooklyn's top minor league team, on which Robinson had starred during the 1946 season. A petition was drawn up by a group of mostly Southern Dodgers players that stated they would not take the field with a black man.

"I'm not signing that," Reese told the ringleaders, who included Dixie Walker, Kirby Higbe, and Bobby Bragan. "No way."

Reese, the soft-spoken but respected team captain, with a Southern upbringing, perhaps surprised the petition-carriers. "I wasn't thinking of myself as the Great White Father," Reese said. "I just wanted to play baseball. I'd just come back from serving in the South Pacific with the Navy during the Second World War, and I had a wife and daughter to support. I needed the money. I just wanted to get on with it."

But there was more to it than the money. And Reese's refusal to sign the petition, many believe, meant the end of the matter.

Robinson played, and endured vicious abuse from opposing teams, from beanballs and spikings to racial epithets and spitting. Robinson had promised Branch Rickey, the owner and general manager of the Dodgers, that for at least his first two years in the major leagues, he would hold his tongue and his fists, no matter the provocation. And one day—it was probably in Cincinnati, Reese recalled, in 1947 or 1948— the attack was so nasty that Reese walked over to Robinson and put his hand on the black man's shoulder.

"Pee Wee kind of sensed the sort of hopeless, dead feeling in me and came over and stood beside me for a while," Robinson recalled, as quoted in the forthcoming biography *Jackie Robinson* by Arnold Rampersad. "He didn't say a word but he looked over at the chaps who were yelling at me through him and just stared. He was standing by me, I could tell you that." The hecklers ceased their attack. "I will never forget it," Robinson said.

Over the years, Reese became perhaps Robinson's best friend on the Dodgers, though there were others who were reasonably close to him as well, including the white players Carl Erskine, Gil Hodges, and Ralph Branca and, of his black teammates, Junior Gilliam in particular.

But Reese's attitude, including that defining gesture of solidarity on the field that they were, in the end, teammates and brothers under the skin, did not come from a save-the-world mentality.

"Something in my gut reacted to the moment," Reese said. "Something about—what?—the unfairness of it? The injustice of it? I don't know."

Reese's son, Mark, a forty-year-old documentary film maker, has wondered where that gut reaction from a man brought up in Southern mores came from.

"I think it might have something to do with that hanging tree in the middle of the town of Brandenburg, Kentucky," Mark Reese said. Brandenburg is about thirty-five miles south of Louisville, and a few miles from Ekron, where the Reese family lived on a farm and where Reese's father, Carl Sr., became a railroad detective.

"When my dad was a boy of about nine or ten years old," Mark Reese said, "he remembers his father pointing out a tree in Brandenburg with a long branch extending out. It was there, his father told him, that black men had been lynched. I believe it was an important thing for my dad, because many times when we visited relatives in Brandenburg, he would point out that tree to me, and tell me about the lynchings.

"He never made a big point about the significance, but there was definitely an emotion in his voice, an emotion that said to me, anyway, that it was a terrible thing that human beings did to another human being, and only because of the color of their skin. And I imagine that when his dad told him the story, there was a similar emotion."

Pee Wee Reese shrugged at this interpretation. It is his innate manner to play down himself and, apparently, his contributions, particularly in the area of Jackie Robinson, where, he feels, he might only be a deflection from the limelight that Robinson deserves.

In the book, *Baseball's Great Experiment*, a thorough study of the black entry into baseball, the author Jules Tygiel quotes Reese telling Robinson sometime before Robinson's death at fifty-three, in 1972, "You know I didn't go out of my way to be nice to you."

And Robinson replied, "Pee Wee, maybe that's what I appreciated most."

"I seem to remember a conversation along those lines," Reese recalled in his home here.

"Sounds right." He laughed.

He recalled the first time he learned about Robinson. "I was on a ship coming back to the States from Guam, in the middle of the ocean, and was playing cards. Someone hollered to me: 'Hey, Pee Wee, did you hear? The Dodgers signed a nigger.' It didn't mean that much to me and I kept playing cards. Then the guy said, 'And he plays shortstop!' My God, just my luck, Robinson has to play my position! But I had confidence in my abilities, and I thought, well, if he can beat me out, more power to him. That's exactly how I felt."

It turned out that Robinson, in his first year as a Dodger, would play first base, and then for the next several years move to second base and team with Reese for one of the brightest double-play combinations in baseball, as the Dodgers won pennant after pennant.

Just as Reese does not give himself undue credit, he seems clear-eyed about others. And while Robinson has been raised in some circles to a near deity, Reese saw the man within.

"Jackie was a great player, a great competitor, and pretty fearless," Reese recalled. "He had only a fair arm, but made up for it at second base by never backing down when a runner came barreling in. And he'd do some things that I wondered about. He would actually taunt some pitchers. He'd shout at them from the batter's box to just try to throw at his head! I told him: 'Jackie, quiet down. They might take you up on it. And if they're still mad, they might throw at me, too!'" Reese laughed. "And after the two years were up in which he had promised Mr. Rickey that he'd turn the other cheek, he became a guy who would stand up for himself. And he could be a tough bench jockey, and he might plow into a guy who was in his way."

One time, after Robinson had been in the league for a few years, he groused to Reese that the pitchers were throwing at him because they were racists. "No," Reese replied. "They aren't throwing at you because you're black, Jackie. They're throwing at you because they just don't like you."

Robinson smirked, and then smiled. Reese could say such things to Robinson because of their friendship, and because Robinson knew where Reese's heart—and mind—were.

After all, it was Reese who was the first Dodger in Robinson's first spring training camp to walk across the field and shake his hand. "It was the first time I'd ever shaken the hand of a black man," Reese said. "But I was the captain of the team. It was my job, I believed, to greet the new players."

But greeting, and associating with, a black man was something different, to be sure. "When I was growing up, we never played ball with blacks because they weren't allowed in the parks. And the schools were segregated, so we didn't go to school with them. And there'd be some mischief between blacks and whites, but, as I remember, it was just mischief. It wasn't hatred, at least not from me."

And it was Reese who first sat down in the clubhouse to play cards with Robinson. When Dixie Walker later took Reese aside and said, "How can you be playing cards with him?" Reese recalls that he replied, "Look, Dixie, you and Stell"—Walker's wife—"travel with a black woman who takes care of your kids, who cooks your food, who you trust—isn't that even more than playing cards with a black?" And Walker said, "But this is different."

Today, Reese, at 5-foot-10, weighs 165 pounds, after losing nearly 15 pounds in a week's stay in the hospital after the surgery for lung cancer (he quit smoking cigarettes about ten years ago). A third of his lung was removed. Doctors believe they have cut the cancer out, but Reese must continue to undergo radiation treatments. He is strong enough, however, to be back playing golf and on Saturday celebrated his fifty-fifth wedding anniversary with his wife, Dotty.

After his playing days, he coached with the Dodgers for one year, in 1959, then broadcast ball games for CBS and NBC and was a representative for the Louisville Slugger bat company. But for Reese, now a great-grandfather, there remain some painful physical reminders of an athletic career. He has an arthritic thumb, perhaps the result of his youth as a marbles champion, from which he derived his nickname. And Reese walks with a slight tilt because of trouble with his knees—he has had one knee replacement and may need a second

The injuries are a result, probably, of a major league career in which he made eight All-Star teams and batted .269 over 16 seasons—10 of those seasons with Robinson. Reese was considered one of the smartest players in the game (remember when he took the cut-off throw from Sandy Amoros and wheeled in short left field as though having eyes in the back of his head and fired the ball to first base to double off the Yankees Gil McDougald to help preserve for Brooklyn the seventh and deciding game of the 1955 World Series?).

At Robinson's funeral, in Manhattan on October 27, 1972, Harold "Pee Wee" Reese, a son of the South, was one of the pallbearers.

"I took it," Reese said, "as an honor."

No, Robinson Wasn't the First, but Cap Anson Provided the Racism

April 6, 1997

He was a handsome man, tall and slender. He was the son of a physician, attended Oberlin College and the University of Michigan, and succeeded in the classroom with such subjects as mathematics, Greek, rhetoric, mechanics, natural philosophy, French, civil engineering, zoology, astronomy, German, botany, logic, and Latin. He was also an athlete, and excelled at baseball.

He was Moses Fleetwood Walker, and he was a catcher. In 1884, he became the first and the last African American to play in the major leagues until Jackie Robinson broke the color barrier sixty-three years later. (His brother Welday, an outfielder, also played six mid-season games on the same team that year.)

As the baseball season begins, the nation celebrates the fiftieth anniversary of Robinson's dramatic arrival with the Brooklyn Dodgers in 1947. A commemorative stamp has been issued, universities—notably Long Island University in Brooklyn—are holding symposiums about the sociological impact of a ballplayer on an entire culture, and every major-league player is wearing a patch on his uniform in honor of Robinson, who helped open the door for the scores of black players who followed him. But little is known, or remembered, about Fleet Walker.

Upon finishing college in 1883, Walker joined the Toledo Blue Stockings, then in the International League. The next year, Toledo moved up to the American Association, and Walker went along. The American Association was considered on par with the National League, but less prestigious.

In *Only the Ball was White*, a history of the black men in baseball (mainly in the Negro Leagues) before Jackie Robinson, Robert W. Peterson writes: "Walker's reception in the big leagues was mixed. If the other players resented his presence, they gave no outward indication of it, and spectators, on the whole, seemed favorably inclined toward him except in the league's two distinctly southern cities."

Those cities were Louisville and Richmond. In Louisville, the Toledo Blade reported, Walker was "hissed and insulted because of his color." In Richmond, Toledo's manager, Charlie Morton, received a letter threatening to "mob" the "Negro catcher" if "he comes on the ground in a suit."

No one will ever know if that threat was real, for Walker did not play that day. In an earlier game, he had suffered a rib injury incurred from a foul tip—chest protectors for catchers had not yet been introduced.

He was released from the team in September, having played in 42 games for Toledo and batted .263. He was considered an adequate backstop, his .888 fielding average being 26th in the league for catchers.

The Toledo team, suffering financial problems, disbanded after that season, and no major-league team picked up either Walker brother (Welday had batted .182).

For the next few years, a handful of black players—including Fleet Walker—played in the minor leagues. But that came to an end on the afternoon of July 19, 1887, in Newark, New Jersey. Adrian "Cap" Anson, first-baseman and manager of the Chicago White Stockings, said his team would not play in a scheduled exhibition game against the minor-league Newark team if Newark, as announced, would send their ace pitcher, George Stovey, a black man, to the mound.

It is a part of baseball folklore that Anson said, "Get that nigger off the field." Newark acquiesced. Stovey did not play. Jim Crow did, and would for years to come.

Some major-league teams tried to circumvent the color barrier in a variety of creative ways. In 1901, John McGraw, manager of the Baltimore Orioles of the American League, sought to sign a light-skinned black second-baseman named Charlie Grant, and called him "Charlie Tokohama, a full-blooded Cherokee." But McGraw's ruse was exposed by Charles Comiskey, owner of the White Sox.

Meanwhile, Fleet Walker had returned home to Steubenville, Ohio. At one point, as a newspaper editor, he urged the emigration of all black people to Africa. Only "failure and disappointment" were in store for "the colored man in America," he wrote.

Moses Fleetwood Walker died in 1924, at age sixty-seven, never having left America's shores.

Larry Doby Crossed the Color Barrier, but in Another's Shadow

February 23, 1997

Larry Doby remembers clearly his first day in the major leagues, that day fifty years ago when he broke the color barrier in the American League. It was eleven weeks after Jackie Robinson had played his first game for the Brooklyn Dodgers in the National League.

Doby remembers the excitement of that day when he became only the second black player in the major leagues—he had hardly slept in four nights leading up to it—and he remembers the dismay.

Saturday, July 5, 1947, a sunny morning in Chicago: Lou Boudreau, the manager of the Cleveland Indians, took the twenty-two-year-old second baseman into the visiting team's locker room in Comiskey Park and introduced him to the players. Each of Doby's new teammates stood at his locker and looked over the young black man who had just been purchased by the Indians owner, Bill Veeck, from the Newark Eagles of the Negro National League. Doby and the manager went from player to player.

"Some of the players shook my hand," Doby recalled recently, "but most of them didn't. It was one of the most embarrassing moments of my life."

As Major League Baseball and the nation prepare for a season of homage to the integration of the game, virtually all of the attention is centered on Jackie Robinson, which is understandable, since he was the first. Jackie Robinson commemorative coins, a Jackie Robinson video, a Jackie Robinson seminar.

"And that's the way it should be," Doby said. "But Jack and I had very similar experiences. And I wouldn't be human if I didn't want people to remember my participation."

Doby went through much the same kind of discrimination and abuse that Robinson suffered—not being allowed to stay in the same hotels and eat in the same restaurants as the white players, hearing the racial insults of fans and opposing bench jockeys, experiencing the reprehension of some teammates.

But while Doby will be honored at the All-Star Game—which, coincidentally, will be played in Cleveland on July 8—and at an Indians game a few days earlier, he in some ways seems the forgotten man.

"Jackie Robinson, of course, deserves all the credit he gets," Boudreau said last week.

"But I really don't think that Larry gets the credit he deserves for being the pioneer in the situation he was in."

When the then-6-foot-1, 185-pound Doby stepped onto the field before that first game with the White Sox, he stood silently in Cleveland uniform No. 14, glove in hand, for what he recalled as five or ten minutes. "No one offered to play catch," he said. Finally, he heard Joe "Flash" Gordon, the All-Star second baseman, call to him, "Hey, kid, let's go." And they warmed up.

Doby, a left-handed batter, was called in to pinch-hit in the seventh inning and after "hitting a scorching drive foul," according to a news-agency report, he struck out.

But he was officially a big-leaguer, one who the following year would help the Indians win the pennant and the World Series. He became the first black player to hit a home run in a World Series, made six straight American League All-Star teams and, at one time or another over a 13-year career, led the American League in homers, runs batted in, runs scored and slugging average, as well as strikeouts. When he retired in 1959, he did so with a .283 career average and 253 home runs.

About Robinson, Doby said: "I had the greatest respect for Jack. He was tough and smart and brave. I once told him, 'If not for you, then probably not for me.'"

Robinson and Doby were followed into the big leagues in 1947 by three other blacks:

Henry Thompson and Willard Brown, who joined the St. Louis Browns in late July, and Dan Bankhead, who came up to the Dodgers in August. Thompson and Brown lasted for only a few weeks (though Thompson returned in 1949 to play several years with the New York Giants), while Bankhead pitched the rest of the season for the Dodgers.

Roy Campanella joined the Dodgers in 1948 and Don Newcombe made it in 1949.

Today, Major League Baseball estimates that about one-third of its players are black or Hispanic, but in 1950, three years after Robinson and Doby broke the color barrier, only five major league teams had been integrated. By 1953 there were twenty blacks on seven of the sixteen teams. And it was not until 1959, when the Boston Red Sox played Pumpsie Green, that every major-league club had a black player.

Lou Brissie, who pitched for the Philadelphia A's beginning in 1947, recalled: "I was on the bench and heard some of my teammates shouting things at Larry, like, 'Porter, carry my bags,' or 'Shoeshine boy, shine my shoes,' and, well, the N-word, too. It was terrible."

Brissie, who was from South Carolina, had been shot and left for dead in Italy during World War II. He pitched with a large steel brace on his left leg and instinctively felt an identity with the young black player. "He was a kind of underdog, like me," Brissie said.

Doby has not forgotten the abuse: the "N-word" being used every day, the calls of "coon" and "jigaboo," the times he slid into second base and the opposing infielder spit in his face.

"I never sought sympathy or felt sorry for myself," Doby said. "And all that stuff just made me try harder, made me more aggressive. Sometimes I'd get too aggressive, and swing too hard, and miss the pitch."

But he cannot forget the sense of loneliness, particularly after games. "It's then you'd really like to be with your teammates, win or lose, and go over the game," he said. "But I'd go off to my hotel in the black part of town, and they'd go off to their hotel."

Doby is now seventy-two, his hair sprinkled lightly with gray. He is huskier than in the old photos of him breaking in with the Indians. He works for Major League Baseball, handling the licensing of former players. Wearing a tie and suspenders and an easy smile and forthright manner, this father of five, grandfather of six and great-grandfather of three reflected on his years as a ballplayer as he sat recently in a sunny twenty-ninth-floor room at the Baseball Commissioner's office in Manhattan.

"When Mr. Veeck signed me," Doby said, "he sat me down and told me some of the do's and don'ts. He said, 'Lawrence'—he's the only person who called me Lawrence—'you are going to be part of history.' Part of history? I had no notions about that. I just wanted to play baseball. I mean, I was young. I didn't quite realize then what all this meant. I saw it simply as an opportunity to get ahead.

"Mr. Veeck told me: 'No arguing with umpires, don't even turn around at a bad call at the plate, and no dissertations with opposing players; either of those might start a race riot. No associating with female Caucasians'—not that I was going to. And he said remember to act in a way that you know people are watching you. And this was something that both Jack and I took seriously. We knew that if we didn't succeed, it might hinder opportunities for other Afro Americans."

Doby had been leading the Negro National League in batting average, at .415, and home runs, with 14, when he was signed by the Indians. He began as a second baseman, but was switched to the outfield, where he would be assured of starting. But he was unaccustomed to playing there, and in an early game, in center field, and with the bases loaded, he misjudged a fly ball in the sun and the ball hit him on the head. It caused his team to lose the game.

After the game, Bill McKechnie, an Indian coach who had befriended Doby, said to him, "We'll find out what kind of ballplayer you are tomorrow." Doby recalled that McKechnie smiled. "It was a challenge and a kind of vote of confidence," Doby said.

"The next day I hit a home run to win the game."

Doby appreciated Gordon and McKechnie and the catcher, Jim Hegan, in particular, who would seek to salve his disappointments and perhaps take a seat next to him after he had struck out or made an error.

"They were tremendous," Doby said. "But there were others who don't remember, or don't want to remember, some of their actions. And sometimes I'd see them later and they'd say, 'Hey, Larry, let's go have a beer.' I thought, 'When I needed you, where were you?' I forgive, but I can't forget. I politely decline their invitations."

Doby spent his grammar-school years in Camden, South Carolina. He recalls seeing the white people riding in fringed horse-drawn buggies through the black neighborhood, and tossing dimes and nickels at the small black children. And then they would rub the children's heads for good luck. "My grandmother warned me never to pick up the money," Doby said. "She thought it was undignified.

"And then I always tried to act in a dignified manner. When I was in the major leagues, some people thought I was a loner. But, well, when Joe DiMaggio was off by himself, they said he just wanted his privacy. And midway through the 1948 season the Indians signed Satchel Paige, and they made him my roommate. Well, he was almost never in the room. I'm not sure where he went. But he was a character and he enjoyed being perceived that way. He'd come into the clubhouse and clown around, and did some Amos 'n' Andy stuff. I didn't think it was right—at least, it wasn't right for me."

Eddie Robinson, the Indians first baseman when Doby broke in, said by telephone from his home in Fort Worth: "I thought it took a lot of courage for Larry to go through what he did. He handled himself quite well."

But when Boudreau put Doby at first base to start the second half of a doubleheader on Doby's second day in the major leagues, Robinson would not let him use his glove. "I didn't want anyone else playing my position, and it had nothing to do with black or white," Robinson said. As Doby recalls, the Indians were able to borrow a first baseman's glove for him from the White Sox.

Doby had been the only black player on the Eastside High School baseball, football and basketball teams in Paterson, New Jersey. He went briefly to Long Island University and Virginia Union before being drafted into the Navy. He first learned of Jackie Robinson's signing with the Dodgers organization when he was on a Pacific Island in 1945.

"I wondered if I might have a chance to play in the big leagues, too," Doby said. "Until then, I thought I would just go back to Paterson and become a high-school coach."

Doby gives talks at schools, and discusses the changes in American life. "I know people are critical and say that not enough progress has been made in baseball, or sports in general, particularly in the coaching or administrative levels," he said. "And I believe there has not been enough progress made either. But when you look at other elements of American society, then sports stacks up pretty good. If Jack and I had a legacy, it is to show that teamwork—the ability to associate and communicate—makes all of us stronger."

In 1978, Doby was named manager of the White Sox, taking over for Bob Lemon midway through the year. He held the position for just 87 games, posting a record of 37–50.

"I was the second black manager in major league history," Doby said, "after Frank Robinson."

Frank Robinson managed the Indians starting in 1975.

"Funny thing," Doby said, with a smile, "I followed another Robinson."

Yogi Berra: Baseball's Oddest Marvel

October 12, 1973

Anyone aware of Yogi Berra's history will not be stunned that he has come out of the National League pennant race smelling like a phoenix.

Berra, too, is a mythological bird who seems to immolate himself, 'and then emerge reborn, bigger and better and luckier than ever.

As manager of the New York Mets, he was on the brink of occupational disaster. His team this season was in last place in the East Division as late as July 8, and 12 games behind the leaders. Incredibly, the Mets went on to win the pennant.

Return with us now, to those thrilling days of yesteryear, when Berra began his daring, death-defying feats of flying past one great opportunity only to land smack in the pot of gold at the end of the rainbow.

The St. Louis Cardinals wanted to sign two local standouts, Joe Garagiola and Lawrence Peter Berra (even then known as "Yogi"—meaning, in his neighborhood, an odd fellow). Garagiola received a $500 bonus; Berra wanted same. St. Louis offered $300. Berra said no. The Cards forgot about him. Enter the Yankees, who signed him.

During Yogi's 17 full seasons as a major leaguer, Berra virtually got rich on the Yankees 14 World Series checks alone. The Cardinals, in that time, won no pennants.

In Berra's rookie year, he was behind the plate in the 1947 World Series. But the Dodgers, with Jackie Robinson, created such base-running havoc for him that he was relegated to right field. Yet in later years he became a Hall of Fame catcher.

One of the most memorable moments of luck and pluck in an athlete's life came for Berra in the shadowy late afternoon of September 28, 1951. He was catching what was most certainly going to be Allie Reynolds's second shutout of the season.

With two out in the ninth inning, Boston slugger Ted Williams popped up. Berra tossed off his mask, nestled under the ball. And dropped it. Almost diabolically, Williams popped up behind home plate again! Berra, in his comical, knock-kneed, dumpy manner, dizzily circled under the ball. But now made proper use of his angelic second chance. No-hitter.

He was named manager of the Yankees in 1964, and the story of how he won a pennant but lost the World Series and, therefore, his job, is an oft-told folk tale.

Few wondered then what might become of the seemingly sad little figure named Yogi, since in his ungrammatical, stumbling way he had amassed much money from shrewd investments.

But he did arise as coach of the New York Mets. His baseball acumen was hardly the sole reason for his hiring. It was thought by the Mets that dear, legendary Yogi would draw fans, even as a first-base coach. Besides, nice things often unwittingly happened to Yogi. For example, when a pedagogical and too logical manager tried to "correct" Yogi's habit of swinging at bad balls, Berra responded, "I can't hit and think at the same time."

And nice things soon did happen to the Mets, whether it was totally Yogi's talisman that did it is a moot point. The once-absurd Mets miraculously won the World Series in 1969.

Last spring, Gil Hodges suddenly died. The Mets needed a manager quick. Berra was chosen, amid moans of many who still considered Berra a fortuitous buffoon, at best.

This season, the Mets were thought to have pennant possibilities. But a series of injuries to key players such as Cleon Jones, Bud Harrelson, Rusty Staub, Jerry Grote, Jon Matlack hurt immeasurably. Berra's critics grew louder. Berra maintained his funny-faced aplomb. "I'm doin' the best wit' what I got," he continued to say.

"There was no word of encouragement from the front office. In fact, Willie Mays, the darling of the owners, came and went as he pleased, thus kicking harder the underpinnings of Berra's authority. The manager withstood.

His wounded players returned to full flower. The Mets made a run for the division title. Hits weirdly began to fall in; a Mets misjudged fly ball mysteriously was blown back toward him, and he caught it; the other team puzzlingly ran into each other in the field. Berra's magic was again on the beam.

All along, he pretended no sagacity. "The game is 50-50," says Berra. "I remember near the end of the season I replaced Jerry Koosman with Tug McGraw. I come back to the dugout, and a fan says, 'Yogi, did you do right?' I says back, 'Dunno, we'll see in a minute.'"

There is no better example of Berra's uncanny ability to survive than when he was the Met first-base coach. He thought he could do greater service for runners if he watched the bag and not the hitter. So Berra stood astraddle on the coach's line, back to batter. Gil Hodges pleaded: either watch the batter or at least wear a protective cap liner. "I never felt any danger," recalls Berra, "so I stayed doin' it my way. Oh, a couple times line drives whistled through my legs, but dat was all."

For Yogi Berra, a Happy Return

March 24, 1986/Kissimmee, Florida

In a period spanning a little more than forty years, Yogi Berra has survived both D-Day and George Steinbrenner, and is alive and well and coaching in Kissimmee.

Lawrence Peter "Yogi" Berra is sixty years old and a long way from when he was nineteen on June 6, 1944, and serving on a Navy landing craft at Normandy—"They called it the suicide squad," he said with a smile. And he is a long way from April 30, 1985, when, just 16 games into the season, Steinbrenner, the Yankees principal owner and noted manager-dumper, dropped Berra as manager.

Berra rarely complains or backbites. All he said about his Steinbrenner past is, "I didn't get a fair shake."

Now, for the first time in his 40-year big-league baseball career, Berra wears neither the vertical blue pin-stripes of the Yankees nor the Mets but the horizontal orange of the Houston Astros, who are limbering up for the season in this tourist haven that is close by Disney World.

"I'm happy to be in a baseball uniform," Berra said. "The only difference now is the stripes are goin' the other way." He seems relaxed and content as he enters the ball field on a recent warm, sunny afternoon before a spring training game.

"Yogi, Yogi, our Yogi," squeals a middle-aged female fan when she spots Berra entering the ball park here. She is one of many who stand imploringly along the low wire-mesh fence that separates the spectators from the baseball folks in the Osceola County Stadium here. They wait and seek an autograph from this gnomic, knock-kneed, accommodating figure, this old, unlikely looking hero, the gold frames of his glasses sparkling in the sun, the sprigs of gray hair extending from beneath his blue baseball cap, his thick neck and wrists and hands browned by the sun, and, tucked under his left arm, a fungo bat with his familiar No. 8 inscribed on the handle.

"Can I get a picture of you with my kids, Yogi?" calls a man in a floppy tennis hat.

Berra pushes back the bill of his cap. When the picture is taken, Berra says to a companion, "Oh, oh, got my toothpick in my mouth."

"How's Elston Howard doin' these days?" someone asked, referring to Berra's former teammate.

"He died," said Berra, scribbling away. "He was young," said the man. "Yeah, he was," said Berra, taking another notepad.

Craig Reynolds, an infielder for the Astros, has joined Berra in signing autographs.

Someone hands Berra an old baseball card.

"Gee, I was young there," Berra said. Craig looks over, appearing incredulous at the youthful Berra pictured on the card. "What year was that?" he asked. "About 1951," said Berra. "I wasn't even born then," said Reynolds, who arrived on this planet in 1952.

Berra didn't add that 1951 was the year he won his first of three American League Most Valuable Player Awards as a catcher for the Yankees. He didn't add that he led the Yankees that year to a World Series triumph over the Giants, one of a record 21 World Series he has participated in, 14 as a player with the Yankees, four as a Yankee coach, one as a Met coach, and one each as a Yankee manager and Met manager.

As Berra is close to finishing with the fans, a woman calls from a short distance, "Yogi, got a minute?" "A minute for what?" he asked. She blushed. Then Berra, realizing after a minute the unintended suggestion, blushed, too.

In the dugout, Berra sat back and spoke about his return to baseball.

"I been at it since I was fourteen, and I don't know what else to do," he said.

He added that he had decided not to accept any offers after being dismissed by Steinbrenner. "It was the first summer I had off in forty-three years, and I thought I'd try to enjoy it," he said. He said that his wife, Carmen, was only slightly reluctant at his decision. "She said, 'Now I'm going to have to cook for you,'" he recalled.

But they also took a cruise, which Berra said he enjoyed, and played in several charity golf tournaments. "It's hard to believe how many charity golf tournaments there are," he said. "You can play in one every day."

He said that John McMullen, a friend and neighbor in New Jersey, who owns the Astros, had asked Berra last summer if he was interested in returning as a coach. He said not now, but maybe later.

"I began to miss the game, and the guys in it," Berra said. "And I don't know what else to do. I been doin' it since I was fourteen years old."

It was when he was fourteen that he began playing American Legion baseball and earning a reputation as a standout hitter while living in The Hill, a section of St. Louis.

It was also at fourteen that he was forced to quit school after the eighth grade and go to work to help his Italian immigrant parents.

He began at the Johansson Shoe Company as a "tack puller," right down the assembly line from a brother who was a "puncher." Later he worked in a coal yard. But in the evenings he played ball, and was signed at age seventeen by the Yankees.

"I wanted to play for the Cardinals or the Browns, to stay in my hometown," he said, "but they didn't want me."

He said that he feels he'll adjust to life away from home and in Houston, as he did when he left St. Louis to play in New York.

His job in Houston will be giving assistance and reminders to the Astros first-year manager, Hal Lanier. Berra's role will be very much like that of Coach Joe Altobelli with Lou Piniella, manager of the Yankees, and George Scherger with Pete Rose of the Reds.

That is, a veteran head to assist the inexperienced new manager.

Berra had been offered a coaching job by Piniella but turned it down. The reason is obvious, though he is circumspect about it. He does not want to work for Steinbrenner.

"But I didn't want to go someplace where the manager didn't want me, and that's why I wasn't sure about going to Houston," said Berra. But Lanier, who thought Berra could be a valuable asset as a baseball mind as well as a cooperative and not ambitious underling, flew to New Jersey over the winter to convince Berra that he was wanted.

And in Kissimmee, Lanier has said, Berra has asked the manager what he could do to help, and he has done whatever he's been asked to do, from hitting fungoes, to operating the pitching machine in the batting cage, and working with the young players, particularly the catchers. In his understated approach, Berra suggested that Al Ashby's "butt is too low" when a batter is about to bunt. Ashby has to straighten up a bit to get a better jump and "become one of the fielders."

"Hi, Yogi," calls an opposing player for that afternoon's game, Bert Blyleven of the Twins, "How's Dale doin'?" "OK," said Berra, "OK." Berra walked past, and said to a companion, "That's one of the old Pirate guys."

Dale, of course, is Berra's son, an infielder for the Yankees, and a former teammate of Blyleven's when both were with the Pirates. Dale was traded to the Yankees and it seemed like the summer of 1985 was going to be an ideal one for the Berras. Yogi would be managing his son, a kind of dream come true; he was the first manager to have his son playing for him since Connie Mack and Earle Mack in the second decade of this century.

But the summer turned out to be one of the most trying in the lives of the Berras. Yogi was dismissed and Dale emerged as one of the major league players who gave testimony under immunity in last summer's headlined drug-related trials in Pittsburgh. Dale admitted to using cocaine. Shortly before a story about the use of cocaine by players, including Dale Berra, was about to be broken, a reporter went to Dale in the Yankee clubhouse and told Dale that the story was going to have to run.

Dale seemed stunned by the information that was uncovered and, knowing that there was nothing he could do to keep it from becoming public, said to the reporter, softly, "Does my father know? "

When this scenario was mentioned to Yogi Berra, sitting now on the Astro bench, he lowered his head and nodded. Someone close to the Berra family had said that Yogi and Carmen "went through a lot of parental anguish" over the drug usage by Dale.

107

"I didn't understand why he did it," Berra said. "I guess, you know, you go to parties and everyone's having a good time. But you gotta be able to say no. I said that if he wants to stay in the game he'd have to kick it. I hear it's like alcohol. You just gotta be able to stay away from it. Dale's brothers got on him, too." Berra has two other sons, Larry Jr. and Tim.

"I think he's all right now," Berra said. "It's hard to follow how he does in the papers because they don't run box scores down here. But I know he hit a home run the other day. I gotta call him tonight. We talk on the phone about every ten days."

The subject changed to happier subjects, like prospects for the Astros, who finished third in the National League West, to improve their lot.

And Berra reminisced about his two score years wearing New York baseball uniforms, and his greatest thrills, such as making the Hall of Fame. "You never think of that when you're a kid," he said. "But egads, you gotta be somethin' to get in." He mentioned catching for Don Larsen's perfect game in the World Series in 1956, and hitting two home runs in the seventh and deciding game of that series; getting the MVP three times, and catching for both of Allie Reynolds's no-hitters in 1951.

"In the second one," said Berra, "Ted Williams was the last batter, and he hit a pop foul.

The wind kinda blew it and I dropped it. I was layin' on the ground and Reynolds had come over." What did they say to each other? "He didn't say anything, but I did," said Yogi, "I said, 'You're stepping on my hand.'" On the next pitch, Williams hit a pop fly in almost the exact same place. This time Berra caught it, clinching the no-hitter.

Now Berra rose to hit some fungoes to the outfielders. As he came out of the dugout, a woman nearby requested his autograph. She handed him a scorecard and a fountain pen. He held them close to his dark blue Astro uniform top as he signed. When finished he noticed that his hands were now stained.

"Your pen kinda leaks," he said to the woman, his eyebrows furrowed. Then Berra turned to a companion and smiled. "Would you believe I got a white shirt on?" he said.

Warren Spahn: War Hero, Baseball Great

November 26, 2003

In the spring of 1942, a twenty-year-old left-handed pitcher who wound up having no decisions in his four appearances with the Boston Braves that season was pitching in an exhibition game against the Brooklyn Dodgers. At one point Boston Manager Casey Stengel instructed the young pitcher to brush back the batter, Pee Wee Reese. He refused.

Stengel immediately dispatched the pitcher to the minors, to Hartford of the Eastern League.

"Gutless," Stengel said of him.

The next year, 1943, the pitcher enlisted and found himself in Europe with the Army's combat engineers in World War II. He participated in the savage Battle of the Bulge and the seizure of the bridge at Remagen, and when it was over, First Lt. Warren Edward Spahn was awarded a Purple Heart for a shrapnel wound and a Bronze Star for bravery and a battlefield commission.

"I said 'no guts' to a kid who wound up being a war hero and one of the best pitchers anybody ever saw," Stengel said. "You can't say I don't miss 'em when I miss 'em." He added, "It was the worst mistake I ever made."

Indeed, Spahn, determined and talented, became one of the best pitchers ever. Though he didn't win his first major league game until 1946, when he was twenty-five—he missed three baseball seasons when he was in the military—he pitched until 1965, when he was forty-four.

He won 363 games, more than any other left-hander, and posted a record of 23-7 and a 2.60 ERA in 1963, when he was forty-two. He was elected to the Baseball Hall of Fame in 1973, the first year he was eligible.

In the last of his 21 big-league seasons, Spahn pitched a part of the year for the Mets, a last-place team, with Casey Stengel as manager, after Stengel's great years with the Yankees. When Spahn played for Stengel and the Braves, the team finished in seventh place.

"I played for Casey before and after he was a genius," Spahn said.

Warren Spahn died Monday, at age eighty-two, at his home in Broken Arrow, Oklahoma.

In the mind's eye, I can still see that quirky kick when he was about to fire a baseball homeward, looking as if he were trying to step over a fence about eye high, a delivery that led to his two no-hitters after age thirty-nine and to his 13 seasons with 20 or more victories. He holds the National League home run record for pitchers with 35, and in 1958 with Milwaukee he joined those pitchers who won 20 games (it was 22) and hit .300 (.333 to be exact) in the same season.

The last time I saw him was in August in Cooperstown at the Hall of Fame induction ceremony. When he was introduced to the audience along with the other Hall of Famers, he appeared from behind a curtain wheeling himself in a wheelchair. He was frail, his hawk nose looked larger than ever on his thin face, but he was there, resolute as ever.

There were times when the old competitor could be curmudgeonly, but as Murray Olderman, who covered baseball in New York in the 1950s and '60s recalled, "He was just fine once you got to know him." In his last season with the Braves, Spahn's manager, Bobby Bragan, accused him of selfishly hanging on for the salary. When he was with the Mets, Stengel thought he was getting a player-coach, but it turned out Spahn was interested in only pitching. When he was out of the big leagues the next season, he couldn't get pitching out of his blood, and played in Mexico.

Jerome Holtzman, the longtime baseball writer, admired Spahn's intelligence, and recalled he had a good eye for the dollar. "They had a Warren Spahn day in Milwaukee and one of the presents was a tractor, for his farm in Oklahoma," Holtzman said. "Spahn had it shipped to Oklahoma, and billed the Braves."

Spahn's death came on the day the Arizona Diamondbacks agreed to trade Curt Schilling to the Boston Red Sox, meaning that Schilling, who has a full no-trade clause, may end his career in the city in which Spahn began his. The two pitchers are similar: classy performers, winning pitchers, strikeout aces. The differences, though, are great.

Schilling, thirty-seven, has pitched 16 seasons in the big leagues and has 163 victories. He has won more than 20 twice. He would need 20 victories a season for the next seven seasons to reach 300. Schilling, among the most successful of his era in pitching complete games, has 79 in 338 starts, 23.4 percent; Spahn's record dwarfs Schilling's, with 382 complete games in 665 starts, for 57.4 percent, more than double Schilling's percentage.

Spahn's career reflects something more than the ultimately superficial aspects of the game, like whose uniform one wears, or the winning or losing of a baseball game, or a championship. It is the tale of one man's grit to remain confident, calm and poised—even though, surely, suffering doubts and fears—in the face of disappointment on the mound. He also displayed valor in a foxhole.

Spahn made 14 All-Star teams and helped pitch three Braves teams into the World Series, the first in 1948. That season, the Braves were in a heated race with the Cardinals and the Dodgers for the National League pennant. Coming down the stretch, the team's two best pitchers, Spahn and Johnny Sain, performed superbly under pressure. Spahn, particularly, was no stranger to pressure.

The *Boston Post* ran a poem by its sports editor, Gerry Hern, that captured the moment as well as leading to a widely quoted phrase:

First we'll use Spahn, then we'll use Sain.

Then an off day, followed by rain.

Back will come Spahn, followed by Sain,

And followed, we hope, by two days of rain.

Lou Boudreau, Once Known as The Boy Wonder

August 11, 2001

Lou Boudreau, the Hall of Fame shortstop who both managed the 1948 Cleveland Indians and played inspired shortstop to lead them to their first American League pennant in 28 years and the World Series championship, died yesterday at a hospital in Olympia Fields, Illinois. He was eighty-four.

He was taken to St. James Hospital and Health Centers yesterday in cardiac arrest and was pronounced dead, said Julie Miller, a hospital spokeswoman. He was hospitalized last month for circulatory problems, forcing him to miss the Indians 100th anniversary celebration honoring their top 100 players.

Boudreau was once known as the Boy Wonder because, at age twenty-four in 1941, he became the second-youngest manager in major league history. He had been the Indians regular shortstop for two seasons when, in November 1941, the team fired its manager, Roger Peckinpaugh (coincidentally, Peckinpaugh, at age twenty-three, was the youngest manager, taking over the Yankees for 20 games at the end of the 1914 season).

Boudreau applied for the job. "I was only twenty-four years old at the time, with just four seasons of professional ball behind me," he later recalled. "I figured I had nothing to lose because I didn't tell anybody about it—not even my wife."

He wrote a letter to Alva Bradley, the Indians owner. "I told him I was qualified to handle the job," Boudreau said. "I thought he might ignore it. Instead, he called me into a meeting of club directors." It was determined that the Indians needed young blood, and Boudreau got the job, shocking the baseball world.

For his first few years, the best that Boudreau the manager could do was help make Boudreau the player better. In 1944 he led the American League in hitting with a .327 average. He also led the league's shortstops in fielding percentage, assists, putouts and double plays. In his first six years as manager, however, his team never finished higher than third and finished in the second division three times.

Bill Veeck took over as owner of the sixth-place Indians in 1946. "My first problem," Veeck wrote in his book *Veeck—as in Wreck*, "was that the best shortstop in baseball was, in my opinion, not the best manager." He added, "I particularly wanted to get Louie out of the manager's office"—and retain him as the shortstop—"because I had Casey Stengel waiting in the wings, ready to sign."

But the reaction to removing Boudreau was so strong—newspaper columnists condemned the change, and more than 16,000 letters of protest from fans inundated Veeck's office—that Veeck backed off. "Louie held all the cards, and he knew it," Veeck said.

Boudreau remained manager. It was among the best decisions Veeck ever made. In 1948, the Indians contended for their first pennant since 1920 with an assortment of outstanding players: outfielder Larry Doby, the first black player in the American League; Bob Feller and Bob Lemon, the ace starting pitchers; everyday stars like second baseman Joe Gordon, third baseman Ken Keltner and catcher Jim Hegan; and the legendary Negro league pitcher Satchel Paige, who was added in midseason.

"It was quite a year," Boudreau recalled. "The pressure kept building and building, until I thought we'd all burst."

Bill McKechnie, who had managed three different teams to pennants, had been hired as a Cleveland coach at Veeck's suggestion, and, Boudreau said, "was a big, big help to me."

"I have never known another year like the one we had in Cleveland in '48," McKechnie said. "Every day was like a final game of the World Series. And that year, Lou Boudreau was the greatest shortstop and leader I have ever seen."

Boudreau batted .355, second best in the league, and he drove in 106 runs, hit a career- high 18 home runs, struck out just nine times in 560 at-bats, led AL shortstops in fielding and was named the league's most valuable player. And he called the shots from the bench and from the field.

After the last game of the regular season, the Indians and the Boston Red Sox were tied for first, setting up a one-game playoff on a chilly afternoon at Boston's Fenway Park.

Boudreau made the unexpected move of skipping Feller and Lemon and starting the twenty-eight-year-old rookie left-hander Gene Bearden, with only one day's rest, against a lineup stocked with left-handed power. "Bearden was one of the finest competitors I had ever known," Boudreau said.

Bearden pitched a five-hitter and Cleveland won, 8–3. Boudreau went 4-for-4: he homered over the left-field wall in the first inning, singled in the fourth to begin a four- run rally, homered again in the fifth and later singled again.

The Indians went on to beat the Boston Braves in the World Series, four games to two, with Boudreau batting .273.

His greatest thrill as a player beyond the playoff game, he said, was helping to end Joe DiMaggio's 56-game hitting streak in 1941. DiMaggio hit two smashes down the third-base line, which Keltner stopped, throwing him out. On DiMaggio's last chance to keep the streak alive in the eighth inning, he grounded a ball up the middle and it took a bad hop. "But I was able to get it and threw him out," Boudreau said.

After the 1950 season, with his skills diminishing and with the Indians having finished fourth, Boudreau was traded to the Red Sox, ending a nine-year managerial reign. He played in 82 games for Boston in 1951 and was named the manager the following year, his last as a player. He managed the Red Sox through the 1954 season and managed the Kansas City Athletics from 1955 to 1957. He then became a WGN radio and television broadcaster for Chicago Cubs games, and in an unprecedented move changed places with Charlie Grimm, the Cubs field manager, on May 4, 1960.

Boudreau returned to the broadcasting booth after that season.

None of the teams he managed after 1948 finished higher than fourth.

Boudreau became known for a 1946 managerial move called the Williams shift, used against Ted Williams, who was a left-handed pull hitter. Boudreau, seeking to throw him off balance, put all four infielders between second base and first and moved the center fielder into right field—only the left fielder remained on the left side of the field—daring Williams to hit to the opposite field. Williams would not concede and wreaked considerably less havoc on the Indians than in previous years.

"There is no doubt," Williams said, "that the shift hurt me."

Louis Boudreau was born in Harvey, Ill., on July 17, 1917. He first made his athletic reputation as a basketball player, leading Thornton High School to the Illinois state championship in 1935, then becoming the captain and star guard at the University of Illinois before leaving to sign with the Indians.

Boudreau, at 5-foot-11 and 185 pounds, had average size, an average arm, less-than-average speed and small hands. But he had deceptive talent, competitive zeal and a good mind. His lifetime batting average was .295, and his wide-ranging skills led him to be inducted into the Baseball Hall of Fame in 1970.

At the induction ceremony were his wife, Della, and their four children, the youngest of whom was Sharyn McLain, wife of Denny McLain, a longtime major league pitcher.

Boudreau retired as a sportscaster in 1988, after thirty years. In the mid-1990s, he moved to Frankfort, Ill., about thirty-five miles west of Chicago.

His baseball legacy remains with a plaque in Cooperstown. "It's something you dream of and think about," Boudreau said when elected to the Hall of Fame. "This is what we all strive for—to reach the top."

Stan Musial: As Good as It Gets

November 20, 2021

Perhaps it was his discipline, among other attributes, including an unsurpassed talent at the plate (well, both plates, as I came to learn), that Musial brought to the Major Leagues when he broke in with the St. Louis Cardinals in 1941, and for whom he played for 22 years, that made him one of the greatest players ever.

To underscore that aspect of discipline: I remember an evening in Cooperstown during one Induction Weekend and having dinner at a restaurant with a few sportswriter friends when Musial, a Hall of Famer, to be sure, and retired for some twenty years, stopped by to say hello. Someone said, "Stan, you look great." He did, at age sixty-three, and appeared as trim as he may have been in his playing days, at 6-feet, 175 pounds. "How do you do it?" he was asked.

The ever-pleasant Musial nodded in appreciation and said, "Well, at meals I only eat half of what's on the plate. I think that makes a difference."

(I once reiterated Musial's contention to an also svelte and retired Sandy Koufax. "I don't know how Stan does it," said Koufax, "but

I generally have to eat everything on the plate—as long as it's tasty." Obviously, Koufax had found another way to stay trim.)

Musial also said, with a wry smile: "I got started too early in baseball. In air-conditioning I could have lasted twenty years longer."

Musial's abilities on and off the field surely led to his lifetime batting average of .331, a seven-time National League batting champion, three-time NL Most Valuable Player and set, among his several NL records, most hits (3,630), RBIs (1,951), and second in home runs with 475, to Mel Ott's 511. Musial played in 24 All-Star Games, which ties the All-Star Game record with Henry Aaron and Willie Mays.

Sometimes one may wonder how it was that Musial hit so well given the quirky, if not even bizarre, "peekaboo" batting stance he employed. The outstanding White Sox pitcher Ted Lyons famously and visually depicted it this way: the stance "looked like a small boy looking around a corner to see if the cops are coming." Someone else saw it as a cobra poised to do damage to the innocent baseball. And yet Musial, with superb eyesight and remarkable bat speed, would uncoil into a magnificent slugger, spraying singles, doubles, triples, and home runs all over ballparks around the country.

One of my favorite quotes about Musial was from Woody Allen, Brooklyn-born and a Dodger fan, who witnessed Musial's numerous outstanding games against his home-town team. He praised "the serene dependability of Stan Musial."

And: Leo Durocher once said, "There is only one way to pitch to Musial—and that's under the plate." Dodger pitcher Carl Erskine said, "I had success with Musial by throwing my best pitch and backing up third base." Mickey Mantle: "Stan was a better player than me because he was a better man than me." Perhaps Mantle was thinking of drinking and carousing days, while there was never an untoward reference to Musial.

In February 2011, at the White House, President Barack Obama presented Musial, wearing appropriately a Cardinal red sport jacket, with the Presidential Medal of Honor, the highest civilian honor that can be bestowed by the US government. Other honorees included basketball star Bill Russell, poet Maya Angelou, and former president George H. W. Bush. In his remarks, Obama said: "These outstanding honorees . . . lived extraordinary lives that have inspired us, enriched our culture and made our country and our world a better place."

Musial died two years later, at age ninety-two.

Part IV: 1950s—Willie, The Mick, and a Heartfelt Call

Willie Mays: Price of a "Hero" Tag

August 14, 1970

Willie Mays walks in a cloak of applause. When he steps out of the visitors' dugout at Shea Stadium and into the shadows of the sunset, there are long wails of "Willeeee" by the fans, even, to be sure, Mets fans, who remember him well when he was a New York Giant, before the team relocated to San Francisco.. He is met by photographers and reporters, too.

"Willie," asks a mustachioed fellow, "could you hold your bat just like that so we could take a picture?"

"Who you with?" asks Mays.

"Don't you remember me? Fifteen years ago in Fairfield, Alabama. . ."

Willie Mays grinned with only his mouth showing emotion. "Look man," said Mays, evenly, not looking at the man. "I see so many people . . . Who you with?"

"Associated Negro Press."

"Well, okay, why didn't you say so?"

Shortly, a reporter comes by and asks Mays if, now, after having passed 3,000 hits and 600 homers, he doesn't feel the safe has been lifted from his back?

"What safe?" says Mays. Another question, another short answer. The reporter asks Mays what's wrong, why so curt?

"Because, man" said Mays, "you start askin' me these questions and you don't even say, 'Congratulations on 3,000 hits, 600 homers. I mean, not many people ever hit that many."

It comes home to the reporter that Willie Mays is not just a household name, not just a sweet man who will always be the "Say Hey Kid" to many, but Willie Mays is a special kind of man; he is a "hero" and almost by definition has suffered the loneliness of walking in the cloak of applause. People take from a hero to feed themselves; a dehumanizing exchange for the "hero."

The reporter and Mays discuss this briefly, and there is an understanding. Now Mays is joking and he seems somewhat more relaxed, more at ease with himself (sure, there are moments where he takes insult when none is meant) than he has in years. He admits that there has had been the pressure of statistics. ("The 3,000 hits was easier," he said, "because the homers are harder to hit.") His body—powerful chest and arm muscles and trim bow legs—is not dragging as it appeared just a few years ago. But his eyes say he is thirty-nine years old, old for a one in his profession.

They are large brown and knowing in a "country-slick" way, as someone once described them. And at the corners are creeping crow's feet,

Mays reminisced about the old days in New York when the Dodger-Giant games had full houses, 55,000 at the Polo Grounds, 32,000 at Ebbets Field, and eight million New Yorkers talking about it. "You had to fight to get into those games," said Mays, proudly. "I knew. I was there."

Governor Nelson Rockefeller was now in the dugout and Giant manager Charlie Fox called to Mays at the batting cage.

"One more," hollered Mays. Then he motion to the governor and said, "Let me hit one out for you." But a plane overhead mopped up the words.

"Let him wait a minute, he's in my ball park now," said Mays, aside, with genuine humor. "When I go downtown then I'm in his ball park."

Mays had one swing coming and the batting practice pitcher, Giants coach Ossie Virgil, threw one high and close and Mays swing and dribbled the ball down to third base. "Hey, this ain't no knock-down," squealed Willie.

Then he departed to see the governor, who was dress dressed in gray pin-striped suit, and gray debonair hair. As they posed arm in arm, there were more wails of Willeeeee. Governor Rockefeller waved.

"So long, Willie," said the reporter, later, as Mays played catch. "I'm off to write a story that will make you famous."

Mays's piping laughter collided with the pop of the ball in his glove.

Willie Mays: From Three Angles: the Greatest, Smartest Play Ever Made

August 13, 2001

Sports fans, cooling themselves these sweltering days in a library or, if not handy, a saloon, invariably get around to telling you about the greatest this or the greatest that they've ever seen.

Well, let me tell you about the greatest play in baseball I ever saw—or thought I saw.

Few recall it, though it was probably the greatest play Johnny Oates, a second-string catcher and later a big league manager, also ever saw—or thought he saw.

Oates was the hapless catcher in the play, which was executed by the wondrous and wily Willie Mays, who incidentally, is in the news, being frequently lauded by his godson, the basher Barry Bonds.

I was reminded of the play at the Baseball Hall of Fame induction ceremonies in Cooperstown last weekend when I saw Mays. I had wondered what he saw on that play—if he even remembered—it being so subtle, so long ago and his career so crammed with highlights.

The play was not, to be sure, the famous, stupendous back-to-the-plate catch in center field off the Vic Wertz drive in the 1954 World Series, or any other of Mays's acclaimed swats or snares.

It took place when Mays was a Met, in a Saturday afternoon game at Shea Stadium in July 1973. The great "Say Hey Kid" was no longer a kid, and no longer even greeting people with, "Say hey." Mays was then forty-two, and in the 22nd and last season of his brilliant, Hall-of-Fame career.

In my mind's eye, sitting in the press box that day, this was the situation:

Close game. I forget the opponent. Late innings. Mays is on second base. The batter—don't remember who—drives a hit to right field. Normally, the runner would score from second fairly easily, but this is no ordinary runner. Mays seems to trudge around third, like, well, an old man, and heads home, cap still on head—remember, in his heyday the cap used to fly off his noggin as if he were in a wind tunnel. The right fielder winds up to fire the ball to the plate, certain to nail Methuselah Mays. But incredibly, Mays picks up steam and there he is racing to the plate like, well, The Say Hey Kid!

He beats the throw and is safe at home. Not only that, but because he drew the throw to the plate, the batter is able to go to second, sitting there now in scoring position.

In an instant, Mays had craftily set the whole thing up in his marvelous baseball brain.

He obviously had run slowly at first to draw the throw, knowing all along he could make it home.

For me, there is nothing quite as exciting in sports as watching a player—particularly an aging veteran—use his experience, his intelligence and his considerable if waning skills to accomplish something remarkable under pressure.

One hesitates to use the word genius in such endeavors—especially with such folks as Einstein, Picasso, Freud, and Frost looking from the stands—but in my view certain athletes performing certain feats may indeed possess a kind of genius.

Some three decades later I recalled the play to Mays, describing it as I remembered it.

Did he remember it?

"Absolutely," he said, in that familiar high-pitched voice. "It was against the Braves. But there's more to it. See, I was on second base and Felix Millan was a runner on first.

Ralph Garr was in right field. But not only did I score, I slid into the catcher—it was Johnny Oates—and I pinned him to the ground so Millan could score, too."

I didn't remember the pinning business, so I later called Oates, at his home in Virginia.

"I always tell that story at banquets," Oates said. "It was the smartest play I've ever seen, and an embarrassing one for me."

I told Oates what Willie told me.

"I was under the impression that it was a sacrifice fly," Oates said. "And I don't remember him on top of me. He made a perfect slide and took my legs out from under me. My recollection is that I wound up on top of him. But definitely we were lying on the plate, and somehow Willie wouldn't let me get up. The throw went over my head, and the runner behind him did indeed score—how he found the plate with us lying on it I don't know."

To check further for details, I called the Elias Sports Bureau, located in Manhattan, the record keeper for Major League Baseball. Elias confirmed the play essentially the way Mays remembered it, with him and Millan scoring on a hit by Wayne Garrett. (Those runs gave the Mets a 7-6 lead in the eighth, but they lost the game, 9–8.)

I like Johnny's version of the play, I like Willie's, and I still like mine. Take your pick.

Along the lines of memorable baseball tales, I've heard two versions of a story that involved Mickey Rivers and Reggie Jackson when they were Yankee outfielders.

Rivers was known to have less than a great formal education, while the voluble Jackson had gone to college. On the team bus one day Jackson was bragging about his IQ.

"Reggie," Rivers said, "you don't even know how to spell IQ."

Version Two: When Jackson boasted he had an IQ of 160, Rivers said, "Out of what, a thousand?"

I recently asked Rivers which version was true. He smiled. "Both," he replied.

Willie Mays at Twilight

March 21, 1973/St. Petersburg, Florida

Willie Mays and his small shadow at his heels created a flurry of activity at home plate. This was the first inning and Mays's first appearance in a spring training game this year. There was a polite—and what may be assumed hopeful—round of applause here at Al Lang Field. The stands were filled with folks from this retirement community who appreciate an old fellow's effort.

Mays and his shadow, which was slight in the early afternoon sun, each acknowledged the reception with a characteristically quick wiggle of the bat.

It was a sultry day. The palm trees behind the outfield fence were still. A clump of dust kicked up by Dodger pitcher Claude Osteen rose heavily. One's shirt grew moist from the exertion of just standing in the sun. Mays will be forty-two years old on May 6. He has played 21 major league seasons, and his terrific career is either over or has one more year, depending, says Mays, on how he swings the bat in spring training.

Right now, he looked lively and light at the plate. His helmet was fastened tight on his head. His knit, concentrating brows, puckered lips and soft Mets cap stuffed in his left back pocket gave the impression that he was still the ebullient "Say Hey" kid of Polo Grounds lore.

The eye deceives. Mays is an aging veteran hanging on. His knees have been mean to him. They must be constantly drained of fluid. And though he holds so many baseball records (only man to twice hit 30 homers and steal 30 bases in a season, 6,992 outfield putouts—which give a hint at his versatility) and is a certain Hall-of-Famer, he seems peevish in his familiar squeaky voice and oversensitive about his declining abilities. He has some reason, however.

He has a manager who, for the first time in his career, would rather Mays got lost. It is difficult, though, to fault Met manager Yogi Berra if you are pragmatic—easier if you are romantic.

Berra and Mays appear to be two men who respect each other but know that the town—the team—isn't big enough for the both of them. They have had two confrontations already this spring. On the first day of spring training Mays showed up late. Berra said practice begins at 10 a.m. Mays said he knows how to train, what his body requires, that he's always in shape, anyway. Berra said all 25 men on his squad get equal treatment, that Mays may exclude exercises but he must be in uniform. Second clash came one Saturday when Mays did not show up at all. He turned up in Arizona, visiting his wife. He was fined $1,000 by Berra. Mays admitted he was wrong in not telling the manager where he was going. Besides having to deal with a separate set of standards for Mays, Berra must also handle ghostly realities. Mays is not the player he used to be ("If I said I was I'd be fooling nobody, including myself." admits Mays) and Berra believes that one of his younger players could be the center-fielder all season. But Mays is trying to prove to himself and Berra that at forty-two he is still better than guys twenty-two.

Berra knows that if Mays wants to play one more season, he must be carried on the club. Mays was bought from San Francisco last spring by Mets owner Joan Payson, a great fan of Mays's. Berra had no say in the deal. But if Mays does stay, Berra must carry a "caddy"—a veteran to take over in late innings—for Mays, and will not be able to keep one promising youngster on the roster. Mays's recent history is that he does well at the beginning of the season, but fades in the hot summer.

Last season, for example, after dramatically winning games with home runs in his first appearance as a Met in Shea Stadium and in Candlestick Park, he played only a handful of games after the July All-Star break because of faulty knees.

Before the game here, Mays saw Dodger manager Walt Alston. "You going to play this season?" asked Alston lightly. Just as lightly Mays retorted, "How come everybody's trying to get me to quit?" There was a serious undertone.

In his first at-bat, Mays took one ball from Osteen, then slammed a high inside fast ball against the left field fence. It lit up the ball park. Glee shot out of the old stands as Willie ended up at second, losing his batting helmet, of course, on his still-quick, dust-puffing, pigeon- toed route.

"That screws Yogi up pretty good," observed a baseball writer for a New York paper, in the press box. "Yogi was hoping Mays would show himself up."

As Mays called time out to retrieve his helmet, one could see with binoculars that his hair is thinning in front and that there are sprigs of gray in his sideburns.

But his body is still powerful and very well-kept, except for his hands, which he says always blister and bleed in spring training, and those well-worn knee hinges.

One also remembered an earlier conversation in which Mays said how lucky he was to be cheered wherever he goes; he said he would be hurt most if he were cheered for what he had been and not for what he can do today. He felt that would be cheating the fans and he would get out of baseball rather than allow that to happen.

On Mays's next time up in his first spring training game, he worked the count to 3-and-2 and then he and his shadow took a mighty swing at an outside-corner curve. "Whooo," went the crowd. But Mays's effort was fruitless. He struck out. He walked back to the bench; his shadow trailed behind. The shadow was longer than before. The sun was lower. It was late in the afternoon.

Mickey Mantle: "Baseball Is All I Ever Knew"

March 15, 1972/Ft. Lauderdale, Florida

Yesterday, all eighteen years of it, roared by much too fast for Mickey Mantle. From 1951 through 1968, he had been a celebrated baseball player for the New York Yankees. When he retired, it seemed he had lost his sense of direction: first base was removed from his life, and the foul line looked barren and limitless.

Mantle had tried some business ventures, as he had in earlier days. The results were similar. A men's clothing chain bearing his name flopped. A drive-in restaurant chain bearing his name flopped. An employment agency he formed with Joe Namath flopped.

Mantle even tried coaching first base for the Yankees in August 1970. He stayed a few weeks before he became bored and returned home to Dallas. This is his fourth year as a "special spring training instructor" with the Yankees here. He doesn't seem much interested in working with young hitters, and is quick to take off for fishing or golf. His job in training camp consists mostly of hitting infield grounders, of being tangible evidence for the "old glory days" which is good for club morale and Florida public relations, and of experiencing again the comfortable, unforgettable joy of lacing on a pair of spikes.

Mantle was sitting one morning recently on a stool before his locker, buttoning the gray Yankee uniform top. One notices that middle- age has been carving lines into Mantle's boyish looks. He was asked what he will do after spring training.

"Go home and have a gall bladder removed," he said. And after that? "I dunno. Rest, Play golf. Make some public appearances." He said he would like to manage, but has had no offers. He had hoped to catch on with the Texas Rangers, his new neighbors. "But nobody there asked if I wanted a job," he said evenly. He still speaks with the twang he brought from Oklahoma to New York City in 1951, along with a $3.95 cardboard suitcase, wide blue eyes, and an enormous baseball talent.

"Playing baseball is all I've ever known," said Mantle. "It makes me kind of bitter that it's all over. You look around and see other guys my age, other guys forty years old, who are just starting to reach their peak in other jobs. And I'm finished."

Mantle thought for a moment, picked at a fingernail. "I wouldn't trade my baseball career. But I'll tell ya, I'd give anything right now to be a lawyer or something."

There is a rumor going around and Mantle has heard it. "Everybody thinks I'm broke or somethin'," he said. "But hell, I paid more income tax last year than ever. I got a $125,000 house all paid for. I got a cabin on the lake. I own part of a cabin-building business. I get $1,500 and up for public appearances. And a lotta other stuff. I'm all right. I got enough."

Looking back now, past the home runs and the three Most Valuable Player trophies and the stirring cheers ("like the roar of some animal," he says), he remembers the quick-talking "agents" with the actual pinkie rings who convinced the young country tow-head to sign on the dotted line fast before all those millions in deals would evaporate. What evaporated were great chunks of his salary over the years.

Perhaps bad business deals hardened Mantle. Whatever, Mantle often was cold if not outright surly. Many sports reporters have experienced Mantle walking abruptly away from them in mid-question. And former teammate Jim Bouton wrote of Mantle slamming down bus windows almost on the hands of kids seeking his autograph.

It was repeated to Mantle what Bob Fischel, Yankee publicity director, said recently: "Mickey's mellowed now. Maybe because all the pressure's off him. But like just the other day he signed autographs in front of the box seats here for thirty-five minutes. And the crowd gave him a standing ovation for it."

"Mellowed?" said Mantle. "That's horse manure. I never thought I was so bad that there was any reason for me to mellow. I heard that a New York writer has done a magazine article, about Bobby Murcer called. 'The Yankees Finally Have a Nice Guy in Center Field.' I don't understand that."

Mantle, unquestionably, is changing physically. Though he still weighs 205 pounds, the same as in his playing days, he says his chest has sunk and he pats his stomach to show where it has sunk to. He said he hadn't taken any batting practice swings this season. "I can't hit no more," he said. "Timing's gone. And when I swing, I get sore here in the chest, and my legs hurt, too."

He will not hit again, he says, until the Old-Timers' Game at Yankee Stadium this summer. There, he can renew acquaintances with "the brotherhood" of teammates he says he misses so much today. And he will again hear the crowd's roar that raises goose bumps on him when his name is announced.

"Yep," Mantle said, "the old days were great while they lasted. They just didn't last long enough."

Remembering Mickey Mantle

August 26, 1996

The sun was high in the sky, the white clouds were pillowed against the light-blue universe, the No. 4 elevated train rumbled somewhere in the distance and the fans at Yankee Stadium were nestling into the furniture. It was a beautiful day for a ball game, and for a sentimental journey. Yesterday the fans had both.

In a ceremony before a cheering crowd of 50,808 that not only preceded but temporarily upstaged the Yankees pursuit of a third straight victory against Oakland and Andy Pettitte's attempt for his 19th victory of the season, a monument in honor of Mickey Mantle was unveiled in an area behind the left-center-field fence.

"This is great day for us," said David Mantle, one of Mantle's three surviving sons, "and a sad one, too."

Mickey Mantle, who died on August 13, 1995, at age sixty-three from liver cancer, was, like the other three Yankees with a monument, a posthumous recipient.

In the nearly century-old history of the Yankees, only four men have been honored with monuments in Monument Park, although many plaques for Yankee stalwarts, as well as two for visiting Popes, have been hung out there. Miller Huggins, the manager of the legendary Yankee teams of the 1920s, was the first to be monumentalized, as it were.

The next was Lou Gehrig and, forty-seven years ago, the third was for Babe Ruth.

The ceremony yesterday included Whitey Ford, Mantle's good friend and longtime teammate in the 1950s and 1960s, unveiling the monument, which was already in place. Ford happily was not asked to carry the slab of granite in, since it weighs 4,500 pounds.

Joe DiMaggio, among several of Mantle's former teammates as well as Mantle family members, was on hand, looking as dapper as ever, though, at age eighty-one, gray-haired, rheumy-eyed and slightly stooped. It was mentioned to him earlier in the day that George Steinbrenner, a certain Yankee administrator, had said that DiMaggio could have a monument out there any time he decided to have it. DiMaggio smiled wanly at the thought. "I'd rather it not be now," he said. "I'm too busy living."

And while the monument would contain the mammoth Mantle statistics, such as 536 home runs in his 18-year career, most World Series homers (18), three-time most valuable player award winner, Hank Bauer would remember something else.

"I think of that interview he gave on television near the end of his life," said Bauer, a former teammate of Mantle's, "when he said to the kids of the country: 'Don't put me as your hero. I'm not a hero.' What he was sayin' was, if I had known I could have played longer, I would have taken better care of myself. I played with him, and I thought that that was outstanding."

Ford said, "He felt he made a bad example of himself with his drinking and carrying on for forty years." But like many, Ford remembered another side of Mantle, one that was warm, gracious and funny. Ford recalled that Mantle, who played center field when the monuments were actually in play near the fence there, used to say, "Whenever Whitey pitched, I'd always have to be circlin' those monuments."

Billy Crystal acted as a stand-in for the legion of Mantle fans, an inspired choice because he was genuine, and because he is good. "Toward the end of Mickey's life," he said, "a new person emerged." Mantle had undergone a liver transplant and in the short life left to him became a strong advocate for organ donors, now reaching past a relatively self-absorbed, sybaritic life into one of greater awareness and humanity. Crystal had come to know Mantle and believed that Mantle then "came to grips with himself. It was perhaps his finest hour."

The outpouring of affection for Mantle from the literally tens of thousands of cards and letters and good-luck amulets seemed to astonish Mantle. He never realized the effect his baseball life had had on so many people. For in imagination he remained the country boy with flaxen hair from Commerce, Oklahoma, the all-America-seeming lad, the guy who, as in the storybooks, hit a ton, ran like the wind and then suffered crippling leg injuries that rendered him sometimes gimpy. As an announcer on a giant-screen replay of Mantle in action said yesterday, the way he played in pain "enhanced his heroic stature, because in the end it made him appear vulnerable, like you, like me."

And this is the Mantle that Crystal remembers when, as a boy living on Long Island, he was taken by his father to his first big league game, on May 30, 1956, and saw Mantle, a switch-hitter batting left-handed, hit a long home run against the right-field facade.

"And I became a Mickey Mantle fan," he said. "I was nine years old and I limped for no reason. I gave my bar mitzvah speech in an Oklahoma drawl."

Crystal concluded that "in my mind's eye, and in all our mind's eyes" Mantle "will always be playing."

Soppy, but with substance. Thus the reality relating to such striking performers as Mantle in such dream-invoking activities as baseball.

And then the current Yankees took the field against the A's. It seemed vaguely anticlimactic.

Whitey Ford and, Yes, Salvador Dali

March 24, 1969/Pompano Beach, Florida

It was a day like many days for Whitey Ford, only a bit different. He had thrown another shutout. Yet he was much less than delighted.

As a pitcher for the New York Yankees, Whitey Ford would dangle a curve ball and opposing hitters would bite like mad, as they racked up zeros on the scoreboard. Now, Ford stepped off the fishing yacht at the Sands Harbor Inn here. The worm on his pole was wet but uneaten. Another shutout.

He turned to his fishing partner, Darrell Shoaff, and said, "Let me know the next time you go fishing, so I can get another windburn." Ford tugged his golf hat and laughed. "I'm thirsty."

Inside the Inn, Ford lounged and discussed his life and good times. In other words, he did not talk fishing. Since his retirement from active baseball competition in 1967, Ford has been one enterprising ex-athlete.

He recently signed to do television color for 40 Yankee games. He also does some coaching for the Yankees. He is part of a group called Trans-National "Communications, Inc. (TNC), which recently paid $4.5 million for the Oakland Seals National Hockey League club; the group includes ex-professional football players Pat Summerall and Dick Lynch.

And lately, one can't tune into Lassie or Here Come the Brides without coming face-to-smiling face with Edward Charles Ford. He is the most prominent TV commercial personality since that other blonde who goes around asking people to take it all off.

He did a baseball commercial in conjunction with a soup company. In it, he plays a first-base coach who is reading a baseball book about the centennial of baseball. A runner gets on, starts asking Ford about the book. The runner gets picked off, and asks Ford why. "Read the book, dummy," says the sage. The soup company has purchased time in the next four months to play this 2,770 times!

Ford's most joyous commercial, though, is the one for Braniff Airlines with Salvador Dali, the eccentric Spanish painter. Braniff is attempting a sophisticated, unusual advertising campaign. They have paired several diverse type like Mickey Spillane and Marianne Moore, Andy Warhol and Sonny Liston, Dean Martin Jr. and Satchel Paige and the pairs sit on a plane and get into a conversation of sorts.

At the end of each segment, one of the stars turns to the camera and says: "When you got it—flaunt it."

Before the commercial, Ford had never heard of Dali. And Dali thought that Ford came in two types—automatic and stick shift.

"He had this terrific mustache and kept twirling the tips of it," said Ford. "He called me 'Vitee.' I said to him, 'Now tell me the truth, don't you think a knuckleball is muuuchh harder to throw than a screwball?' He says, 'Oh no, no, no, no Vitee.' He mumbles something about how to pitch.

"Then he says, 'When you got it—flaunt it.' And I say, 'Tell 'em, Dali, baby.'" Ford laughed about it. "Actually, Dali wrote his line on a cheat card. He wrote it just the way he spoke it: 'Ven you god id—flaund id.' Ron Holland, who's one of the heads of the advertising agency who did the commercial, took the card and had Dali sign it. He said he now has an original Dali."

Ford got up, he had to get to the ball park at nearby Fort Lauderdale, where the Yankees are in spring training. He asked Shoaff for a comb.

"For what?" Shoaff needled.

With a flourish Ford removed his golf cap and ran his hand through a thick head of white-blond hair.

"Ven you god id—flaund id," he said.

Hank Aaron: Up From Obscurity

August 20, 1973/Atlanta, Georgia

First of all, Hank Aaron's swing is all wrong. He hits on his front foot. The great hitting textbook in the sky says you swing with the weight more on your back foot to get—the irony for Aaron—more power.

This is not so bad as when he first played in the Negro Leagues in 1952 and batted cross-handed. That's right, cross-handed; like your Aunt Fanny at the family picnic.

And Hank Aaron looks so passive at the plate, no trace of the cobra he is. "Henry Aaron is the only ballplayer I have ever seen who goes to sleep at the plate," said former big league pitcher Curt Simmons. "But trying to sneak a fast ball past him is like trying to sneak the sunrise past a rooster."

Aaron's nap is a ruse. He has become one of the greatest hitters in history, and is one, two, three or four in runs scored, hits, total bases, runs batted in, extra base hits, home runs and doubles among Ruth, Cobb, Speaker, Musial, Wagner, Mays . . .

Yet he has been buffeted with the faint praise of, of all things, bland consistency. He has been so uniformly out standing in all areas of play for the last twenty years that, until two years ago when he began to seriously challenge the "legendary" career home-run record of 714 held by Babe Ruth, Aaron was playing in spectacular obscurity.

Aaron had always admired Joe DiMaggio's "cool perfection." But Aaron was cool in the shadows, while DiMaggio was in the glaring cynosure of fame. Aaron is reserved like DiMaggio, smooth like DiMaggio, talented like DiMaggio, versatile like DiMaggio.

But he did not play in New York like DiMaggio. And he is not white like DiMaggio.

Whenever he would hear talk of the greatest players, he—was never included. "I'd hear Mays and Mantle and Killebrew and Clemente and Frank Robinson," he says. "I'd never hear me." The lack of recognition rankled.

When professional baseball celebrated 100th anniversary with a gigantic banquet in a Washington hotel before the 1969 All-Star Game, the All-Time team, as selected by writers and broadcasters, was announced. The All-Time "Living" outfield was Williams, DiMaggio, and Mays.

"That wasn't so bad," said Aaron, who was on the National League All-Star team that year, "but I wasn't even invited to the dinner."

At the 1970 All-Star Game in Cincinnati, Aaron came to the hotel where the baseball headquarters was and asked for a room. He had made a reservation. The clerk checked and checked and said, "Sorry, but we have nothing in your name, we've never heard of you." (This, says Aaron, did not peeve him so much. He has enough perspective of himself to say, "There are a lot of people walkin' the streets who nobody knows.")

"The thing about Hank," says Eddie Mathews, Aaron's one-time teammate with Milwaukee and Atlanta and later his manager, "is that he does everything so effortlessly, so expressionlessly.

"He runs as hard as he has to, for example. His hat doesn't fly off the way Mays's does. Clemente ran, and he looked like he was falling apart at the seams. Pete Rose runs hard everywhere, and he dives head first. Aaron runs with the shaft let out, but you'd never know it. Yet when the smoke clears, he's standing there in the same place as the others."

Aaron has wondered, though, why only recently has he been discovered by the nation. He believes that his blackness was the most important reason. There is a feeling that the white press wants to promote white players. And when one counters that he played in comparatively small towns like Milwaukee and Atlanta, he asks why Johnny Bench is so famous.

Even now he feels sensitive about the diminishment of his achievements. In Atlanta, Babe Ruth chase or no, the team is going poorly and attendance is only slightly more than 11,000 a game.

The letters of racial slurs against his run for the record also, of course, disturb him. And in a lesser way, so do the little slights. Bowie Kuhn, after "warning" pitchers not to groove pitches to Aaron, does not send Henry a congratulatory telegram on hitting No. 700. President Nixon does send a telegram, but he sends it to the Milwaukee Booster Club, of all places. ("Maybe he didn't know my address," said Aaron. He also remembers that President Nixon sent him a Christmas card addressed to "Mr. Frank Aaron.")

An Atlanta paper runs a series on "The Truth about Ruth." One line reads: "While Braves right fielder Hank Aaron will probably break Ruth's home run record this year, no one has yet come close to matching the magnetism of the Babe."

Says Aaron, with a grimace: "No BLACK player has yet come close to matching the magnetism . . ."

Besides that, Aaron is now the Braves "left fielder." He is thirty-nine years old. He was shifted this season from right field" because, he admits, "my arm is not what it used to be."

He also knows he is no longer the player he was ten years ago, "or even five years ago," he said. "It used to be that before a season, I'd know I'd hit over .300, steal 25 bases, bat in 100 runs, score 100 runs and hit over 30 homers. Now I know I will hit over 30 home runs. That's all.

"I'd probably have retired by now if I wasn't going for the record. I'd probably be bored, what with the team 20 games out of first place, and me not able to do all that I once could. I wouldn't want to be an old man hanging on. But this record is so prodigious that I'm going to stay until I break it."

Aaron hit his 714th and 715th homers early in the 1974 season.

Hank Aaron Still Wields a Hammer

February 24, 1991

Hank Aaron has a long memory, longer to be sure, at age fifty-seven, than any of today's athletes, a sometimes unconcerned and "selfish" group, he says. His memory is long because some of the slights and hardships and pain he experienced as a black man in a racially divided nation are indelible, long because he feels it is important that he doesn't allow himself to forget. Long because he isn't permitted to forget.

The man who broke Babe Ruth's celebrated career home-run record will walk into a store today accompanied by a white man and the white salesperson walks over to the white man and says, "Can I help you?" Aaron sits in a restaurant with a white man and the waitress looks at the white man and says, "Can I help you?" But when or if it is learned that this black man is Hank Aaron, baseball slugger, the mood changes. "Then," he said, "their eyes get big, and they want to shake my hand and get my autograph. Happens all the time."

Aaron sees these incidents as often unconscious slights, but it demonstrates for him the need for the struggle for blacks to be seen, literally and figuratively, as equals to everyone else.

He remembers when the racism was even more blunt. He recalled times in the mid-'50s when he barnstormed through the South on a baseball team that consisted of some of the other black major league stars of the period, Willie Mays and Ernie Banks and Roy Campanella and Sad Sam Jones. At night after a game, when the black-owned restaurant in Mississippi or Georgia or Alabama had already closed, the team had no choice but to seek food from a white establishment.

"Sam Jones used to save us," Aaron recalled last week, while in New York to promote his new autobiography, *I Had a Hammer*, written with Lonnie Wheeler. "We'd park our bus on the edge of town and send

Sam for food. He was very light-skinned and so we put a hat on him and he took a cab to the white hotel. Sam could pass for white, except for when he talked. So at the hotel restaurant he acted like he was a deaf mute. He pointed to his mouth to show that he couldn't speak, and then handed over a list of sandwiches we'd ordered. He'd get the sandwiches, hail a cab, and return to the bus."

But on the ball field, none of those players was invisible, or, under their baseball caps, disguised. Aaron, for one, was the subject of one of the most appealing descriptions in sports.

Curt Simmons once said: "Trying to sneak a fastball past Hank Aaron is like trying to sneak the sunrise past a rooster."

Aaron smiled when the line was repeated to him. He sat now in a coffee shop, in sport jacket and white shirt opened at the neck, and looked typically husky and fit.

"Curt and I go back a long ways," Aaron said. "The first time I ever faced him was in a game in spring training in Bradenton, Florida, in 1954. I was a twenty-year-old rookie with the Braves and he was with the Phillies, and already a veteran pitcher. He threw me a fastball and I hit it for a home run. From then on, he'd never throw me a fastball to hit. Sometimes I'd see a fast ball, but it was way outside, or inside, to try to set me up for his junk stuff.

"He'd give me a little dink curve here, and a little dink spin there. Well, he became one of the hardest pitchers for me to hit. So one day, late in his career—must've been around 1966 and he was with the Cubs—I came up with the bases loaded. I had said to one of my teammates, 'He's going to give me more of that damn junk.' But instead he threw me a fastball in the strike zone, and I hit it out of the park."

For Aaron, that was just one of his 755 regular-season homers over a 23-year career for the Braves and the Brewers (41 homers more than Ruth), a career filled with remarkable, consistent achievement that landed him in the Baseball Hall of Fame. It was recalled that

Joe DiMaggio, discussing professionalism, said he always played hard because someone in the stands might be seeing him for the first time, and he didn't want to disappoint.

"I did the same thing," said Aaron, "except I thought it might not only be the first time for that, it might be the only time."

Aaron is now a vice president for the Atlanta Braves and a consultant to the owner, Ted Turner. From 1976 to 1989, he was the Braves farm director, one of the few significant front-office jobs in baseball held by a black man.

He noted with satisfaction that Bill White is the president of the National League, and that there are two black managers, Frank Robinson and Cito Gaston. "And I believe that one of the American League teams has a woman who is a comptroller, and there's another black in administration somewhere else, but other than that," said Aaron, "I don't see a great deal of movement for blacks off the playing field in baseball.

"We still can't even get a black coach on third base. Over on first, OK, but not on third. I've seen maybe two black third-base coaches in my 37 years in baseball. I don't understand why. Do people really think a black man can't give signals like a white man, or be able to tell a runner to score or hold up? We do in the field, don't we?

"America is a great country, and I wouldn't have been able to do what I've done anywhere else, but the problems are still great, too. Some of the younger black athletes today don't want to hear any of this. They don't seem to care what the history is behind all this big money they're getting. There are still many, many blacks struggling because of racism, and these athletes often don't speak out about it, or enough, or give back to the community.

"It bothers me that even though players today may have heard of Jackie Robinson they don't know what Jackie Robinson went through: the abuse, the death threats," said Aaron. "Too many of the black athletes today think the battle is won. It's not won, not by a long shot."

Whew! Rizzuto Talks Circles Around the Hall

August 1, 1994/Cooperstown, New York

Somewhere in his acceptance speech into the Baseball Hall of Fame yesterday on a hot day behind a school beside a cornfield, like something out of *Field of Dreams*, and with who knows how many thousands of people because a lot were sitting, many were standing and many others lolled on the hilly grass, somewhere in that speech Phil Rizzuto, speaking without notes and without what sometimes seemed a semblance of rhyme or reason—not that anybody in the loving, laughing audience seemed to care, least of all the Scooter himself, who in his inimitable and wondrous digressions and ramblings actually began with "Holy cow!" since it took him thirty-eight years after the end of his baseball career in 1956 to finally make the Hall of Fame.

Anyway, somewhere in the speech he told about leaving home in Brooklyn for the first time when he was nineteen years old and going to play shortstop in the minor league town of Bassett, Virginia, and he was on a train with no sleeper and when he got his first taste of Southern fried chicken and it was great and it was also the first time that he ever ate—"Hey, White, what's that stuff that looks like oatmeal?"—and Bill White, his onetime announcing partner on Yankee broadcasts, and, like all his partners, never seemed to learn their first names, though he knew the first and last names of a lot of the birthdays he forever is announcing and the owners of his favorite restaurants even though as he admits he often talks about the score or the game, but after 38 years of announcing games and after a 13-year playing career with championship Yankee teams few seem to care about this either, well, White was in the audience and stood up and said "Grits."

"Grits!" announced Rizzuto. "That's right. And I didn't know what to do with them so I stuffed it in my pocket."

141

There isn't enough space here to get into Rizzuto's whole recitation of being raised in Brooklyn and his family that means so much to him, especially his wife, Cora, and his baseball career or his time in the Navy during World War II when he even got seasick on the ferry from New Jersey to Virginia and people said, "He's going to protect us?" and how he said he starts stories at the end and goes back to the beginning and winds up in the middle but he paid tribute to many, including two he was inducted into the Hall of Fame with, Leo Durocher and Steve Carlton, and told a story of Durocher being a great bench jockey as well as a great manager and when he popped a ball straight up and the catcher caught it in a World Series against the Dodgers, Durocher hollered, "That's a home run in an elevator shaft!"

And Carlton, sitting right behind him on the dais with some thirty Hall of Famers, threw back his head and laughed, old Stone Face and old Mum Mouth to the reporters, even though they voted him into the hall on the first ballot and he did thank them for it, but Lefty to the ballplayers who loved him if he was their teammate and hated him if they had to face his wicked slider and fadeaway fastball said that everything seems to come in cycles.

It was at Cooperstown in an exhibition game during induction week in 1966 that Carlton was called up to the St. Louis Cardinals after having been sent down to the minors to pitch on that day to the Minnesota Twins and he struck out 10 batters in seven innings and went on from there to strike out more batters than anyone in baseball history outside of Nolan Ryan and also performed the amazing feat in 1972 of winning 27 games for the Philadelphia Phillies, a forlorn, last-place team that won just 59 games altogether that season and also said another old Phillie, Richie Ashburn, should be in the Hall of Fame. (Ashburn indeed was elected in 1995 to the Hall by the Veterans Committee.)

But—where were we?—oh, yes, Carlton said that he didn't talk to the news media because he needed to focus on pitching and couldn't be distracted, something Rizzuto never minded, and after about twenty minutes of his thirty-minute confabulation, Rizzuto said that if his voice held up—it was getting hoarse and he was also embarked on combat with a few flies at the podium—that he could talk for a long time and if anybody wanted to leave they could and Yogi Berra and Johnny Bench, laughing like everyone else, got up and started to walk out and Rizzuto explained, "They took so many balls in the mask."

Someone in the crowd asked whose birthday it was and Rizzuto, looking natty in his blue blazer and silver hair, mentioned Ruby Sabattino, "who is getting along in age," he said, "and was a little under the weather and couldn't make it up to Cooperstown and, oh, the cannolis, the cannolis came last night—a day without cannolis is like a day without sunshine!"

And then he said that this was the last part and he had written something down and adjusted his glasses and said he can't read it and doesn't want to start crying, though he knows it's OK in a situation like this—just before him was the actress Laraine Day accepting for her late husband Leo Durocher, often a bad actor on the ball field, and beside her their son, Chris, who broke down when he said it was unfortunate that his dad couldn't be here for this honor but felt "my father stands here with us because he got time off today for good behavior."

Rizzuto was able to read now, gravel-voiced and emotional, and said: "I had the most wonderful lifetime any man can possibly have. And I thank you for this wonderful game they call baseball."

And everyone understood this perfectly, and laughed between tears, or cried between laughter, or just stood and cheered. Baseball was never better.

The Phone Rings for Nellie Fox's Widow

March 6, 1997

In her home in Chambersburg, Pennsylvania, Joanne Fox anxiously awaited the phone call that would say whether her late husband, Nelson Fox, would finally make the Baseball Hall of Fame.

The call would come after the vote of the Veteran's Committee, which was meeting yesterday in Tampa, Florida. Fox, the former Chicago White Sox second baseman, had come so close in 1985, his last eligible year on the baseball writers' ballot, getting 74.68 percent of the vote. He needed 75 percent.

Last year, he came in second to Jim Bunning on the fifteen-member Veteran's Committee ballot. Joanne Fox waited in the home she shared with her husband until his death from skin cancer in 1975, at age forty-seven. She waited in a room that contained one of the bottle-handled bats he used, as well as, on a wall, the most valuable player plaque he won for leading the White Sox to the 1959 American League pennant.

One of Fox's teammates, pitcher Billy Pierce, had called every year after Fox failed to make the Hall, to share her disappointment—along with the Nellie Fox Society, an organization of fans in Chicago, which campaigned for his election.

And for those of us in Chicago in those exciting baseball years starting with the "Go Go Sox" of 1951, when such players as Chico Carrasquel and Minnie Miñoso and Jim Busby and Fox scratched out runs and challenged the mighty Yankees, the image of Fox remains vivid—the intense, crouching left-handed batter choking up on the thick bat, and the comical, stout wad of tobacco in his cheek.

'Nellie was very annoying," recalled Jerry Casale, a former Boston Red Sox pitcher and the owner of Pino's Restaurant in Manhattan. "He'd never strike out and he might foul off 20,000 pitches. He could hit to all fields, and he was a great bunter. He could do a million different nice little things."

Fox was exceedingly competitive, and tricky. "Fox played a good game in the field at second base," Casey Stengel once said, "and he'd stand up at the plate and barber and keep the boys irritated. And he'd even walk by and step on the resin bag for our bats, and make the resin run out."

And Ted Williams, in his autobiography, *My Turn at Bat*, wrote: "You couldn't underrate that Fox. He was always blunking or blooping one to win the game in the ninth inning."

The way it all began was with that old pickup truck rattling into the dusty driveway of the ramshackle ball park in Frederick, Maryland, in March 1944. The Philadelphia A's were preparing for the season there because major league teams couldn't go south to train during the war. The truck came to a stop and three people emerged from the cab, a moon-faced lad of sixteen with a big cigar in his mouth and his parents. They had made the fifty-mile trip from their home in St. Thomas, Pennsylvania, in order to meet Connie Mack, the A's manager, and present them with their son, Nelson Fox, a first baseman.

The youth was relatively short for a first baseman, at 5-foot-9 and rather slight, at 150 pounds. He was a first baseman, he would tell Mr. Mack, "because, well, I have the mitt." Mack gave the kid a look, and liked what he saw, and signed him. He sent him to the minor leagues and switched him to second base. Mack brought him up to the A's in 1947—the Foxes were married shortly after that—primarily kept him on the bench, and then traded him in 1950 to the White Sox.

It was there, under Manager Paul Richards, that Fox developed into one of the best second basemen of his time, a 12-time AL All-Star, four times leading the league in hits and finishing a 19-year big-league career with a .288 batting average.

Fox's manager in his later years with the White Sox, Al Lopez, said yesterday, "He was a good man for me." But Lopez had found some fault with Fox. Lopez thought he could be a selfish player, and when Lopez was a member of the Veteran's Committee, it was known that he did not cast his vote for Fox.

Then yesterday came the news: Tommy Lasorda, the extroverted former manager of the Los Angeles Dodgers, was voted into the Hall of Fame on the first try. And an old Negro Leaguer, shortstop Willie Wells Sr., also made it.

And then the phone rang in the home of Joanne Fox. After a moment, she picked up the receiver.

"Nelson Jacob Fox," she was informed, "has been voted into the Baseball Hall of Fame."

"Thank you," she said. "Thank you."

Robin Roberts in an Unforgettable Doubleheader

May 30, 1991

With the recent rash of managerial firings—despite it being so early in the season—and the heat being turned up on the seats of several others, including the one in Queens, the most unusual ousting of all was recalled, when Phil Cavarretta was bounced as manager of the Cubs in spring training 1954. No manager, alive or dead, was ever fired so early.

Cavarretta met in Mesa, Arizona, with the owner, Phil Wrigley, and since the club had finished next to last the year before, said they needed help at catcher, and in the infield, and in the outfield, and, oh yes, with pitching, too.

"Defeatist attitude," said Wrigley to Cavarretta, and Cavarretta was history.

"I'd never had a defeatist attitude in my life," said Cavarretta, who, at age seventy-four, is now retired in Florida. "Mr. Wrigley was wrong."

And anyone who watched Cavarretta play understood that to be true. For me, one moment in particular stands out.

It happened, coincidentally, in the same year, 1951, in which Bobby Thomson struck that blow to win the pennant for the Giants in the National League playoffs, and which Roger Angell, in his piece in the May 27 issue of the *New Yorker*, says, probably aptly, "stands as the most vivid single moment, the grand exclamation point, in the history of the pastime."

I didn't see Thomson's homer, but I did see another that remains more vivid. Many of our most cherished memories are those of our youth, when we were most impressionable and the flotsam and jetsam of life's events hadn't yet cluttered up our heads. And so I recall when I was eleven years old in Chicago, and watching a Cub game on television in my living room.

Nineteen fifty-one for Cub fans was different from what it was for New York fans. The Dodgers and the Giants were battling for the National League pennant; the Yankees were winning their third straight in the American League. In Chicago, the Cubs were in a dogfight with the Pirates for last place. But the Cub fan rooted hard for the stray win, and hope was always just around the corner—a corner never quite turned.

The date of my particular recollection was July 29, a Sunday. It was the second game of a doubleheader with the Phillies. The Cubs had switched managers a week before this doubleheader, firing Frank Frisch and elevating Cavarretta, the veteran first baseman, to player-manager.

In the first game against the Phillies, Cavarretta hit a two-run triple off Robin Roberts to help the Cubs win, 5–4, and end yet another long losing streak.

For the second game, Cavarretta replaced himself at first base with Dee Fondy. In the seventh inning, the Cubs rallied for two runs to tie the score, 4–4. There were two outs and the bases were loaded. Philadelphia brought in their ace, Robin Roberts, to relieve Curt Simmons.

Roberts almost never relieved, and had pitched the first game. He had won 20 games the previous season, leading the Phillies to the National League pennant, and appears on his way to another 20-win season. The twenty-four-year-old Roberts, at 6-feet, 190 pounds, and with a blistering fast ball and enviable control, now was perched on the mound.

At this point, Cavarretta, the fledgling manager, looked around and chose himself to pinch-hit for the pitcher, Dutch Leonard. It was late afternoon; Wrigley Field was already in shadows and much of the crowd had departed. You could hear on TV the periodic boomlet of heels crushing empty cups in the stands.

Cavarretta was a big Cub hero, now in his 18th season with the team, and had once even led the league in hitting. And here he came to the plate. Oh, this was exciting! This was dramatic! I must have leaned forward on the couch. Maybe I chewed the antimacassar. I don't remember.

Cavarretta had a strange habit of wiping his bat between his thighs before he got into his stance. I didn't know why then (he later explained to me that he'd spit while in the on-deck circle and try to hit the flying saliva with his bat to work on his timing) but it didn't matter.

Tension mounted. The dark-complexioned, left-handed-hitting Cavarretta stepped in to the batter's box. Roberts wound up and threw. Cavarretta swung, and whacked Roberts's first pitch into the right-field bleachers for a grand slam!

Jack Brickhouse, the announcer, went nuts. So did I. I jumped and screamed. Mr. Heifetz, who lived in the first-floor apartment directly below us, beat his ceiling with a broomstick. Despite all this, Cavarretta coolly circled the bases.

The Cubs won, 8–6, to sweep the doubleheader. The thrill of victory was fleeting, however, since the Cubs soon fell into last place, where they concluded the season.

Cavarretta said he wasn't nervous about calling upon himself in that situation. "I always loved a challenge," he said. "And if I had struck out? Well, they'd have to say I at least had the guts to try. That was anything but defeatist, wouldn't you say?"

I would say, absolutely.

* * *

Roberts finished the 1951 season with a 21–15 record, and a 3.02 ERA. Roberts's Hall of Fame plaque reads in part: "Won 286 games over a 19-year career. Won 20 games 6 years in a row for the Philadelphia Whiz Kids . . . started 5 All-Star Games. Major League player of the Year, 1952 and 1955." Yet, one wonders if that doubleheader against the Cubs had caused him a few sleepless nights.

Minnie Miñoso: "The Cuban Comet"

December 6, 2021

On May 1, 1951, Saturnino Orestes Arrieta Armas Miñoso, nicknamed "Minnie," as a play on "Miñoso"—and would soon be called "The Cuban Comet" for his speedy skills at stealing bases and running out triples— came to bat for the first time in a Chicago White Sox uniform. He had been traded to the Sox from the Indians, for whom he had played sparsely—and getting a cup of coffee, as it's called, with the Indians in 1949—but was still classified as a rookie. On the first pitch to him by the Yankees Vic Raschi, Miñoso met a fast ball solidly and sent it 415 feet into the Comiskey Park left-field seats for a two-run home run.

It was, to paraphrase the Humphrey Bogart character (Rick Blaine) speaking to the police captain at the conclusion of the film, *Casablanca*, it was the beginning of a beautiful major-league career. A career that as a left-fielder and sometime third baseman covered 17 seasons, over five decades (1949–1980) and concluded with a .299 lifetime batting

149

average, with 83 triples (league-leader three times), 205 stolen bases (league-leader three times), 195 home runs and just 584 strikeouts in 6,579 at-bats, led the league in assists for a left-fielder six times, and in putouts and double plays four times, named to nine all-star game teams and a three-time Gold Glove winner and four times was in the top 10 of Most Valuable Player voting.

And Miñoso was the American League career leader in being hit by a pitch, a total of 192 times, until Don Baylor surpassed him in 1985. In his rookie year with the Sox, the 5-foot-10, 175-pound, well-knit Miñoso was plunked by pitches 16 times, to lead the league. And then, in this weirdest of bruising baseball arts, he would go on from there to lead the league nine more times—his total of 10 remains an American League hit-by-pitch record, as is his record of six consecutive seasons in which he took one, as the saying goes, "for the team."

In 1951, I was eleven years old and living in Chicago, and rooting for both local teams, the Cubs and the Sox, and became a fan of Miñoso, who, though his overall plate statistics were superior to those of Gil McDougald, came in, disappointing for me, second to the Yankee infielder for AL Rookie of the Year honors (McDougald, for the record, was hit by only four pitches that season, and batted .306 to Miñoso's .325).

I followed Miñoso not only because he brought an elan to the team that, now with players like Nellie Fox, Jim Busby, Eddie Robinson, Billy Pierce, Saul Rogovin, and Marv Rotblatt, rose from the second division to first-division status, but also because he was a ground-breaker, becoming the first Black to play for a Chicago major-league team (two years later, in September, the Cubs would call up Ernie Banks and Gene Baker from the Negro Leagues). It was in Miñoso's second season with the Sox, 1952, when he began his strange streak of league-leading hit by pitches: 16, 14, 17, 16 (only 10, and a second-place finish, in 1956) and then topping the league with 23, 21, 15, 17, 13, 16.

As a Little Leaguer, Pony Leaguer, Liberty Leaguer, an American Legion and high-school first-baseman, I sought NOT to be hit by a pitch. And when I did, it hurt! My befuddling observation of Miñoso in those days was that he took a stance nearly on top of the plate and then he seemed to delight in the assortment of bruises that he subsequently surely suffered.

Miñoso, who grew up picking sugar cane alongside his father in a plantation outside of Havana, explained his hit-by-pitch philosophy in a *Sports Illustrated* article:

"What was I doing wrong in the game, that they'd purposefully want to hit me? They didn't do it because I'm nice looking, and I didn't do it to get the record. I crowded the plate because, if you only have to look middle-outside, you can kill a pitcher, and if it's outside, it's a ball.

"My father and my mother taught me there was a way to pay somebody back, if they tried to break your arm or break your face. Pay them back on the field with a smile on your face. I used to keep my teeth clean all the time, just to make sure that's how I gave it back to them that way all the time."

He also endured racial taunts of varying degrees. Once, an opposing team released a black cat in front of him and called it "Minnie." In segregated America, Miñoso often couldn't stay in the same hotel or eat in the same restaurants as white players. Yet, he overcame. How many of those pitches that smote him were intentional—out of animus or simply to intimidate or try to nudge him off the plate—is impossible to know.

On his good nature, even when receiving those taunts and racial abuses, or being hit by a pitched ball on the arm, or leg, or back or, alas, the head, which happened a few times but he was able to shake it off, Miñoso said: "When you come from nowhere—cutting sugar cane in Cuba—and get somewhere, you have to be happy."

I once interviewed Don Baylor in 1985 on the subject of being hit by pitches. He had passed Miñoso's American League record that season, and seemed to identify with Miñoso's curious talent. "Over the years," said Baylor, "I started creeping closer and closer to the plate. Now, if I backed up even a little I'd feel I was in the other team's dugout."

He added, "Pitchers try to destroy a hitter's confidence by throwing inside and backing him up. They try to intimidate him. It doesn't work with me." He maintained that he had no fear at the plate. "If you're going to be an effective hitter, you just can't be afraid. You lose the edge. . . . I feel sore sometimes. But it's not from being hit by pitches. When I'm sore, it's usually from jet lag."

After his retirement from the major leagues in 1964, he played and managed in the Mexican leagues. But at age fifty (or thereabouts, his age within a two- or three-year span was invariably in dispute, Miñoso saying he made himself older when coming to play in America from Cuba at age nineteen in order to be perceived as more mature), was called up to the White Sox by his friend, team owner Bill Veeck. And again in 1980 at age fifty-four (or so). He went 1-for-10 (getting a single) in those appearances, which may or may not have been classified as stunts to entice fans to turn through the turnstiles.

Many thought that Veeck was overplaying his carnival antics (remember, for example, when Veeck was owner of the St. Louis Browns, in 1951, he had a midget pinch-hit in a game). In 1976 Veeck refuted that claim. "Minnie's in remarkable condition," said Veeck. "if he doesn't gets a hit, he'll get hit by a pitch."

Miñoso had become known as "Mr. White Sox," and continued to live in Chicago and was a kind of Good Will Ambassador for the team and continued to be adored by Sox fans.

When Veeck died, in 1986, Miñoso, to honor his friend, came to the funeral wearing his White Sox No. 9 team jersey and the Sox baseball cap.

When Miñoso died, on May 19, 2015, he was ninety years old, or in that neighborhood.

Part V: 1960s—A Galaxy of Hurlers Amid Brilliant Batsmen

Sandy Koufax and Hank Greenberg: Stars of David

April 2010

Sandy Koufax, at age seventy-three in 2009, hair salt and pepper, more salt than pepper, yet looking as fit as though he still might be able to hurl a few shutout innings in a tight ballgame, wearing a Navy-blue blazer, white button-down shirt and wine-red tie, natty in that understated but warmly appealing manner that his millions of fans surely would recognize quickly, sat for a film interview. It was for the documentary, *Jews and Baseball: An American Love Story*, for which I was the script-writer. The interview was conducted by Peter Miller, the director of the film, and in his apartment on the west side of Manhattan. Miller and Koufax were seated facing each other, a video camera above the shoulder of Miller and focusing on Koufax. The conversation turned to Koufax's striking out 15 New York Yankees in the first game of the 1963 World Series, a World Series record.

Yankee Stadium, that sunny October afternoon, looked immense to Koufax. "You're playing the Yankees in Yankee Stadium, which is an amazing feeling," he recalled. "The Stadium is so tall and then so close to the field, as opposed to other ball parks, it almost feels like you're at

153

the bottom of the Grand Canyon." Whitey Ford, the Yankees starting pitcher, "came out and struck out the side in the first inning," continued Koufax. "So I came out and struck out the side. It kind of made it feel like, OK, the game is on. . . ."

And so it was. Koufax began to dominate. Yogi Berra, who was coaching at first base for the Yankees, remembered feeling "lonely there." "No one was coming to see me," he recalled, because most of the Yankee batters were returning to the dugout, their bats useless against Koufax's sizzling fast ball and tumbling-off-a-table curve ball. To say nothing of his knee-buckling change-up and control that would make pub dart-thrower envious.

I was sitting on a couch nearby, a few feet away from Koufax, and beside his wife, Jane. During a break in filming I took the opportunity to speak with Koufax.

"Sandy," I said, "are you aware of James Thurber's line that the majority of American males go to bed at night dreaming of striking out the Yankee batting order?"

"No," he said. "I hadn't heard that."

"But you did it."

He shrugged, as if to say, that's nice.

"Did you ever dream of doing anything like that?" I continued.

"No, I never have."

That response hung in the air for a moment.

"Well, Sandy" I said, "what *do* you dream about?" A throw-away line, to be sure.

He smiled. "Her," he said, pointing to Jane.

Everyone in the room laughed. Jane beamed. Koufax, not known for his prowess *at* the plate, had hit this one out of the park.

I tell this story because it is so revealing of Koufax, and the Jewish condition and tradition in America.

Here was a "clutch moment," of sorts—Koufax was certainly used to dealing with crises, with games on the line—and perhaps this was also a moment of indecision, and the Jewish baseball icon chose the right thing to say, and came at it from an unusual or unexpected angle, underscored with a, well, Yiddish sense of humor, as he deflected the question away from himself. One may be taken back over six thousand years, when Jews, by brains, by innovation, by wit, by self-possession, even by, yes, muscle, sought to overcome or resolve or side-step situations, sometimes with their lives hanging in the balance—which, to say the least, wasn't quite the case with Koufax's response to my question.

At one end of the spectrum, it was nothing more than a cute, though surely sagacious, response. On the other, however, it might well be fodder for, as almost everything else, a Talmudic discussion,

From earliest times in America Jews faced a preponderance of obstacles amid strivings, from   when Jews their first attempt to settle these shores in the seventeenth century (initially barred from entry by Peter Stuyvesant, the antisemitic governor of New Amsterdam, later called New York, who referred to Jews as "a repugnant race") to their various travails in Columbus' Land, as immigrants were wont to refer to America, to their entrance into, and discovery, as it were, of the world of baseball. The National Pastime would take a passionate hold among newly arrived Jewish citizens and, surely, their off-spring, a hold that continue to the present day. It was to this notion that the esteemed scholar and author Jacque Barzun, French-born but an Americanized citizen, wrote in 1954, "Whoever wants to know the heart and mind of America had better learn baseball."

Mark Twain had a similar take when, in 1890, he commented that baseball had become "the very symbol, the outward and visible expression of the drive and push and rush and struggle of the raging, tearing, booming nineteenth century." Bart Giamatti, the late commissioner of baseball, echoed both earlier writers in 1998, when he stated that in the early part of the twentieth century, "baseball became business as Business and wealth and population boomed across the country, as millions of immigrants poured in, as the tempo of life quickened and the country flexed its muscles. Baseball, increasingly played with increased skill, caught the mood of America and rode it. . . . for the immigrant, the game was a club to belong to, another fraternal organization, a common language in a strange land. For so much of expanding and expansive America, the game was a free institution with something for everyone."

Jews, as well as other new arrivals from all over Europe, blacks, and Hispanics and Asians, found that there was significant truth to baseball opening doors to feeling American. For example, in the 1920s Jews flocked to the Polo Grounds to see the rookie second-baseman Andy Cohen play for the New York Giants while Italians cheered Yankee second baseman Tony Lazzeri, one of the first Italian star major-leaguers, calling from the stands, "Poosh 'em up, Tony" in the hope that their Italian hero would advance the runners whenever he came to bat. Growing up in Chicago, I remember going to Wrigley Field with my father in 1948 to see the Cubs play the Brooklyn Dodgers. I remember the great block of Negroes (as blacks were generally referred to in those days) all sitting together in the right-field grandstands (and nowhere else in the ballpark), attired in their Sunday-best suits and dresses and hats, and heartily, if politely, cheering for Jackie Robinson.

One of the first players to receive money for playing baseball—$20 from the Philadelphia Athletics in 1866, was a Jew of Dutch origin, the outfielder Lipman Emanuel Pike. When the first professional baseball league was organized in 1871, the National Association of Professional Baseball) Players, Lipman Pike was its star. He led the league in home runs the first three years of its existence, hitting as many as six home runs in a season.

When Barry Bonds became the all-time leader in career home runs in 2007, I was charmed to come across a time-table of big-league career home run leaders. Bonds broke Henry Aaron's record of 755, Aaron broke Babe Ruth's record (714) and down it went to the very bottom, to the first career home-run leader, Lipman Emanuel Pike, known as "Iron Batter" for his stunning ability at the plate. Pike hit a total of 20 home runs in his 16-year career, a seemingly low number, but baseball was different in those days, the ball softer, the outfield stands more distant, a variety of pitches he saw like the spitball that are disallowed today, yet he still sent more baseballs soaring over the fences than any of his contemporaries.

It has not been recorded, to my knowledge, whether Pike endured antisemitic treatment. He was respected enough to be named a player-manager, for the Troy (New York) Haymakers, the first Jew to become a professional baseball manager. Still, it is instructive to know that big-league players in the early part of the twentieth century (some with very short careers, if only a handful of games, and others that played for a number of years) such as the 5-foot-4, 145-pound St. Louis Cardinals shortstop Reuben Ewing (born in Odessa, Ukraine), Philadelphia Phillies pitcher Harry "Klondike" Kane, Chicago White Sox pitcher Ed Corey, Cincinnati Reds star infielder Sam Bohne and Yankees third baseman Phil Cooney all decided to change their names when they entered professional baseball. Each one of them, it happens, was born "Cohen" or "Cohn." At the time that Harry Kane made his debut in the major leagues, on August 8, 1902, a story in *The Sporting News* noted, "His name is Cohen and he assumed that of Kane, when he became a semi-professional, because he fancied that there was a popular and professional prejudice against Hebrews as ball players."

One who did not change his name was second baseman Andy Cohen, who came up to the New York Giants in 1926. He once told me a minor league game in which he was being berated by a fan who loudly called him "Christ killer." Finally, Cohen had his fill of it. He went to the edge of the stands and, bat in hand, shouted, "Come down here and I'll kill you, too!"

Hank Greenberg, who would become the first Jewish baseball superstar, first came up to the major leagues in 1930, when the nation was in the throes of the Great Depression, antisemitism was rife in America and, with the rise of Adolph Hitler in Germany, would grow to unimaginably tragic proportions in Europe.

The 6-foot-4 Greenberg was named the American League's Most Valuable Player in 1935. He was continually being sought for appearances, dinners, and other events by the Detroit Jewish community. The child of Orthodox parents, he had grown up in the Bronx, where he sought to be "a good baseball player, not a good Jewish baseball player." He tried to shrug off that burden—an added burden, as he saw and felt it. "While I was very aware not to do anything that would embarrass the Jewish people," he once told me, "it was still hard enough trying to hit a major-league fast ball without thinking that the Jewish community was looking over my shoulder."

That changed by 1938, when he pursued Babe Ruth's hallowed record of 60 home runs in a single season. As he was belting home runs 52, 53. 54, 55, he said he was acutely aware of the plight of Jews in Europe. "As time went by, I came to feel that if I, as Jew, hit a home run, I was hitting one against Hitler," he said. With five games to go in the season, Greenberg had 58 home runs. He did not hit another, though he got several hits and some long outs and foul balls. He was walked a handful of times, but no more than any other slugger of his caliber. It is widely thought by conspiracy theorists that the opposing pitchers did not want a Jew to break Babe Ruth's record, so they pitched around him—"didn't give him anything to hit."

Greenberg, who died in 1986 at age seventy-five, disputed that supposition. "I had enough chances," he said, "I just didn't do it." The facts, as I understand them, bear that out. One example Greenberg liked to tell was his 57th home run, against the St. Louis Browns. He had driven a ball over the centerfielder's head—it bounced against the wall and rolled back toward the infield. Greenberg, not a speedy runner, thought he could get an inside-the-park home run. The third-base coach tried to hold him up, but Greenberg ignored him, thinking he could beat the relay. The throw came in to the catcher and, recalled Greenberg, "I was out by a mile." However, the home plate umpire, an Irishman named Bill McGowan ("my good friend," said Greenberg), called him safe. The Browns catcher leaped up and protested. To no avail. Home run No. 57 was entered into the record book.

In 1956, Greenberg became the first Jewish player to be elected into the Baseball Hall of Fame.

"Hank Greenberg was the perfect standard bearer for Jews," Shirley Povich, a Jew who was the great sports columnist for the *Washington Post*, said. "He was smart, he was proud—and he was *big*."

This piece began with an anecdote about Sandy Koufax, and it seems fitting to end it with one that may say something about how being Jewish shaped his identity. The fact that Koufax did not pitch on Yom Kippur, which happened to fall on the first day of the 1965 World Series, was a matter of pride for the Jews across the country. "I had always taken Yom Kippur off, and felt I should do the same, even if it was the World Series," Koufax said. Koufax pitched Game 2 against the Minnesota Twins, lost, then won Game 5 and returned with just two days rest to pitch a three-hit shutout, 2–0, to give the Dodgers the World Series victory.

I had heard an anecdote about that Series and wondered about its veracity. Don Drysdale, the other ace on the Dodger pitching staff along with Koufax, started Game 1 and was removed by manager Walt Alston in the second inning in the midst of a six-run scoring outburst by the Twins. One day in the 1980s, when Drysdale was a broadcaster, I ran into him and asked if the story was true. "Yes," he said. "When Alston came to the mound to take me out of the game, I handed him the ball and said, 'I know, Skip, you're wishing I was a Jew.'"

I think we should go with the way Drysdale told it to me.

This is not the only example, to be sure, of how Jews have often succeeded in America and in the National Pastime, but few, from where I sit, are funnier.

* * *

From chapter on "Shaping Identity" from *Chasing Dreams: Baseball and Becoming American* (National Museum of American Jewish History)

Drysdale Could Laugh at Himself

July 5, 1993

I saw Don Drysdale for the last time two months ago at a formal baseball dinner at the Waldorf-Astoria. He was still looking very large at 6-foot-6, about 220 pounds, large enough, strong enough, young enough, even at age fifty-six, that in the mind's eye I could see him back on the mound, alone under the stadium lights as cool in his black tuxedo as he had ever been in his Dodger blue.

There he was, winding up, wheeling and coming in sidearm with his fearsome fastball that sizzled over a corner of the plate, when it wasn't rattling the beak of the batter's cap, or bouncing off his shoulder. "The trick against Drysdale," Orlando Cepeda once said, "is to hit him before he hits you."

That's how Drysdale performed in his 14-year major league career, all with the Brooklyn and Los Angeles Dodgers, from 1956 through 1969—a career that led him into the Hall of Fame.

160

On Saturday, Donald Scott Drysdale was found dead of a heart attack in a Montreal hotel room. He was with the Dodgers, working as a broadcaster for their games with Vin Scully. Drysdale would have been fifty-seven on July 23. The shock of his death reverberated through the sports community, and beyond. Beyond to his family, of course, and to his wife, Ann Meyers, and his four children. Meyers is in the Basketball Hall of Fame; they are possibly the only husband and wife to be in sports halls of fame.

Drysdale was not only an important baseball pitcher who ended up with a 209–167 won-lost record and a 2.95 earned run average and six seasons of 200 or more strikeouts. He was the one who with Sandy Koufax held out in tandem for a fairer salary and thus helped open the doors to the salaries of today. But I also remember him as a man who could laugh at himself, a rare and wonderful trait.

A few years ago he told me this story: Drysdale started Game 1 for the Dodgers in the 1965 World Series against Minnesota. Koufax had originally been scheduled to pitch but the game fell on Yom Kippur, the Jewish high holiday, and Koufax sat out the game in deference to his religion. The Twins scored one run off Drysdale in the second inning and six runs off him in the third and there were still only two outs when Walter Alston came out of the dugout to remove Drysdale. As the manager approached the mound, Drysdale said: "I know, Skip. You're wishing I was a Jew."

Drysdale, the strapping blond kid out of Van Nuys, California, broke into the major leagues when he was nineteen years old, after having pitched only 44 games in the minors.

He had a lot to learn, and Sal Maglie, who had been bought by the Dodgers from the Indians for pitching insurance, helped teach it to him. Maglie tutored Drysdale in the art of knocking down batters. Drydale said that Maglie instructed: "It's not the first one, it's the second one. The second one makes the hitter know you meant the first one."

And Drysdale developed a philosophy of his own: "My own little rule was two for one—if one of my teammates got knocked down, then I knocked down two of the other team.

And if they knocked down two, I knocked down four. I had to protect my guys."

In 1965, Koufax was 26–8 and Drysdale 23–12, the best pitching duo in baseball. In contract negotiations the Dodgers had usually played one against the other. This time, the two pitchers decided to do something unique. They presented themselves during spring training of 1966 as an entry, asking for $1 million over three years, and holding out. They also hired an agent. This had never been done successfully before.

The Dodgers owner, Walter O'Malley, grumbled. "I have never discussed a player contract with an agent," O'Malley said, "and I like to think I never will." But he did. And while the pitchers didn't get what they asked, each nearly doubled his salary, Koufax getting $130,000, Drysdale $115,000.

Marvin Miller, who became executive director of the Major League Players Association in April 1966, said the Koufax-Drysdale holdout set the stage for the free agency of players that came about ten years later. "It was a kind of educational tool to the other players," Miller said. "It showed how banding together might get them something that individuals acting alone never had."

Drysdale once said that the three things people often associated him with were his record in 1968 of pitching a string of 58 scoreless innings (subsequently broken by Orel Hershiser in 1988), of "my reputation for being mean, or the fact that I was durable and never missed a turn." For nine years in a row he pitched in 40 or more games, sometimes coming in in relief if he was asked to in a pennant drive.

The irony of his death is that he was so relatively young and, just two months ago, still seemed able to strike out the side, even in black tie.

Roberto Clemente's Legacy

February 25, 1974/San Juan, Puerto Rico

Except for the threat that always lurks of a brief outburst of tropical rain, it was a glorious day.

Bright kites soared in the blue sky. On the green ballfield below, a high school band, all tasseled, high hatted and white booted, practiced a merengue to the beat of a drum, the toot of a whistle, and the perky tinkle of a xylophone. In more serious matters, Little Leaguers warmed up by tossing and chasing baseballs and baseball caps.

And soon, the highlight of this sun-splashed February morning: Mrs. Vera Clemente was scheduled to throw out the first ball of the official opening of the new Roberto Clemente Little League in the old quarter of San Juan.

Members of the nine teams were assembling. One eleven-year-old center fielder wearing a floppy Dodgers uniform carried a tube of Ben-Gay in his back pocket. He explained that the ointment made his throwing arm feel good.

Nearby, leaning against a palm tree as he slipped on spikes, was Angel Ramos, the brightly smiling umpire. "I grew up with Roberto in a barrio in Carolina," he said. Carolina is a small town just west of San Juan. "I remember we were on a baseball team together. He was thirteen years old, and he did not play much. We say it is 'eating bench.' This is very bad, to 'eat bench.' People fight when you say it to them. But one day Roberto was called to bat and he hit a double. From then on, it was 'Roberto, Roberto, Roberto.'"

The location of the ballfield in the Old San Juan is beside El Motto fortress, a sixteenth-century battlement that kept Corsairs from invading the island. Today, the fortress holds back only the sparkling waves of the Atlantic Ocean.

It was into this ocean that Roberto Clemente's plane vanished shortly after takeoff, two years before, on New Year's Eve, 1972. Clemente was taking food and clothes he had collected to Nicaragua, where he had once played winter ball, and which had just suffered a devastating earthquake.

For days after the plane fell, Vera Clemente walked the beaches searching for a sign of her husband.

Angel Ramos, the umpire, was asked if anything was ever found.

"Nunca," he said, "not even a shoe."

Why?

"The sharks," he said."

Angel Ramos told how a wreath had later been placed on the waters where the plane went under. "And the wreath disappears soon too," he said.

It was getting into midmorning, and Mrs. Clemente still had not arrived at the ballfield.

Most of the boys on the nine teams of the Roberto Clemente Little League of the Old San Juan knew the Pittsburgh Pirates Hall-of-Fame outfielder personally. He often organized baseball clinics where he taught them the finer points of the game.

What did they learn? Angel Ramos called over his young nephew Ricky, and asked him. "Cogelo suave," replied Ricky. The phrase is Spanish slang for "keep cool." Ricky adds, "He tells us always to get along with teammates, and when we lose, not to fight with someone. The most important thing is fun of competition."

Clemente had long been a popular figure on the island. He was more than just a countryman who brought pride because he had become a famous baseball player. "He grew up poor and he died trying to help the poor," said Ricky.

Before he died, Clemente was working to realize a dream of his, a sports city for Puerto Rican youth. It would house about 1,500 boys and girls who would get expert instruction not only in sports but also in crafts. "Roberto," said Angel Ramos, "felt such activities could help unite humanity."

As the Little Leaguers lined up along the foul lines for the opening ceremonies, one notices that no number 21 was worn. "No one in Puerto Rico is allowed number 21, Roberto's number," explained Angel Ramos. "It is out of national respect."

The ceremonies began without Mrs. Vera Clemente. Sponsors of the teams were introduced. Polite applause. The lady with sequined glasses who was translating the Little League rules from English into Spanish was introduced. A painting showing Roberto Clemente's strong, dark face on a "baseball in heaven was given to Mrs. Clemente's stand-in, the secretary of the Clemente Sports City project. She bit her lip to hold back tears.

There had been no stir when it was announced that Vera. Clemente would not come this day. It seemed that all understood. She had been under great strain. "Everywhere," explained Luis Mayoral, a Sports City Official, "it is 'Roberto, Roberto, Roberto.'" He related how she must go to Pittsburgh to arrange exhibition games with major league teams in San Juan. She goes to Cooperstown. She helps filmmakers on a Roberto picture, spends time with magazine writers and book authors, attends dinners to raise Sports City money, and sifts requests for appearances.

"She has long had the virus, maybe for three months," said Luis Mayoral. "But mostly it is the end of the year and the remembrances of Roberto. So Vera, she is in a depression during the holiday season. And she knows that she must spend more time with the children, Robertito, who is eight, Luisita, seven, and Enrique, four. For a long time they were like in a vacuum, especially Robertito, who understands best what happened.

"They only have one mommy and one daddy and they need a great deal of mommy now. She has done all this with the marvel of a champion—breathtaking. And I think the family has finally defeated this past year."

The band again struck up a merengue in the infield dust. Kites bobbed in the sky. The ocean rolled against the thick fortress. And a baseball game was about to begin in the new Roberto Clemente Little League in the Old San Juan.

Bob Gibson: Only His Pride Hasn't Changed

March 26, 1975/St. Petersburg, Florida

A pair of old baseball crocks met on the sidelines before a recent spring training game here.

Vada Pinson, trying to hang on in the big leagues now with Kansas City, was discussing aging with Bob Gibson, the St. Louis Cardinal pitcher who is one year shy of being a quadragenarian.

"When you get old," said Pinson, "it takes longer to heal."

"When you get old," said Gibson, "you don't heal." Then the pair creaked off to their respective jobs. Gibson has announced that this is his final baseball season. Although he is the winningest pitcher among active players (248 career victories), 1974 was the worst statistically of his 14 full big-league seasons. He had his first losing record of those years, 11 and 13. His earned run average was his highest (3.83), and his strikeout total was his lowest (129).

"I'd be a damn fool if I said I'm as good as I've ever been," said Gibson. "But I wasn't all that bad last season, either. There were six games, for example, in which I was removed from the game with a lead. And we lost that lead. We win those games and I have 17 wins for the season."

It is time, though, he says, to quit.

"I've been playing ball for something like 30 years—30 years!—and I'm tired.

"Oh, once you get on the mound, the challenge comes back, and it's fun."

His eyes, shaded under his bright red Cardinal cap, are alive now. His voice is quick and rather high.

"There is that sense of power on the mound, like you know everything pretty much depends out there on how you do. Or don't do. That's something I'll miss when I finish playing ball."

He says that being one of the best at his profession was something he strove for. He says he knows that whatever is next—possibly broadcasting, possibly business, he has enough money to make a leisurely choice—he may not reach the heights he did as a ballplayer.

"I don't think that that will be frustrating—not being the best anymore," he said. "I mean, I will always know that there was something I could do as good or better than anyone else. That's satisfying. My records are important in a relative way in this regard. I've had accomplishments and there they are for all to see.

"I'm proud of them, and sometimes even now I'll think about, oh, my no-hitter in 1972 or that 1968 season and a smile will come to my mind." In 1968, he had a 1.12 ERA, an all-time big-league low, and won 22 games, led the Cardinals to a pennant and a World Series win; he broke the Series record in the first game in 1968, striking out 17 Detroit Tiger batters.

"But when it's over, I hope not to dote on the past," he said. "And I won't be going to any of those Old-Timers games. I'll tell you that. I've sat around and heard these guys talking about how good they were and how the players today ain't nothin' like they used to be.

"Hell, we're better than they are, and the players to come will be better than us. It's the way things are."

Being tired is both a mental and physical thing for Gibson.

"Last season, I had my knee drained 22 times, before almost every start, and that's tiring," he said. "Also, playing for so long, I can't get as fiercely excited before a game as I used to. But losing—man, I still can't get used to that."

There is another change apparent to Gibson and that is the difference in the treatment of blacks.

"I remember when I first came down here to spring training in 1958, the black players couldn't stay at the same hotel as the whites. And there was no place for us to keep our families. So they stayed home. That has changed.

"Also, I think more people think of me as Bob Gibson, ballplayer, instead of Bob Gibson, black ballplayer. I believe that because of my mail, which is a lot less racist than it once was.

"But still there is an undercurrent. You get it in little things. For example, I was in an elevator in a hotel recently. A couple gets on. Now I'm in a suit and tie. The man says to me, 'I want the twenty-second floor.' He thought I had to be the elevator operator.

"I said, 'For all I care, mister, you can take the whole hotel!'"

Brooks Robinson: A Touch of Gold

December 23, 1982

Brooks Robinson playing third base was, like a rainbow, routinely marvelous. He didn't always look beautiful, however. He had a wobbly, heavy-footed way of locomotion.

Once, the former track star Jesse Owens tried to show him how to run better. "But he gave up," Robinson would recall. "He said I ran like a duck."

But Brooksie, as he was called by friends and fans, didn't play like a duck. In 23 seasons in the major leagues—all with the Baltimore Orioles—he set an armful of records for third basemen, including highest career fielding average (.971), most chances, most assists and most putouts. He won the Gold Glove for fielding excellence 16 times.

He could also hit. He often did so in streaks, though Earl Weaver, the manager during his last 10 seasons at Baltimore, said that Robinson, from the seventh inning on and with the game on the line, was one of the best hitters ever.

Robinson finished with a career .267 average and 1,357 runs batted in. And his 268 home runs were, until Graig Nettles passed him, more than any other American League third baseman ever hit.

Robinson was in the news the other day because ballots for the Hall of Fame had been mailed to the voting members of the Baseball Writers Association of America, and Robinson, who retired five years ago, is eligible for the first time. A headline noted that B. Robinson tops hall list.

Alphabetically, of course, he does not top the list. Dick Allen, Luis Aparicio, Jim Bunning, Lew Burdette, and Orlando Cepeda, all bona fide candidates, do that. But, of the forty-six former players on the ballot, Robinson is considered to have the best chance of getting elected. He will head this voter's ballot to join his longtime teammate F. Robinson—Frank—who made it into the hall last summer, in his first year of eligibility.

Perhaps B. Robinson's single most famous play was also the best example of his style. It occurred in the sixth inning of the first game of the 1970 World Series, Orioles versus Reds in Cincinnati's Riverfront Stadium. Robinson was at third for the Orioles, wearing swatches of charcoal under his eyes to protect against the sun, when Lee May hit a bouncer down the third-base line. Robinson hurried over and speared the ball after it had already gone past him.

"He was going toward the bullpen when he threw to first," recalled Clay Carroll, then a relief pitcher for the Reds. "His arm went one way, his body another, and his shoes another."

The ball arrived in Boog Powell's glove at first base on a bounce but got the batter, who had had sugarplum visions of a double. The play dashed a Cincinnati rally.

Robinson also hit the tiebreaking homer in that game to give the Orioles a 4–3 victory.

He continued in each of the succeeding games—Baltimore won in five—to dominate the Series as no one man had since, it was said, Pepper Martin, also a third baseman, some forty years before.

To a baseball fan, watching Robinson at third was pure joy. Here was a man working to the best of his ability and performing better than anyone else did, or perhaps ever would. Excellence is thrilling to see, whether in a Robinson or a Rembrandt or a plumber.

This fine artisan's tool, his glove, has preceded its owner to the Hall of Fame. In the World Series exhibit in Cooperstown is the Rawlings KBG-3H Pro Model that Robinson used in the 1970 Series.

Picking it up in the locker room before one of the Series games, a reporter was surprised at how old it seemed even then. The color was a tobacco-juice brown from heat, sweat, dust, line drives and spit. It was cracking in the pocket and ripped inside from summer perspiration. The wool on the underside of the wrist flap was dark and shrunken.

Robinson had traded for the glove. Ballplayers often do that. He had got this one a couple of years before from Dave May, an outfielder who at the time was a teammate. "I picked it up and liked the feel of it," said Robinson.

Neither Robinson nor the glove was perfect, to be sure. In the final game of the 1970 Series, for example, he was angry at himself for not gobbling up a ground ball by Tommy Helms. It had ticked Robinson's glove. "I didn't get a jump on it," he said, "because I wasn't concentrating."

Unusual, because if he had a particular secret of success—beyond extraordinary reflexes and timing—it was his power of concentration at third base, a position that, because of the proximity to righthanded sluggers, is sometimes only a little less dangerous than being a member of a bomb squad.

That was while playing. Off the field, Robinson, now a television color commentator for the Orioles and involved in a consulting firm for players, was and is well known for his decency.

"I've never seen Brooksie hurt anyone's feelings, intentionally or unintentionally," said Weaver. "And I never saw him lose his temper. And I've only seen him get mad at one person, himself. I think he's a fella who knew how to handle success."

It seemed he could also handle rough times.

On July 6, 1976, Weaver performed what he would later call one of the hardest tasks of his managerial career. He told Robinson, then age thirty-nine, that a younger player, Doug DeCinces, would be starting in his place.

Weaver recalled, "All he said was, 'If you need me, I'll be here.'" One year later, on August 21, 1977, the Orioles had to make room for Rick Dempsey's return from the injured list, and the man they dropped was Brooks Robinson, making him a coach. Some people felt that the Orioles had virtually ripped the uniform off his back. If Robinson felt that way, he never said a word about it.

On September 18, though, the Orioles had a "Thanks Brooks Day." A crowd of 51,798 streamed into Memorial Stadium to honor him. It was, up to that time, the largest regular-season crowd in Baltimore history.

For the game on the following day, the Orioles drew 3,325.

Addendum: Brooks Robinson led the Hall of Fame balloting in his first year of eligibility, with 92 percent of the vote. The only other player voted in in 1983 was Juan Marichal, with 83.7 per cent, and in his third year of eligibility.

Harmon Killebrew: The Big Surprise

January 14, 1984

It was the summer of 1955 and the Landon School in Bethesda, Maryland, a suburb of Washington, was having its annual Father-Son Alumni softball game. Bob Wolff was asked to announce the event on the public address system. Wolff, now a sports commentator for the Madison Square Garden Network, was then the main radio and television announcer for the Washington Senators.

"I've got an idea that could really liven up the affair," Wolff told one of the fathers. "I'll ask Harmon Killebrew if he'd like to come and pinch-hit. We won't tell anyone, and then when he promptly knocks the ball out of the lot and is coming around the bases, I'll tip off that he is the great slugger of the Senators."

"That sounds great," said the father.

"Sure," said Killebrew, when Wolff suggested it, "I'd be happy to go."

Killebrew was then eighteen years old, the Senators publicized "bonus baby," having signed the year before for $30,000. He had gone directly from high school in Payette, Idaho, to the big leagues.

"The Senators," Wolff said, "were probably in last place at this time—actually, I don't ever recall them not being in last place—and Harmon was being hailed as the big hope for the Senators. You know, Killer Killebrew, maybe the greatest home-run hitter since Babe Ruth. He was going to be like Joe Hardy and take the Senators to a pennant.

'But outside of the ball park, few people would recognize him. He looked a lot older than he was. His hairline had already receded a great deal and he was barrel-chested and quiet, and in a sport jacket and tie he appeared a lot older than he was. I was going to pass him off as one of the fathers."

172

The game was played in the afternoon. Wolff drove Killebrew to the field and would take him back for the Senators game that night at Griffith Stadium.

"I became friendly with Harmon from the time he came off the train and joined the team in Chicago right out of high school," said Wolff. "He had never seen a big league game before this. I used to write a column for all the newspapers in towns that carried the Senators broadcasts. And I had Harmon write something in it. He wrote it on hotel stationery, and it was really quite nice.

"He told about this dream come true for a kid, and that it was also his father's dream for Harmon to make the big leagues, and he wished that his father, who had died the year before, could be alive to see this. And he wrote: 'I know I must make good and not let my family and friends on the ball club down.'"

When Wolff and Killebrew arrived at the boys' school, Wolff noticed that a microphone had been set up behind a little backstop. He looked at the diamond and noticed that the outfield was ringed by woods—it looked like a snap for Harmon to belt one into the trees and really give the folks a show.

There were a few hundred people there and as each father or alumnus came to bat, Wolff gave him a fluffy send-off, "So-and-so, a sparkling line-drive hitter," etc. "I made it sound like a game I was announcing for the Senators," said Wolff.

"I remember there were men on base and I decided this was the time for Harmon.

"'And now, folks, a pinch-hitter for the father's team,' I said, 'John Thomas.' Or something like that. No one recognized him. He took off his sport jacket and loosened his tie.

"He tipped the first pitch, then took a big swing and missed the second pitch. This had to be a fluke. The ball was as big as a watermelon and it was being tossed in real slow. I wasn't worried. The next pitch came in looking bigger than ever. Harmon cranked up and took a mighty swing, and missed. Strike three. Oh, God! 'Wow,' I said, 'he just barely tipped the ball. He's got another swing coming.' Nobody seemed to really take notice. He was just another father up there.

"The next pitch he topped easily to the pitcher and was thrown out. I said, 'Well, fans, I've got a surprise for you. The man you've just seen at bat is not one of the fathers but the great Harmon Killebrew, who undoubtedly will become one of the most feared home-run hitters of all time.'

"I said, 'Harmon, would you give the fans a demonstration of your might?' Now everyone perked up. And Harmon went back to the plate and proceeds to miss some pitches, pop some up and hit grounders. He can't get the ball out of the infield.

"Now the hole's getting even deeper. Now, you can feel that the natives are getting restless. Either I'm lying or they want the game to go on. "So I finally say, 'Harmon, why don't you just fungo some out yourself.'

"They give him the ball and he swings at this elusive object. He manages to hit some line drives and a couple of hard ground balls, but he never gets under one to really lift it up in the air.

"The gimmick has about run its course now, and I say, 'Harmon is always a great sport, fans, and he doesn't want to break up the game by losing your softball. So let's give him a hand!'"

"There was polite applause and pretty soon we got out of there.

"Poor Harmon. All the way back I had to console him. 'Don't worry,' I remember telling him, 'you hit a hardball real well. This is just a different sport.' And he nodded his head.

"Of course, Harmon went on to hit 573 home runs in the big leagues, and only four guys ever hit more, Ruth, Henry Aaron, Willie Mays and Frank Robinson. I was reminded of all this last week when Harmon was elected to the National Baseball Hall of Fame. And he deserved it.

"But I can kid Harmon now about that game at the Landon School nearly thirty years ago. I remember telling him once that he's going to make the Baseball Hall of Fame one day, and he deserves to. But he'll never make the Softball Hall of Fame. He looked at me and smiled. He said, 'You're right.' A honey of a guy."

Harmon Killebrew: A Gentle Giant Comes Back

September 3, 1974

Bald as brass, he has done hair shampoo commercials. Mild-mannered, he is known as "Killer." Second only to Babe Ruth in number of homers per times at bat, he remains relatively anonymous. Aging, after a 20-year big-league career, he was recently given up for dead as a ballplayer—yet is again rattling fences. He is the baddest ghost going.

Harmon Killebrew is a burst of contradictions. He has indeed made an impact, but as quietly as the Abominable Snowman. He is gracious, smiling, gleaming (check his shiny pate), bland but awesome. He is fifth in all-time home runs hit (nearly 560) behind Hank Aaron, Babe Ruth, Willie Mays, and Frank Robinson.

However, most impressively, he has hit a home run better than once every 14 trips to the plate. Only Ruth's one for 11.76 at-bats is better. ("Pretty fast company," is as much as Killebrew says on the matter.)

As this season began, though, it looked like curtains for "Killer" Killebrew. He was thirty-eight years old, had in 1973 his lowest major league homer total since 1955, five, after having suffered torn cartilage in his left knee.

Last winter, Twins owner Calvin Griffith, the notorious curmudgeon, callously chose to cut Killebrew's $90,000 salary. (Meanwhile, Killebrew, though embarrassed, worked with weights to strengthen his knee.)

175

A Twins highlight film was released and there was no Killebrew to be seen on it; the one-time hero was being transformed into a nonperson.

In spring training, more woe: He tore ligaments in his right shoulder and progress back was slow. He had been the rock of the team for nearly two decades, but now at first base he covered as much ground as the Rock of Gibraltar.

As the season got underway, he was hitting poorly. The Twins called up a new, big young first baseman named Craig Kusick. Now Killebrew was spending most of his time switching off with Tony Oliva as the team's right-handed designated hitter.

These were bleak but still stoic times for Killebrew, who had been making mush out of fast balls since he was a teenager in the semipro leagues around his hometown of Payette, Idaho. (He had been discovered when Idaho Senator Herman Welker went back to Washington and told his friend, then Senators owner Clark Griffith, about this kid Killebrew in his constituency.)

This June, as the snows began to melt in Minnesota, and the sun warmed his virtually Pleistocene bones, Killebrew grew renewed. He would step into the batter's box and take his cut as of old, his massive torso and back and forearms leveling into the pitch like a no-nonsense lumberjack felling a great oak.

From the mid-July All-Star game until the last week in August, he hit around .350 and had busted for the season 11 home runs.

He was given a "day" at home in Metropolitan Stadium (he agreed to it only if his gifts were sent to a Children's Hospital in Utah and "day" money donated to a leukemia-research lab in Minneapolis). He got two singles that day, driving in two runs and scoring the winning run.

But surely his most satisfying hit this season, and ranking certainly among his career favorites, came at the end of July in Anaheim against the California Angels.

It was the second game of a doubleheader. The Angels, with new manager Dick Williams, had lost 14 straight home games. They had been winning this one 8–4 going into the eighth inning. Then Bobby Darwin hit a three-run homer. Now, with two outs, the Angels winning by only 8–7, Killebrew came up to pinch-hit. Williams strode out to the mound to change pitchers. He imperiously signaled for his fire-balling ace, Smokin' Nolan Ryan. This was Ryan's first relief appearance this season. It seemed to some that Williams was saying, okay, now we'll show 'em, our young phenoms'll turn that fat old man to butter.

On a 2-and-2 pitch, Killebrew swung mightily and ripped a high hard one so far so fast it crashed into the left field seats before anyone hardly even heard the crack of the bat.

The Twins bench went wild. Later, Steve Braun, the youthful Twins third baseman, said it was the biggest thrill of his life. Killebrew himself was so tickled that a little grin could be spied as he creaked lumberingly home.

"And Dick Williams," recalled Pat Reusse, the *St. Paul Pioneer-Press* sportswriter covering the game, "I think Dick Williams choked on his mustache."

Al Kaline Wondered If He Should Have Been a Doctor

April 10, 2020

Funny how sometimes you remember most saliently a particular instance—perhaps a little thing, an otherwise unnoticed moment—that illuminates, or symbolizes, the whole.

And so it is with me in regard to Al Kaline, the Hall of Fame outfielder, 18-time American League All-Star, 10-time Gold Glove winner for fielding excellence, who died on Monday at age eighty-five, and who played his entire 22-year career with the Detroit Tigers, from 1953 to 1974.

I recall one afternoon his running out a double, usually an unremarkable event. As he raced down the first-base line, rounding the bag and then heading for second, he did it with such lightness of foot, with such grace and swiftness, that upon observation it seemed his spike marks would be no deeper in the dirt than those of a bird's imprint.

Billy Martin, who played for the Tigers in 1958, once said: "I have always referred to Al Kaline as 'Mr. Perfection.' He does it all—hitting, fielding, running, throwing—and does it with an extra touch of brilliance."

"You have to watch him every day to appreciate what he does," said the pitcher Johnny Podres, once a Kaline teammate.

Kaline never spent a day in the minor leagues. He received a $15,000 Tigers contract when he was an eighteen-year-old senior at Southern High School in Baltimore, signing on his prom night. He became a Tigers regular the following season, and when he was twenty years old, he led the majors in batting with a .340 average, becoming the youngest batting champion in history.

Kaline began playing baseball when he was nine, and by age twelve, he was considered a prodigy, in the way Itzhak Perlman was as a violinist, or Picasso as a painter.

Fifty-one years ago, in the summer of 1969, I sat with Kaline before a game in the home dugout at Tiger Stadium. It was his 17th season in the big leagues. At age thirty-four and 6-foot-2, he was lean and hard-muscled. There were light tufts of gray in his brown sideburns under his navy blue baseball cap. As I recall, I asked him about his longevity, still playing at an all-star level. His answer surprised me.

"Sometimes I wonder what I'm doing, if I've wasted my time all these years," he told me, his eyes thoughtful. "And sometimes I think I have.

"I would like to have more to contribute to society. I don't know, maybe a doctor. Something where you really play an important part in people's lives.

"But I never had much education. I had always wanted to be in the big leagues, since I was a kid. And boom—I was there before I knew it."

He went on.

"Once in a while I'll sit in the dugout and look out on the field and wonder: What good is all this, thinking about me, me, me, my batting average, my fielding average? Oh sure, you care about the team. You have to. But in the end you're worried about you.

"So I have to think of myself as an entertainer, really. Maybe kids can draw inspiration from what I do. Maybe people who come out to the park can forget their problems for a while by watching me play.

"The difference between ballplayers and entertainers—actors like Richard Burton or Marlon Brando—is that actors do different things—comedy, drama, musicals, television, movies. A ballplayer just plays ball.

"But don't get me wrong. A ballgame is never a bore to me. Oh, geez, it's great. I love it. Every day there's something new—the different situations, the different pitches."

He paused.

"You know, I was a very good outfielder. I'm still a good outfielder, but I don't run as fast as I used to and I don't throw as well. And I beat out 12 to 14 hits a season in the hole at shortstop. Now I'm lucky to beat out one or two a season.

"I feel great so far this season. But the hot weather is coming, and that tires me some. I'll play next year for sure. After that, I don't know. I'll sure miss baseball and the people in it. And when I'm done and gone, I think I would like for people to say, 'Al Kaline? He was a real good outfielder.'"

Kaline played five more years, retiring at thirty-nine with a career batting average of .297, 3,007 hits, 399 home runs and 1,583 runs batted in. He was elected to the Baseball Hall of Fame on the first ballot in 1980. He spent much of the rest of his working life as, first, a Tigers broadcaster and then as an assistant in the Tigers front office.

Yes, history will show—has shown—that Albert William Kaline was indeed a "real good outfielder," but it will also show that he was irrefutably a wonderful entertainer, right up there with Burton and Brando.

Vince's Story, with an Assist from Mickey Lolich and Al Kaline

December 25, 1986

When the holiday season rolls around and talk of miracles is in the air, Mickey Lolich sometimes remembers a boy named Vince, and wonders what happened to him.

In fact, the thought of Lolich was triggered by the arrival recently of the ballot for the Baseball Hall of Fame. One of the names on it for the third straight year—he has received only a modest number of votes in the past—is Mickey Lolich, who pitched for 16 years in the big leagues, mostly with the Detroit Tigers.

Besides having won 25 games in one season, and having started, completed, and won three games in the 1968 World Series—in the seventh game he defeated Bob Gibson and the Cardinals, 4–1, and was named the most valuable player in the Series. Besides all that, Mickey Lolich stood out because, from the neck down, he looked like Santa Claus in a baseball uniform.

Six feet tall, and weighing as much as 225 pounds in his playing days, Lolich sported a pot belly ("Got it from home cooking," he said, "I rarely drank beer"), but still threw hard and well and long.

He could hit (he had a home run in the World Series) and he could field. "That belly of his never seemed to get in his way when he was on

180

the mound," said Rod Carew. "But I always marveled at how well this chubby guy bounced off the mound after bunts or taps. I always thought that the fatter he got, the faster he got. He seemed to defy the law of nature."

"The fatter you get," Lolich said recently, with his easy laugh, "the faster you get in perpetual motion. I'd come off the mound to field a bunt and just let my weight propel me. But I pitched a lot—one year I threw 376 innings—so you can't tell me I was out of shape." Lolich now earns a living from, perhaps not surprisingly given his penchant for munching, the Mickey Lolich Donut Shop in Lake Orion, Michigan, some fifty miles from Tiger Stadium, the scene of many of the triumphs.

Lolich was someone many guys in the stands could relate to. "People used to say to me," Lolich recalls, "'Hey, it's nice to see you in the major leagues. You look human, and not like all those Golden Gods.'"

But Lolich and his teammate Al Kaline were gods to Vince, who in 1977 was fourteen years old. Lolich and Kaline ran a one-week baseball camp for boys, in Ypsilanti, and Vince was one of the campers.

"He was a black kid who lived with his mother, was overweight for his age, and mentally handicapped," said Lolich. "He didn't know how to put a key in a door. He was confused about things like that. When he put on a T-shirt, he put it on backwards.

"We didn't know about Vince, and just accepted applications and let it go at that. We really didn't notice him the first day at check-in, but we discovered on the second day that basically he could do nothing in the way of sports."

Lolich and Kaline became "quite concerned" that Vince might get hurt, and their attorney suggested that Vince be sent home. The attorney called Vince's mother, and she broke down in tears.

She said Vince idolized the Tigers, and that he worshiped Al Kaline and Mickey Lolich. Vince would sit in front of the television set and watch ball games wearing his Tiger cap and baseball glove.

"He lives and breathes the Tigers, and exists only for baseball," she said. She said she was a cleaning lady and living on that and welfare. Vince had never been to a Tiger game because she couldn't afford it, and she had to take odd jobs to come up with the money to send Vince to the camp.

"It would be the greatest blow to him if he were sent home," she said. "I don't know what effect it would have on him."

"When Al and I heard the story," said Lolich, "we said, 'What choice do we have?'"

So Kaline and Lolich called a meeting of the ninety or so campers—all but Vince, who was taken for a walk by one of the counselors. "Al and I explained the situation to the kids, who had been teasing him and calling him 'Fatty' and 'Stupid,' the way kids can be cruel when there's someone different among them," said Lolich. "We told them it was Vince's life dream to be here, and we'd appreciate it if they could accept him and try to help him.

"They did immediately. They helped him get dressed, and put food on his tray at each meal, and took him to the ball field. One couple of kids would stand around him to protect him in case of a line drive. It was really something to see. He couldn't play, but he coached first base, and he cheered hard. Vince was a great cheerleader. He was in his glory, he was having the time of his life.

"On the last day, I pitch to all the campers, and Al and I decided to let Vince bat. He had tremendous problems making contact with the ball. Al was on the on-deck circle, and called advice: 'Get your hands up, Vince, get your bat back.' And he'd walk over and show him.

"I had moved in, but I still threw overhand. The first pitch was a strike down the middle, and the umpire naturally called it a ball. Vince swung at the next pitch and missed. And then, lo and behold, on the next pitch the miracle happened. Vince hit the ball! He tapped a slow roller to the shortstop.

"Vince chugged to first, and the shortstop—God bless him, I wish I could remember his name—juggled the ball on purpose, and threw to first just as Vince was one stride from the base. Vince beat the throw and both teams were jumping up and down, yelling and screaming.

"Later that night, there was an awards banquet, and Vince got the award for most improved player.

"Vince was given a standing O, and he put his arms around Al and me and gave us a big hug. He said, 'I'll never forget this as long as I live.' And that's when Al and I both cried."

* * *

While Kaline is now an inductee of the Hall of Fame. Lolich has never received enough votes for enshrinement.

"Cubs Family" minus "Mr. Cub," Ernie Banks

June 14, 1983

Ernie Banks smiled. It is perhaps the most famous smile in sports. Once he would greet someone with, "It's a beautiful day today, let's play two." That was in a different life.

Banks's hair is thinning now, and he wears steel-rimmed spectacles for reading some of his business papers. He had on a dark tie and a vest from a blue business suit as he sat in his office at the Equitable Life Insurance Company on Michigan Avenue.

He was a standout infielder for the Chicago Cubs for 19 years, and was elected to the Baseball Hall of Fame in 1977. He had a career average of .274 and hit 512 home runs—and became the greatest power-hitting shortstop of all time. Twice he was named the Most Valuable Player in the National League, in 1958 and 1959.

He was called "Mr. Cub." And that was the title of his autobiography. No more. Retired for twelve years, Banks, now fifty-two years old, has stayed with the Cubs during that time in one capacity or another. Most recently, it was on a part-time basis in the team's promotional department.

On Saturday, the Cubs announced that Banks will no longer be a member of the "Cub family." The reason is that Banks, according to Cub management, had missed several scheduled appearances over the years, and that he was "unreliable."

Is that true? "I had missed some," said Banks. "Not a lot, but two or three in a hundred. And when I did, I'd send a note of apology afterward, and maybe a Cub cap and a ball. I didn't want them to think I ignored them intentionally."

Was this the first time he had been the subject of negative remarks from the Cub office?

"No," he said. "In 1980, they had said similar things about my not showing up." Was it justified? "I had missed some engagements, yes." The Chicago papers used words like "Cubs snub Mr. Cub," and a story castigated the Cubs for treating an idol in such a "callous" manner. A statement issued from the Cub office today said in part, "There are always two sides to every story. The Ernie Banks story also has two sides, and he apparently has chosen to let the newspapers do his talking for him."

Banks has said the split was amicable. "They said that they had to make budget cuts," said Banks. "And they did make me an offer, but then my attorney made a counter-offer, and the next thing that happened was that Dallas Green wrote me a letter." Green is the Cubs general manager.

"He said that the Cubs just couldn't afford what I was asking, and that he hopes there's no hard feelings. I told him that I was getting deeply involved in the insurance business, and he wished me luck."

Banks has not had a particularly easy time of it since he retired. He was a coach for two years, and he was in the marketing department of the Cubs, and then he tried the banking business, going to work for the Bank of Ravenswood in Chicago.

"They put me through an entire program, starting with teller," said Banks. "And I enjoyed it. I love people, love being around them, and I could have been even a teller for the rest of my life. But I hoped to rise in finance, and took courses at several colleges. But sports always seemed to take me away from it.

"They always thought of me as Ernie Banks, the ballplayer. It was hard to make a new identity. There was always the company softball team, and racquetball with the bank president, and functions to attend.

"I think I had a fear of failure in doing something outside of sports, like a lot of athletes do. And people don't help, because they keep talking to you about your past. They are trying to be nice, but they don't understand the problems an athlete has in adjusting to a new career.

"The bank had a social psychologist, and employees go to see her. I told her my problem, and she said, 'You can't change what you were, and you can't change the way people look at you. So why don't you just enjoy it?' And that's what I try to do now."

Banks retired after the 1971 season, just before free agency, when the truly big money for baseball players began. The most he ever earned in one season was $65,000. He was, though, able to save a substantial amount. But much of that is gone.

"But I spent it the best way you can," he said. "I put my three kids through the best private schools, and then helped them each go to college."

Money remains a factor, however. "Wherever I go in Chicago," he said, "people are always coming up to me—just like a woman this morning in the drugstore, and saying, 'Ernie, I'm still a big fan of yours. I want to thank you for all the pleasure your playing ball gave me.' I think that's great, that they still remember me and wish me well after all these years. But, you know, that doesn't put any money in my pocket.

"I have no regrets, though, and I hope to make a success now in insurance. I have a temporary salesman's license, and on the 24th of this month I take the test to be certified as an agent. It's tough, and there's a lot of studying to do, but it's something I like and want to succeed in."

And the Cubs? "I feel I'll always be a Cub. And I feel if there's anything I can do for them, I'll be happy to do it. They've been a part of my life for 30 years. I'd be happiest, probably, if I could stay with them for another 30 years."

The Hands That Caught Nolan Ryan's Heat

July 21, 1990

Jeff Torborg talked about his left hand, the hand that caught most of Nolan Ryan's booming fastballs in 1973 when the two players were with the California Angels. It was the year that Ryan, with his 100-mile-per-hour heater (give or take a mile or two per hour of smoke on a given outing), established the major league record for strikeouts in a season, 383.

"The index finger of the left hand, right where the joint meets the palm, is much thicker to this day," Torborg said recently by telephone, seventeen years after having speared Ryan's fastball for the last time. "Of course, that wasn't just from catching Nolan. I caught Sandy Koufax at the end of his career when I was with the Dodgers. And there were other hard throwers along the way. The swelling was cumulative.

"But no," said Torborg, "Nolan didn't help this hand. He could certainly do damage."

Torborg, now the manager of the Chicago White Sox, was at the end of his major league career in 1973, but memories of Ryan, who last night with the Texas Rangers gained the 299th victory of his career, are indelible, just as they are with two other retired catchers, Jerry Grote, formerly of the Mets, and Alan Ashby, the ex-Astro.

Those three catchers hunkered behind the plate during a good portion of the games that Ryan, now forty-three and still formidable, has pitched in his 24 years in the major leagues with, first, the Mets, and then the Angels, the Astros and the Rangers.

That trio of catchers also, of course, caught a large number of the record 5,000-plus strikeouts Ryan has amassed.

"I caught Nolan when he first came up to the majors in 1966," said Grote, now a sales manager of a real estate company in San Antonio, "and for his four years with the Mets after that. I caught him with padding, of course, and with my forefinger out of the glove, for extra cushion. So my hand was pretty well protected. But, yes, sure, the finger portion of my hand still took a bit of a beating."

Ashby, newly retired from baseball and living in Houston, recalled that Ryan sometimes hid the catcher's mitts, tossing them under the dugout bench. "I used to like to catch with old rag gloves," recalled Ashby, "and Nolan hated them. He was like most fastball pitchers. He wanted you to use new leather so that there was a louder pop to his pitches. He'd say, 'Aw, c'mon, make it at least sound right.'

"That's a big part of the psychology of pitching. A bigger poom! can scare hitters.

"Everybody sitting in the dugout looks at each other and says, 'Jeez, he's throwin' good tonight.'"

When catching Ryan, recalled Grote, he couldn't squat in the normal receiver's position.

"You had to get up a little straighter," he said, "otherwise there was no way you could get to his fastballs at the letters. We had some very hard throwers on the Mets in those years: Seaver and Koosman, for example. But none threw quite as hard as Nolan. I'd say it boils down to about a two-foot difference."

In the year that Ryan broke the single-season strikeout record, 1973, one of his victims was Ashby, then a rookie with the Cleveland Indians. "I remember I got a hit off him the first time," said Ashby, "and the next time I maybe took too big a swing. I think I swung hard and spun around. It was like I was saying, 'I'm in charge.' On the next pitch, he cleaned off the inside of the plate a little bit. It was a fastball, high and tight, and I hit the ground. I said to myself, 'Oh, oh, I'd done something wrong.' And he was saying, 'Hey, kid, if you wanna spin, I'll be the one to spin you.' I found that he's the greatest guy off the field. But between the lines, he's the most serious player there is."

"What's made Nolan so effective is his curveball," said Torborg. "It was the same with Koufax. Major league hitters can begin to time even the best fastball. And earlier this year, when Nolan pitched a one-hitter and struck out 16 of our batters, it was the curveball that was killing us. And he's improved that considerably since I last caught him."

Grote talked about Ryan's excellent pitching mechanics, his low "drop-and-drive" delivery; Torborg mentioned his work ethic and his superb conditioning, and Ashby marveled at his competitiveness.

"I remember when Pete Rose was going for the National League all-time base-hit record and needed two hits to break it," recalled Ashby, "and he had predicted that he'd do it on a certain day. And on that day he was facing Nolan. Rose got a base hit his first time up, and then Nolan struck him out the next three times. And after the last—everyone in both dugouts had been standing to see what would happen—Pete turned to Nolan and doffed his cap, and then walked on.

"I'm sure that all the rest of the players felt like doffing our caps to Nolan, too."

Nolan Ryan, Satchel Paige, and Rules For Keeping Young

March 9, 1991/Port Charlotte, Florida

The only time Nolan Ryan met Satchel Paige was in the mid-1970s in Los Angeles, and the old pitcher—now the late old pitcher—gave the younger man a piece of advice.

"One of the best pitches is the bow-tie pitch," Paige said.

Ryan looked at Paige, then about seventy years old. Ryan was close to thirty and already an experienced big league pitcher, but he was puzzled. "What's a bow-tie pitch, Satch?" he asked.

"That's when you throw it right here," said Paige, drawing a line with his hand across his Adam's apple. "Where they wear their bow tie."

This was sound advice, Ryan believed, and he has not been above using the bow-tie pitch to keep batters off the plate and make them reluctant to dig in. Of course, Ryan's pitches remain bullet-fast, which also makes the batter wary, whether he's concerned about a baseball landing on his bow tie or not.

Last season, Ryan's 24th in the major leagues, he was still one of baseball's best pitchers.

Among other achievements, he was third in the American League in strikeouts—adding to his career strikeout record, which stands at 5,511—and he flung his seventh no-hitter, three more than anyone else in history. Now, at forty-five, an age when most old ballplayers are home clipping coupons or out hooking drives, Ryan looks forward to yet another remarkable year on the mound.

While his hair is thinning, and there are the little crow's feet about the eyes, the rest of him looks pretty fit. "And my arm? My arm is just fine," he said the other day in the clubhouse here at the Texas Rangers spring training camp.

Can he top the seniors' mark of Satchel Paige, who pitched in the majors when he was forty-seven years old?

"I don't know, but then no one really knows how old Satchel was," Ryan said. "He might have been fifty-seven. At least I have a birth certificate. And I have people who could verify it, though not as many as there used to be."

Ryan isn't certain why he has had such staying power—especially throwing as hard as he does at the age he is—but he believes genetics probably has something to do with it, as well as diet, exercise and attitude. Ryan said he had once read Satchel Paige's rules for keeping young and thought at the time that they were "applicable" to him.

In the interest of public service and the field of geriatrics, enduring concerns of this column, Ryan was asked to comment on Paige's six famous points to promote health and longevity:

Paige: "1. Avoid fried meats, which angry up the blood."
Ryan: "I think from a cardiovascular standpoint, Satchel's right. I stay away from fried foods now, even though I grew up in Texas where a frying pan was always sitting on the stove. Nowadays I have my food broiled. I stay away from fatty foods, and chocolate cakes and chocolate pies, which I used to love. But I don't know anything about angrying up the blood."

Paige: "2. If your stomach disputes you, lie down and pacify it with cool thoughts."
Ryan: "I take naps when I can, and I always try to get seven or eight hours' sleep a night. You want to keep relaxed. I tried to teach my kids that. They've been around the clubhouse since they were little bitty tykes. And they've seen a lot. They've seen players get into fights, they've heard cussing, they've seen managers go crazy. I told them: 'That's not how we act. There are a lot of different type people in the world. But we're not like that.'

190

"Also, don't let things upset you that you can't control. And try to make any difficult situation better. Last season, for example, we brought up a rookie catcher, Ivan Rodríguez, and he caught me in his second game. We weren't in rhythm, because that takes time. But I set my mind beforehand not to get upset, and to work with him. So I shook him off until he called the pitch I wanted, and it didn't throw off my concentration."

Paige: "3. Keep the juices flowing by jangling around gently as you move."
Ryan: "My assessment of that is, basically, stay loose by stretching. At this age, you tend to stiffen up when sitting in one place for too long." What about jangling? "Sure, if you know how to jangle. I'm not sure I do."

Paige: "4. Go very light on the vices, such as carrying on in society. The social ramble ain't restful."
Ryan: "Very true. You can do a lot of things with the body, but do everything in moderation." How does Ryan characterize "social ramble?" "Bar hopping, staying out late in a joint or something. Over-indulging. Listen to your body. Sometimes the rumble is because of the ramble."

Paige: "5. Avoid running at all times."
Ryan: "Here I disagree with Satchel. I think a pitcher needs to run to build up stamina and to strengthen the legs, the hips, the knees, the lower back. But I don't run for distance any more, and maybe I run 40 percent of what I used to. The recovery rate to bounce back gets longer. If this keeps up, there's a good chance that when I'm forty-seven I won't be able to run at all. So Satchel might be right again."

Paige: "6. Don't look back. Something might be gaining on you."
Ryan: "I take Satchel to mean that you can't start worrying now. You know there's always some kids behind you. Let them worry about it."

Then Ryan went over and climbed on the stationary bicycle. And one was reminded that Satchel Paige's exercise machine was also stationary. It was a rocking chair.

Satchel Paige: "A New Generation is Taking Over"

March 25, 1969/West Palm Beach, Florida

One flamingo-thin leg was wrapped around the other and two long leathery fingers cradled a cigarette in a V. Satchel Paige rocked back in his locker-room chair, curled his lower lip onto his anchovy mustache. He raised his eyebrows, nearly spilling a couple eyeballs over drooping horn-rimmed glasses. His forehead furrowed like Venetian blinds.

"I couldn't have taken it the way Jackie done," he said. "No siree. The first time someone called me a black SOB I would quite naturally have been a little peeved. There woulda been a fuss, sure.

"They wanted some youth, someone who wouldn't go feudin'. Jackie had a top education, too. Me, I didn't have nothin' but the ninth-grade and mother wit and twenty years throwin' a baseball all over the world every day for every one of them years."

So Satchel Paige was not the first black to break the color barrier in the major leagues. Jackie Robinson, in his twenties in 1947, was.

"Now you look at Jackie," said Paige, dangling his long, wide, flat baseball shoe, "and his hair's white and you'd think he was my great grandfather. And I'm sixty-three."

Late last season the Atlanta Braves signed Paige, who started his professional baseball career in 1926 with the Chattanooga Black Look-outs, to a contract as a pitcher.

He did not see game action. The Braves move was mainly a good-will gesture. Paige had needed 158 days to complete five major league years, thus qualifying for the baseball pension.

192

The baseball strike hassle this winter resulted in, among other things, lowering the pension qualifying to four years. But the Braves have kept Paige as a coach.

In 1962, Paige wrote an autobiography entitled *Maybe I'll Pitch Forever*. It did not seem out of the realm of possibility then.

"Forever is a pretty good while," said Paige. "And I'm like a fire horse in olden days. I hear the bell and I run under the harness. I can still get anyone out for three or four innings. My onliest problem is they bunt on me, and my wind's short. If I'd pitch, I might bring back the old lost art of bunting, all by myself.

"People here are doubtin' my vision, too. My eyes do give me some troubles now and again. And maybe I'm just too old and gentle to pitch no more.

"Besides, here come another generation altogether. It's all changed over, saw it happen with my own natural eye. The colored man's accepted now like never before. But times are rough now, real rough. The world's in too big an uproar.

"Lotta things are bad, but some are good. I ain't heard the word 'Nigger' in ten years, and I been from one end of the United States to the other.

"And these white boys here. Look 'round. Not a one would ever dream about a lynchin' or pourin' gas on a colored man. That's why I don't like to talk much about problems that used to be. Just let dead dogs lie.

"I think about other things. Like maybe some day gettin' in the Hall of Fame. The whole world wants me in it. But I didn't play in the major leagues long enough—that's how it's wrote up, even though for years and years I was the world's greatest pitcher.

"I pitched in the Negro Leagues and barnstormed against the best white hitters like Musial and Williams and DiMaggio and Pepper Martin and the Waners—Oh, Lord, I forget who else. Kept 'em all in the park, too.

"Maybe some day I'll fall into the Hall of Fame, like I done the pension. But I'm not sayin' they'd change the rules for me. Maybe some day before I die I could sorta sneak in. You know, for good conduct or somethin' like that."

Leroy "Satchel" Paige—who, starting in 1948, pitched six seasons in the major leagues for the Indians, the Browns, and one game for the Kansas City A's in 1965, in which he gave up one hit in three scoreless innings at age fifty-nine—was named to the Baseball Hall of Fame in 1971, opening the way for numerous other deserving Negro League players to join him over the years in the Cooperstown shrine. Paige died on June 8, 1982, a month short of his seventy-sixth birthday.

Jim Bunning: Standing on the Bully Pulpit

August 5, 1996/Cooperstown, New York

Jim Bunning, the right-winging right-leaning Congressman, took time away from his Washington concerns yesterday afternoon to accept his induction into the Baseball Hall of Fame.

Earl Weaver took time away from the golf course to do the same.

On a hot day, before a crowd of some 8,000 in a meadow here called Clark Field, Bunning, a conservative Republican from Kentucky's Fourth Congressional District, and once a chafing, side-arming pitcher, received the highest of baseball honors.

Weaver, whose battles with umpires were legendary and amusing, and who became one of baseball's most successful managers, was there alongside the Congressman.

Bill Foster, a star pitcher in the Negro Leagues in the 1920s and '30s, and Ned Hanlon, a standout manager at the turn of the century, were also inducted.

194

On a day when most of the issues were tinged with nostalgia, as well as praise for families and friends and coaches and teammates, Bunning did have strong words for the baseball establishment.

"Get your house in order," he said. "Stop going to the players and asking them to foot the bill. And get a commissioner—a real commissioner. Come up with a way to share the revenues, and mutually hire someone. Restore the power of the commissioner.

"For over four years now, baseball has been rudderless. Find a rudder before Congress gives up on you and intervenes."

Rudderless? It is just the way the owners want it, with their so-called acting commissioner, Bud Selig, the owner of the Milwaukee Brewers. The last thing the owners want is a commissioner with independent powers. Fay Vincent can tell you that.

And for the fourth straight year, there was no commissioner in attendance at the Hall of Fame induction ceremonies, which carry perhaps the greatest symbolism for the sport, whose yesterdays are as alive as its present, at least.

Oddly enough, while Selig did not make an appearance, Marge Schott did. The recently suspended owner of the Cincinnati Reds, who managed to make the trip despite having left her usually ubiquitous pet Saint Bernard, Schottzie II, at home, showed up to support Bunning, whose home in Southgate, Kentucky is just five miles from Riverfront Stadium.

As for Congressional threats, the owners have heard it all before. It comes as no secret to the honorable Representative, meanwhile, that baseball teams are private enterprises, though some owners, like Selig, give lip service to it being a "quasi-public trust." And owners like Selig then threaten to move unless the public builds them stadiums.

Among those in attendance who were introduced were Len Coleman, president of the National League, and Gene Budig, president of the American League. One of those in attendance not introduced was

Marvin Miller, also there to pay tribute to Bunning. It was Bunning, along with Bob Friend, Robin Roberts, and Harvey Kuenn, who were on the search committee in the late 1960s that chose Miller as the executive director for their players union.

Few people have made as great a contribution to baseball as Miller, whose brilliance and leadership helped raise salaries, pensions, benefits and playing conditions. From the nonplayers' side, he is the most deserving person not in the Hall of Fame.

From the players' standpoint, Bunning, in his remarks, cast votes for pitchers Don Sutton and Phil Niekro—"Do you baseball writers know how hard it is to win 300 games?" he said sternly—as well as Tony Perez, the runs-batted-in great.

In a curious note, of the two living men who were inducted yesterday, the one who entered as manager did not succeed as a baseball player. And the other was inducted as a player but was unsuccessful as a manager.

Weaver toiled 10 years as a minor league infielder, never getting past Class AA. Then, after 10 more years as a minor league manager, he got his chance with the Baltimore Orioles, winning four pennants and one World Series.

He was known as a bane to umpires.

"I want to give credit to the group of people who seldom get the credit they deserve," Weaver said in his acceptance speech yesterday. "The umpires."

The crowd laughed, but Weaver was serious. "The game has succeeded because the umpires' integrity has been beyond reproach," he said. "And in the 13 years I managed the big leagues, they must have made a million calls. And they were wrong just 91 times."

The 91 times, that is, that he was tossed out of games. Now he was smiling.

Bunning, after a 224–184 record—winning 100 or more in each major league—tried managing in the Phillies organization, but the tough approach that served him so well as a pitcher was found unsuitable in handling the modern young player, and he gave it up after three years. He eventually found his way into the halls of Congress.

After the ceremony yesterday, Bunning spoke about his work in Washington, including his having voted for passage of a welfare bill last week.

Weaver, deeply tanned from his play on the Miami links, was asked if he had an opinion on the welfare bill.

"Are you kidding?" he said, with a look of disbelief. "No."

Orlando Cepeda Is a Hero to Kids at P.S. 83

December 6, 1967

At the end of last baseball season, signs popped up all over St. Louis reading, "Congratulations, El Birdos." The reference was to the Cardinals, World Series champions, and the corrupted Spanish honored Orlando Cepeda, the Puerto Rico-born first baseman who would soon be named the National League's Most Valuable Player.

Recently, another sign, this one in Public School 83 in Spanish Harlem, paid tribute to the Cardinal slugger. It was tacked on the stage of the auditorium: "Orlando Cepeda Day in El Barrio."

Cepeda had come at the request of MEND, Inc., a local antipoverty group. At 2 p.m. about 350 students, fourth through sixth graders, trooped in to see the baseball hero. About three-quarters of the students of the school are of Puerto Rican descent. Cepeda was born in Santurce, and is known as Peruchin, "Baby Bull." His father was known as Perucho, the Babe Ruth of Puerto Rican baseball.

197

Not everyone in the moppet audience had heard of the guest of honor, however. "Who is this Orlando Cepeda?" asked one girl. Her friend replied, "A football player."

On stage, Cepeda, looking trim and strong in a natty gray suit, sat with the school's principal, the Bronx borough president, a "representative" from Mayor Lindsay's office, and a few others.

The program began with the glee club singing two Latin American songs, including "El Coqui" (The Frog), and one non-Latin tune, "Supercalifragilisticexpialidocious." The soloist was Angel Valentine, a bespectacled tyke the size of Cepeda's bat. Cepeda was introduced by another student. Harry Olivarez, head lowered, shyly said, "He is a great man from our same background. Now I will give my speech."

Cepeda rose to applause. He spoke first in Spanish. Then he reiterated in English. "My English is not too good-looking," he said, "but I'll try.

"We are all brothers. We come from a very small place. We should always try to put Puerto Rico very high.

"It is a place where the boxing champion Carlos Ortiz is from, and Junior Cordero, who broke race track records as a jockey, and Roberto Clemente. Very much to be proud.

"And for me, I work very hard and challenge the world to make something of myself. I had two bad knee operations. Doctors told me I would never play baseball again. But I had not much education, so I told myself I had to play. I wanted to follow in my father's steps. With God's will and my will, I do them.

"But you need education. High school and college. With that, you can challenge the world, too."

As the students filed out, one boy was asked his reaction.

"Good, except for one thing," he said. "How come he didn't wear his uniform?"

Another was asked his favorite player.

"Mickey Mantle," he said.

National loyalty, it seems, goes only so far.

Juan Marichal Remembers Bumbo Ramos, His Idol

June 23, 1971

The late, legendary Bumbo Ramos must be tossed as many bouquets as anyone for the San Francisco Giants quick start this season.

Bumbo was killed in a plane crash some years back, but he left a prize legacy. It was Bumbo who turned Juan Marichal into a pitcher. And Marichal is the backbone of the Giants staff.

When Marichal was a lad of ten, he went to see Bumbo pitch for the best amateur team the Dominican Republic has ever had, according to Marichal. Bumbo was from Marichal's home town, Montecristo.

"I was a shortstop then," said Marichal in front of his locker recently. "Then I saw Bumbo. Ooooh. The next day I was a pitcher.

"He threw sidearm and he would turn around and all the batter would see was his number. He would talk to the batter, too. 'You better hit this one because if you don't you won't even see the next one.' You wouldn't either. He was very fast. He was my idol."

Once, Marichal would stand on the mound and imagine that he was Bumbo. That was when he was an amateur, he said, and when you could have fun. As a professional, however, Marichal says that it is too serious, and so many things come to mind so quickly about the batter that he no longer has time for reminiscing.

He is so intense that he wears batting gloves when changing from mufti to business knickers. Two days before this season started, Marichal was rummaging in his shaving kit and cut his naked finger on a blade. The cut bothered him for three weeks. That's why he wears gloves before a game nowadays.

He is also serious about his role as an idol.

"The kids, they expect so much from you," said Marichal. And so, he says, he does not drink or smoke and never goes to a bar where trouble might pop up and give you a black eye. "It would not look too good in the paper," said Marichal. His 1970 record did not look too good to him in the paper, either. He won 12, lost 10, and had his highest earned run average, 4.11, of his 11 big-league seasons. He said that a reaction to a penicillin shot caused much of his misery last year. But he still became only the third active pitcher to win 200 games. Something neither he nor Bumbo dreamed possible years ago in Montecristo.

"But I did love baseball so much," said Marichal. "I saved bubblegum cards. My two favorites were Sal Maglie and Carl Hubbell. Especially Maglie, because he was a right-handed pitcher like me. And I liked what they called him, "The Shaver." Once the Dodgers played in my country and I liked Duke Snider. They called him "The Destructor."

"And maybe I missed school two days in a row to play baseball in a backyard. My mother would catch me. 'Tell me, what you gonna get from baseball?' She would be mad. All I could tell her was that someday she will hear me play on radio, just like Bumbo Ramos because in those days every house in the Dominican Republic listened to those games. I never thought of the major leagues.

"But she wanted me to get my education. When I was fifteen, I was playing with the men. She didn't like that either. She thought I would get hurt, that one of the big men would run over me.

"It is easy for me to remember those days. I remember the time I was so proud of my older brothel Gonzalo. He was a very good baseball player. He was an outfielder and a pitcher and he played the infield, too. I think I was eleven years old and I was watching the game in this open field. Somebody said, 'We have no catcher.' And Gonzalo said, 'I can catch.' I did not know he could do this. When he put the equipment over his head I got the goose pimples on my arm. It was the greatest feeling I ever had. He did something nobody knew he could do. Like Superman."

Young people still concern Marichal. "In America, the kids like autographs," he said. "And sometimes I feel so bad when a little kid is in a crowd and gets crushed. In my country they don't care so much for autographs. But they really follow you inside. They want to run like Willie Mays, steal bases like Maury Wills."

And pitch like Juan Marichal? he was asked. He laughed. "Let me tell you. If these kids could have see Bumbo Ramos. They would have had some idol."

Nonetheless, each time Juan Marichal pitches now the game is broadcast by a station in the Dominican Republic. Homes all over the country are tuned in, including Mama Marichal's.

The Day They Entered Baseball Heaven

July 24, 1989/Cooperstown, New York

The man yesterday remembered the boy: In the eighth grade, in the small town of Binger, Oklahoma, in about 1950, he was 5-foot-2, had size-11 1/2 feet and a head and hands that were as big as they are now—and right now one of his hands can hold seven baseballs in it.

"I told people I wanted to become a baseball player," the man said yesterday, "and everybody laughed. And I guess Barnum & Bailey would have been the only people interested in me at the time."

The man is Johnny Bench and one day he indeed got to the Big Time, and was forever grateful it wasn't the Big Top. And yesterday afternoon, standing on the gaily bedecked porch of a well-known museum here in this perfect-seeming little village, the man, now grown to 6-foot-1, and two other former players, Carl Yastrzemski and Red Schoendienst, and an umpire, Al Barlick, received the highest level of recognition for their endeavors: induction into the Baseball Hall of Fame.

Bench struck a chord that was sounded by the two other ball players, and that was a dream was realized, one that took sweat, but that couldn't have been realized without the help of others, from parents and wives to coaches and teammates. Sometimes, as the players remembered, their voices cracked with emotion. "No man," said Yastrzemski, "is an island." It was warm and sunny, and some 20,000 lively and often quite vocal onlookers in the area called Cooper Park greeted them with, "We love ya, Yaz!" and "Number one, Johnny!"

On the porch and seated behind the inductees were twenty-six returning Hall of Famers—stars like Ted Williams, Stan Musial, Bob Feller, Roy Campanella, in his wheelchair, Joe Sewell, holding a cane, Warren Spahn, Ralph Kiner, Cool Papa Bell, Willie McCovey, Johnny Mize, Duke Snider, and Charlie Gehringer.

Bench, in charcoal-gray suit with red pin stripes and red tie and red breast-pocket handkerchief, and still looking young enough to catch a ball game at forty-one, spoke glowingly about the man who hit the longest home run he ever saw, and was the greatest ball player he ever saw—he paused—"My father," he said. Bench recalled a time as a boy when his father hit a ball into the cornfield beside which they were playing, and, Bench said, "We never did find that ball."

Yastrzemski was introduced by the commissioner of baseball, Bart Giamatti, who read the inscription on Yaz's Hall of Fame plaque, which begins with a tribute to his "graceful intensity," and ends with his having led the Red Sox in 1967 to the "Impossible Dream" pennant.

"I remember it well," said Giamatti quietly to Yastrzemski, as he handed him a framed photograph of his Hall of Fame plaque.

Giamatti, having grown up in Massachusetts and being a devoted Red Sox fan, said he was speaking for all the memories of all the fans in every corner of the baseball world.

Yastrzemski recalled his rookie year with Boston in 1961. He was handed a task that he was unprepared for; he was to replace Ted Williams, who had retired the year before, in left field in Fenway Park.

"I was a scared rookie and hitting only about .220 after three months," he said. "I was doubting my ability, and thinking I could never play major league baseball." He then begged Tom Yawkey, owner of the Red Sox, to get Ted Williams, to help him if he could.

Yawkey said that Williams was fishing some place in New Brunswick, but that he'd get him.

"Ted came the next day—I don't know how he got there that fast," said Yastrzemski, "and he watched me take batting practice for two days." Williams, Yaz recalled, didn't say much, except to "follow the ball."

"But he really helped build up my confidence. I hit .300 for the rest of the season."

Yastrzemski talked about how lucky he'd been, particularly with his choice of parents, his father, who was there, and his mother who is deceased.

His father, he said, had been a great ball player, but had to suppress his desires to earn a living for the family. He "sacrificed for others" during hard Depression years, and his son, now looking down at him from the podium, said he appreciated it very much.

"I'm often asked how I could stand up to the rigors of the pressure of baseball," said Yastrzemski. "I say, 'What pressure?' Pressure is what faces millions of parents every day in bringing up their families, and giving them comfort and devotion and love."

Schoendienst, whose Hall plaque will read that he was a "sleek, far-ranging second baseman," recalled how forty-seven years ago he and three friends hitch-hiked a ride on a milk truck from Germantown, Ill., to try out with the St. Louis Cardinals. "And I never thought that that ride would lead to Cooperstown and baseball's highest honor," he said.

There was another ride that was significant to him. "It was forty-five years ago that I was on the Grand Avenue street car in St. Louis and met Mary O'Reilly. Two years later, I signed her up." In the audience, Mary O'Reilly Schoendienst stood. Later, she would recall,

"Well, we outlasted that street car." And their four children and nine grandchildren were there to attest to that.

Schoendienst, who has worn a baseball uniform for 47 straight years, as player and manager, remains with the Cardinals today as a coach.

"It's still a thrill to put on my uniform," he said, "and still a thrill to every day hear those wonderful words, 'Play Ball!'"

The Victory Laps of Johnny Bench

July 15, 1983

Eighteen years ago last month, Johnny Lee Bench gave the valedictory speech at his high school graduation in Binger, Oklahoma, a town of 600. The speech was titled "How the Youth of Today Will Be the Leaders of the Next Generation." It is just the kind of subject on which seventeen-year-old kids are expert.

Bench, the Cincinnati Reds veteran player, recalled the speech the other day with slightly arched eyebrows. "I don't remember much about it," said Bench. "Oh, there were some vague thoughts about making the world a better place to live. But I was a naive kid, and I only had thoughts of becoming a major league baseball player." He smiled. "I decided very early to back out on the Presidency."

Bench, as the sporting public knows, succeeded mightily in his ambition. He became one of the best catchers in the history of the game.

The Reds are making their last swing of the season through the Eastern cities of the National League, and it is Johnny Bench's last swing as a player. Last night's game against the Mets was his last in New York. He has announced his retirement at the end of the season.

And now, in the 16th and final season of his major league career, he is taking curtain calls, perhaps not with the frequency of Sarah Bernhardt's numerous farewell tours, but receiving, one might imagine, similar warmth and admiration.

Before Wednesday night's game at Shea Stadium, a decorous ceremony was held at home plate, and Tom Seaver, a friend, a onetime teammate and a once and current opponent, presented him a "token of appreciation" from the Mets, a diamond-studded pendant in the shape of his uniform number, 5. The fans and the players on both teams stood and applauded generously.

And Bench, at age thirty-five, doffed his long-billed red cap and waved, revealing a still-young- looking face and, as he turned, a small bald patch on the back of his head.

After another night in New York, the club would be on to Philadelphia, where some of Bench's teammates with the old Big Red Machine now play: Pete Rose, Tony Perez, Joe Morgan. "I know the Phillies are planning a little something too," said Bench.

Last week, he was honored along with Carl Yastrzemski, also retiring, at the All-Star Game in Chicago. Many of the old Hall-of-Famers were there, and at a luncheon they gave Bench a standing ovation. Bill Dickey, the former star catcher of the Yankees, came by and said to Bench, "Joining the rest of us, huh?"

"That," Bench recalled later, "was a real thrill." On September 17, the Reds are playing Houston at Riverfront Stadium in Cincinnati, and it has been designated Johnny Bench night. Bench is scheduled to be behind the plate, for old times' sake.

Two years ago, after 13 seasons as a catcher, he told the club that he could no longer play there. He would be available for third base and first base. Backstopping had taken a terrible toll on his body: His knees ached, his back ached, his shoulders and throwing elbow ached. "I've been shot up with so many painkillers to stay in the lineup," he said, "that if I were a race horse I'd be illegal."

He had caught 100 games or more for 13 straight seasons, a major-league record he shares with Dickey. For his last game as a catcher, he'll have to warm up his body and especially his arm for two weeks in advance, he said wryly. "Nowadays," he added, thinking of trying to throw out stealers, "all the base runners wear track shoes."

And now his playing career is nearly ended, a career that was begun and nurtured in the tiny town of Binger. "You start out not being able to go to the proms or buzzing around all day in a car, because you've got to be on the field, practicing, practicing," Bench recalled, "and dreaming about becoming Mickey Mantle or Willie Mays."

Indeed, he became a national sports figure, much as they had. But what about the valediction, about becoming a leader of the next generation? Did he think he had fulfilled some of that promise as a baseball player?

"When people heard I was retiring," said Bench, "I got a lot of letters from kids and adults saying, 'Thanks.' They said I had helped them get over some humps, especially after I had had surgery for lung cancer in 1972. I was only twenty-five years old. And I came back to play regularly. I think that gave some people encouragement, seeing that if I didn't let something like that get me down—well, too down, because I was scared -then they wouldn't let whatever problems they were having keep them down, either.

"I'm glad I could help some people. I feel good about being in some way a part of their lives. "Of course, I didn't make everyone happy—like some of the catchers in the Reds minor league system." He also learned about the fickleness of the fans. He recalls a period in 1971 when he was being booed regularly by the hometown crowds. During one particular game, which his father was attending, Bench struck out twice and popped up in his first three times at bat. "The boos for me were rocking the stadium," recalls Bench.

"My last time up, I got two strikes on me. Boo. Boo. Then I hit a home run to win the game. My dad jumped up and shouted, 'Boo now, you bums.' They didn't hear him. They were cheering."

Bench laughed. "But I have no complaints," he said. "I've gotten all the recognition anyone could dream for, and I've got financial security and helped my parents and went around the world and met all kinds of people. I've even been invited to the White House.

That was 1969, and I met Mr. Nixon."

How had he felt about that? "Great," Bench said. "It was almost as good as meeting Willie Mays."

The Winter of Yaz's Content

January 18, 1968

For Carl Yastrzemski, this has been the Winter of His Content. He has capitalized on winning the American League's triple crown and as the Boston Red Sox' World Series hero. Several times a week, he has made appearances at banquets and benefits, been on television and radio shows, put his name to products from cereals to toys to T-shirts and has started "Yaz Industries."

However, there is one thing he won't do. That is go skiing. Recently, Boston's ace pitcher, Jim Lonborg, tore knee cartilages while sweeping down the slopes.

"I'm not saying that Lonborg shouldn't have skied," said Yaz, at dinner in Manhattan, "all I'm emphasizing is that I wouldn't have. Each player has a moral obligation to the team to stay healthy and be in shape for the season.

"We'll be in trouble if Lonborg isn't ready to pitch right from the beginning. He may be out for the first month of the season.

"But I also have an obligation to my family." I have a wife and three kids. Maybe if I were single I'd go skiing, too. Maybe."

Besides enlarging his wallet, Yaz said he also feels a responsibility to do something for baseball. Along with Ted Williams, he is co-chairman of the Jimmy Fund. He also does work with mentally handicapped children. He will even speak at places like the father and son dinner of Cub Scout Pack and Troop 20 in Livingston, New Jersey.

"He'll be lucky if he gets eighty bucks for that," said a friend of Carl's. "Sure, he likes the big money functions. But he's also a guy with a heart."

Shortly after the Series, Yastrzemski visited a Navy hospital. He told of the impact one sailor had on him.

"He was just back from Vietnam. He was in a cast to his neck. But he seemed so enthusiastic about life. I invited him to a Red Sox game when he got out of the hospital.

"I told him that he should keep up his spirits, that America was behind him and the other boys in Vietnam. Only a loud handful was dissenting. And even if people don't agree with the war, they're still our boys fighting there. I left the place almost in a daze. You know, I've been asked what effect I have when I make appearances and visits. It should be the reverse. It's me who is moved."

Getting back to baseball, Yastrzemski said that two elements contributed to his great season—no study hangover and a fine team behind him.

"I had promised my parents I would complete college," said Yaz, who matriculated first at Notre Dame, then signed a pro contract and finished in the off-seasons at Merrimack College. "Before, I would end the season, get to school a couple weeks late and have to cram all winter. By spring training I was exhausted. This year, for the first time, I was relaxed.

"Most important, though, was the team. I'm not a strong man like Mantle or Mays. I can't do it alone. I need all the help I can get. I need men on bases and good hitters following me to get good pitches.

"Also," he added with a grin, "the wind was blowing out more last season than it ever had."

In A Slump, Richie Ashburn Took His Bat To Bed with Him

May 29, 1983

Richie Ashburn, the Phillies broadcaster and former center fielder who spent most of his 15-year major league career with Philadelphia, and was a two-time National League batting champion, remembers one horrible slump, going 0-for-33 in the mid-1950s. He did everything he could to snap out of it, he said, including taking his 34 1/2-inch, 33-ounce Louisville Slugger bat to bed with him.

"I've seen guys in the dugout pour gasoline on their bats and burn them, but I took mine to bed," he recalled. "I wanted to know my bat a little better, and it me. Sounds a little weird now, I know, but in a slump a player will do anything."

Ashburn, though, is convinced that he beat the slump by chewing tobacco. "A teammate named Bill Nicholson gave me a chaw," said Ashburn. "The first time I tried it, I walked up to the plate and I was gagging. I was trying not to swallow the juice and I was getting sick. I started worrying more about not vomiting than about hitting. And I got three base hits that game, and broke out of the slump."

The Mets—and Ashburn—Twenty Years Later

April 14, 1982

Sherman "Roadblock" Jones, amid snowflakes, was the starting pitcher for the original Mets in their home opener in 1962 in the old Polo Grounds.

Yesterday, at Shea Stadium, under sunny skies, he was the designated honoree—survivor, as it were—to memorialize the twentieth anniversary of the Mets entry into the National League. It was a team that would be recorded as the worst in baseball history and, as hopeless underdogs, one of the most adored.

Richie Ashburn remembered those days. He was one of the Phillies announcers yesterday, but he was the Mets center fielder playing behind Roadblock Jones twenty years ago.

Ashburn, thirty-five then, and at the end of his 15-year career, was one of the players—young and old—who were on their last legs for the 1962 Mets, an expansion team of castoffs and callow rookies.

"I was the leadoff hitter and I don't remember exactly what I did, but I know I made an out," he said, during the rain delay. "I guess I set the pattern. It's strange, but I had a pretty long career and finished with a .308 batting average. But the thing most people seem to remember is that I played for the worst team in history."

Ashburn recalls the last day of that season. "It was against the Cubs, in Chicago, and it ended on a triple play. In the clubhouse afterward, Casey tried to make us feel better after this disastrous season. He said, 'Fellas, don't feel bad—it was a team effort. No one or two guys could have done it alone.'"

Perhaps the highlight of that season was, said Ashburn, the day Marvelous Marv Throneberry hit a triple. "The story's been told before but it's absolutely true," Ashburn said, recalling an episode with Throneberry and the Met manager, Casey Stengel. "The bases were loaded and it looked like the game-winning hit. Marv goes sliding into third—it was like a dust storm. In the dugout, we saw Marv miss first base. But Casey didn't—he was too busy jumping up and down. The first baseman—I think it was Ernie Banks of the Cubs—asks for the ball, and tags first, and the umpire calls Marv out, and no runs count.

"Casey goes running onto the field, screaming that he's being robbed. Dusty Boggess was the umpire at second base, a nice old guy, and he puts his hand on Casey's shoulder and says, 'Casey, I hate to tell you this, but he also missed second base.'

"Casey looked at him for a moment, and said, 'Well, I know for damn sure he didn't miss third!'"

* * *

Ashburn was elected to the Hall of Fame in 1995.

Gil Hodges and the Saints of Lost Causes

May 22, 1989

Twenty years later they were different, of course, grayer, rounder at the belt, and with noticeably less spring in their step. No longer did they appear, as one of them, Ron Swoboda, the outfielder, said back then, like "the saints of lost causes."

On Saturday at Shea Stadium, the 20th reunion was held of the 1969 world champion New York Mets, "the Amazin's," as some called them, or even "Destiny's Darlings."

But the manager of that team was, however, missing, and sorely missed, having died of a heart attack three years after that memorable, year, on April 2, 1972, at the still young age of forty-seven, The star pitcher of that Mets team, Tom Seaver, in discussing Hodges with me after the '69 season, said. "He said a model manager, Gil obtained and retained the respect of all 25 players by making every player feel important, that he's contributing to the team . . . If I ever become a manager, there are two rules that Hodges follows that I'm sure I'd keep. One is that there are no prima donnas; the other is that you do not blast one of your players publicly.

They won the title in only their eighth season as a franchise, a franchise that in its early years was a national joke, a team so upside down that their first manager, Charles Dillon Stengel, once turned in the dugout and asked, "Can't anybody here play this game?" and for whom, as a sportswriter named Dick Young noted, "a superstar was someone who could put on his baseball shoe without spiking himself."

In the previous year, 1968, they finished 9th, and before that, 10th, 9th, 10th, 10th, 10th, and 10th.

But the 1969 Mets turned out differently, led by the young, broad-shouldered, bright, laughing and hard-throwing pitcher from Fresno, California, Seaver, also known as "Tom Terrific."

I was in the manager's office near season's end when the first baseman Donn Clendenon came in and said to Hodges, "You're a genius. Every move you've made has been right."

"Oh, I make mistakes," said Hodges, with a wry smile, "I just don't admit them."

It was a remarkable time in America, and the world. The war in Vietnam was raging, and protests to get the military out of Southeast Asia were shaking up this nation. The city of New York was suffering financial problems. Racial conflicts continued. And less than three months before the Mets won the title, men had walked on the moon.

Everywhere, though, people looked for hope out of the morass of their daily lives, and some saw the Mets as providing this hope.

You'd read that the Mets had pumped optimism into the lives of the downtrodden, the working stiff; these people, said some social observers, could now grasp a straw of hope. The Mets were the ragamuffins of baseball until then. It was Horatio Alger revisited, but with a bedsheet flapping from the mansion window. The sheet was inscribed: "Macy's Long Island Warehouse Loves the Mets."

And a City Councilman stated publicly that the Mets were the power that kept the city peaceful that summer; that is, the town was too busy following the Mets to fool around with race riots and the like. (Skeptics, though, said that a rainy summer, not a winning summer, kept the fires from burning.) And others said that if the Mets could win a championship, the city could get its affairs in order. The man on the street wondered if the Mets manager, Gil Hodges, shouldn't run for mayor of the five boroughs, and all their bridges and potholes, too.

Pamphlets were circulated in front of Shea Stadium with Seaver's picture on them and a reprint from a newspaper story in which the pitcher said that if the Mets won the series he would take out the following ad: "If the Mets can win the Series, the United States can get out of Vietnam." (Seaver, upon learning of these pamphlets, was irked that his name had been used without his permission.) All this was also reminiscent of the celebration for the three Houston Astro fans who went to the moon. This wasn't just one small step for a man. But it was one giant step for mankind. And people said: "It just goes to prove what we can do if we set our minds to something. Let's fix the country the way we fixed up the moon shot."

The Mets, in that day, were the moonwalkers of baseball.

They beat the Braves in three straight games, and the Orioles in five games, for the championship. Ron Swoboda, that elephantine outfielder, momentarily turned into a swan and made a diving catch in right field that would forever be the envy of saints of lost causes. And the team's greatest hero, Seaver, would lose the opening game of the Series, and win the fourth, but could keep things in perspective afterward. "Well," he said, "I'm the only pitcher in Mets history to lose a World Series game."

The same with the manager. Although winning the World Series was, understandably, Hodges's greatest thrill as a manager, he had said that his most glorious personal moment in a baseball uniform was the first time at bat for Brooklyn in the seventh game of the 1952 World Series. After having gone six games and 17 times at bat without a hit, the popular first baseman received a standing ovation from the Ebbets Field crowd. To no avail. He went 0-for-4 and became the only regular in World Series history not to get a hit in seven games. Yet he was the ever dependable rock at first baseman for the contending and pennant-winning Dodgers of the late '40s and '50s, alongside Robinson and Campanella and Reese and Snider and Erskine, batting a career .273, with 370 home runs, two Gold Gloves, and making eight all-star teams in during his 18-year playing career.

That 1969 season was a merry time, a thrilling time for Mets fans, and it may not be a stretch to include most baseball fans, but, in the light of history, not necessarily a meaningful time. The Amazin' Mets winning the World Series meant no more and no less on the world stage than the Miracle Boston Braves of 1914, who went from last place in July to sweep the powerful Philadelphia A's in the World Series.

The Braves couldn't keep us out of World War I. And the Mets couldn't get us out of Vietnam. For that matter, though, neither could the men on the moon.

Yet the Amazin's served a significant purpose. They indeed brought a great deal of joy to Gotham. Joy: something we can all embrace, and often. Thanks, Gil. Thanks, guys.

Part VI: 1970s—Triumphs and a Tragedy

Tom Seaver Goes for 300th Win

August 5, 1985

The day began with a bat in Tom Seaver's bedroom. Not a Louisville Slugger, but an airborne mammal who had found his way through a window into the Seaver family's house in Greenwich, Connecticut.

It was about 5:30 yesterday morning when Seaver and his wife, Nancy, were awakened.

They jumped out of bed and flung their arms, grabbed a broom and gave other appropriate signals to the intruder that he was not wanted, especially at this hour, and especially on this day.

The bat finally took the hint and winged off. The Seavers returned to bed, to continue perchance the dream of what he called "the story-book touch."

This was the fitful morning before the memorable afternoon in which George Thomas Seaver would attempt to earn his 300th victory as a major-league pitcher. He was pitching for Chicago, but he was back in New York, where he began his major league career nineteen years ago and where, it seems, his heart is.

215

Seaver has had two stretches with the Mets. Each time he left, he did so with heavy heart. He has maintained his residence in the metropolitan area.

It would make Seaver only the seventeenth pitcher in baseball history to win 300 games. He is among the career leaders in earned-run average and strikeouts and class, and if he doesn't get elected to the Hall of Fame on the first ballot, there are some fans who might justifiably call for a Congressional investigation.

Looking well-rested despite his bout with the bat, Seaver was in the White Sox clubhouse at Yankee Stadium later that morning, answering questions from reporters, accepting congratulations from the White Sox owners Jerry Reinsdorf and Eddie Einhorn and autographing some baseballs.

"This one," said a clubhouse man, "is from Rickey Henderson." Seaver, seated on a stool before his locker, looked up.

"No kidding," said the clubhouse man. "He gave me the ball for you to sign."

At 2:09 p.m., Seaver came out of the dugout to walk across the field and headed for the bullpen in left-center to warm up for the game. Fans in the area cheered. They were cheering an opponent, yes, but they were cheering a man who for eleven-and-a-half years had been one of the most popular and accomplished athletes in New York history.

As a pitcher with the Mets, he won three Cy Young Awards and helped pitch them to two pennants and one World Series victory.

Despite a list of exceptional days in his career, this was special, and there was no disguising that. So special that he had his father, Charles Seaver, and his father-in-law, Dean McIntyre, fly in from California for the game, to join Nancy and their two children, Sarah, fourteen, and Annie, nine.

The crowd of 54,032 noisily greeted Seaver as he came out to pitch the first inning against the Yankees. "My head hurt, I was so nervous," Seaver would recall. "I talked myself into its being just another game, but deep down you know it's not just another game."

Most of the fans cheered, but there was a smattering of boos. "I can't believe all the Met fans out there screaming for Chicago," said a Yankee fan in the stands.

He would have been closer to the fact if he had said "baseball fans."

The category "Seaver fan" was well-represented, too, of course, and no better constituents exist than the five seated immediately to the right of the White Sox dugout, the four Seavers and the McIntyre.

Seaver's first pitch of the game, a strike to Henderson, was greeted with appreciative applause from his daughters. Nancy, though, leaned forward and held onto the top of the low wall in front of her. After twenty-one years of marriage to a hurler, she understands that one pitch does not a game make.

Under generally clear skies and a warm sun, they cheered when the White Sox threatened to score in the first, the second, the third, the fourth, and the fifth innings, but came up empty each time.

Annie held her White Sox cap with two hands and Sarah sat with her head resting in the palm of her hand when the Yankees scored a run off Pop in the third.

The Seaver contingent was on its feet when the Sox scored four runs in the sixth to give the old man a thick cushion on which to work.

It was an ambivalent crowd. It cheered the Yanks when they had scoring opportunities, but they booed the White Sox pitching coach, Dave Duncan, when he walked out to the mound in the eighth to talk to Seaver. With two on and two out, the dangerous Dave Winfield was coming to the plate. The crowd didn't want Seaver removed. And he wasn't.

The count ran to 3-and-2 on Winfield. Seaver, partly in the Stadium shadows now, wound up and fired home, following through in that long, low, familiar stride.

Winfield swung and missed mightily to end the inning. The crowd roared, and the five in the Seaver group leaped to their feet in exultation.

The old man calmly walked off the mound, seemingly cool as could be, the unexcitable professional, but, surely, as happy and relieved as his kin.

Now, in the Yankee ninth, he would just finish off the next three batters.

But not so fast. Dan Pasqua, the Yankees first hitter, lined a single off the right-field wall. Seaver struck out the next batter, but Willie Randolph followed with a smash that Harold Baines grabbed when he crashed into the right-field wall. Another White Sox conference on the mound.

"I was beat as hell," Seaver would recall, "but there wasn't a chance in hell I was coming out, not on this day." He stayed. But the tired Seaver walked Mike Pagliarulo.

Now Don Baylor batted for Bobby Meacham. The formidable Baylor represented the tying run with the score 4–1. He swung hard and lofted a high fly to left field. Reid Nichols came in, then went back.

And Nichols had it. And so did Seaver. Number 300 was his.

As his White Sox teammates hurried over to congratulate him, Seaver headed for his family. He hugged his wife, the girls, and his father and father-in-law.

Meanwhile, most of the fans had not left the park and they stood, some with tears, and continued to clap.

Yesterday, for that one day, anyway, most of the people at Yankee Stadium felt just like the five in the first row, like family.

The Tom Seaver I Came to Know

January 7, 2021

I call it the night that Tom Seaver and I slept together, but it was a great deal more innocent and monumentally less risque than it sounds. The story:

It was the last Sunday in January 1970, when Tom Seaver and I, along Joe Louis, the former great heavyweight boxing champion, and Curt Blefary, a journeyman major-league outfielder most recently with the Yankees, rushed from the Baseball Writers dinner at the Waldorf-Astoria to catch a train.

The four of us raced from the banquet, where Seaver had been awarded Player of the Year by the New York baseball writers, to Penn Station in hopes of arriving in time to catch the 10:30 overnight train to Rochester. There Seaver, who had compiled 25 wins and a 2.21 earned run average and led the Mets to a World Series championship, was to receive the 1969 Professional Athlete of the Year Award, and Louis would get a Lifetime Achievement Award, both presented annually by the Hickok Belt Company, with headquarters in Rochester.

I was then the thirty-year-old sports columnist and sports editor for Newspaper Enterprise Association, a Scripps-Howard feature syndicate, and tagged along to write a story about Seaver. I don't remember what Blefary was doing with us—maybe he got lost, he had been noticeably drinking—but he would soon make his presence felt.

We luckily quickly grabbed a cab at the Waldorf curb, and made the train, with little time to spare. In the hurry, and as the train began to chug north, Seaver realized he had forgotten to take his overcoat from the hotel. The twenty-five-year-old, 6-foot-1, 200-pound hurler would stoically have to make do with his sport jacket and tie.

Well, Louis went to bed early and the three of us stayed up late talking sports. I remember the conversation came around to "greatest athletic feat," and Seaver said, "Sandy Koufax, for having pitched four no-hitters."

The organizer of the Rochester event, who made the sleeping arrangements, had Tom and me sharing a compartment with bunk beds. The room was so small that it seemed if you turned around you'd bump into yourself. Tom and I shrugged and flipped a coin. He got the lower berth and I the top one. "Now I know what Rube Walker meant," said Seaver, referring to Rube Walker, the Mets pitching coach, "when he said you really came to know your roommate when teams used to travel by train."

Only a few hours later, jostled and dreamy, we emerged onto the Rochester platform. It was raining in the dark before dawn and Seaver and the rest of us waited for the chartered bus with the bad memory. Blefary, in an act of kindness that only a hitter might perform in respect to a star pitcher, took off his coat and draped it over Seaver's right, pitching shoulder. Tom expressed surprise, but also gratitude.

And so ended the night that I slept with Seaver—rather slept above Seaver. But it was the beginning of a lifetime friendship. Now, a journalist should, in the best of all possible worlds, remain objective, regardless of the affection one might feel for a subject. But a particular circumstance, in this case, changed that worthy dictum to a significant degree for me.

The following baseball season, in April 1970, three months after that train ride, NEA hired Seaver to write a once-a-week column. I was to shepherd the column. I'd call Seaver and we'd discuss a subject and then, using his words, I'd fashion a column.

He was thoughtful and often generous as he was, for example, to Gil Hodges, the Mets manager, who was, he said, "my most important influence in professional ball. He was a pro's pro. He held that there were no prima donnas on this ball club.

He had one important rule: Everyone is treated alike."

220

Seaver also had a great admiration for the professionalism of Henry Aaron, and recalled the first time he faced the legendary slugger, as a rookie Mets pitcher in 1967: "The first time I faced him, I was a rookie. I got him to hit into a double play on a sinker down and in. I could have lit up a victory cigar. I was so proud of myself. I figured I had his number. And he figured I was figuring that, too, because I threw him the same pitch in the same spot the next time he came to bat and he whacked it into the left-field seats for a three-run homer. Another piece of education."

And through the years I covered Seaver as objectively as possible, and sticking to what I saw and how he performed, with that long, powerful stride off the mound and so low to the ground that his right knee would drag through the dirt, be- smudging his pants leg, as he went, in his luminous 20-year major-league career, from the Mets to the Reds, back to the Mets, to the White Sox to the Red Sox and, finally, enshrined in the Baseball Hall of Fame in Cooperstown, with 311 wins against 205 losses and a 2.86 earned run average, sixth all-time in major-league strikeouts with 3,640 and three Cy Young Awards as best pitcher in the National League.

We shared meals and we shared laughs. He could be silly, with a rather goofy giggle. I saved a photograph of us on the Busch Stadium field in St. Louis before a 1982 World Series game between the Cardinals and Milwaukee, when I was now covering as a columnist for the *New York Times* and Seaver was working as an analyst for NBC-TV. He made a silly face with scrunched up mouth for the photographer and later sent me an autographed copy of the photo, with the inscription: "To Ira—Are you proud to know the mature #41. Best as always, Tom Seaver #41" (his uniform number).

Seaver, who had lived with his wife Nancy, and two daughters, in a house in Greenwich, Connecticut, then moved to Calistoga, California, where he joyfully produced quality wines. In the fields, he contracted

Lyme Disease. It affected him in numerous ways, including increasing loss of memory. In 2013, I ran across a publicity photo of the two of us in the NEA office when he began the column, and it showed Tom behind a typewriter and handing me a supposed draft. I sent the picture to him to be autographed, and wrote "My best to Nancy, and with hopes of good grapes and fond memories."

About a month later, he sent back the photo autographed and with it a note. The note read, in part, "Sorry for taking so long to get back to you, but this Lyme Disease is no fun." The autograph on the picture read: "To Ira—A long-standing friend! Between us—311 W's in the 'Bigs.' Best, Tom Seaver." Needless to say, there had never been any "Bigs" in my past.

On August 31, Tom Seaver, who had become reclusive the last few years, died from complications of Lyme Disease, Lewy Body Dementia and Covid-19. He was seventy-five years old. I have framed the photo of two of us together in the NEA office, two young friends, exactly a half century ago.

(Silurian News, published by Silurian Press Club, New York City)

Reggie Jackson: Old "44" Returns to Yankee Stadium

April 28, 1982

At 3:30 yesterday afternoon, under the threatening sky, Reggie Jackson came out of the visitors' dugout at Yankee Stadium to take batting practice. He was carrying his familiar black bat and wearing his familiar mustache, but the uniform was not the customary one.

It was the red and white of the California Angels and not the blue pinstripe of the Yanks.

This was his first time back to New York City in a baseball uniform of any kind since the World Series last year.

Now it was a full four and a half hours before the start of the ball game. Earlier in the day, at a news conference for a baseball shoe he is sponsoring, Jackson said he was feeling "skittish" about returning to New York. "I've got butterflies," he said.

The end of a turbulent and dramatic five-year career with the Yankees came over the winter when the owner of the team, George Steinbrenner, a shipbuilder by profession, did not renew his contract.

The stands were empty now, and the loudest sound was the rumble of the Woodlawn elevated train just beyond the park. There were no cries of "Reg-gie, Reg-gie," as there had been for the last five years in which he was a Yankee. The chant had continued this season as well whenever the Yankees fell behind. The fans hoped that Steinbrenner the Shipbuilder would hear their displeasure over the loss of the slugger.

And there was no one now floating through the stands wearing a Yankee cap and a white bedsheet with No. 44 on the back. Stepping into the batting cage now was no ghost, this was the real thing—or what has been passing for the real thing.

Reggie, after all, was hitting only .173 this season, with no extra base hits—he had nine singles—and only four runs batted in—and three of those RBIs coming when he made outs.

"I had heard about the chants and the guy dressed like a ghost," Reggie had said. "I'm just glad they don't read the stats." Jackson hit for forty minutes off Coach Bobby Knoop, sometimes lunging at pitches and sending them up to stick in the screen of the batting cage, and sometimes, with that powerful, rippling stroke, driving balls crashing deep into the blue right-field seats.

After the batting practice, Jackson was brought into a room for another news conference. He was affable, even mellow. "I guess it's a matter of maturity, of getting older," he said. He will be thirty-six on May 18. Jackson has had difficult personal experiences with the Yankees, from battles with Billy Martin, the former Yankee manager, to Steinbrenner the Shipbuilder. And now he is trying to do well with a new team and struggling.

"I've been not wanting to come back and then wanting to come back," he said. "New York City is still the place I'm very familiar with, still like very much. And the people have been great, warm and receptive.

He was asked what's wrong at the plate. "I'm just not feeling comfortable at the plate, in my home turf—and I don't know why." Was he trying too hard? "That's part of it, I'm sure. I'm trying to hit three home runs at one time at bat." Are you sorry about leaving New York? "I would have loved to finish my career here. But George didn't think it was the thing to do." Jackson had become a free agent after the 1981 season. Was he ever made an offer by the Yankees? "No." He went on: "I was kind of made a fool of. George cast doubts about whether I could play anymore, about my worth, and quality and character to be a Yankee.

"I got tired of being run down by him." Reggie's voice softened. "I didn't want to prostitute myself to come back, I wasn't going to bow down to the guy." Now the Angels were about to take official batting practice. And when Jackson came down the runway to the dugout, he stepped on white towels—the old white-carpet treatment—set out by Rod Carew. Carew introduced him to the assemblage of photographers.

Jackson laughed, fooled around at the bat rack for several minutes, then stepped out onto the field. The small early crowd cheered as they saw Reggie's number: 44 On the scoreboard, the digital clock read 6:44.

When Jackson ran out to play right field in the bottom of the first inning, the crowd of 35,458, most holding colorful umbrellas against the thin rain, gave him a standing ovation and the familiar Reg-gie chant. Later, a guy in a T-shirt would run out and present Jackson with a bouquet of yellow flowers.

In the second inning, batting in the sixth position against Ron Guidry, he popped up very high to second base. He was clearly trying to drive the ball out of the park, and he was clearly disappointed.

In the fifth, Jackson singled past second base. It was a good shot, but it wasn't what he wanted.

By the seventh, the rain was coming down harder. Jackson would be leading off.

Manager Mauch was out talking to the umpires, trying to get the game called since the Angels were ahead, 2–1.

But the game continued. Jackson toweled off his black bat, wiped his glasses and stepped into the batter's box. On Guidry's first pitch, he swung. The crack of the bat resounded through the park. The ball rocketed. Jackson dropped his bat, clapped his hands in pure and unadulterated delight. The ball was into the right-field upper deck for a home run before he had taken three steps.

There was a moment of shock, then the fans thundered applause. And chanted his name, and kept chanting it so that, after he had ducked into the dugout, he was forced to come out into the rain and wave his arms to them.

When Jackson departed into the dugout, shortly another chant began, starting slowly, and then swelling until the entire ball park was throbbing with it. It was an obscenity directed at Steinbrenner, who was in the ball park—and repeated over and over. It was chilling: "Steinbrenner Sucks! Steinbrenner Sucks!"

After the inning, Jackson was replaced in right field by Juan Beniquez. For Jackson, though, the game was complete. And on this rainy, miserable April night, the home run was a moment to remember—his first extra-base hit of the season.

Reggie Jackson: "Mr. October" is Now "Mr. Cooperstown"

August 2, 1993/Cooperstown, New York

On a hot August afternoon, Mr. October rose to the occasion—again. Center stage, as we had come to expect of him, all alone, and in front of a huge crowd of some 10,000 people, Reggie Jackson became the 216th member to be inducted into the Baseball Hall of Fame.

Shouts of "Reg-gie! Reg-gie!" rang out from fans on a sprawling meadow. And the man in the dark suit, white shirt, aqua tie and broad shoulders standing under the canopy acknowledged the familiar chant with an empyrean nod, befitting this moment of ascendance into baseball's Olympus.

He came armed with a speech filled with emotions, with memories, with personal moments, with viewpoints about the state of the game and with a sense of appreciation and even gratitude for what he was, as well as who he became. It was a home run. A rather long home run, about thirty minutes in length, but isn't that what we had come to expect from Reggie, too?

Among the thirty-eight Hall of Famers who returned to Cooperstown for the event was Catfish Hunter, a teammate of Jackson's with both the Oakland A's and the Yankees. Hunter preceded Jackson to the Yankees. "Reggie hit the clubhouse talking," said Hunter, "and guys on the team asked me, 'How come nobody killed this guy in Oakland.' I said, 'Just listen to him for two minutes and then walk away. He'll still be saying the same thing an hour later. But it doesn't matter. He'll help you win.' At the end of the year they said, 'Cat, you were right.'"

George Steinbrenner, who courted Jackson as a free agent and signed him to a $2.96 million contract for five years in 1977, was in attendance. "I think it's appropriate that Reggie is alone as an inductee," said Steinbrenner. "Fits his personality." Steinbrenner said that Jackson was "the definition of a star."

But Jackson unexpectedly defused what in times past resembled an ego as great as any of the towering blasts he cracked.

"You remember a player with the Yankees named Mickey Rivers?" asked Jackson. "Well, he said I had a white man's first name—Reginald—a Spanish middle name—Martinez—and a black man's last name. And that's why you're so fouled up."

And when he introduced his father, Martinez Jackson, a former tailor who is ninety years old and lives in Philadelphia, he asked him to stand. His father did and waved to the crowd. "Dad," he said, "no more applause. You're stealing my thunder."

It was his father, he said, who was his greatest influence, who taught him pride in being a black man, even though his father lived in a time when he was considered a second-class citizen, but who instilled in his son the dream of "climbing the ladder of equality."

And it was his father who reminded him that he had to speak correctly, to form his words so that they would fit his thoughts. "And no ununh, no nope, no yep," said Jackson.

Reggie, though, would grow up in a different generation from Martinez Jackson, when he could be anyone he felt he wanted to be. And of the athletes of his time, Reggie said that Muhammad Ali, who was making his presence known in the early 1960s while Jackson was a college student at Arizona State, was a guiding light. Ali talked, regardless of the perceived effect on the listener. Jackson listened and learned. "He gave me the confidence to speak out and to be proud of who I am," said Jackson.

While Jackson wasn't in a league as a figure in racial matters as Ali had been, or, another of the models that Jackson referred to yesterday,

Jackie Robinson, he took personal stands against what he saw as unfair treatment by a manager—Billy Martin, particularly—or Steinbrenner. And he saw himself in historical perspective. As he said, "I'm a real fan," and he remembered the struggles of black predecessors, including those in the Negro leagues. "It was a time when they knocked at the door," he said, "but nobody let them in."

While he played for the A's, the Orioles, the Angels, and the Yankees, it is as a Yankee that he enters the Hall of Fame, a bronzed Yankee cap resting on his bronzed image on his Hall plaque. And while there may have been some deal between Steinbrenner and Jackson for a job as a consultant to the Yankees principal owner, for the greater glory of both, Jackson still talks most movingly about his experience as a Yankee. "When you play in New York, everything is intensified a thousand times. And the fans there play a special role. I'll never forget you. You're the best."

Earlier, Hunter had recalled when the fans once pelted Jackson with his Reggie! candy bars, which shot briefly across the chocolate firmament. But, after a homer or two, they were again eating out of Reggie's hands.

Jackson took a look at the game today and was concerned. "The humanity of the game" cannot be lost. "The game of Williams and Mantle and DiMaggio and Clemente" should not be overcome "by the economics."

Returning to himself, he said, "I know I wasn't the best—just look behind me and I know that"—seated behind him on the podium were folks like Musial and Spahn and Feller and Frank Robinson. "But when the roll is called, sooner or later they've got to call my name."

As Mickey Rivers might have noticed, Reginald Martinez Jackson, the man with a profusion if not a confusion of names, had got it right.

The Goose (Gossage) in His Old Nest

June 4, 1988

We remember him with the Yankees, for six years from 1978 through 1983, when Goose Gossage was possibly the most fearsome man in baseball.

He was built more like a walrus than a goose, big and beefy, wearing a drooping mustache the ends of which were as long as tusks. His ball cap was pulled down so far on his face that hitters saw only the lower parts of his eyes.

He was 6-foot-4 and 225 pounds and when he strode in from the bullpen with the game on the line and climbed the mound—"In the crunch, that's when I go crazy," he once said—and unfurled, he released smoke, and somewhere in that smoke, speeding toward the plate, was an aspirin tablet.

At one point when he was still with the Yankees, the Goose, that most menacing creature, was asked: Was there anyone who intimidated him?

"Yes," he said. "Waiters in New York restaurants." Anywhere in particular? "All over."

He recalled this the other night in Shea Stadium, where he was in town with the Chicago Cubbies, with whom the Goose, now in his 17th season in the big leagues and who will be thirty-seven years old next month, still attempts to strike fear in the hearts of batsmen, sometimes with success, and, as on Thursday, sometimes without.

He entered the game in the 10th inning with the Cubs ahead, 1–0, and gave up a run on two singles and a stolen base to allow the Mets to tie the game. He left after pitching a scoreless 11th, but he opened the opportunity for the Mets to win, which they did in the 13th, on Howard Johnson's solo home run.

"The game is over," Gossage said afterward. "You go on to the next one."

Despite Thursday night's game, he remains effective, having been credited with six saves this season, tied for fifth in the league. He is striking out an average of one batter per inning, as he has for much of his career, though his fastball isn't the express it once was and he relies more than ever on his slider.

He had been traded last winter from San Diego to the Cubs, and says he's happy to be in Chicago where baseball tradition is great, the fans are knowledgeable and pleasingly obnoxious, unlike "laid-back San Diego," but like, he noted, fans in New York. "I don't mind being hooted," he said. "It makes me you feel like it's real baseball."

He says that he'll "always have a soft spot" for New York and that his six years with the Yankees were among "the happiest of my big league career."

It would seem that absence just might make the heart grow fonder, for he had problems in New York, with Billy Martin, with George Steinbrenner, with the citizenry, but, he says, he lived and learned.

"In New York," he said, "everything is a struggle. You go to a restaurant, it's a fight. You walk down the street, and people bump you. I took my kids to a merry-go-round in a mall in Paramus, New Jersey, and normally people would stand in line, but here they're pushin' and shovin'." What did the Goose do? "I started pushin' and shovin', too. You gotta stand your ground. "Then you drive through all that traffic, and by the time you get to the ball park you're mentally prepared for the battle."

Nor did things get much easier in the ball park.

"With the Yankees in those days, it was a veteran team, and everybody ragged everybody," he said, smiling. "Nothing was sacred. I mean, if your mother messed up, they'd get on your mother." Not Mother Goose, too? "Yep. That's how they were—Catfish and Mickey Rivers and Piniella and Nettles and Reggie and Munson.

"When I first got to the Yankees there was a lot of pressure on me. I took Sparky Lyle's job, and he had won the Cy Young Award the year before. We started the season on the road, and I think I lost three games. So now we come in to Yankee Stadium and I'm called into the game and Munson walks out to the mound and says, 'Well, how you gonna lose this one?'

"I looked at him. 'Just go back and catch the ball.'

"He said, 'I haven't been catching many lately.'

"Another time I'm getting ready to pitch and Munson calls time out and comes out and says, 'Check Rivers.' I look around and Mickey is in a three-point stance, like a track runner, with his butt to me, ready to chase down the ball.

"Then one time I'm called in from the bullpen in center and I climb in the car, the door opens and Rivers jumps on the hood and spread-eagles himself. 'Don't let him in the game!' he hollers. 'Don't let him in the game!' I roll down the window, and holler, 'Get off that car or we'll run you over!'

"It was like when you're a kid, and you're having fun. That's the way baseball should be played."

But some of it began to pale for the Goose, and in 1983 he opted for free agency. He had said he no longer desired to play for Steinbrenner, that he was embarrassed when the Yankees principal owner apologized to Yankee fans about not winning the 1981 World Series and management "started messing with the lineup and messing around every other way, too—all this off-the-game junk, in elevators and that stuff."

But in San Diego, he apparently began to appreciate the Yankees principal owner. The Goose criticized San Diego management when it banned beer in the clubhouse after games and accused it of wanting "choir boys." He also gave no stars in his review of the hamburgers sold by Joan Kroc, owner of the Padres and the McDonald's fast-food chain.

"George," says Gossage, "wanted to win. I couldn't say that about Joan Kroc."

So New York now is a fond memory for Goose Gossage.

Even, he was asked, Steinbrenner's remark in 1982 that the Goose should do more pitching and less quacking?

He laughed and tugged at his baseball cap.

"Even that," he said.

Joe Morgan and Jim Palmer Weather the Weather

August 6, 1990/Cooperstown, New York

It was a leaky afternoon yesterday in this hamlet by the lake, just the kind of wet and gray day on which no one here would ever have considered inventing baseball.

Umbrellas, yes. But not the national pastime.

Sun was predicted for this morning, and Abner Doubleday no doubt would have rejoiced, for that was his kind of weather. And heirs to fellow townsman Doubleday, the officials of the Baseball Hall of Fame, decided that the induction ceremonies for the newest members, Joe Morgan and Jim Palmer, would have to be postponed until the following day.

When Bill Guilfoile of the Hall made this announcement to the scattering of folks who waited in the persistent rain around the park outside the National Baseball Library, he was met with a chorus of boos, the loudest came from the group to one side who sat nestled under a mushrooming of orange-and-white umbrellas.

These are the colors of the Orioles, and these were fans from Baltimore, the team for which Palmer pitched his entire 19-year major league career.

Suddenly, there were cheers. Morgan and Palmer came out of the double doors of the library and onto the covered steps and waved.

Joe Leonard Morgan wore an olive suit and James Alvin Palmer wore a blue blazer with gray slacks, and both also wore broad smiles. And each looked so fit that if a ball game happened to break out between now and tomorrow, they'd be able to get in there, the tall Palmer, at age forty-four, with that patented high ostrich kick in his windup, and the small Morgan, at forty-six, with that left elbow flapping like a loose shutter at the plate. And they'd raise their customary havoc among the opposition.

When the pair went back inside, others in the rain shouted, "Encore! Encore!" The inductees were taken into a theater in the museum where a news conference was held.

Both said they were disappointed that the event had to be postponed, but both said they promised to hang around until the next day.

"I think when I walked out and waved just before," said the 6-foot-4 Palmer, "maybe for the first time since I learned about my election to the Hall of Fame I really the emotionality of it. Seeing all those Orioles umbrellas. And I thought about all the great things that have happened to me in my life, going back to the Little League, but not just in baseball, in everything.

"And there was nothing better than the people who adopted me, when I was born, and having parents that loved me. And I thought about my mother, who passed away a few years ago, and how much she would have enjoyed all this.

"But my father, Max"—Palmer paused to smile about the man who had helped raise him after his first father had died when Jim was ten years old—"he doesn't want this weekend to end. He's been signing autographs the whole time."

Morgan, who had played second base for 22 years in the major leagues with the Astros, the Reds—for which he was best known and a two-time most valuable player—the Giants, the Phillies and the A's, spoke about his parents, too, Leonard and Ollie Morgan of Oakland, California.

"Last month," he said, "I received my bachelor's degree. It took me 22 years in the major leagues to get to a plaque in the Hall of Fame, and it took me 27 years to get my degree.

But I'm thrilled to have both.

"The reason the college took so long, was that when I graduated from high school, I was offered a pro contract. My father wanted me to take it. My mother wanted me to get an education. I said to her, 'If you let me sign, I promise I'll get the degree.'"

So he went about going to night school, and taking courses during the off-season, and sometimes not doing any course work for five years at a stretch. "I was majoring in business in college," he said, "but I was also in various businesses for real, and so I thought I didn't need it. But then I thought I'd keep going, for my mother. And I thought college was important. And finally, I got the degree."

At California State at Hayward now, Morgan had changed majors, to physical education, a subject he was not unfamiliar with.

"I had thought that my mother had forgotten about my promise," said Morgan. But she said she hadn't, though she was surprised—and elated—that her boy had kept his promise. Morgan talked about his height—5-foot-7—and that it wasn't a handicap but an impetus. "It made me have a good work ethic," he said, "because I knew that if I was going to succeed, I'd have to work hard. "I didn't have all the tools, like Jim did—" "I didn't know I had all the tools," interjected Palmer. "Nolan Ryan, he had all the tools."

"How tall were you?" asked Morgan, smiling. "Well," said Palmer, "taller than you." And both laughed.

Palmer recalled that he had to overcome difficulties, too, particularly injuries. He suffered arm problems so severe that after three seasons with Baltimore, he struggled back and forth in the minor leagues, and in 1969, at age twenty-three, he thought he was finished.

But emotional support from pitching coach George Bamberger— "Just give it one more month, Jim," he said—and the discovery of an anti-inflammatory pill, helped Palmer return and, at his apex, win 20 games in eight of nine seasons.

Morgan also mentioned briefly the help he got as a rookie from the veteran second baseman Nellie Fox. Later, Morgan, now a star with the Big Red Machine, made an emotional visit to Fox, who was dying of cancer in a hospital. "But I'll leave that story for tomorrow," said Morgan. "Yes," said Palmer, "tomorrow."

Joe Morgan Was Barred from an All-White Golf Course

August 14, 1990

Rusty Staub and Joe Morgan were teammates and friends with the Houston Astros in the mid-1960s and shared an interest not only in doubles and double plays, but in drivers and divots, too. So Staub, a member of a nearby country club, had naturally taken Morgan as his guest to play golf at this club a few times.

After the last time, Staub received a phone call from one of the heads of the club.

"Rusty," the man said, "you can't bring Joe Morgan to the club anymore. Some members complained."

It was not that Morgan comported himself in an unsavory manner in the clubhouse or on the greens, or that he was a bad player. Morgan shot in the 80s. And it wasn't because Morgan was short. After all, it was not a club only for tall people. But Morgan was black. And the country club was only for white people.

Morgan and Staub recalled this at an outdoor barbecue party on the weekend of the recent Baseball Hall of Fame induction ceremonies in Cooperstown, New York, where Morgan was the new electee along with Jim Palmer, and Staub, now the noted restaurateur, was the party's caterer.

"I wondered what had been bothering you all day," Morgan said to Staub about that incident some twenty-five years ago.

"Telling you you couldn't come to that club anymore was one of the hardest things I've had to do in my life," Staub said.

The discussion came up over the controversy of the PGA Championship at the Shoal Creek Country Club near Birmingham, Alabama, where the founder of the club, Hall Thompson, had told a local reporter that "we don't discriminate in every other area except the blacks."

Curiously, when *Nightline* with Ted Koppel did a segment on the issue of discriminatory golf and country clubs, and the fact that a public institution like the Professional Golfers Association would hold its tournaments and championship in such places, one of the guests was Jackie Burke, co-owner and co-founder of the Colonial in Fort Worth.

Burke defended in a peripheral way the all-white membership at his club, and, by extension, many of the other clubs like his, by saying that blacks don't apply for membership there and he can't go out onto the streets and "lasso" them.

"You know," Morgan said to Staub, "I don't know what all the fuss is about now. This stuff has been going on for years."

There was irony in his tone because Morgan hardly condoned the action of Staub's old country club, or Hall Thompson either, and looked right through Burke's statement about his country club in Texas.

But because of a curious chain of events, this little section of the world—that is, the esoteric, exotic, exclusive, and often perniciously exclusionary world of country-club golf—may be changed forever. And it will not be, as Payne Stewart, said the other day, all "water under the bridge."

After Hall made his remarks, after a local black religious leader raised the issue of a protest and a boycott, after television sponsors "sensitive to minority patrons" withdrew, and after a black was named an honorary member of Shoal Creek to keep the peace, it was at about this time that the ruling bodies of golf decided that they would be more picky about future sites for their golf games.

On television Sunday afternoon, while people like the surging Wayne Grady and the collapsing Fred Couples were knocked around the Shoal Creek course, Deane Beman—the commissioner of the PGA Tour—was interviewed. He said he had already begun talking to the local sponsors of the 118 Tour events, and to the heads of the 130 golf courses that are eligible to hold events, about discrimination on their premises, and not just relating to color, or religion, but in regard to women, too.

"We're encouraging these people to work on their recruiting," Beman said. "And we hope that this issue will be relegated to the back pages."

There are some who have said, as did Joe Morgan, but coming from a different slant than Morgan, "Why the fuss now?" The reason is that Thompson's remarks created an opening. This development, in the esoteric but not isolated world of sports, might have broad effects.

In 1947, Jackie Robinson broke the color barrier in major league baseball. And America changed. In 1967, another protest arose at the Kentucky Derby, successfully led by the Rev. Martin Luther King Jr., concerning open housing in Louisville, which was too often "closed housing to blacks." And America changed.

None of that was just water under the bridge. There was more to come. It's a wide bridge.

On Sunday, Nick Faldo, who finished 13 shots behind the winner, Wayne Grady, said, "No more Shoal Creek for another ten years." He was talking about the difficult rough grass on the course.

Others hold the same sentiments. But not just for ten years. For them, it's for all time.

A Vote For Hoyt Wilhelm

December 8, 1984

The year was 1969, and Hoyt Wilhelm, a relief pitcher then with the California Angels, was in town for a series against the Yankees. It was late morning of a summer's day, and the renowned knuckleballer sat on the edge of a rumpled bed in his hotel room, one bare foot tucked under a dangling leg, the way he might have sat forty years before while fishing in a creek near his home in Huntersville, North Carolina.

He was then the oldest player in baseball, at age forty-six with a receding hairline. But he was still so effective with a knuckleball that no one—not the pitcher, not the hitter and not the catcher—knew which way it would break.

"I remember once when I was with the White Sox, this rookie catcher said he didn't need no mask to warm me up," Wilhelm said in his easy drawl. "I didn't say a word, but the other players began yackin' at him like players will do.

"So a day or so later, I was goin' to throw batting practice, and who's warmin' me up but this rookie fella, without a mask. The second pitch I throw caught him as fair in the eye as if you'd a stuck it there. It was swollen before he hit the ground."

Wilhelm came to mind recently when his name was noticed on the ballot for the Baseball Hall of Fame which just arrived in the mail.

He is now a minor-league pitching instructor for the Yankees, but for 21 years was perhaps one of the best pitchers in baseball, and surely one of the most extraordinary.

In last year's balloting for the Hall of Fame, 303 votes were needed for entry. Harmon Killebrew, Luis Aparicio and Don Drysdale each received the necessary votes. Wilhelm fell thirteen short. This will be his eighth year on the ballot, and the concern is that, with such fresh blood as Lou Brock, Catfish Hunter and Elston Howard entering the eligiblity ranks, Wilhelm might never muster the necessary votes within the ten-year limit.

One is reminded that Gil Hodges was close so often in the balloting but never quite got over the hump and into the Hall. It would be a gross injustice if this happened to Wilhelm. For pure grit and effectiveness, there could hardly be anyone better.

He was a rookie at age twenty-nine when many players are winding up their careers. It was 1952, and he had spent seven years in the minor leagues, with time out to fight at the Battle of the Bulge in 1944, where he was awarded the Purple Heart.

In his first major league season, as a reliever with the New York Giants, throwing in that effortless manner and sending the ball fluttering and dipping madly across the plate, he won 15 games and lost 3. He led the National League in percentage that season, with .833, and in earned run average, 2.43. No rookie had ever accomplished that distinctive double.

Wilhelm had been a starting pitcher for his entire minor league career, but Leo Durocher, the Giant manager, needed a reliever and gave Wilhelm a chance at the top.

Wilhelm overcame a concern that his floating knuckleball would allow base runners to steal with impunity. "The trick," he said, "is not to let them get on in the first place." And also to have a deceptive motion to first base.

For most of his long major league career, Wilhelm was a relief pitcher. However, he did start numerous games, and in 1958, with Baltimore, he pitched a no-hitter against the Yankees. The next year he won nine-straight starts and finished the season with 15 victories.

He played for nine major league teams, and, each time he was let go, management had decided that he was simply too old. But, as Wilhelm has recalled, almost every time he was dropped he had led the team in earned run average.

Someone else always took a chance on the old man, until 1972, when, one month short of his forty-ninth birthday, and after having pitched in 16 games for the Los Angeles Dodgers that season, he was cut for the final time.

Now, John Picus Quinn, born, for some strange reason, John Quinn Picus and called "Jack," was forty-nine years old when he pitched in 14 games for the Cincinnati Reds in 1933. And Satchel Paige, born, it is assumed, sometime after the Battle of Hastings, was rather wintry when cranking it up for the St. Louis Browns in 1953. (According to *The Baseball Encyclopedia*, he was then forty-seven years old.) Beyond that, no major leaguer has rivaled Hoyt Wilhelm, born James Hoyt Wilhelm, for playing regularly at such an advanced age.

Wilhelm still holds the major league career records for most games pitched, 1,070; most innings pitched by a reliever, 1,870; most games finished, 651—a mighty figure, because he was frequently in games that were on the line and wasn't on the slab simply to mop up—and most victories in relief, 124. The save, which is now often a yardstick to measure a relief pitcher's effectiveness, was not an official statistic for the first 17 years of his career, or until 1969.

As for Wilhelm's career earned run average, it was 2.52, and in six of seven years, from 1962 through 1968, it was, stunningly, under 2.00.

There are pitchers in the Hall of Fame, such as Stan Coveleski and Waite Hoyt, who did a considerable amount of relief pitching, but no one who was primarily a reliever has ever been selected.

The relief specialist, invaluable to a team, has been sorely mistreated by the sportswriters who finger deities for the Hall. There should be a place in the pantheon for one like Wilhelm.

And what was it that made him so successful?

"Well," Wilhelm said when he was with the Angels, "I never went into a game and got all flustered up. I try to take a close game and men on base in stride.

"I've always thought baseball was just a game—and I enjoy it. And ever since I was a boy and learned that knuckleball, I've thrown it with a lot of damned determination."

* * *

Wilhelm was elected to the Hall in January 1985.

Rod Carew Is Next in Line For the Hall

December 26, 1990

One night Rod Carew came to dinner and the hostess laid out a nice table, as was her custom. Among other items, she placed a slab of butter beside the sliced bread. Carew, in conversation, reached for the butter and stopped, his knife and his sentence suspended. He had suddenly noticed there was only a small piece of butter on the tray.

"Am I using up all your butter?" asked Carew, with genuine concern.

The hostess glanced at the dish, and smiled. "Oh, don't worry, Rod," she said, "there's plenty more butter in the refrigerator."

The hostess, my wife Dolly, has never forgotten that little, gentle moment, which to her encompassed all of the criteria that are listed in the 1991 rules for the Hall of Fame ballot: "Candidates shall be chosen on the basis of playing ability, integrity, sportsmanship, character, their contribution to the team on which they played and to baseball in general."

Carew, who retired as an active major leaguer five years ago, is on the recently released ballot for the Hall of Fame, having become eligible for the first time. And one would think, based on his extraordinary record at the plate—on the ball field and in the dining room—that he is a cinch to gain entrance. But things don't always work out so smoothly.

Each of those particulars, from playing ability to character, can be debated, perhaps endlessly, for they are all in the eyes of the beholder. Character on the field, or off the field, or both? Who can judge? And on the field, are the tricks of the trade, even nefarious ones, good, bad or accepted sportsmanship?

Meanwhile, just because Carew led his league in hitting seven times—only four men have bettered or equaled that, Ty Cobb with twelve, Honus Wagner eight, and Rogers Hornsby and Stan Musial seven each—finished with a .300 batting average in 15 of his 19 seasons, had a .328 lifetime average, and compiled more than 3,000 hits, he is not guaranteed admission to that quaint shrine on Main Street in Cooperstown, New York.

Questions arise for some of the 450 or so baseball writers who get ballots—an electee must receive 75 percent of the vote—whether Carew, not a home-run hitter, drove in as many runs as some believe a Hall of Famer should have.

"Everyone has a job to do on the field," said Carew recently, from his home in Anaheim, California. "My job was to get on base and to score runs, and to do everything I could to help my team win. That included all the little things, like moving a runner over and stealing a base."

Was Carew pouty as a player? "I was hot-headed when I was younger, especially," he said, "but when I was at the ball park I was all business. I hope that some writers don't hold that against me."

Ted Williams remembers seeing Carew for the first time and he thought he looked too lackadaisical. "But that's his style," said Williams.

"Some guys—Pete Rose is one, and I put myself in this category—have to snort and fume, to get everything going. Carew doesn't."

Carew, who played second base and first base for the Twins, and later the Angels, was not only surprisingly graceful, but could be fearless, too. He was one of the great stealers of home and shares with Pete Reiser the record of most steals of home in a season, seven.

"Stealing home can be dangerous," said Carew, "and that's why most guys don't do it. The batter might not get the signal. Once, I thought Harmon Killebrew was about to swing as I was racing home. But he held up. Otherwise I would have been a double down the left-field line."

Another on the Hall ballot for the first time is Rollie Fingers, the relief pitcher with the mustache as wide as long horns, who has a relatively good chance of getting elected, being the career leader in saves. Rusty Staub is on for the first time, too, and he drove in as many runs as many in the Hall, but was he versatile enough, some ask? He appears to be borderline, at best.

Four players, though, who linger on the list, and who have gotten quite close in recent years, may miss again, the pitchers Gaylord Perry, Ferguson Jenkins, Jim Bunning (this will be his last of fifteen years on the ballot), and the first baseman Orlando Cepeda. Based on their baseball records, all should be in the Hall of Fame.

But Perry, who admitted he threw a spitball (may candor be a virtue?), Jenkins, who was once arrested for transporting drugs, and Cepeda, who served a jail sentence relating to drugs, may have been penalized by some voters for those reasons.

"But if a player performs on the field," said Carew, "you just can't take that away from him."

As for Perry, who won more than 300 games, Carew says he was one of the great competitors. "He wasn't the only one to throw a spitter, either, and still isn't," said Carew. "But a lot of guys worried about his spitter. I never cared if he threw it wet or dry. I told them I was just going to hit it on the dry side."

* * *

Carew was elected to the Hall of Fame in 1991.

Rod Carew: A Baseball Legend Confronts a Moral Reckoning

July 1, 2020

The tumult of recent weeks has made my thoughts turn to Rod Carew, whose past life as a Minnesota Twin speaks to present days in Minneapolis, and the country.

In a tweet the other day, the *New York Times* sportswriter John Branch (my former colleague, since I've been retired from the paper for thirteen years) quoted something I had said in a panel discussion on race a number of years ago, which he obviously and chillingly found pertinent to the news of today, in which Black men are targets of the police, from casual racial discomfort to killings.

Then Carew came up again with the news that Twins management had decided to take down the statue of a former team owner, Calvin Griffith, in front of Target Field, the team's ballpark, because of racist remarks he made at a speaking engagement in 1978.

Griffith had moved the Senators franchise from Washington, DC, to Minnesota for the 1961 season. "I'll tell you when I came to Minnesota," he said. "It was when we found out that there were only 15,000 Blacks here. Black people don't go to ball games but they'll fill up a wrestling ring and put up such a chant it'll scare you to death. We came because you've got good, hard-working white people here." Griffith later apologized for his remarks.

I called Carew and found him magnanimous, as usual, and also direct about Griffith and the current protest movement against racism.

It was clear he was working through the news about Griffith. He had issued a statement recently, which read in part that he "understands and respects" the Twins decision to remove the Griffith statue, but he also remembers "how supportive" Griffith was to him, a young Black rookie second baseman in 1967, and beyond. Carew wrote: "In 1977, my MVP year, I made $170,000. When the season was over, Calvin called me into his office, thanked me for the great season, told me that I had made the team a lot of money, and handed me a check for $100,000. Could have knocked me over. A racist wouldn't have done that."

Carew, however, then still uncomfortable playing in Minnesota and, presumably, for Griffith, sought a trade that landed him in 1979 with the Angels, in Southern California, where he now lives.

Yet Carew recalls that when he was told he had been elected to the Baseball Hall of Fame in 1991, "The first person I called was Calvin." He also reasoned, "While we cannot change history, perhaps we can learn from it."

Now seventy-four, Carew sounded strong. A few years ago, he went through a heart transplant and a kidney transplant—both at the same time. "I've recuperated, been given a clean bill of health," he said, "and I'm feeling great." This year, he published a memoir, *One Tough Out: Fighting Off Life's Curveballs*.

Like most of the country, he has been deeply troubled by the racial tragedies regarding white police officers and Black men that have been recorded. He has lived through discrimination both in his native Panama and in the United States, but maintains a cautiously optimistic outlook.

"It's a way of life, but I do think things will change, at least some-what," he said. "Almost everyone has a camera on their cellphones. Now, cops are being watched like never before. I personally haven't had any run-ins with police in recent years, but I'm still aware that you have to be careful."

He learned that lesson a long time ago.

When I helped Carew write his autobiography, *Carew*, which was published in 1979, he told me then, "I've also been hassled by white cops when they've seen me driving a nice car," adding, "They think you've got to be a pimp." He recalled one particular instance which he told me was a specific that characterized the general.

"After a Twins game in Met Stadium"—or Metropolitan Stadium, the former ballpark in Bloomington, Minn.—"a few years ago, I'm driv-ing down 35W near my home and going fifty in a fifty-five-mile zone. Two cops in a squad car pull me over. 'You know the speed limit, boy? You think you're going to be burning up the road with this fancy car you're driving?'

"They asked for my driver's license. My first instinct was to tell them that I've got my license in my pocket and if they want to take it out. Among Blacks, white policemen have a reputation that as soon as you go into your pocket, they think you're going to pull out a gun. They could jump me and pull out their guns and it's all over.

"I told them my doubts. One cop said, 'Do it slowly.' When he saw my name, he starts shaking his head and says, 'Well, Rod, you're nuts for going over the speed limit.' I said: 'I know I wasn't going over the speed limit. I knew you guys were behind me. And I knew you were going to stop me.'" It ended without further incident. "I'm Rod Carew, but the bottom line is I'm still Black."

That event happened more than forty years ago, but reads like it could have happened yesterday.

There's a lot of growth in this country. We've come a long way. And we still have a long way to go.

Gary Carter Gives the Signs of Confidence

May 12, 1986

The ground ball that resulted in a double play to end a game last week also ignited the catcher. Like some over-armored knight, he bounded madly to the pitcher's mound, his shin guards clanking, his chest protector flapping and his square jaw going. He was shouting at the pitcher. The pitcher was Dwight Gooden. The catcher was Gary Carter.

What was he shouting? "You're the best, Doc, you're the best!"

Carter sat placidly a few days later before his locker in the Mets clubhouse. He was caparisoned only in the long, curly blond locks that fall to his neck, and the scar on his forehead and the scar on his right knee and the bumps on both thumbs, which were once broken—byproducts of his arduous and risky occupation. He recalled that recent moment of exaltation, after Gooden had hurled a two-hit shutout against the Astros. It was one of the Mets numerous victories in their quick start to currently lead the National League East by four games, with a 20–5 record.

"You've got to pump up the pitchers, and keep 'em pumped," Carter said, "even when the game's over. It's one of the good catcher's most important responsibilities, and the kind of thing you never will find in a box score."

He added: "Even a great pitcher like Dwight, he's got to be told he's good, too, like everyone else. It gives you just that much more incentive."

There was the starting pitcher who felt the manager lacked confidence in him because he was always being removed in close games. "I had to reassure him," Carter said. "I told him: 'Listen, he wouldn't be putting you out there every fourth or fifth day if he didn't have confidence in you. He just feels that he can preserve the win for you, rather than having you leave with a tie game.'"

Conversely, he must calm the super-pumped. "Relax," he said, arriving at the mound to soothe the young, intense Ron Darling. "Take a deep breath. It's a simple game. Keep it simple." But inevitably there's the little motion of an upthrust fist when Carter is crouching behind the plate and the pitcher is about to go into his windup, a motion that says, "Let's go!"

"Pitchers have fragile personalities and egos," said Frank Cashen, the Mets general manager. "You have to be able to encourage them. And a pitcher is more likely to believe encouragement from a veteran like Gary than from some rookie catcher."

Carter, now in his 12th full big-league season, came to the Mets from Montreal before last season in a trade for four younger players. The Mets sought him because, Cashen said, they were looking for a right-handed power hitter to bat between "Keith and Straw"—Keith Hernandez and Darryl Strawberry. "And we got a bonus," Cashen added.

"Gary's arguably the best defensive catcher in the National League, exactly what a young staff like ours needs."

Another factor not reflected in box scores that is essential: Carter is a deft blocker of pitches. "For a young pitcher, that's really important," Rick Aguilera said. "You've got a lot to think about out there without having to worry that with men on base, if you bounce a curveball in the dirt it's going to get past your catcher."

And having been in the league so long, Carter knows the hitters, knows their strengths and weaknesses, and is wise enough to keep them off-balance.

The pitchers don't often shake off one of his signs, but on occasion they do.

"Someone like Dwight, who has a lot of pride in his fastball, well, he wants to throw it a lot," Carter said. "And if I call for more curves than he wants, he might shake me off. He might get a little demoralized that I'm not showing confidence in his best pitch. But I explain to him that I'm showing confidence in his other pitches as well. It's a matter of communication."

Darling says: "He might call pitches that aren't to the batter's weakness in his first and second trip to the plate. But then when the game is on the line, he'll go to the weakness. Say it's a fastball high. If we had been throwing there earlier, the batter just might have made an adjustment and been looking for it."

Darling smiled. "But sometimes he's wrong, too. But who isn't?"

But when giving an example of Carter's signal-calling—a time when the catcher was right—came to mind first.

"It was against the Cardinals last season, in that tough extra-inning game in the last week of the season," Darling said, "and Ozzie Smith was up. He was batting left-handed against me, of course, and we know he was going to try to pull the ball. So we worked it so the ball Ozzie bit at was a sinker away, and he bounced it back to me for a double play."

Aguilera also mentioned Carter's experience in relation to umpires. "He knows them and they know him, and I think they respect him, the way they do a Pete Rose, so you might get the benefit of the doubt on a close pitch, where you might not with another catcher," he said.

What Carter said he tries to do in relation to umpires is "not show them up." "I'm not going to be turning around all the time and arguing, or looking to the dugout," Carter said. "But if they start missing too many, I might say, 'Weren't those pitches a little close?' or 'Where's your strike zone tonight?'"

Carter has the confidence not only of the pitching staff, but of Manager Davey Johnson as well, and Johnson allows him to make all the pitch selections. On some teams, the manager will signal most of the pitches in a game. Johnson, though, relies on Carter to be a kind of second manager on the field.

"He's the heart of the pitching staff," Johnson said. "We'd be lost without him."

And yet there is the constant threat of losing him. Not altogether, but losing him to the outfield. He has been through a decade of accordion-like crouching behind the plate, the collisions with flying baserunners, and the rain of foul tips against his shoulders, throat, hands and toes. It has exacted an enormous and painful toll on this otherwise healthy-appearing specimen 6-foot-2, 210 pounds, thirty-two years old.

Last season, for example, he was playing with torn ligaments in his left ankle, torn cartilage in his right knee and a cracked ninth rib (ribs No. 11 and No. 12 had been cracked previously). He missed the All-Star Game, and there was a question of just how much longer this $1.9 million-per-year catcher could remain in the lineup.

He didn't complain, but on occasion he did wince, which told the story. Yet he continued to catch, continued to run, and continued to hit so well that in September, that clutch month for the Mets in their pursuit of the Cardinals for the division title, he had the best month of his career. He belted 13 homers, drove in 34 runs, and hit .343 in 27 games.

(For the season, he had 32 homers, 100 RBIs, and a .281 batting average in 149 games. And, in the matter of little-discussed but significant statistics, he was the seventh hardest batter to strike out in the National League.)

When the season was complete, he underwent arthroscopic surgery on his right knee for the second time (he has had surgery on his left knee once). Now, before a game, he spends twenty minutes in the trainer's room being taped with all the care of a valuable package being sent parcel post. He is resigned to knowing that no matter how well wrapped his knee is he will always be playing in some pain.

"Gary obviously has a high threshold of pain," Johnson said. "But I know that we've got to rest him some from behind the plate. And since we don't want to lose his bat, he'll play some left field for us. But it's tough to even think to rest him early on, when we want to get off to a good start. As the season goes on, I know we'll have to give him more rest from behind the dish. But not now. We know, and he knows, that a hurt Gary Carter is more use to us than a healthy anybody else."

With all his injuries, there was another physical pain early in the season. It was a sore throwing arm, and there was some concern among observers that runners were beginning to take advantage of Carter on the base paths.

"They run on the pitcher," said Johnson, which is an oft-repeated notion. But sometimes they run on the catcher, too. "But the guys who were running—people like Vince Coleman—they run on everyone."

"The arm was tender," Carter said, "but it isn't anymore. It's fine, now."

Oddly, for one of the best catchers in baseball, he spent his first year and a half in the big leagues in right field. The Montreal Expos, the team that signed him out of Sunny Hills High School in Fullerton, California, in 1972, had a catcher they liked named Barry Foote, whom Carter would eventually beat out.

Carter was an all-America high school football quarterback but saw his future as a baseball player. And he didn't play catcher until the last few games of his senior year in high school. Scouts had told him that the quickest way to the major leagues was as a catcher. Before this, he had played shortstop and had pitched.

He went first to Jamestown, New York, for a two-week tryout, and then to Cocoa, Florida, in the Florida East Coast Rookie League and began to learn to play catcher, having to first learn to throw with a snap from behind the ear, instead of that longer quarterback-style fling. But he was still having problems even the following year, when he had moved up to Quebec in Class AA ball. He still hadn't learned something fairly crucial.

"What are you?" asked his manager, Karl Kuehl.

"I'm a catcher," responded the nineteen-year-old Carter.

"That tells me one thing," Kuehl said. "If you're a catcher, you're supposed to catch the ball."

Carter recalled this with a laugh in the Mets locker room. "I was dropping a lot of balls," he said. "I was sort of slapping at the ball, instead of bring it in nice and gentle. Karl started fining me a quarter for every ball I dropped. He kept a record, and it was starting to mount. It got up to about $25, and when you're only making $600 a month, that hurts. I started to concentrate more than ever on catching the ball, and I began to get the hang of it. And Karl never asked me to pay up the fine. It was just his way of getting my attention."

Now Carter has little trouble catching a baseball behind the plate. In fact, it appears he has mastered most of the elements of that demanding position, including the mastery over himself, and this translates into his unceasing and generally infectious enthusiasm behind the plate.

"He always gives the impression that he's excited to be out there," Aguilera said. "Some catchers have a bad day at bat, and they get down. That's not helpful. A young pitcher needs all the help he can get."

Carter works at maintaining that enthusiasm. "The thing I learned very early is that offense is secondary to a catcher," he said. "If I don't get a hit, but I catch a winning game, if my pitcher throws a shutout, then I come home and I've got to be happy. I have to feel that I've done my job."

Luis Aparicio: Switching Sox, From White To Red

July 16, 1971

At the crack of the bat, Luis Aparicio, no spring chicken, pops out of shortstop as if newly hatched. Wispy arms aflutter. Dusty, pigeon-toed scutter. Hard dart of a peg! He was voted the 1971 American League All-Star shortstop by the fans, despite the worst hitting slump he's ever endured. "I voted for Mark Belanger myself," said Aparicio. "He's the best in the business now."

No, he was not embarrassed about being picked first at short. "I'll quit when I get embarrassed," he said. In fact, he felt honored. "The fans chose me, I think, because of my career."

He has played over 3,000 big-league games at short. More than anyone in baseball, from Appling to Zimmer. At 5-foot-8, 157 pounds (one pound more than when he broke into the majors with the White Sox in 1956), Aparicio appears fragile from afar. Batboys are often bigger. Close up, he is not callow at all.

Thirty-seven years old, silvery streaks in fine black hair, good cheekbones, soft eyes, easy smile, body wound firm as hemp. Signs of fraying, though: Began wearing glasses lately, bursitis in throwing elbow, back muscle pull has forced him to miss more games than usual, stole only two bases by All-Star break (stole eight last season, but still holds major league mark for most consecutive years leading league in stolen bases, nine), sad slump.

In the locker room before a game, he excuses himself with a smile. "They're going to put this body together, it's falling apart." Trainer Buddy LeRoux rubs him down twice before each game. Aparicio groans in pain from the hot balm on his back. He also gets daily diathermy and whirlpool treatments. He never forgets his vitamins, either, says LeRoux.

"I guess I've lost a step or two," said Aparicio. "But my legs are still strong. I think I'm playing the best shortstop I've played in ten years."

Up to the All-Star Game, he had made only five errors. Hitting was another matter. On June 9, he had dropped to .151, after having gone 2-for-65 from mid-May, with one streak of 0-for-44—this coming on the heels of his best season batting, .313 in 1970.

He got lucky coins, statues, mementoes, religious charms, well wishes, advice and, sadly, only a few loud fouls. Finally, Rico Petrocelli discovered that Aparicio had been dropping his bat and pulling his elbow back. When Aparicio broke the streak with a single in Fenway Park, the crowd of 10,266 rose and applauded warmly.

"The fans never booed me, the whole time," said Aparicio.

The Red Sox had been in first place throughout that period and that, said Aparicio, took much of the pressure off. He also did not make an error during that 15-game hitless streak. "That's what kept me from going crazy," he said. His plate performance was depressing also because the Red Sox had traded for him over the winter to bolster an anticipated pennant drive. The day after he broke his somber streak, he received a letter from a fan in Washington, DC. The fan, the year before, had called Aparicio "indestructible." It had made the papers. Now, the fan wrote to congratulate Luis and told him that he, too, was once in a slump and then hit a home run. Signed, Richard M. Nixon, 1600 Pennsylvania Ave.

Aparicio went on a hitting streak the last couple weeks before the All-Star break. He bad raised his average more than 50 points to .206.

His 16-year career has taught him, he said, that baseball is a very tough game, that you can learn something new every day, that nothing comes easy. And so he worries about the welfare of his body.

"I want to play three or four more good years," he said, in his nearly conquered Venezuelan accent. "I just hope I don't break a leg. I keep my fingers crossed."

Ted Simmons's Case: Cause Without a Rebel

July 3, 1972

"It's kinda weird," said Ted Simmons. "I mean, I think I know how the guy felt who was the first to climb Mount Everest."

Ted Simmons is also a first. Simmons, the St. Louis Cardinals regular catcher, is the only playing holdout in baseball history.

He may also change the course of baseball history, in a way that Curt Flood could not.

Simmons wants more money than the Cardinals are willing to pay. He is still trying for it, and continues negotiations with the front office when he is not crouched and waggling his fingers for the edification of the pitcher.

"I'm no crusader," said Simmons in the Cardinals clubhouse recently. "I don't even have a lawyer. All I want is more money."

If he doesn't get what he wants, he may take his case to court. And Simmons's case has elements that the Flood case did not.

Flood challenged the reserve clause, which states that a player is bound to a club for an indefinite period. The Supreme Court recently upheld a 1922 ruling which allowed baseball to remain outside the anti-trust laws. So Flood lost.

Simmons's case, however, is undeniable proof of the change in baseball. First, Simmons was picked by the Cardinals in the free-agent draft. Therefore, could not sign with any other team (unless he waited a year and was drafted by another club then).

Flood, on the other hand, had a choice of signing with any team that would have him. He signed with Cincinnati in 1956, before the free-agent draft was instituted. Simmons is getting $25,000 for this season, having received a raise of $7,500 from last season when he hit .304 in what was his first full year in the major leagues. But he wanted

$30,000 this spring. Two Cardinals, Jerry Reuss and Bob Burda, also were unhappy with their contracts and were also playing holdouts. Both were traded by Cardinal president August Busch. And both have since signed standard player contracts.

Simmons will be challenging the "renewal clause," if he doesn't receive the $5,000 he has been bargaining for.

If the Cardinals invoke the renewal clause, then Simmons says he will probably take the case to court. The Cardinals, in essence, would be reactivating his 1971 contract, forcing Simmons to play under terms not agreeable to him. They could also cut his pay as much as 20 per cent.

"I'm not trying to force the issue, and I'm no troublemaker," said Simmons. "But I am frustrated."

He says he is frustrated because he receives no hope or satisfaction in his contract negotiations. He says he speaks frequently with "Mr." Busch, and "Mr." Jim Toomey, and "Mr." Richard Meyer and "Mr." Bing Devine, all front office men.

In the end it is Busch who pays the bills and he has been an outspoken critic of the "younger generation." (Simmons is twenty-three.) When Busch heard that the players were going to strike this spring, he blustered, "Let 'em strike. I won't give them one more damned cent."

Simmons says he likes St. Louis and has established roots there— an apartment, friends, business associates. He has lived with a fear of being traded. But the encouragement from fellow players buoys his spirit.

"Like a satisfied paranoia," he said.

He also is not critical of the baseball establishment, as was Flood. "In fact," said Simmons, "the Cardinals have treated me very well. For example, in 1970 I was released from the Army and got married the next day. My wife and I came through St. Louis on the way to Tulsa, where I was going to play that season. Well, the Cards put us up in a St. Louis hotel for four days. And picked up all the bills. That was great.

So was my bonus for signing." (He got $50,000.) However, Simmons says he is standing firm in his contract hassle. "It gives me satisfaction to know that I haven't compromised my principles, and that I haven't faltered under the pressure.

"What pressure? From fans, who write that I should sign. And the fears of being traded."

Simmons said that all his life he has stood up for what he believed, and that he has usually got what he wanted.

He said, "I remember when I was a kid and wanted a motorcycle. My mother was afraid of them and didn't want me to have one. So I did odd jobs, like some rough carpenter work, and saved $800 in four years. When I was sixteen, I bought myself that motorcycle.

"My mother let me keep it. And everything turned out fine. I think she was proud of the way I earned it. I never got hurt on it, and I didn't turn into a Hell's Angel."

Billy Williams Says No

November 7, 1987

A first-base coach in baseball must know how to blink not only with one eye, but with two. These are among his essential functions, along with being nimble enough to dodge foul balls.

Signals to a runner on first, similar to those flashed for Paul Revere, are sometimes one blink for a steal and two blinks for a hit-and-run.

A third-base coach must be even more clever. He has to interpret the manager's signals and relay them all the way to the batter: whether to bunt or to swing. He must determine if a runner can take an extra base against an outfielder's arm, and he has to make sure the runner on third doesn't fall for the hidden-ball trick or some other nefarious gem. And of course, he, too, has to dance out of the way of foul balls.

And a manager? He's got to know when a pitcher is tired—usually the other team helps him decide this because it is blasting the ball. He also has to make out the lineup card and determine if a batter should hit second or first.

In the clubhouse, he must, as Casey Stengel once said, try to keep some of the players from killing each other—and from killing the manager. And on occasion, even while sitting in the relative safety of the dugout, he'll get plunked by a foul ball.

A lot has been written about how smart coaches and managers must be. But in the end, the necessary brainpower for a field leader in baseball is generally slightly less than that required of someone, say, performing surgery on the cerebrum, or maybe even sailing a boat.

Billy Williams, a sometime first-base coach for the Chicago Cubs and the team's batting instructor, is intelligent enough to understand this. He is also smart enough to comprehend that the primary requirement of a baseball manager is to have good baseball players.

This profundity alone should qualify Williams for the Baseball Hall of Fame. But he was also bright enough to develop his natural talents and become a terrific hitter, one who understood how to figure out pitchers, and how to run the bases wisely. He learned the one-blink and two-blink signals of the first-base coach and the arm motions of the third-base coach, and how to shade various hitters while playing the outfield. Last summer, he was inducted into the Hall of Fame.

It took ability, certainly, but it also took observation, it took experience—he has been in the game on a professional level for 30 years—and it took effort.

Because of these qualities, he felt he should at least be considered for the job of manager of the Cubs, a position recently rendered vacant. In fact, some have felt that it has been vacant for a very long time, even when it was supposedly filled. The Cubs, after all, haven't won a pennant since 1945, and haven't captured a World Series since 1908.

Williams saw that John Vukovich, the Cubs third-base coach, was possibly being groomed as the skipper. Williams, meanwhile, had been offered the job of manager of the Cubs Triple-A team in Des Moines, Iowa. But this week, he refused it.

He said that last season he had managed for a month in the Arizona Instructional League, and was satisfied that he did well enough to manage in the big leagues.

Vukovich's managerial experience also consists of one month in the Instructional League.

The differences, perhaps, are that Vukovich was a third-base coach, with all that responsibility—and that the third-base coach is usually a pal of the manager. Thus, by baseball standards, he's better qualified to be a manager.

There is another difference between Vukovich and Williams, and between every third-base coach in baseball—except Ozzie Virgil of Seattle—and Williams. That is, Williams is black, and all the rest, save Virgil, are white.

When the furor broke last season over what many construed as racist remarks by Al Campanis of the Dodgers, a move was launched by the commissioner's office to get more blacks into management in baseball.

Only three blacks had ever managed in the big leagues—none with the Cubs—and not any do presently.

At the end of last season, the Kansas City Royals offered an interim managing job to Hal McRae, but he turned it down because he wanted a two-year contract.

Now Williams, seeking the Cubs job, is told he needs more experience. He looks around and sees that several big-league managers, including Pete Rose and Bobby Valentine and Whitey Herzog and Jim Fregosi, were originally hired as managers without having managed a day in the minor leagues.

Most managers have served a minor-league apprenticeship. But experience in the minors—or in the majors, for that matter—is not a guarantee of success.

Look at old Connie Mack, who made the Hall of Fame. He once managed his A's to last place in seven straight seasons. Of course, this followed his selling all of his best players from two straight pennant-winning teams. Still, he felt secure in the dugout. He felt secure because he happened also to own the team.

And if experience was so important, then Gene Mauch, a big-league manager for 26 seasons, would have won at least one pennant. He hasn't. And Tom Kelly wouldn't have won a World Series with the Twins in his first full season as a big-league manager.

It's an unhappy fact, but a fact nonetheless: Blacks in big-league management are still pioneers. And as difficult as it might be for proud men, men of achievement, the view here is that they shouldn't pass up these opportunities—even as an interim manager, even as a minor-league manager.

Owners would begin to adjust to a black in the manager's office, and, on the bench, to his flashing the sign to bunt or to swing away.

Catfish Hunter, Who Pitched in Six World Series for the A's and Yankees, Dies at 53

September 10, 1999

Catfish Hunter, the Hall of Fame right-hander who helped pitch the Oakland A's and the Yankees to six pennants in the 1970s, hurled a perfect game and was part of an economic revolution in sports, died yesterday at his home at Hertford, North Carolina. He was fifty-three.

He had been struggling for the last year with amyotrophic lateral sclerosis, the progressive and ultimately fatal neurological condition also known as Lou Gehrig's disease. He had also been hospitalized after falling and hitting his head on concrete steps outside his home August 8. He was sent home Saturday.

Hunter was a premier pitcher of his era, a 6-feet, 190-pounder who did not have overpowering speed but possessed outstanding control, an assortment of superb pitches and a winner's poise.

He won 224 games in 15 major league seasons from 1965 to 1979 and won at least 21 games over five consecutive seasons, from 1971 to 1974 with Oakland and in 1975 with the Yankees. He won the Cy Young Award as the American League's top pitcher in 1974 and was an eight-time All-Star. In compiling a record of 224–166, he had an outstanding career earned run average of 3.26.

Although an unassuming ballplayer who rarely took himself seriously, Hunter was wise enough to become the first big-money free agent.

An arbitrator freed him from his contract with Charlie Finley's Athletics after the 1974 season, and the Yankees signed him to a five-year, $3.35 million contract that was the largest in baseball history at that time.

While his case did not directly lead to free agency for other players—a ruling in an unrelated case the next year led to that—it showed the players what they, too, might command from the baseball owners.

"He paved the way for me," said Roger Clemens, who will earn $16.1 million with the Yankees over 1999 and 2000.

James Augustus Hunter was born on April 8, 1946, on a farm near Hertford in Perquimans County. He said he was taught to pitch by his older brothers.

"My three brothers taught me to throw strikes," he said when inducted into the Baseball Hall of Fame in 1987, "and thanks to them I gave up 379 home runs in the big leagues."

Hunter was overstating things a bit, having given up 374 homers. And the control he developed by throwing baseballs at a hole in the barn door—the last brother to hit the hole had to do the chores—would pay off.

A Yankee teammate, pitcher Pat Dobson, once said about Hunter: "He can put the ball where he wants it—or within an inch or two, which is just about as good. From that one capacity stems everything else."

On occasion, Hunter's family would travel to Baltimore to watch major league baseball. "I remember once we were watching Robin Roberts there," Hunter said, "and my father said, 'Hell, I could hit him; he's not throwing that hard.' We were sitting behind the plate, and Roberts really did look as though you could murder him. But nobody seemed to do it. I admired the heck out of Roberts. I just naturally patterned myself after him, and eventually I learned to do it, too."

Major league hitters would feel the same way about Hunter as Hunter's father had felt about Roberts. "I could never understand why I couldn't hit Hunter," said Ed Herrmann, an opponent who later became a teammate on the Yankees. "Even when you're up at the plate, you think, just give me one more of those and I'll clout it out of here. But I rarely did."

Hunter was known all his life as Jimmy in his home area. Finley, the A's flamboyant owner, gave him the nickname Catfish and apparently manufactured a story to go with it. "Around here, we never call him Catfish," Ray Ward, editor of the *Perquimans Weekly*, once said. "We call him Jimmy. Jimmy's mother has been upset about the nickname." The story created to go with the name: Hunter had once run away from home and come back with two catfish. "His mother was irritated that somebody would believe her little boy ran off," Ward said.

During Hunter's senior year at Perquimans High School in Hertford, he was wounded in his right foot when his brother Pete's shotgun misfired, destroying his little toe and leaving the foot full of pellets. The Kansas City Athletics signed him anyway, for a $50,000 bonus, and sent him to the Mayo Clinic for surgery. He spent the 1964 season on the disabled list, but the foot did not bother him after the operation even though about fifteen shotgun pellets remained.

Hunter never pitched in the minor leagues, starting the 1965 season with a cellar-bound Kansas City team that had eight rookies. He had an 8–8 record that year and was 55–64 in his first five seasons, never finishing above .500. Despite his mediocre won-lost records with mostly mediocre A's teams, Hunter was named an American League All-Star in 1966 and 1967.

In 1968 Finley moved the A's to Oakland, and on May 8 of that year Hunter retired all twenty-seven Minnesota Twins he faced, the first regular-season perfect game in the American League since 1922.

The fortunes of the A's improved dramatically after their move to Oakland, and they quickly developed into a powerhouse that won three straight World Series from 1972 to 1974. Hunter also improved, in part because of a slight modification to his pitching motion, and he became the steady center of a swaggering, squabbling club that featured larger-than-life characters like Reggie Jackson, Vida Blue and Rollie Fingers. In his last five seasons with Oakland he compiled a record of 106–49, and he was 4–0 in seven World Series appearances.

Jackson, a teammate of Hunter's with both the A's and the Yankees, would recall, "When we started winning in Oakland, Cat was the father of those teams." Hunter was only twenty-six when the A's won their first World Series championship.

Lou Piniella was another teammate on the Yankees. "The main thing about Cat is that statistics didn't mean much to him," Piniella said. "The only thing that mattered was victories. He didn't have overpowering stuff, but he knew how to pitch and how to beat you. If there was a game you had to win, he's the guy you wanted on the mound."

After he won the Cy Young Award in 1974 with a record of 25–12 and a league-leading 2.49 ERA, Hunter uncovered a violation of his contract with Finley and the A's that allowed him to become a free agent.

The A's were to send half of Hunter's $100,000 annual salary to a North Carolina bank as payment on an annuity, but Finley did not comply.

At season's end, with the guidance of the players' association, Hunter took a grievance to arbitration. He won and was declared a free agent, unfamiliar words in baseball in 1974.

When he learned of the decision by telephone, Hunter hung up and, shaken, turned to his wife, Helen. "We don't belong to anybody," he told her.

"I was scared," Hunter recalled. "I didn't have a job. I didn't realize the implications."

His case was an anomaly; it was the next year before Andy Messersmith and Dave McNally would challenge baseball's reserve clause and win, establishing the players union's power and spurring a tremendous escalation in athletes' salaries. But Hunter was about to show baseball players what their services were worth on the open market.

Hunter was the most accomplished veteran player ever to become a free agent, and soon teams were clamoring for his services in an unprecedented bidding war.

Among those who sought to sign him was Gene Autry, the singing cowboy of the movies who was the owner of the California Angels. Autry was so eager that he traveled across the country to meet Hunter in Ahoskie, North Carolina, sixty miles from Hertford.

"Gene Autry came down here handing out records of 'Rudolph the Red-Nosed Reindeer,'" Hunter once recalled. "That was the biggest thing that ever came to Ahoskie."

Twenty-three of the twenty-four teams in the major leagues—all but the San Francisco Giants—bid for Hunter's services. George Steinbrenner's $3.35 million offer to pitch for the Yankees for five years, which included a $1 million signing bonus and various insurance policies and annuities, was the most appealing, and the Yankees announced the signing of Hunter on New Year's Eve 1974.

The $150,000 annual salary Hunter received from the Yankees did not even rank among the top 10 in baseball—Dick Allen of the Chicago White Sox had received $250,000 in 1974. But the total package was the largest in baseball's history, and it made Hunter, at age twenty-eight, one of the three or four highest-paid American athletes at a time when rival leagues in hockey and football had already begun to drive up salaries.

But it was not just the money that brought Hunter to New York. "We'd had better offers, but New York was closer to home and they played on regular grass," he said. Coming to the Yankees also meant rejoining Clyde Kluttz, the scout who had signed Hunter to his first contract with Kansas City.

Hunter again led the league in victories in his first season with the Yankees, winning 23 games. He was 17–15 the following season, when the team won its first pennant in 12 years, and he compiled records of 9–9 and 12–6 for the Yankees World Series winning teams of 1977 and 1978, despite spending time on the disabled list during both seasons.

He was a humorous and a stabilizing force in the clubhouse for the Yankees, as he had been for the A's. While his jokes to teammates could be pointed, they were usually taken well. When Jackson had a candy bar named for him, Hunter said, "When you unwrap one, it tells you how good it is."

When Hunter was elected to the Hall of Fame, Steinbrenner, the Yankees principal owner, said: "You started our success. You were the first to teach us how to win. Other Yankees continued that leadership role, but you were the one who first showed us what it means to be a winner."

Hunter retired from baseball at age thirty-three when his contract expired after the 1979 season, having suffered problems with his pitching arm. But he found it no hardship to leave the limelight and return to his roots. Shortly after he joined the Yankees he had said: "I don't like New York much, either. I had to live in a hotel downtown for a couple of months until my wife got here. Hated it. Now I got this nice home in Norwood, New Jersey, and I just drive straight from there to the ball park. Never go downtown. Nothing for me to do down there."

Hunter and his wife, Helen, his high school sweetheart, lived in the same house outside tiny Hertford for more than twenty years. But their 100 acres had increased to 1,000. He was a full-time farmer in his corn, soybean, and peanut fields for ten years after he retired from baseball, and then he turned it over to a friend who leased the land.

He was an avid fisherman and hunter, keeping a kennel of deer hounds and bird dogs and shooting quail, pheasant, rabbit, and deer in the winter.

The financial package from the Yankees in 1974 included $25,000 payments for annuities for college tuition for his two children, Todd, then five, and Kimberly, two. His son Paul was born five years later. "I forgot I might have one more after baseball," Hunter said. "I have to pay for him myself."

In addition to his wife and three children, Hunter is survived by three brothers, three sisters and a grandson.

Hunter was a fierce competitor, but he kept his perspective and his unruffled disposition, understanding that baseball was just a game. "Golf's the only thing that makes me mad," he once said, with a smile.

Hunter entered a hospital in Baltimore last September after experiencing difficulties with motor skills, and amyotrophic lateral sclerosis was diagnosed. He did not appear in public outside his hometown again until March, when he attended the Yankees first spring training game in Tampa, Florida. He joked with reporters but had difficulty shaking hands.

"I've got no strength in my arms and my hands," he said last fall. "I can't do the routine things like button a shirt anymore."

Helen Hunter helped him with cutting his food and tying his shoes. "I'm putting a lot of work on her and she's strong," Catfish Hunter said. "But once in a while we sit here and cry together."

For many of his friends and family and teammates, Hunter's charm was memorable.

After he lost a game with the Yankees in the 1977 World Series, for example, he was unhappy but not distraught. He understood that there are good days and bad.

"The sun," he said, "don't shine on the same dog all the time."

For Ferguson Jenkins, Another Tragic Twist in the Road

January 3, 1993/Guthrie, Oklahoma

In the morning, Ferguson Jenkins had noticed that the hose to the large red vacuum cleaner was missing, but he paid little attention to it, never once imagining what terrible use it might be put to.

Then in the late afternoon, around five o'clock, the phone rang in the kitchen of his ranch house here. The date on the calendar on the wall was Tuesday, December 15, 1992, two days after Jenkins's forty-ninth birthday. Jenkins was outside, smoothing the red clay in the driveway with a shovel, when his ranch foreman, Tommy Christian, answered the phone.

"Sheriff Powell!" he called to Jenkins from the doorway.

"Sheriff Powell?" Jenkins recalled thinking. "What can he want?" The last time he had spoken to Doug Powell was two years earlier, after a robbery at the Jenkins ranch.

From the driveway, Jenkins could see that the sun, weak all day, was disappearing behind the hills and two man-made lakes on his 160 acres. It was getting cool as a wind picked up in this isolated area of the plains, about eight and a half miles north of Guthrie, the nearest town, and about forty miles north of Oklahoma City.

Jenkins was wearing a green windbreaker, green baseball cap, jeans and work boots.

This is a working farm, with eight horses, fifty-two head of beef cattle, and sixty acres of wheat, and Jenkins dresses for it. So did his fiancee, Cindy Takieddine, who lived with him, his adopted twelve-year-old son, Raymond, and his three-year-old daughter, Samantha, the child he had with his wife, Maryanne, who was seriously injured in a car crash in December 1990. Her death in January 1991 came just four days after the announcement that Fergie, as everyone calls him, had been named to baseball's Hall of Fame.

The election had been the culmination of a 19-year career in the major leagues, mostly with the Chicago Cubs and Texas Rangers, in which Jenkins won 284 games, was a 20-game winner seven times, won the National League Cy Young Award in 1971, and the American League Comeback Player of the Year Award in 1974, and then finally retired in 1983.

Jenkins is a big man. At 6-foot-5 and 225 pounds, he is about twenty pounds heavier than in his playing days, but he carries his weight well, with a graceful, slope-shouldered walk. Having learned that the sheriff was on the phone, he entered the two-story redwood house, walked past the Christmas tree that Cindy had decorated for three days, took the receiver and was told that the sheriff wanted to see him in Guthrie. Within fifteen minutes, Jenkins arrived in town in his pickup.

"I have some horrible news, Mr. Jenkins," said Sheriff Powell. "And there's no easy way to tell it.

"Cindy Takieddine and Samantha Jenkins were found dead of carbon monoxide poisoning. They were found in a Bronco pickup on a rural road near Perry."

"No, you're wrong, sheriff," said Jenkins. "You're wrong. I'm picking up Samantha at 5:30 at her daycare nursery." He looked at his watch. "In about ten minutes."

"It was a positive ID, sir. And a note was left."

"Call the day-care center," said Jenkins. "You'll see; Samantha's there."

Powell called the center for Jenkins, and put the call on a speakerphone. Samantha Jenkins was not at the nursery.

"Mr. Jenkins was devastated," recalled Powell. "This was one of the hardest things I've ever had to do as sheriff, or deputy, in Logan County. Mr. Jenkins is highly admired here. He's been a model citizen, and always willing to speak at civic or school or church groups. As famous as he is, that's how down to earth he is. He rode up to Perry with my undersheriff to identify the bodies, about thirty miles. All the way there and all the way back he never said a word."

It was back in Powell's office that he learned that Cindy, a tall, forty-four-year-old blonde, had stopped at the day-care center and picked up Samantha, whom she had dressed at home that morning in a green party dress with white sash and white stockings and black shiny shoes, saying it was for a Christmas party at the nursery school. But no party was scheduled.

Before Cindy and Samantha left home that day, Jenkins went to town to buy groceries.

It was the last he saw them alive. "There were no arguments," recalled Jenkins. "We were civil to each other."

"She didn't look or act no different," said Christian, the foreman.

After picking up Samantha at the daycare center, Cindy would drive to the deserted road. She affixed the vacuum cleaner hose to the exhaust pipe of the Bronco, ran it up through the back window, sealed the window with the duct tape she had taken from home along with the hose and, with the ignition still running, climbed into the back seat, and held Samantha in her arms. The coroner's report estimates that this happened around noon.

A few hours later, a pumper on a nearby oil rigging spotted the car, with two bodies slumped in the back seat, and he phoned the police.

On the day after Christmas, twelve days after the tragedy, Ferguson Jenkins loaded his pickup truck with unwrapped Christmas presents, and returned them in Guthrie to Walmart Sam's Wholesale Outlet, and Anthony's Clothing Store. They included a jogging outfit and sweaters for Cindy. For Samantha, there were Cabbage Patch dolls, a Minnie Mouse towel set, a *Beauty and the Beast* towel set ("She loved *Beauty and the Beast*," said Jenkins), coloring sets, a large box of crayons, a sweater that had Santa Claus and reindeer and the word *Christmas* across it, and matching socks.

When Jenkins returned home from the stores, his three daughters from his first marriage, to Kathy Jenkins, were in the house. The girls, Kelly, twenty-two, Delores twenty-one, and Kimberly, fifteen—all in college or high school—had come down from their home in Chatham, Ontario, where Jenkins was born and raised, to celebrate Christmas with their father, as they did every year. But this year, they had also come to go to the funeral of their three-year-old half-sister.

Jenkins's eighty-six-year-old father, who is in a nursing home in Chatham, had not made the trip for the funeral. "Said he couldn't take it," said Jenkins. It was his father, Ferguson Jenkins Sr., to whom Jenkins dedicated his induction into the Hall of Fame and who sat proudly in attendance in a wheelchair.

Jenkins had told the gathering at Cooperstown: "My father was a semipro ballplayer and he played in the Negro leagues, but he didn't make the major leagues because he was limited by history"—the color barrier in big-league baseball that existed until 1947.

"But he has outlived that history," Jenkins continued. "I always told him that anything I do in baseball, I do for the two of us, and so now I feel I'm being inducted into the Hall of Fame with my father."

Jenkins's mother, Delores, has been dead for several years. She had become blind after complications while giving birth to her only child. "I remember she always walked with a white cane and always made sure that my baseball uniform was sparkling clean and my baseball shoes were polished," Jenkins has recalled. "I'm not sure how she knew, but she never let me out of the house to play ball unless I was all in order."

Jenkins grew up playing baseball and hockey and basketball, and was often the lone black in those leagues in Chatham. "I heard 'nigger' a lot," he recalled, "but I was always determined to make people respect my abilities. I always wanted them to say, 'Hey, watch that black guy, he's good.' And I did get into some fights, mostly in hockey, and lost a few teeth. But I came out of it."

He left home after signing a contract with the Philadelphia Phillies when he was eighteen, having just graduated high school, "a tall, skinny kid of 155 pounds," he said. "My father was a cook on shipping lines in the Great Lakes, and my mother was home alone a lot. I've always felt kind of guilty leaving her, but I knew I had to pursue my career."

Three years later, at the end of the 1965 season, he was called up to the Phillies, as a relief pitcher. In his first game, he replaced the veteran Jim Bunning, whom, he recalled, he had badgered for pitching help.

"How do you grip the ball? How do you throw your slider?" Jenkins would ask Bunning.

The next season Jenkins was traded to the Cubs, and Leo Durocher made him a starter.

Jenkins would learn his craft well while pitching in Wrigley Field, the smallest ball park in the major leagues.

With the often lackluster Cub teams, he pitched in bad luck. He still shares a record for the most 1–0 losses in a season, five, in 1968, in games against pitchers that included Bob Gibson and Don Drysdale. Still, he won the Cy Young Award in 1971, with a 24–13 record, leading the league in complete games, with 30, innings pitched, 325, and strike-outs, 304. He won 20 games six straight seasons for the Cubs, and then fell to 14–16 in 1973. The Cubs responded by trading him to Texas in a move that stunned him, and much of baseball.

The next year, 1974, Jenkins won 25 games and the American League's Comeback Player of the Year award. Like his former teammate Ernie Banks, he was never on a pennant-winner. He came close, however, during the 1969 season when the Cubs, leading for much of the season, faded in the stretch as the Mets won the National League's East Division, and then the pennant and World Series.

Jenkins was traded to Boston in 1976, traded back to Texas in 1978, released after the 1981 season and then signed as a free agent by the Cubs. He pitched two more seasons and then retired, two months short of his fortieth birthday. He caught on as a pitching coach in the Rangers organization, where he spent several years with their Oklahoma City Class AAA team before being given his release three years ago.

Jenkins was always one of the most gentlemanly of ballplayers, and was thrown out of a game only once, when he threw a few bats onto the field in a pique. "Fergie, I'm sorry," said the umpire. "I'm going to have to ask you to leave." Jenkins had one other incident of greater notoriety. In August 1980, he was arrested in Toronto on a charge of carrying in his luggage small amounts of hashish, marijuana, and cocaine.

He was suspended by baseball Commissioner Bowie Kuhn, but soon was reinstated by an arbitrator who said that Kuhn could not rule on Jenkins before the courts did.

But while Jenkins was found guilty of possession of drugs in December 1980, no police record exists. At sentencing in the Ontario Provinicial Court, Judge Jerry Young told Jenkins: "You seem to be a person who has conducted himself in exemplary fashion in the community and in the country, building up an account. This is the time to draw on that account." Judge Young then wiped the slate clean for Jenkins.

It was while he was with the Oklahoma City team that he found that ranch house. He and Maryanne, whom he had met and married while with the Cubs, had loved the house at first sight, he said. Both liked the solitude it afforded, and the beauty of the landscape there. Her son, Raymond, by a previous marriage, was then eight, and his father had died and Jenkins had adopted him. "I call him Fergie usually," said Raymond, a bright, good-natured youth, "unless I want something. Then I call him Dad."

Ray, who had known only cities, had to make adjustments to farm life, and did, getting to learn how to care for and ride horses, and, at paternal urging, to paint posts, too, not always with pleasure.

Adjustments for him, and for Jenkins, would grow increasingly harder when Maryanne was injured in a car accident near their home, and, after a month in intensive care, died of pneumonia. Samantha was then six months old.

When Cindy Takieddine, divorced and working as a secretary in a law office in Los Angeles, read about Jenkins's election to the Hall of Fame, she called the Cubs to try to locate him, to congratulate him. She managed to get his home phone number. She had met him when he was a young player with the Cubs and she was nineteen.

They had struck up a friendship, although Jenkins says it was never a romance, and he hadn't seen her in about fifteen years. When she learned from Jenkins on the phone that his wife had died, she offered to come with a girlfriend to Guthrie on her vacation, and help him any way she could. He accepted.

"They cooked, they took care of the house and they watched over the kids," Jenkins recalled. The girlfriend soon went back home, but Cindy stayed and they fell in love.

Six months ago they became engaged. He said she started feeling pressure from friends about marriage. "It'll happen, just not right away," Jenkins told her. Meanwhile, she was a great mother and, essentially, a great wife, Jenkins said. She traded her white slacks for farm overalls. She was a talented decorator around the house, putting, as the foreman, Christian, called it, "the woman's touch on it, with all them frills and friggles."

He added, "And she was always a lady."

Cindy kept the checkbook in order and looked over the endorsements and the personal-appearance schedule for Jenkins, who flew periodically to card shows, fantasy camps and speaking engagements. She grew to be a loving and concerned mother to Raymond and developed a close bond with Samantha. Cindy also seemed to take to farm life, and was active in classes in town, particularly ceramics. She made angels and deer heads and a Santa Claus for Christmas that was placed on the mantel above the fireplace in the living room.

"There were some spats between Fergie and Cindy, sure; what couple doesn't have spats on occasion?" said Lemoyne Hardin, a family friend. "But it was pretty clear that they got along just fine."

A lot of mail came to Jenkins, much of it asking for autographs, and sometimes Cindy would open it up, see that it was from a woman and throw it away. When Jenkins found out, he said that was not right, that it was his personal property. If she wanted to open his mail, he would be happy to do it with her.

Tension seemed to increase when a sports reporter from Cincinnati called the Jenkins home in early December and Cindy answered. He asked whether it was true that Jenkins had accepted a job as a pitching coach in the Cincinnati Reds organization. Cindy had known nothing about it, and it angered her.

"Cindy knew I was talking with front-office people," said Jenkins. "But I hadn't told her about the Reds, hadn't shared it with her. But I hadn't signed the contract. I still have the contract, unsigned." At his kitchen table recently, he took out a briefcase, and two pink contracts, and showed them still unsigned.

"I told her that baseball had been my life, and that I still had a dream of one day being a pitching coach in the major leagues," he said. "But I said nothing is certain yet, I hadn't made any definite decision about baseball. But she was concerned. She said she was nervous about having to spend eight months alone at the ranch, and she wasn't sure how she could manage the place.

"I told her that she could come visit me wherever I was. It appeared I'd be with the Reds minor league club in Chattanooga and that things would work out. Not to worry. I think that's what troubled her. I think so. I don't know for sure. I never will."

Jenkins sighed. "I sit here and I seem calm," he said. "But my mind is racing ninety miles an hour. The other night I woke up about three in the morning and came down here and just looked around. I said, 'Why? Why? Why did she have to do it? Why if she's unhappy, chop off her life like that? And take the baby with her?' OK, be angry at me, but don't punish the baby."

After Jenkins had returned the Christmas presents, he remembers "getting short" with his daughters. The suicide and homicide, the Christmas season, all of it was bearing down on him, "smothering me," he said.

"I apologized to my kids," he said. "I told them, 'Your dad's just not having a good day.'

They understood, I think. I said to myself, 'Fergie, get a grip.'

"But I knew I needed help, needed to talk to someone. I thought of calling 911. But then I thought about a chaplain I'd met in the hospital where Maryanne had been. I needed answers and I thought a clergyman might know. I called and told him it was urgent. He said to come right over. We talked for about three hours.

"He told me that God will not put more pressure on an individual than he can handle. Well, I don't want any more pressure. I don't want any more grief, any more sorrow. I really don't know how much more

I can take. But talking to him was a big help. And I had talked to a priest, too. He told me he thought that Cindy had had a chemical imbalance. But I'm going to be going to some support groups now. I think it's important."

Jenkins is a Baptist, and says that despite his agonies he has maintained a belief in God.

"People tell me that God has his reasons," he said. "I'm hoping somewhere down the road he lets me know. I certainly can't figure it out."

The suicide note that Cindy left on the front seat of the Bronco provided no answers for him, either, he said. He took out the letter that was written in pen on the back of a lumber-company receipt. It read:

"My last statement. My name is Cindy Backherms Takieddine. My address is in my purse. Contact Ferguson Jenkins. He can claim the bodies.

"Fergie said opening his mail is a gross invasion of his privacy—truly immoral. But ruining someone's life and telling them to get out the best way they can—that's immoral. I am to leave with what I came with. I was betrayed.

"I cannot leave and go away without Samantha. I love her more than life itself and cannot envision my life without her. She has been my child for almost two years.

"To all those who love me and Boog please forgive me—I had no way out." Boog was Cindy's nickname for Samantha.

"We had been talking," said Jenkins. "We talked a lot. We worked things out a lot. I never wanted her to leave. I never said that. I don't understand what she meant by betrayal. I just don't know. I just don't know. I've got so many questions. And no answers."

Jenkins was now on the white porch overlooking his property, as the sun, on an unseasonably warm day, reflected on the lakes and the cattle that were grazing, and on the horses. "My uncle Coleman said I should blast the house, that it's unlucky," he said.

"I even thought of it. But this is my home, where I'm going to stay. And I'm going to have a priest bless it."

Jenkins ran a hand against his graying temple and looked out at the farm that he loves so much. "It's much quieter now with just me and Raymond," he said. "But we're trying to make it, trying to get things done. And I'm trying to be his dad as much as I can."

Jenkins said he still isn't sure about the Reds job, and who will stay with Raymond if he does go. "I still have things to figure out," he said.

Later that evening, in the dark, he drove for dinner into town to a pizza parlor with Raymond. The lights from the pickup truck reflected on the red clay farm road. Raymond seemed to be doing all right. His father talked now about the computer game Raymond had been promised for Christmas if he did well in school, in the seventh grade. He had produced a 96 average, and received the game. Raymond talked about the computer game and what he wanted to do when he grew up. "Probably mess with computers," he said. Jenkins smiled.

"Oh, Raymond," said Jenkins after a moment, "it's supposed to start getting cold and rainy tomorrow. I think you'll have to take the horses into the barn."

"OK, Fergie," he said, quietly and respectfully. "I'll remember."

Father and son sat, lost in thought. Jenkins, in his green baseball cap, was silent behind the wheel. The only sound in the night was the rattling of the truck on the road.

Tony Oliva: A Neglected Name on the Hall Ballot No More

December 22, 1989

The 1990 Baseball Hall of Fame ballot is before me and must be mailed soon. Forty-four players are on it—a voter can mark up to ten choices—and two, both new on the ballot, will almost certainly and properly be elected. They are Jim Palmer, the tall, elegantly effective pitcher, and Joe Morgan, built, as Russell Baker once wrote about someone else, like an ambulatory fireplug, but he played like a dream.

Others have been on the ballot for one or more years, and some deserve inclusion, like Bunning, Cepeda, Jenkins, Gaylord Perry, and Wills. Others may fall just short, like Flood, Lyle, Kaat, Kuenn, Mazeroski, Miñoso, Munson, Santo and Pinson.

But the eye stops at another name: Tony Oliva. And a moment is recalled. It is a May morning in 1973, Oliva, in town with the Minnesota Twins seemed oddly ebullient for a man whose career, at the age of thirty-two, was in danger. He was having breakfast in his hotel coffee shop. "When the weather comes good all over," he said, "my knee won't be stiff no more. Then I start to hit the bullets."

Oliva, born in Cuba, had a history of hitting baseballs that, to the naked eye, looked like missiles from rifles. But he had injured his knee diving for a ball in right field, undergone surgery and had missed virtually all of the previous season.

"I don't play for so long my timing is not too good, either," he said. "But I have the confidence still at bat. One thing I always know: if one time I miss, the next time I go smoking for sure."

Oliva, 6-foot-2, 200 pounds, never again smoked quite the way he had been accustomed. He played a few more years, and exclusively as a designated hitter, since he could barely run on his damaged knee. No longer was he the left-handed-hitting terror who, for eight straight seasons, beginning in 1964, was among the very best in baseball.

Three times he led the league in batting average, including his first two years in the major leagues, and twice he came in second and, another time, third. He was the *Sporting News* Player of the Year in 1965 and 1971. And a Gold Glove winner, too.

In his memoir, *A False Spring*, Pat Jordan, a minor leaguer in 1960, recalled: "One day a farm team of the Minnesota Twins came to camp. Its star, a nineteen-year-old Cuban refugee named Tony Oliva, had already fashioned a legendary reputation in the minors as a 'pure hitter.' Players drifted away from their diamonds to watch Oliva hit against the best pitchers in camp. He went 7-for-9 in a doubleheader, hitting nothing but line drives.

"After each line drive the players watching from behind the home-plate screen shook their heads in disbelief. Oliva batted with a knock-kneed stance. As he waited for the pitch, his weight rested on his front foot, the one closest to the pitcher. He lunged at the ball.

"It was all wrong, argued the players watching. You're supposed to keep your weight on the back foot. Someone grabbed a bat, assumed a stance behind the screen and demonstrated. Others argued. Ted Williams says. That's Ted Williams interrupted another. Meanwhile, Oliva, unnoticed, steps into the batter's box and lines the first pitch six inches over the cap of our pitcher, who dives to the ground."

Oliva had been signed by the Senators (before they became the Twins) and left home in Pinar del Rio, Cuba, without knowing a word of English (but a language that he has developed to a conversational extent). In the Appalachian League, his manager wrote two messages on a piece of paper so Tony could order in a restaurant. One message read, "ham and eggs," and the other, "fried chicken." That's all he ate for three months—that and he feasted off pitchers.

He soon learned to order other items, but for more than a decade his diet concerning hurlers remained the same.

Then he suffered torn cartilage, and had to change his stance. "I'd be asleep," recalled Rod Carew, when they were roommates, "and wake up and hear Tony cry like a baby in the night because of the pain. He'd get up and wander all over the hotel trying to find ice to put on his knee.

He had been such a beautiful hitter, such a powerful hitter, and now it was awful to watch him this way."

When it was over, after 11 full seasons, Oliva had a .304 batting average—one of the best in recent years. Some Hall of Fame players have long careers. Others, like Sandy Koufax and Dizzy Dean, have, because of injury, shorter but still stellar ones. Oliva is in that category.

He has been on the Hall of Fame ballot for nine years, and keeps coming up short. He has been grievously overlooked. It's time that Tony Oliva, who "smoked for sure," got his ticket to Cooperstown.

* * *

Thirty-four Decembers after the column above was written, on December 5, 2021, Tony Oliva, at age eighty-one, was voted into the Baseball Hall of Fame.

Part VII: 1980s—Record Breakers and Then Some

Dave Winfield: One Definition of a Winner

August 28, 1986

George Steinbrenner recently said that, yes, he had paid too much for Dave Winfield. Before the 1981 season, he signed Winfield for nearly $20 million for 10 years. "It was much too much," said Steinbrenner recently. "For that money, a man must be a genuine superstar."

No one, as far as we know, gave Steinbrenner the ultimatum that either he sign Winfield or they'd sink his boats. It all came out of Steinbrenner's own mind, and willing wallet.

Obviously, he thought Winfield was a genuine superstar from his record at San Diego, where the outfielder played eight seasons, from 1973 through 1980.

And so the question raised by Steinbrenner's remarks are: Did he get the player he thought he signed? Or did he get a reasonable facsimile? Or not so reasonable, like an Elvis impersonator.

Now in his sixth season with the Yankees, Winfield's statistics with the Yankees compared with those when he was with the Padres are instructive. The following statistics were graciously compiled by Peter Hirdt, co-author of the annual *Elias Baseball Analyst*.

281

Winfield's overall batting average with San Diego was .284. With the Yankees, it is .289. With the Padres, he drove in 91 runs for every 162 games played, and hit one homer for every 26 times at bat. With the Yankees, Winfield has driven in 116 runs for every 162 games, and hit one homer for every 22 times at bat. There are two statistics generally considered good barometers of clutch hitting. One is a player's overall batting percentage with runners in scoring position. With San Diego, Winfield's was 32 percent. With the Yankees, it has been 36 percent—putting Winfield sixth among active players. Of the other stars in the American League, George Brett is 18th and Jim Rice 53rd.

Another significant percentage is driving in runners from scoring position in late innings—seventh inning onward—with the team at bat either tied, or one, two, or three runs down. These percentages have been kept only since 1975. And for Winfield's last six years with San Diego, he hit 28 percent of the time in that situation. With the Yankees, it has been 42 percent. That's 50 percent higher. Winfield is fifth, behind the leader, Eddie Murray. Don Mattingly is 16th, and Rice is 61st and Brett 91st.

Steinbrenner has often compared Winfield's clutch hitting unfavorably with that of Reggie Jackson, when Jackson was with the Yankees. In Jackson's five years with the Yankees, he hit 34 percent of the time with runners in scoring position, 2 percentage points under Winfield, and hit only 28 percent in late-inning clutch situations.

So Winfield has produced more in average and in power with the Yankees than he did with the Padres, and over a full season has been an outstanding clutch hitter. Steinbrenner, though, has frequently disparaged Winfield as a clutch hitter, and done so since Winfield's poor championship series and World Series in 1981.

Steinbrenner never mentions that Winfield was outstanding in the division series—it was the strike year, remember—when he hit .350 as the Yankees beat Milwaukee in five games.

It is true that in the Oakland championship series and the Dodger World Series, he got only three hits and three runs batted in.

And for those three series, he went 10-for-55, for a .182 average. Now, is it fair to take 55 times at bat in a player's career as indicative of his abilities? Especially when he has come to bat more than 7,000 times? (Don Mattingly, in a year that he batted .324, had a streak when he was 10-for-54.) Or did Winfield have the bad luck to go into a slump at a bad time? It was, recall, the only playoffs and World Series he has ever been in. And numerous great players have had miserable postseason appearances.

Mickey Mantle, for example, batted 6-for-46 for a .130 batting over three World Series, from 1961 to 1963. Ty Cobb, in his first World Series, batted .200. So did Ted Williams, in Williams's only Series. In Eddie Murray's first World Series, he hit just .154. Frank Robinson batted .188 in the 1969 Series against the Mets. In the 1922 World Series, the unfortunate Babe Ruth could muster only a .118 batting average, with one RBI and zero home runs. Perhaps the most famous and prolonged frustration in a World Series was in 1952 when the Dodgers slugger, Gil Hodges, went 0-for-21 in seven games.

Even Mr. October, who has been superb in postseason play, has bumbled, hitting just .111 for California in the championship series against Milwaukee in 1982. Reggie went 2-for-18 with one homer and two RBIs in that series.

As for clutch hitting down the stretch with the Yankees, Winfield's September performances hold up. Winfield has been involved in two pennant chases with the Yankees, 1983 and 1985. In the first, he hit .324 during September, and drove in 20 runs. In the other, he batted .261 but drove in 24 runs.

Now, this season, his production overall has been down, but he still has six weeks to improve.

And beyond Winfield's hitting, he is perhaps the best right fielder in the game, covering ground not only in the field, but in the stands, too, robbing hitters of homers by leaping into the fourth row. He frequently wins the Gold Glove, and his powerful arm saves games by flinging runners out at the plate. He is one of the better base runners, often turning singles into doubles, and routinely going from first to third on hits. "When I'm pitching," said Dave Righetti, "I love to see Dave Winfield in the game." So the question raised earlier—Has Steinbrenner got his money's worth out of Winfield?—comes down to this:

If Winfield was worth the money based on the assumption that he would play as well for the Yankees as he had for the Padres, then the answer must be no. Steinbrenner didn't get his money's worth out of Winfield. He got more. Winfield has been an even better player for the Yankees.

Based on Steinbrenner's own criterion at the time of signing, the conclusion is clear: Dave Winfield is underpaid.

George Brett: The Eternal Pine-Tar Case

August 9, 1983

The George Brett bat issue remains as sticky as, well, you fill in the blank.

Last Friday, the American League office determined that four Royals—Brett, Manager Dick Howser, a coach, Rocky Colavito, and the pitcher Gaylord Perry—who argued vigorously over the original call have been thrown out for the last four outs of the game, if there will be four outs, or more or fewer.

The American League president Lee MacPhail is expected to decide later in the week if, when and where the game will be replayed. The two teams are not scheduled to meet again this season. So when to play? On an off day? But teams in the division race need a breather.

After the regular season? But what if one team is eliminated and thus disinterested in the game?

Meanwhile, the original incident continues to intrigue people from such diverse backgrounds as Prof. David Halivni, a rabbi and Talmudic scholar at the Jewish Theological Seminary, to Alfred Manuel Martin, former Berkeley, California, street kid and now New York Yankee baseball scholar and manager.

Professor Halivni was reluctant to be quoted, since Talmudists concern themselves with philosophical matters that generally don't include baseball. However, even though he says he knows little about sports, Professor Halivni admits he was attracted to the situation because of its moral dimensions: the spirit of the law versus the letter of the law. What did the pine tar on the bat have to do with the essence of the game? Was chicanery involved? Was there simply a cunning way of taking advantage of the rules?

Mr. Martin was attracted to it for more practical reasons. The result could cost him a ball game.

The episode and its ramifications are still debated two full weeks after the fact. It seems it will continue, and get steamier, if either the Yankees or Royals, or both, have their respective division races decided by a single game.

The details, in brief, in case you haven't heard:

With two outs and a man on, Brett hit a home run against the Yankees in the ninth inning at Yankee Stadium that gave the Royals a 5–4 lead. Mr. Martin protested that Brett's bat had more than the eighteen inches of pine tar from the bat handle that is allowed in the rule book. The umpires agreed, and Brett was called out, ending the game.

But later, MacPhail overruled them and said, yes, there was indeed a home run, and the game is not over.

MacPhail cited the spirit of the law over the letter. Pine tar in itself doesn't help a batter hit the ball better or farther. It is commonly used by batters only to improve their grip on the bat. It reminded Professor Halivni of a story in the Talmud. A man sold his house because he was moving to another country. The contracts were signed. Then something occurred, beyond the man's control, and he had to change his plans and remain where he was. The decision of the rabbis was that he did not intentionally violate the contract, and he was given his house back.

Common sense, it is obvious, must apply in all matters.

Aristotle said, "It follows logically that it is equitable to look not to the letter of the law, but to the intention of the legislator."

Confucius said, "Language should be made such as fully to convey one's meaning but no more."

St. Paul said, "For the letter killeth, but the spirit giveth life."

And Billy Martin said, "This is highway robbery."

He added, "What should we do, throw out the rule book?" He said that Brett knew the bat had too much tar on it, and was told so, but he still used it.

Mr. Martin, however, also knew that there was too much tar on it—having spotted it two weeks before in Kansas City—but had waited for the opportune moment to object.

Talmudists say that if one uses technical grounds to perpetrate chicanery, then it is anti-moral. Or, as in the pine-tar episode, contrary to the essence of the game.

But technicalities, contends Mr. Martin, are integral to baseball.

"If a man doesn't touch a base, he's called out," he said, "and if a pitcher goes to his mouth, he's penalized." In each of those cases, however, an unfair advantage could result from the attempt. To gain an unfair advantage was not why Brett put pine tar on his bat.

Although Mr. Martin assumes a choirboy's innocence about tricks he may use in a game, he might be better served if he would opt for the argument that clever ploys and gambits are a part of the essence and history of baseball, and often much admired.

A runner who can force a pitcher into a balk, and thus advance a base, is within the rules. So is the hidden ball trick.

The recent play by Julio Cruz, the White Sox second baseman, is a case in point. He knew a short fly was going to drop, but called to his right fielder as if he could catch it. The Tigers runner on first, heading for second and not seeing the ball, heard Cruz, and ran back to first. The right fielder picked up the ball and threw to easily force the runner at second. So Mr. Martin waited for just the right moment to point to the fine print in the rule book.

Now, Billy Martin asks, if Brett and the three other Royals will not participate in the pine-tar game, how about Dan Quisenberry?

He noted that Quisenberry, the Royals ace relief pitcher, had pitched five innings the day before. "He was too tired to work that day," said Mr. Martin. Now, he wonders, should Quisenberry be allowed to pitch in the resumed game?

The rules say that any eligible player on the roster can participate in a game.

Mr. Martin may have a valid point. But as it has been written, more or less, a manager can cite the letter or the spirit of the rule book for his purpose.

Mike Schmidt Has Impeccable Credentials

April 5, 1982

Mike Schmidt used to swing and miss so much that one of his Philadelphia Phillies teammates called him "Ah-tchoo," because he made people sneeze from the breezes he stirred.

Schmidt also made some Philadelphia fans grow hoarse, they booed him so much. Schmidt, a right-handed power hitter, batted only .196 in his first full season in the major leagues, 1973. And in the next three seasons, although he led the National League in home runs, he also led in strikeouts.

It wasn't just his numerous strikeouts as a result of swinging for fences, but the nonchalant way he seemed to accept the whiffs that drove the fans wild.

"Mike," one could almost hear the fans pleading, "do something!" He did, though improving was, he would say, "a dogfight." Now, as he prepares for his 10th full major league season, which begins when the Phillies play the Mets tomorrow night, Schmidt, by most accounts, is the most dominant player in the major leagues. He has won the last two most valuable player awards.

Unlike his early years, Schmidt, thirty-two years old, is becoming the model of professional consistency. Last season he batted .316 and led the National League in home runs and runs batted in—the second straight season he's done that—and led in slugging percentage, total bases, runs scored, total walks received and intentional walks. Strikeouts have been cut down. And for the sixth straight year he won the Gold Glove award for fielding excellence at third base.

"He can hit for average, hit with power, has a great throwing arm, can field his position better than anyone else and he can run—if they wanted him to steal bases he could do that to, he once stole 29 in a season," said Ray Shore, a top scout for the Cincinnati Reds. "He's the best all-around player in baseball today, and just might become one of the all-time best."

Those sentiments are shared by many others. Schmidt is also the highest paid player in the National League—his contract calls for $1.5 million a year through the 1987 season. What he isn't is a nationally recognized personality—even though he has been the National League's highest vote-getter for the last three All-Star Games. His baseball statistics and accomplishments are impressive, but for a player of Schmidt's stature he is much less than a household name. And therein lie mixed feelings.

Recently, in the nearly empty Philadelphia clubhouse at Jack Russell Field in Clearwater, Florida, the Phillies spring training site, the attendant, John Hurley, was hanging up laundered uniforms in the players' wooden cubicles. As he placed Schmidt's white pinstriped No. 20 on the hook, Hurley was asked if there was anything in particular that Schmidt likes concerning his uniform. Some players, for example, like the shirt tapered a certain way, or the knickers styled.

"Yes," said Hurley, "Mike likes his uniform washed." Schmidt sticks to the basics. "I go about my business on the field in the only way I know how," Schmidt said. "I guess it would be called quiet. Sometimes I know it looks like I don't care. But when I'm doing poorly, when I strike out when I shouldn't have, I'm fit to be tied. I remember when I was a rookie and I had struck out three times one game, I was talking to Ernie Banks the next afternoon. He said that I reminded him of Hank Aaron. He said: 'You've got the wrists and the temperament like Hank. And when Hank struck out, he'd just walk back to the dugout and hand his bat and helmet to the batboy. But you knew he couldn't wait to get up the next time.'"

He was wearing a short-sleeve red knit shirt, jeans and white sneakers. His concessions to fashion were the two gold chains around his neck. He is rangy and redhaired, with a red mustache. The red color of the shirt adds to his ruddy complexion, and the fit highlights the substantial musculature of the 6-foot-2, 200-pound ballplayer.

Pete Rose offers salutation. "Hi, Herbie." "Hi, Hulk," Schmidt responds, deadpan. Rose calls Schmidt Herbie because he feels it symbolizes Schmidt's low-key manner. Hulk is for "Incredible Hulk," a character Schmidt believes Rose resembles.

"I don't really have a nickname that flashes on the scoreboard, like a Reggie Jackson," said Schmidt. "Or the flair, I guess. I mean, when Reggie gets brushed back, he flops around in the dirt, he asks for a towel, wipes off his glasses, then digs back in in the box. When I get brushed back, I rarely fall down. I just step back in—I might be mad, but I'm not going to give the pitcher the satisfaction of knowing it, or thinking he's intimidating me. Some people think that's bland.

"I think it would distract from my game if I was any different. I mean, sometimes when you develop a flamboyant style, it can irritate the other team. Baseball is tough enough to play well, why rile up the other team unnecessarily?

"Sometimes I think I'd like to be better known outside of Philadelphia. But you wonder at the price you'd have to pay, and whether it's worth it.

"It's not to me. I'm basically a family man." He and his wife, Donna, have two children, Jessica, three, and Jonathon, one and a half. "Baseball is important to me, of course, but it's secondary to my marriage and family."

The significance of a prominent national name has another side for Schmidt. And that is where the ambivalence comes in. "I feel I have something to say to offer people, especially young people," he said. "They look up to athletes, and athletes can serve as a model. In 1977, I became a Christian. This has given me a foundation, a balance in life, that I never had before. I don't want to belabor this issue, because sometimes pressing a point could have an opposite effect of the one you're trying to get. But it has been vital to me. Oh, I sin. Don't get me wrong. I'll celebrate with a few beers at a disco—you know. I'm not saying I'm a saint now, but a Christian."

He said that he admires people like Steve Garvey of the Dodgers and the golfer Jack Nicklaus, not only for their excellence as athletes, but as human beings.

"The people who criticize Garvey for being 'too good,' are just jealous, I think," said Schmidt. "And Nicklaus—his humanity just shines through. It's interesting now that when he's in a close match with a young player, for example, the underdog who you'd think fans would root for, they don't. They're cheering Jack.

290

"They didn't used to. But he's proved himself over many years."

Schmidt says he would enjoy that kind of recognition. Schmidt is considered by his peers not only one of the strongest and best athletes among ballplayers—he is a crack golfer, tennis player, swimmer, and basketball player—he is also one of the more articulate persons in his profession.

Schmidt was born and grew up in Dayton, Ohio, the son of an ice cream salesman. He was a standout high school quarterback and defensive back. In 1967, he enrolled at Ohio University. But because of surgery on both knees because of football injuries, he stayed solely with baseball.

He began to major in architecture but switched to business administration in his sophomore year. "I had a talent for baseball," said Schmidt, "that could lead me to being a professional. I had loved architecture, but I also realized that to be good it would demand most of my creative time. So I had to make a decision. I chose baseball."

Schmidt was the Phillies No. 2 pick in the 1971 free-agent draft. After two years in the minor leagues, he came up in 1973, and suffered.

His .196 batting average in his rookie year was bad, but his strikeouts were even worse, 136 in 367 times at bat. His 18 home runs and 52 runs batted in, however, showed promise.

Danny Ozark was the Phillies manager, and he and Schmidt had problems. "No one wanted me to succeed more than Danny," said Schmidt. "But he tried to change my hitting style. We fought about that. I'd cock my elbow high—it gave me leverage. He wanted me to lower it. I refused. I once walked out of the batting cage when he insisted, and told him that he could sent me back to Class A.

"I can still remember him after a game when I'd strike out several times, or make an error in the field, he'd beckon me with a crooked finger to come into his office. 'C'mere, you dumb Dutchman.' I hated that."

Schmidt is of German extraction. Ozark says he knows that. "I don't think I ever called him dumb, but I did call him stubborn," said Ozark, now a Dodger coach. Schmidt analyzed the pitchers, and dissected his hitting. Ozark told him he thought too much. In Schmidt's second season, the Phillies acquired Dave Cash, an infielder, from Pittsburgh. "We had been a losing team, with a losing attitude," said Schmidt. "Dave came from a winning team, and with a winning approach. Everything was positive with him. A guy like Willie Montanez would come by me and say, 'Ah-tchoo,' because of my strikeouts. Cash never would do anything like that. He told me he thought I could be a star. For a young guy like me who was being booed, who was going through all kinds of inner doubts, words like that meant a lot."

In 1974 Schmidt drove in 116 runs, batted .282, and hit 36 homers. He led the league in homers, and in strikeouts, with 138. He would lead the league in each of those departments for three straight years.

"I'd be inconsistent, striking out, going through long ohfers"—that is hitless in a number of times at bat—"and suddenly I'd break out with something really outrageous. I hit four home runs in one game, and then I hit three home runs the last three times up in a game and a home run the first time in another game. No one in history ever hit four straight homers twice."

But consistency was a problem which he began to solve in 1979, he said. "I was hitting the long ball but I had never hit for average," Schmidt said. "I felt that if I got, say, 25 hits more a season, I'd drive in about 25 more runs a season. The question was, if I did that, would I have to cut down on my power. I thought I'd try.

"It was at the All-Star break in Seattle, and I got into the batting cage and moved back from the plate—I used to stand very close—and extended my left foot. It was 'wham, bam, bam, wham.' Right from the start. I began to spray the ball all over, and hit with power, too. I kept the stance." He hit 45 homers that season, but averaged only .253.

But in 1980, he raised his average to .286, and hit 48 home runs, breaking Eddie Mathews's record by one for most home runs in a season by a third baseman. And his league-leading 121 RBIs were the most he had ever had.

In the strike-shortened 1981 season, he lifted his average to over .300–.316—for the first time in his career. He struck out only 71 times.

But it was in 1980 that Schmidt established himself. He led the Phillies to their first pennant since 1915. He had 17 game-winning RBIs, second best in the league. And he batted in the winning run in four of the team's last five victories. His extra-inning homer against Montreal clinched the division title.

It is the afternoon before the sixth game of the 1980 World Series, against Kansas City, at Veterans Stadium in Philadelphia. The Phillies are ahead, three games to two.

Mike Schmidt and Tug McGraw, the Phillies relief pitcher, are driving to the game. They are neighbors in Delaware County, Pennsylvania. McGraw recalls the conversation: "For the last month—including the pennant race and the playoffs and the Series—I'd been on the front page of newspapers and magazines, jumping up and down on the mound.

"Mike says, tongue in cheek, 'You know, Tug, I've been playing every day and getting hits and you come in in relief once in a while and your picture's always in the paper and mine never is. I'm tired of this. Tonight I've got a feeling that you're going to come in in relief and strike out the last batter and we win the Series.'

"I said, 'Gee, that sounds great.' he said, 'Then I'm going to race across the field and dive on you and when everyone is taking pictures, I'll be on top of you and smiling right into the camera.'

"Of course, I gave that a big laugh. I mean, Mike is so quiet on the field, never does anything strange, the perfect professional, cool and reserved.

"So now it's the top of the ninth, I've been called in to relieve Steve Carlton. We're ahead, 4–1. I've loaded the bases, and there's two outs.

Willie Wilson is up. I strike him out. Just as Mike predicted. We win the Series.

"I start to jump up and down and then I stop. I turn suddenly to third base. And, oh my God, here comes Schmidt racing across the field at me! And he makes a swan dive right on top of me, with a big, 'Whop.'

"If you look at the pictures, you'll see him on top of me, and smiling into the cameras." Schmidt later said to McGraw, "How did you remember?" And McGraw replied, "How did you remember?" Cool, reserved Mike Schmidt had decided that for once in his career, he would let show on the outside what he was feeling inside.

Lou Brock: High-Speed Data Analyst on the Base Paths

July 20, 1982/Washington, DC

When Lou Brock broke the major league base-stealing record for a single season with 118 steals in 1974—the record Rickey Henderson of Oakland seems certain to break this season—he was thirty-five years old. At an age when most ballplayers are on their last legs, Brock was romping like a colt.

His legs were still good, but his head was even better, and it was the latter that made the difference. Brock mulled and analyzed and plotted the entire art of larceny on the bases. He figured to the tenth of a second the throws and movements of pitchers and catchers, the idiosyncrasies of first basemen, how many feet he needed for a leadoff.

He was revolutionary. He clocked the pitcher's movements with a stopwatch from the dugout, he even took films of the pitchers. Once, during spring training, he set up a camera along the foul line to look over Don Drysdale.

"What are you doing?" asked Drysdale. "Oh, taking some home movies," said Brock. "Get outta here," said Drysdale. "But it was too late," said Brock. "I could spend every night with him and his motion stuck in a frame so I could study it. And there was nothing he could do about it."

Brock was in town for the Cracker Jack Old-Timers Game last night. He sat in his hotel room in gold Bermuda shorts and gold knee-length stockings, and the muscles in his thighs and calves appeared firm enough to still send him barreling toward second in a puff of smoke.

He was saying that he had learned some base-stealing techniques from discussions with Maury Wills, who had broken Ty Cobb's base-stealing record that had lasted forty-nine years. Wills stole 104 bases in 1962. He was thirty-one years old, also a relatively advanced age for a base thief.

Brock had heard that Wills had a little black book detailing the most arcane intelligence about pitchers. "He was supposed to have information on every pitcher," said Brock. "Whenever I'd see him, I'd put my hand in his pocket looking for the book. But of course none existed. If there was such a book with that kind of information, it would have to be as big as an encyclopedia.

"No, all you need to know about pitchers is that they are in one of two categories, the two-motion pickoff throw to first or the three-motion throw. Soon as you can read the pitcher well enough, you can eliminate the catcher. He won't have a chance of nailing you."

Brock said that Henderson is ahead of him and Wills concerning information on base stealing that is available. "Rickey came through St. Louis, where I live, over the winter," said Brock, "and we had dinner. One thing we talked about was that you can have no fear of failure if you're going to steal a lot of bases. You have to have a certain arrogance.

"You know, you're always on the verge of disaster as a base stealer. If you're thrown out, you could be wiping out a potential rally. But you have to have utter confidence. You've got to figure that you'll steal four out of five times. And if they catch you, well, then they owe you four.

"Something else, you've got to love it. You have to love the spotlight—the visibility factor, I call it. Rickey has that passion. It was like when I was doing TV broadcasting and I asked George Brett, when he was trying to hit .400, when he gets to the ball park. He said, 'Get to the park? I never want to leave.' Another point, said Brock, that is often overlooked in base stealing is the pain factor for the hand.

"You brace your slide—if you slide feet first—with your hand. Pretty soon, the pain is terrible. At one point in 1974, I could hardly hold a glass of water.

"A few years ago, Ron LeFlore had 97 stolen bases, and then leaned his hand against a wall and broke his wrist. When I saw Omar Moreno in 1980, his right hand was twice the size of his left.

"Rickey usually slides headfirst, and that could cause even more damage to the hand. I remember I saw him last year and I said, 'I just have one question for you, how's your hand?' No one had asked him that question. He just smiled."

Brock seems early on in his career to have had a bent for the analytical, and to appreciate the little thing that might mean a lot. When he was traded from the Cubs to St. Louis in 1964, the Cardinals had a reputation for sound fundamentals. Out in left field, he noticed that the third baseman, Ken Boyer, would put his glove behind his back and wiggle it. Brock would move this way or that, following the wiggle.

"I thought Boyer was brilliant," said Brock, "because I always seemed to get a better jump on the ball. So a few years later, wanting to pass it onto some of our younger outfielders, I asked him what the process was.

"He looked at me, and asked, 'What process?' "To shift the outfielders—when you put your glove behind your back and wiggle it." "He said, 'Process? That's no process. That's just a crazy habit I have.'"

Paul Molitor's Hitting Streak: "It Was Fun While It Lasted"

August 29, 1987

Someone asked if the news gatherers—they had begun to arrive from all across the nation—weren't simply grasping for something to gather with regard to the hitting streak, only recently concluded, of Paul Molitor. Was it too much too soon? At the end, Molitor was still 18 games removed from breaking Joe DiMaggio's mark of 56 straight games, set forty-six years ago. Molitor, gaining ever-wider attention when his hitting streak entered the early 30s, was still, in historic distance, hardly out of the Ice Age.

Eighteen games is a far piece in a record of this nature. At game 37 or 38, Las Vegas announced the odds on Molitor overtaking DiMaggio. The odds posted on the big board were 100-1.

Only six men in baseball history ever had longer hit streaks than Molitor.

The nation was excited in 1978 when Pete Rose drew to 44 straight games—tied for the National League record and the second best consecutive hitting string ever. On the road to the major league record Rose had entered, what, the Age of Reason? But still it was a long way from the Age of Rock Videos.

Despite this, there was great curiosity about the Molitor streak and, for the most part, cheering for the Milwaukee designated hitter to keep the streak alive.

Sure, the news gatherers had begun to report this event and maybe, surprisingly enough, even milk it a little.

But they were feeding a nation hungry for this kind of thing, hungry for the good news. And if you can't get the good news from sports—especially baseball—where can you get it?

Browse through a newspaper and what do you get? Warmongering in the Persian Gulf, money-mongering on Wall Street and ego-mongering in the front office at Yankee Stadium.

If you stay long enough in the sports section, you'll notice that the big-time college athletic directors and football coaches are crying that the National Football League wants to prevent some of their amateurs from staying amateurs. In other words, the colleges, where principles are supposed to reign, and where sophistry ought to be out, are trying to prevent some of their students from pursuing employment before they—the schools—deem it time. What arrogance. What nerve. What self-serving nonsense.

It's claptrap of this sort up with which the average sports fan and news observer must put. Now came Paul Molitor onto the scene—a fine player, but doubtfully a future Hall of Famer. He began hitting baseballs that bounced onto untended patches of village greens in Arlington, Texas—and Chicago and Baltimore and Cleveland and Milwaukee.

Every day for nearly six weeks he performed those feats. Soon he appeared to be challenging a harmless record, some figure computed by someone among a maze of figures. For if there is anything a baseball fan loves more than his baseball, it's his baseball statistics.

And this was a good one, established by one of the best players in baseball history, Joseph Paul DiMaggio, who, it is believed, developed an ulcer from the pressure of maintaining that streak.

A hit is a positive thing, unless you're the pitcher who served it up. It's one man's achievement, earned honestly, with help from no one. It is an individual feat, combining a lifetime of blood, sweat and batting practice.

You're alone, and the pitcher's alone, and all you have is a ball and a bat and a will between you.

The chances of getting a hit are never in your favor to begin with. The best hitters fail two out of three times. And as Molitor drew closer to the record, the percentage of time that he was expected to fail increased proportionately. But so did the hopes and expectations of the number-less fans that he would defy the mountainous odds.

Even if you root for the other team, one hit is not necessarily cause for a loss, so even rivals can root for a record like this. No one was get-ting swindled or demeaned or mugged or drugged.

Rose's 44 was like that, and so was the record that he established in 1985 when he passed Ty Cobb's career mark for hits, which was 4,191. This chase of the DiMaggio record was different, though, and surely, as it might go on, more dramatic. There was virtually no doubt that Rose, barring injury, would get that longevity record when he got close to it. Rose could go for the collar and still have the following day to gain on the career record.

Not so Molitor. One hitless day and he had to return to Go. It was a tightly contained drama. It was clean, it was joyous, it was genuine, it was happily unexpected. In sports or out of sports, this kind of thing doesn't happen too often these days.

And so we wondered, and watched, and rooted. As they say in the theater, it was, or was becoming, one of those mysterious cathartic exaltations.

Then, it ended. As suddenly as it had begun. Molitor, trying for his 40th straight game with a base hit, went 0-for-4 Wednesday night in Milwaukee against a rookie pitcher for the Indians named John Farrell.

With Molitor on deck due to bat next, Rick Manning singled to win the game for the Brewers in the 10th, 1–0.

"I went up to congratulate Rick," Molitor recalled afterward, "and he said, 'Sorry.' I said, 'Sorry? you won the game.'"

"The irony is the distortion of priorities," Molitor added. "You have the home team win in extra innings and the crowd goes silent. The streak was an emotional and humbling experience, and in a lot of ways it's disappointing. But Farrell pitched well."

The next night Molitor banged out two hits, and a new streak was born. But all those news gatherers, from all across the nation, had gone home.

Eddie Murray: 3,000 Hits Later, a Few Reluctant Words

July 2, 1995

For 19 years, Eddie Murray, despite his excellence as a major league baseball player, a man whose attainments have placed him in the category with Aaron and Mays and Pete Rose, has been a virtual mystery man to the public.

On Friday night, Murray, hitting from a low crouch, became only the twentieth player in major league history to gather 3,000 hits. And while there were headlines and an acknowledgment by the sports world of this grand achievement by the Indians thirty-nine-year-old first baseman and designated hitter, there was little that generally seemed to touch the heart.

But this was not true for everyone, to be sure, for there are two faces to Eddie Murray, he of the scowling, intimidating eyes; he of the gentle, generous eyes.

"Years ago, Eddie had decided not to talk to the press," said Murray's agent, Ron Shapiro, "and I think for that reason he has been underappreciated. When you don't commit yourself in words, people tend to look at you in a negative way. It's not until he does something so positive that it's overwhelming is he recognized.

"But did you ever in his 19 years in the major leagues ever hear about Eddie Murray in trouble? Or any scandal associated with him? No. All you know is that he plays every day, plays hard and plays well."

Murray's achievements could fill a book, or at least several pages in the Indians media guide. And some of the most impressive facts are not only his number of base hits, but his clutch hits—he is hitting .418 for a career with men in scoring position. And his 469 home runs and 1,781 runs batted in put him in the top tier in both categories. He is only the second switch-hitter—the other is Rose—to attain the 3,000-hit club.

After the game Friday night, Murray allowed himself to be interviewed. He seemed somewhat uncomfortable in a setting in which he had to talk about himself, and he seemed genuine. He laughed easily, and somewhat shyly.

"It was nice," he said, when asked about the milestone. "But 3,000 is just a number. It's not something that I focused on. I've never looked at personal goals that way."

Did he know that he was only 1,245 hits from Pete Rose's record?

"How many years did Rose play?" he asked.

Twenty-four, he was told.

"He's got me," said Murray, smiling above his thick brush mustache. "No chance at that one."

"There are two records that mean the most to me," said Herb Score, the former Indians pitcher and now a sportscaster for the team. "One is that he has played in 150 or more games for 15 seasons. Only Pete Rose has had more. And that Murray has had 75 or more runs batted in for 17 seasons. Henry Aaron holds the record at 18."

One record interested Murray when it was mentioned in the news conference. He has a chance to become only the third player ever to get 3,000 hits and 500 home runs (he is 31 homers short). The other players are Aaron and Mays.

"That's some company," he said. "Maybe I can reach that one someday."

"There really hasn't been that much excitement around the club about Eddie's 3,000 hits because Eddie hasn't wanted it that way," said Indians Manager Mike Hargrove. "He has just stressed winning."

But Murray, despite protests that he was taking the milestone in stride, struck out twice and grounded out on Thursday night after getting hits No. 2,998 and 2,999 on his first two at-bats. "He swung at some bad pitches, which isn't like Eddie," said Twins Manager Tom Kelly. "I think he was getting a little nervous."

There are two perceptions of Eddie Murray that seem to coexist. One is the image of him as someone who can be stubborn, unforgiving, nasty—"a cancer on the ball club," the line has gone. The other is that of a guy who is a leader on and off a baseball team, and who may lead by both example and words.

The first time that Murray was publicly called difficult was by Edward Bennett Williams, the late owner of the Baltimore Orioles. He told reporters one day that Murray was "doing nothing," that he might be a bad influence on some of the younger players.

Williams later apologized for the remark, but Murray never forgave him. Murray went to the Dodgers and then to the Mets, where the "cancer" business got its legs.

"But when I wanted a big bat to hit behind Albert Belle, and I wanted a veteran who had been in big games, the first name on my list was Eddie Murray," said John Hart, the general manager of the Indians. "I had known Eddie in the Orioles organization, where I was a coach and a manager. I knew the man. Turned out I couldn't have made a better choice. He's been great. He's a clutch, clutch hitter and has been a superb influence on our young players."

Kenny Lofton, the Indians center fielder, is one of those younger players. "I don't talk to Eddie Murray a lot about baseball," he said. "But I watch what he does. He's a true professional and cares about even the little things. Like the way he gets the extra base, going from first to third.

He'll slow up around second to lull the outfielder to sleep, and then puts on a burst of speed and winds up at third."

As for his off-the-field advice, Lofton said he remembers going to Murray with a problem. As a young man who had suddenly come into a fat contract worth a million dollars, Lofton wasn't sure how to handle all of the family members and friends who made financial requests on him. Murray experienced something similar as a young player out of Los Angeles.

"Eddie made it simple for me," said Lofton. "He told me, 'You have to understand the difference between what's wanted by a person, and what's needed.'"

If Murray was going to give short shrift to anyone, it would seem to be someone he was competing with for playing time. "I had heard all the stories about him, the negative stuff," said Paul Sorrento, the Indians other first baseman. "And I was concerned. But from the first day he came over here last year, he has always been willing to help me. He's taught me how to hit in the clutch, what to look for. His main thing is patience at the plate. Don't try to do too much. Don't overthink. And with, say, the bases loaded, he's looking to drive in one run, rather than three. Helps him stay loose, and what usually happens is that he drives in three runs."

If Murray doesn't like something, he'll give an intimidating look, like the old fight champion Sonny Liston. But sometimes he does it in jest, also like Liston. "I might be talking with a reporter, and he'll look at me with those eyes," said Hart. "But I know he's kidding, and I crack up."

There is something else about Murray, whose wife, Janice, and 10-month-old daughter, Jordan, were at the historic 3,000th-hit game. He is involved in numerous community and charitable activities, from United Cerebral Palsy to sickle cell anemia. "When he signed his first big contract in 1979," said Shapiro, "Eddie said, 'I want to do something with this money to help kids.'" From that came the Eddie Murray

Foundation, which helps provide health, educational and recreational needs for inner-city youth across the country.

"He is," said Kirby Puckett, the Twins star outfielder and off-field friend of Murray, "one of the kindest men I have ever known."

What was he going to do with the ball he hit for No. 3,000? "I'm glad I was able to get the ball back," said Murray, who is planning to auction off about thirty balls on which he got hits this season for charity.

Not only fans and sportswriters, but also ballplayers sometimes have a hard time placing Murray in the elite of players, and, presumably, a future Hall of Famer.

"As good as he is," said Sorrento, "I don't look at him as a superstar. I look on him as friend, and it probably won't be until I retire and look back on things will I think how fortunate I was to play alongside him."

* * *

Murray was inducted into the Baseball Hall of Fame in 2003.

Unflappable Bruce Sutter

October 11, 1982

In the old days it would've been the cavalry—horses pounding across the dusty horizon—that was coming to the rescue. Now, it's a man with a mess of curls spilling out from under a funny red cap and a beard and an even, though determined walk. He is Bruce Sutter. He is a one-man cavalry. He is more than enough.

And every time a game for the St. Louis Cardinals needs saving in the late innings, their ace relief pitcher will be summoned out of the bullpen.

And extricate them he does. He did it tonight again, in the third and final game of the National League playoffs. The Cardinals had built what seemed a comfortable lead, 5–0, after seven innings. But in the home half of the seventh, the Braves, a team that made a habit of coming back all season, threatened.

They scored two runs off the starter Joaquin Andujar, and had runners on first and third with two outs when Sutter was called into the game.

Throwing his unusual split-fingered fastball, he quickly disposed of Bruce Benedict on a fly ball to center for the third out. Just as swiftly, he went right through the next six Brave batters—the last, Chris Chambliss, was retired on a fly to left—and gave the Cardinals the National League pennant.

It was business as usual for Sutter. He had won the game in relief Saturday night and now he added a save. Over the 1982 season, he saved 36 games—one short of the National League record held by, yes, Howard Bruce Sutter.

He also won nine games. That's 45 in the victory column, nearly half of the Cardinals 92 victories as they won the National League East championship by three games.

Manager Tommy Lasorda of the Los Angeles Dodgers says that Sutter is so good he should be outlawed. "You only play seven innings against the Cardinals," Lasorda said. "Because the last two innings belong to Sutter."

Sutter does all this with just one pitch—a split-fingered fastball —only a few warmups and an impressive confidence. Even when he experiences setbacks, when his split-fingered fastball is not jumping but instead is being met squarely and resoundingly, Sutter maintains aplomb. Or seems to.

"He has a special temperament for his job," said Jim Kaat, a veteran pitcher and teammate. "When he goes into a game, it is usually in a crisis. I mean, when he leaves the game, it is either won or lost. But he always has the attitude, 'Give me the ball.'"

"Bruce has told me," said Glenn Brummer, the Cardinal reserve catcher, "that he always thinks he's going to get a batter—somehow, some way. Even if it's a line drive and the left fielder has to make a diving catch for it." Looking Toward Tomorrow

Sutter says that that's true. "I know that you'll always have differences one day to the next," said Sutter. "So if I get hit one day, I know it's a good chance it won't happen again.

"That's what's nice about my job. Tomorrow's another day." He sits in front of his locker, an average-sized man, casual, approachable, patient. In a crowd, he would hardly be set apart. Unless he heard a bugle call, of course.

He is often such a dominating force, but earlier this season he was being rocked, and he didn't know why. "Sometimes you go along and suddenly you are doing something differently—I mean from a mechanical standpoint—than you were before. I just went out of the groove.

"A lot of guys offer suggestions and comments, but you begin to hear so many it gets confusing. "So what I did was call Mike Roarke in Boston." Roarke was a pitching coach for the Cubs when Sutter played for Chicago.

"Mike is a part-time pitching coach for the Pawtucket team in the Red Sox organization now, but he still knows me better than anyone else as a pitcher. He asked me some questions over the phone about my windup. I answered the best I could, but we decided that he would fly in to see me."

Roarke observed Sutter and determined that he had dropped his arm slightly upon delivery. Usually, Sutter throws nearly straight overhand. Now it was closer to three-quarters.

"Also, I guess because I was starting to get a little tense from several failures," said Sutter, "that I had begun to hold the ball tighter and my wrist wasn't as flexible as before."

Apparently, that was it, because a few days later, on Sunday, June 26, Sutter came in at the end of both games of a doubleheader against the Cubs, and saved them both, 4–1 and 2–1. From the All-Star break in July, Sutter's earned run average was stunning—1.47.

Sutter learned his unusual pitch from Freddie Martin, a Cub minor-league pitching coach, in 1973 when he was just beginning his career in Quincy, Illinois.

The ball is gripped wide between the index and middle fingers. Few pitchers can throw it well. Sutter has mastered it, though, like knuckle-ball pitchers, he does not know how it will break, or when.

"I don't try to throw at corners or high or low," he said. "I just try to throw the ball right down the middle." When it's breaking well, the ball will, as Bob Horner noted, "jump right over the bat when you're swing-ing." During most of the early parts of games, Sutter sits in the dugout instead of the bullpen. "That's because a lot of fans want to come down and talk to you out there, and I want to concentrate on what's happen-ing in the game," he said.

At about the fifth or sixth inning, he says he can tell by the way the game is going whether he'll see action. That is, if it's a close game.

"That's when I get butterflies, when I think I'll be used later—and not when I'm coming into the game," he said. He begins to flex his arm with a metal ball that's wrapped in tape.

Then, in the seventh or eighth inning, comes the call. He hustles down to the bullpen, throws a few throws—there often isn't time for much more—and then he strides to the mound, coming, yet again, to try to save the day.

And the kettle drums roll.

Steve Carlton Tries a Comeback

March 18, 1989/Tampa, Florida

He was not like the rest of them, older, to be sure, and off by himself. He came alone, at 8:45 yesterday morning, earlier than most, through the back way.

The day was already warm and the broad sky a seamless blue when he opened the green chain-link fence at Yankeeland, the Yankees minor league complex here, and then closed the gate.

He was tall, standing about 6-foot-5, and lean. He wore a maroon and white T-shirt, the colors of the Phillies, a team he once played for, and gray, pin-striped Bermuda shorts that appeared cut from baseball pants.

A white towel was draped over one shoulder, and he carried a tan gym bag. Beside a batting cage, he knelt and changed from sneakers into baseball shoes.

No players were yet on the field. The few groundskeepers watering the infield nearby took no notice of the older man, of Steve Carlton, now forty-four years old, the only pitcher to win the Cy Young Award four times, who pitched for 24 years in the big leagues, the second-most winning left-hander ever, with 327 victories, and second to Nolan Ryan on the career strikeout list with 4,136.

But last season Carlton pitched in just four games, for Minnesota, finishing with an 0–1 record and a disastrous 16.72 earned run average.

Over the winter, Carlton underwent surgery to remove bone chips in his pitching shoulder. He asked several clubs for a chance to pitch again, saying that his shoulder was feeling fine. He was turned down.

Then he called Dallas Green, the new Yankee manager, whom he played for in Philadelphia. Green agreed to give him a place to throw, but gave no promises.

It's hard for old ballplayers to hang up their spikes, and Carlton perhaps more than most. He looks fit. Also, there have been reports that he is broke, his agent having lost millions in investments.

The other players, the Yankee minor leaguers, all youth and strength and dreams, were arriving at the complex, and disappeared into the clubhouse.

A catcher in a Yankee uniform named Glenn Sherlock, a reserve last year with Columbus, came onto the field and met Carlton at a mound in a distant part of the field. Sherlock was assigned to catch Carlton, as he has been doing for the last three weeks while Carlton has tried to round into shape.

On the mound, Carlton smoothed and tamped the dirt, making himself at home again.

"He's not throwing hard," said an observer, after a while, to George Bradley, the Yankees vice president for player development.

"It takes a long time to come back from an operation," said Bradley. "And each arm responds differently."

The soft pop in the catcher's mitt from Carlton's half-speed throws sounded across the field.

A pitcher named Tim Layana, with Columbus and Albany last year, emerged from the clubhouse.

"It's weird seeing him out there," said Layana. "I guess guys like him and Tommy John and Ron Guidry still have the dream to pitch in the big leagues, like we do who've never been there. On one hand I resent it. I mean, they've had their time, now step aside and give somebody else a chance. But I can understand their desire. If I could still throw at their age, I'd wanna be competitive and try to get people out, too."

Carlton and his young catcher stopped a few times to chat. "It's a thrill," Sherlock would say later. "We talk about how to set up a hitter, about location, and I learn so much. Like a batter who holds the bat straight up should be pitched to differently than one who holds the bat flat."

Sherlock noted that Carlton rarely threw anything but strikes. "And when he'd throw a ball you could see on his face how unhappy he was."

"That's it," called Carlton. And they were done, after about 45 minutes. The young catcher hustled across the field to the clubhouse, and the old pitcher, wiping his face with his towel, walked back out through the green gate.

Two autograph seekers asked Carlton to sign their baseballs. He did.

"I've been trying to get his autograph for ten years," said one.

"It's been eight years for me," said the other. "I guess he's mellowing."

Carlton, who didn't speak to reporters for much of his career, even spoke to one in the parking lot. "How's the arm?" he was asked. "Comin' along," said the pitcher.

"Those shorts, were they cut from Yankee pants?"

He laughed as he climbed into his Bronco van. "No, they're from the last team I was with, Minnesota. Wish they were the Yankees, though."

Then the old pitcher said, "Gotta go," closed the door and drove off.

Ryne Sandberg and Wade Boggs: Heartfelt Induction

July 31, 2005/Cooperstown, New York

In his acceptance speech at the National Baseball Hall of Fame induction ceremony on a hazy, hot afternoon Sunday, Ryne Sandberg, the former Chicago Cubs second baseman, related the following tale:

A man comes upon a bottle on a beach, pops the cork and a genie appears. The genie grants the man one wish. The man says he wants to see peace in the Middle East and hands the genie a map of the region.

After studying for hours and hours, the genie replies, "This is impossible," and suggests that the man give him another wish.

"I always wanted to see the Cubs in a World Series," the man says.

The genie replies, "Hmm, let me have another look at that map."

This drew a great laugh from the forty-nine other members of the Hall of Fame sitting behind Sandberg, as well as some 20,000 fans sitting and standing on the field adjacent to the Clark Sports Center. Few had to be told that the Cubs have not been in a World Series since 1945, and have not won a Series since 1908, as long a championship drought as there is in team sports in the United States.

It was coincidence, and a nice twist, that the two new inductees into the Hall, Sandberg and third baseman Wade Boggs, who went into the Hall wearing a Boston Red Sox cap, played the major part of their careers with franchises that were famous for frustrating their fans with futility. It was not until last season, of course, that the Red Sox won the Series for the first time since 1918.

Perhaps it will be an inspiration to the Cubs this season; they are in contention for the National League wild-card spot. Cubs fans turned out in huge numbers Sunday, wearing Cubs jerseys and Cubs caps.

"We love you, Ryno!" someone called out during Sandberg's remarks, and he halted his speech to say, "I love you, too."

It seemed there were few Red Sox fans in the crowd—if there were, they were relatively subdued. They might not have forgotten that Boggs, who played for Boston for 11 of his 18 major-league seasons, signed with the Red Sox' archrival, the Yankees, as a free agent before the 1993 season. He was the Yankees third baseman on the 1996 World Series championship team. When he took a victory lap on a police horse around Yankee Stadium, it might well have added insult to injury for Boston supporters.

But much of that was in the background as Sandberg and Boggs made moving, even inspirational, speeches about their struggles to, as each said, "realize a dream," of not only playing in the major leagues, but of making it to the Hall of Fame. They said they were in awe to be in the company of those seated on the stage, among them Stan Musial, Willie Mays, Bob Gibson, Yogi Berra, Bob Feller, Sandy Koufax, and Tom Seaver.

Boggs spent six years in the minor leagues before making the Red Sox in 1982 as a utility infielder. He holds the distinction of being the oldest position player since 1950 to make it to the major leagues, at two months shy of twenty-four, and then to the Hall of Fame.

"Life is about obstacles," he said, adding that it did not matter what adversity was faced, but what someone made of the situation that counted. He went on to win five American League batting titles, four consecutively, winding up with a .328 lifetime average and 3,010 hits.

Sandberg spoke about "respecting" the game and never taking "a single day for granted."

He said that he had tried to play the game the "right way," the "team way," and that he believed that with no outs and a runner on second, it was "a great thing" to hit a ground ball to second base to move the runner to third, where a flyout might drive him in.

Sandberg, who could hit for power and average and steal bases, was also an outstanding fielder, winning nine consecutive Gold Gloves. He finished his 14 full seasons, and parts of two others, with a batting average of .285 and one Most Valuable Player award.

He added that he was happy to be a part of two Cubs teams that made the playoffs, but was sorry for the devoted Cubs fans that he could not help get them to a World Series.

A particularly sweet moment during the ceremony occurred when the Hall of Famer Gary Carter, the former catcher for the Montreal Expos and the Mets, followed the playing of the American national anthem by singing the Canadian national anthem, mostly in French. Another occurred when Musial, a longtime harmonica player, delighted the crowd with "Take Me Out to the Ball Game."

Wade Boggs: "Magnitude" Is a Very Big Word

March 1, 1989

I rolled over in my mind the word *magnitude*.

I began this mental gymnastic when I came upon the word in a story reprint sent to me by publicists for a national periodical. The story concerns the courtship of the wed Wade Boggs, a conceded baseball Romeo, and Margo Adams, his bachelorette Juliet. It will appear in the April issue of a magazine known for its fierce intellectual integrity and its photographs of naked women.

The word *magnitude* was used in the following context by the author of the piece, David D. Shumacher: "Not until I read the lawsuit and spoke (off the record) with several major-league baseball players did I realize the validity and magnitude of this story."

This appears early in the first of a two-part series of interviews entitled "Designated Swinger."

It is Ms. Adams who reveals the off-the-field gambols of Wade Boggs, the five-time American League batting champion with halo askew, and some of his Red Sox teammates. This is offered to the magazine's clientele as "magnitude."

She contributed this in her spare time, and for a reported $100,000 payment from the magazine, while awaiting trial in her quest to wring

$500,000 from Boggs, contending that she lost time away from her office job while she and Wade trysted. She had originally sought another $11.5 million for anguish, but a court last week ruled that she would not be entitled to it.

Now, it is one thing for the magazine to run an article and boast that this is great, sleazy stinkbug stuff that will titillate its readership.

But when they cart in the word *magnitude*, I sit up.

In the news these days we learn, for example, about a head of state seeming to impersonate Tony "Big Tuna" Accardo and putting out a hit contract on an author, though to be fair to the original Big Tuna he was never known to have ordered a scribe rubbed out.

The effects of such an order by the head of state had serious repercussions concerning the First Amendment in this country, and the health of the author. That's magnitude.

We read of child abuse increasing. And drug abuse increasing. And high school students who graduate with fourth-grade reading levels. That's magnitude.

We read about possible drinking problems of one whom the President believes to be the most qualified person to head the Defense Department. In other words, he'd be the man in charge of protecting the populace. That's magnitude.

Meanwhile, the magazine informs us that the Boggs and Adams wrangle is magnitudinous because it is "one of the greatest scandals to hit the game."

Maybe it is, and maybe, like one of the definitions of "magnitude" in the Random House Dictionary, it is of "great importance or consequence: affairs of magnitude." But somehow this affair doesn't seem on a plane with the Black Sox scandal, when players dumped the World Series for cash from gamblers. Nor is it on a level with the pitcher Denny McLain running a bookmaking operation from the clubhouse of the Detroit Tigers.

And it hardly equates to the unspeakable policy of owners, until after the Second World War, to bar blacks from playing organized baseball, or, in recent times, their sluggishness in hiring black and Hispanic managers or front-office staff. That's Scandal. That's Magnitude. In regard to interpersonal relationships, the word magnitude might better be applied to, say, presidents or presidential aspirants involved in liaisons that possibly threaten the well-being of the nation.

Magnitude in regard to amorous affairs is a practice, it seems safe to assume, that was not invented by Adams and Boggs, and would surely include such non-baseball luminaries as Henry VIII and Anne Boleyn, Napoleon, and Josephine, and all those persons who run around undressing each other on *Dynasty*. To say nothing of Adams's namesake, and Eve.

This, though, is not to minimize the private magnitude of the Adams chronicle. Adams and Boggs aside—after all, the twosome entered not blindly into that risky state of woo—the pain that all this inflicts on Boggs's family, and those innocent bystanders mentioned in the article, and others dragged in, is real, considerable, and probably indelible.

The article ends. But just below it is what mag editors term "the teaser." It reads:

"Next month: Margo bares all—sensational pictures, plus more on baseball wives and groupies and sizzling locker room intrigue."

That is, more magnitude.

Ozzie Smith: Acrobatic Shortstop

October 18, 1985

Marvella Smith's son, Osborne Earl, says that when he was growing up in the Watts section of Los Angeles, his mother gave him the most important piece of advice in his life. "Son," she said, "always put your heart in whatever you do."

315

The lad had dreams of becoming a big-league baseball player, but he was rather small. He would grow to be no taller than 5-foot-9 and weigh no more than 155 pounds.

And there were people who didn't give young Smith a chance to succeed at his dream.

"Those were people I didn't listen to," said Smith.

Mrs. Smith's son is thirty years old now and known to a large segment of the Western Hemisphere as Ozzie Smith, or the "Wizard of Ahs," shortstop without peer. On Wednesday, he was voted the most valuable player in the National League Championship series. He will lead the Cardinals into the World Series against the Royals Saturday night in Kansas City.

Anyone who has watched him play baseball in his eight big-league seasons would surely agree that he has followed his mother's counsel to the letter.

He has become famous as a glove man: He is in the first year of a $2 million-a-year contract for four years, and got that loot primarily for his defensive play, because his career batting average going into this season was .238.

But this season was his best at bat. He hit .276 with six home runs (he previously had only seven homers for his entire big-league career), and it was his work with the bat, as much as that with his glove, that made the difference in the last two games of the championship series.

In Game 5, he hit a dramatic home run in the bottom of the ninth inning to snap a tie—the first left-handed homer in this switch-hitter's big-league career. Then in Game 6 he banged out a triple in the seventh inning to score a run and tie the game. In the ninth inning he kept alive a rally by walking on a 3-and-2 pitch and set the stage for Jack Clark's pennant-winning homer.

"People have always underestimated Oz's ability at the plate," said Manager Whitey Herzog of the Cardinals. "His role, batting in the eighth spot in the order, is to get on base, and if the pitcher batting behind him can't get him to second, he can steal second."

But his offensive ability remains secondary to his defense. For Ozzie Smith is considered by some to be the greatest fielding shortstop in the history of baseball.

His play in the field is simply spectacular: He leaps, he dives, he whirls. He seems to appear behind second base as if popping from underground; he can soar and stay aloft like a hummingbird and wait for a line drive to arrive.

He has won four straight Gold Gloves for fielding excellence. In 1980 he broke the season record for assists by a shortstop with 621, a testament to his great range. The previous record, 601, was set by Glenn Wright of Pittsburgh in 1924.

"What is overlooked about Ozzie," said the Cardinal second baseman, Tommy Herr, "is that he always makes the routine plays. Most guys can make a lot of good plays, and a lot of guys can sometimes make a great play, but they'll blow the easy ones, and that hurts a team. But Ozzie has tremendous powers of concentration. He won't take the easy ones for granted, and that's how they get muffed up."

Smith agrees that he has a high level of concentration.

"Because I wasn't born with a lot of size," he says, "I've had to maybe work harder than some others. Or concentrate harder. You play like you practice, and so I just don't go out in infield practice for the sake of taking some ground balls. I have a purpose in what I'm doing out there—testing the infield bounces, working on my moves."

Considering that he isn't blessed with an extraordinarily strong throwing arm, he still has great success with throws. "What I try to do when, say, I pick up a grounder over second," said Smith, "is have my body somewhat turned to first base before I catch the ball. In this way I can throw faster than otherwise.

"My mother also told me that if you don't put anything into something, you won't get anything out. I want to look back and say, I got everything out of all I had, and I never cheated anyone who paid me to play, or paid to see me play."

Smith was not drafted by any major-league team after he graduated from high school. He went to California Polytech in San Luis Obispo, was a walk-on on the baseball team, and soon earned a scholarship.

He was drafted after his junior year by Detroit, but didn't like the Tigers offer, so he decided to return to college, where he majored in social science.

The next year, the Padres drafted him.

"I thought I'd give myself five years and if I didn't make the major leagues by then, I'd quit baseball and, I don't know, maybe teach social science," he said.

After 68 games at Walla Walla in the Northwest League, San Diego called him up. After a contract dispute in 1981, the Padres traded him to St. Louis for Garry Templeton.

In his first year with the Cardinals, he led the team to a pennant and the World Series championship.

Before the seventh game of the Series, before a packed crowd at Busch Stadium, Ozzie the acrobat (as a child he liked to jump on a trampoline and dive into a sawdust pit in a nearby lumberyard) ran out to his position and performed a handspring and a back flip. And then he helped defeat the Brewers in Game 7.

Phil Niekro: Trying To Pitch Forever

September 5, 1987

About a year ago, Ted Turner, the television mogul who has boats and a baseball team to play with, wondered about Phil Niekro, his former

318

knuckleballing employee on the Atlanta Braves. Niekro was then seeking to hang on as a pitcher in the major leagues.

"When is he going to learn," said Turner, "that you can't pitch forever?" Personally, I wish he'd never learn. Niekro, or "Knucksie," as he is known in diamond circles, is forty-eight years old, about nine months older than the sportswriter who is taking up space here. Niekro was the last major league ballplayer who is actually older than the writer.

We get older—the world around us gets older—marking time in various ways, and not simply by the calendar.

Trees do it by their rings, tigers by their teeth, and some of us one day look around and wonder how it is that cops have suddenly got so young.

Mark Twain saw it another way. He made rare visits back to Hannibal, Missouri, and in his last, at age seventy-seven, he returned to the house on Hill Street in which he was born. "It all seems so small to me," Twain said. "I suppose if I should come back here ten years from now it would be the size of a birdhouse." For many Americans, time is marked, not necessarily by the shrinking of their old houses, but by the aging of their baseball heroes.

There was a time when the ballplayers all seemed so much older, men we once noticed standing outside of the clubhouse waiting for autographs after a game, who smoked cigarettes and wore bright sport coats and slicked back their hair.

Now if, as seems plausible, it is indeed the end of the road for Philip Henry Niekro, born on April Fool's Day, 1939, then all of the ballplayers, every single last tobacco-plug one of them, will be younger than the writer.

Last Monday night, Knucksie was given his release by the Toronto Blue Jays, who only about a month before had purchased him from the Indians for the stretch drive.

Now Niekro, the white-haired hurler of 20 vintage years and four teams in the big leagues, has gone home to Linburg, Georgia, conceivably never again to float a baseball seriously in a ball game. But it is the decision of others, not his.

When would Knucksie learn that you can't pitch forever? Well, after the Braves released him at age forty-four—and he had the second-best pitching record on the team—he went to the Yankees and won 32 games in two seasons.

His last victory for the Yankees, before they released him, was the final game of the 1985 season. He beat the Blue Jays, 8–0, and did it with the utmost style. At age forty-six, he wanted to prove that his fastball could still win games. And so he stored the knuckleball that he had thrown almost exclusively for his entire professional career.

And he set the Blue Jays down inning after inning.

Niekro's brother, Joe, also a pitcher then on the Yankees, queried him about the knuckleball in the fifth inning. "When you gonna throw one?" he asked.

"Not even my brother believed I could do it," Phil Niekro recalled. "I just looked at him and laughed."

But Knucksie threw two knucklers, the last two pitches to the last batter of the game, Jeff Burroughs, and struck him out. "I just couldn't see pitching the most important game of my career without throwing one," he said. In 1986 Niekro was signed by the Indians, and had an 11–11 record with one of baseball's worst teams. This season he was 7–11 before being dealt to Toronto. He pitched three games there. "He did well in the first two," said Howard Starkman, the Toronto public relations director. "But he didn't win. And then the third game, last Saturday, Oakland bombed him for five runs in two-thirds of an inning."

Knucksie ached for a chance to get into a World Series, his first. He had been in two league championships series—both with Atlanta, in

320

1969 against the Mets and 1982 against the Cardinals—and his club lost in three straight both times. He had hoped for this chance with Toronto. It was not to be.

When Toronto got Mike Flanagan from the Orioles—they wanted another southpaw—they found their forty-eight-year-old right-hander dispensable.

Niekro had said several years ago that it made him mad when he had lost five games in a row and people said he was finished. He complained that they don't say that about younger pitchers. "But with me, two losses in a row means curtain time," he said. Exactly. He was 0–2 with Toronto. In his autobiography, *Knuckle Balls*, Knucksie wrote that it also riled him that people kept asking him the same question, "When are you going to retire?"

"I don't know when I'm gonna retire and nobody can convince me why a forty-seven or forty-eight-year-old man can't continue to play baseball," he said. "Someone has to be the oldest player in the game and I guess that I just have to be that person."

While he was still that person, in 1985, Niekro recalled being in the Yankee clubhouse on Old-Timers' Day. "When ya look in the players' eyes, as they see all their boyhood heroes appear before them, it looks like you're lookin' into the eyes of a twelve-year-old," Niekro wrote. "I feel the same way. God, I feel like a forty-year-old again, bein' around these guys."

Now he's gone, and the writer wonders, what next? How will the world look and behave when he is older than every major leaguer striding the earth? After Knucksie, the deluge?

* * *

Phil Niekro retired after the 1987 season, his 24th year in the big leagues. He died in 2020, at age eighty-one.

Gaylord Perry: The Lonely Quest For Victory No. 300

March 1, 1982/Williamston, North Carolina

The lavender blue telephone rang and Gaylord Perry, the elderly spit-ball pitcher without a team, picked it up before it had a chance to ring again. Any call now could be the one. It was late morning, and he was sitting at his desk in his home here, having recently come in from performing considerable chores on his peanut farm. He still wore a yellow cap that covered a baldish head, and a plaid shirt, blue jeans, and work shoes, which he had washed off with a hose before entering the house.

"Hello," he said into the phone. Then, "Oh, how ya doin', Bob." Perry told the caller that he still hadn't found a team to play with this year, but was still working on it, still thought it would happen.

"Uh huh, twenty-two-pound bags," said Perry, writing down the man's order. "Right, a picture of me pitching and a tractor and my signature is on the burlap bags. . . .

"He what? You sure? . . . They taste good, can use 'em for cookin', too. . . . Well, uh, OK. And thanks, I'll get 'em right out." Perry hung up and turned to a visitor. "That was Bobby Feller, the pitching coach with Cleveland, calling from Arizona," he said. "Remember him? He had a pretty fair fastball." Perry smiled. "Feller" sounded like "Fuller" in Perry's clipped North Carolina drawl. "He has a friend who's a baseball collector, wants to buy twenty peanut bags—but no peanuts."

Perry takes pride in his peanuts, as he does in his pitching. He is selling peanuts -and peanut bags—but he was having no success selling himself as a baseball commodity.

Last season Perry, who is now forty-three years old—he will be forty-four on September 15, was the oldest player in the major leagues. After the season, the Atlanta Braves released him.

Perry and his agent, Alan Hendricks of Houston, are trying to get him hooked up with a club, and they will be happy to take less than the

Three hundred thousand dollars a year he was earning with Atlanta. Is he interested in any particular club? "At this point," he said, "I can't be too choosy. I'm on the phone at least a few times a day with my fella in Houston."

This is the first time in twenty-three years that he has not gone to spring training with a major league club. Although, according to Perry, four teams have expressed some interest in him, none seems particularly eager to sign him. Strange, because Perry won eight games for Atlanta in the strike-interrupted 1981 season, tying him for second best on the club; he also pitched more innings than any Braves pitcher. And tempting, too, is the fact that he is just three victories short of 300 victories for his major league career.

Only fourteen pitchers in history have reached that lofty number, the last being Early Wynn nearly two decades ago; and each of those pitchers is in the Baseball Hall of Fame.

"I've been having to prove myself every year since 1971, when I was thirty-three and the Giants traded me because they said I was too old," said Perry.

So the following season, 1972, with Cleveland in the American League, all he did was win 24 games and the Cy Young Award. In June 1975 he was traded to Texas, and the old man had a winning season that year and two more for the Rangers. In 1978, at age forty, after having been traded again because he was thought to be too old, he won 21 games for the San Diego Padres, and again received the Cy Young Award in the National League—becoming the only man to win the coveted pitching award in both leagues.

"So now I'm forty-three, and I'd have to prove myself again," he said. "But teams say they want to give their younger kids a chance. I can understand that, but I feel I can still help teams—good teams that need a veteran in the pennant race, and poor teams that could use an older guy to steady the young pitchers. A few teams said they want to see how their young guys work out in spring training, and then if they need me, they'll call."

Perry, a 6-foot-4, 230-pound right-hander, has had numerous weird experiences as a pitcher. On the mound, it has become common for plate umpires to come out and frisk him. Opposing managers have come running out of the dugout screaming "Spitter, spitter."

For a long time he had been suspected of throwing the nefarious, illegal spitball—a pitch that comes in like a fastball and then breaks sharply downward as it reaches the plate. It is a nasty pitch to hit.

Perry is not the only pitcher in baseball to practice this "black art," as it is called, but he has developed the most infuriating twitches. Umpires, checking for foreign, moist substances such as Vaseline or slippery elm or grease have inspected under his belt, under his arms, behind his neck, up his sleeves, in his hat.

They have found nothing but sweat. So umpires have brought out towels and wiped him off, like geisha girls. Other times, the game has been held up while Perry was forced to return to the clubhouse and put on a new uniform top.

A few years ago, Perry decided to end the mystery and wrote a book with a Cleveland sportswriter, Bob Sudyk, titled *Me and the Spitter: An Autobiographical Confession.*

Perry tells how it all began. He was signed by the Giants for a $90,000 bonus in 1958. He would follow his older brother Jim to the major leagues. Gaylord came up to the Giants at the end of 1962, not in time to make the Giants World Series roster. For the next two years, he was a mediocre pitcher. "I was the 11th man on an 11-man pitching staff," he said. "The 12th man was in Tacoma."

He knew that he didn't have much of a major league future if he continued like this. He had a good fastball and a pretty good slider, but he obviously needed something else or, he said, "be gone.".

"In this game," he said, "you gotta do what it takes. If it takes bein' mean, you be mean. If it takes brushin' a hitter back, you brush 'im back. If it takes bein' wet, you moisten up."

His pitching coach in 1964 was Bob Shaw, who, Perry says with a gleam in his eye, was "the master of dirty pitches." Shaw taught Perry a few.

Perry experimented. He said he spent hours in front of a mirror practicing how to surreptitiously "load up" with saliva or something else to get the proper wetness.

He tried it in a game against the Mets. He walked the first batter. Then Galen Cisco, the Mets pitcher, came up. "Cisco didn't have a chance," Perry recalled in his book. "He bounced the first pitch right back to me. The son-of-a-gun was still loaded. It slipped from my grip when I threw to Jimmy Davenport covering second base. He made a great leaping catch and came down on the bag. He leaped again to avoid the runner and threw to Orlando Cepeda at first, who dug it out of the dirt. That ball had enough on it to last three throws."

From then on the pitch was a significant part of Perry's repertory, he says, and it has made him one of the most consistently successful pitchers in baseball. His 20-season major league career, with 297 games won and 239 lost and a 2.99 earned run average, has included tying or leading the league in victories three times, winning 15 straight games (one short of the major league record) in 1968, pitching a no-hitter, leading the league in shutouts and complete games and pitching for both the National and American Leagues in All-Star Games. He also has had tremendous stamina, missing only six pitching turns because of injury—once because of a sprained ankle and once because of a back spasm. Never for a sore arm. He has always kept himself "physically fit."

He says that he also has a psychological edge. "Just the idea that batters think I'm throwing the spitter when I might not be helps me," he said. "Some of 'em worry more about whether I'm throwing it than about hitting it."

It is one thing to say you are doing something illegal, it is quite another to have it proved. And Perry has been clever enough to never have been caught throwing the spitball.

"Spitball? You mean, 'forkball,'" said Perry to a visitor. "Right, Jack?" And he nudged a light elbow into the chest of his fourteen-year-old son. Jack offered a noncommittal grunt. They were in the family's Ford pickup truck; Perry was driving his son to school. It was shortly after noon, and Jack, with a cold, had stayed home that morning.

The son, self-possessed and unawed, perhaps had his mind on school—he held two notebooks and books for English and algebra—or on basketball practice after school. He is a starting forward on the junior varsity team.

"You think I should scrimmage or just shoot on the side?" he asked his dad. "Just shoot on the side for today, what with your cold," said Perry, driving up a little hill on Highway 125. The conversation returned to pitching. "A pitcher's got to protect himself," said Perry. "The rules makers are against you. They lower the mound, tighten the strike zone, shorten the fences, put in Astroturf, and liven the ball. Right, Jack?"

"Yeah," said Jack, blowing a bubble with his gum. "And the batters, they put cork in their bats. So you gotta do somethin'. I load up. "Once, I even tried a resin ball. You know the resin bag got all this dust. So I threw the ball and big puffs of dust came off. Oh, they got mad. When was it, Jack, '78?"

"I don't know, I think so." "But they disallowed it. They didn't like it wet, and when I went dry, they don't like it dry." He laughed. Jack, the visitor asked, what would you like to do when you get out of school? "Probably be a baseball player if I can," he said. "That seems like fun." Is there anything negative about it? "You're away from your family a lot, that's about it." Perry pulled up into the Hobgood Academy parking lot. Jack handed him his notebook opened to a blank page. "I need a note," he said. "Just say I was sick or whatever."

Perry wrote, "Jack wasn't feeling well this morning—that's why he wasn't in school. Thanks. Gaylord Perry."

Blanche Perry put the box of groceries down on the butcher block in the kitchen. Gaylord Perry's wife and the mother of their four children—three of them girls—is a tall, lean woman with dark short hair and a direct, friendly manner. She was once a schoolteacher.

How would she feel if Gaylord didn't get a chance to win 300 games? "When he got his 3,000th strikeout, the world didn't change," she said. "It's purely a personal feeling, but I'd rather have him at home. Maybe he's done his part.

"For a long time," she said, "Gaylord didn't really understand—or want to understand—what it took to run a house. He was off playing baseball and living in hotels where he'd lie in bed and they'd bring him breakfast.

"We'd travel to see him, and stay with him in some cities during the summer, but the moving and shifting was always hard on the family. And it was lonely a lot of times. Any wife in sports will tell you that.

"And sometimes we'd be home and Gaylord would stop for a day or two on the way to playing ball. He'd try to get the house in order in one day. I said to him it wasn't as easy as he thought. He said, 'You just don't know how to run a hotel, anyway.' I said, 'Ah ha!' He had slipped. He just never realized how hard it is to bring up four kids, run a house and be out chasing the cows half the time, too."

The large living room of the Perry home has a regulation basketball hoop hanging from the second-floor landing. "It's not there for decoration," she said. "The kids and Gaylord shoot at it. And they throw the baseball and football around. That's why everything looks crook-sided and fallin' down." Actually the room appeared orderly, perhaps because there was no workout in progress.

The walls are covered with baseball pictures and paintings of Perry, and along one side is a long, museum-like glass enclosure containing a flood of baseballs from most of the games Perry won from his junior high school days to the present, and uniforms, caps, gloves and plaques.

"Well, there was nowhere else to put the stuff," she says. "And I like to think we've put it in perspective now. Gaylord has a pretty healthy ego, and I guess you have to in his business. How you gonna pitch to a Mike Schmidt if you don't have a strong sense of yourself? And we allowed him certain liberties, because we understood. As his pitching day got closer, he'd get tighter, and he'd get meaner and meaner and yellier and yellier. Once, the kids were worried because he was nice. One of our daughters said to me, 'Oh, oh, daddy's gonna get bombed.'

"But you can only take so much of nastiness. And Gaylord has mellowed in the last few years. Why? Because I told him that if he didn't, he was gonna grow old alone."

Blanche and Gaylord share a great many things on the farm, which contains 400 acres—"as big as Manhattan," says Gaylord. It grosses $200,000 a year. There are also two full-time farmhands to help grow the peanuts, soybeans, and corn, and to raise the thirty-six head of cattle for market.

Perry helps feed the cows, and assisted recently in the birth of one, Vanessa. He is overseeing the cutting down of trees to extend the grazing area.

With Blanche, he has developed the peanut business. She handles orders. They also do exercises together. "Every morning at 6:30, we put on this exercise program and follow the instructor," she said. "But when it gets to the aerobic dancing, Gaylord leaves. He falls down when he dances. So he goes and pulls on the wall weight to strengthen his arm."

In early February, Gaylord begins to throw lightly outdoors. The person he throws to is Blanche. While he limbers up he thinks about where his career is going. "I remember when Warren Spahn joined the

Giants, coming over from the Mets, in 1965," said Perry, about the left-handed pitcher who won 363 games.

"He was forty-four and still a good pitcher. He lost games, 3–2 or 2–1, but after that season no one ever gave him a chance to pitch again. It was a shame that he couldn't do what he wanted to do, and what he was so very good at."

Perry said he prefers to think positively, that the right phone call will come, that he will be back pitching, going for 300 victories.

Meanwhile, he plays catch with Blanche in their backyard. "The only problem is when she throws the ball back, it's usually over my head or to the side someplace," he said. "So I've gotta chase it down. I guess she does that to keep me bending and in shape."

"No," said Blanche, "it's because the ball is wet, and hard to grip." "Wet?" said Perry, with a little smile. "Spit," said Blanche. "Just like an umpire," said Perry. "It's nothin' but dew, honey, dew."

* * *

Perry ended his twenty-two-year major-league career after the 1983 season, with 314 wins against 265 losses. He was inducted into the Baseball Hall of Fame in 1991.

Bert Blyleven and His Magical Beard

October 18, 1987/Minneapolis, Minnesota

When Bert Blyleven first joined the Minnesota Twins in 1970, recalled Tony Oliva, now the Minnesota Twins batting coach and then the team's slugging right fielder from Cuba, "he was nice young man, nineteen year old, but he pitch like thirty year old. He had big-league arm and big-league fastball and big-league control and he was like today, except no beard, they no allow it."

"I didn't have a beard then," Blyleven recalled, with an upraised brow, "because I couldn't grow one."

The team also didn't allow it. No facial hair was a club policy, perhaps with the idea that someone who had facial hair, despite such esteemed hirsute precedents as Jesus and Abraham Lincoln and Siggy Freud, would be a recalcitrant influence.

It wasn't until sixteen years later, after he had been traded to the Texas Rangers and then the Pittsburgh Pirates and then the Cleveland Indians, and then back to the Twins in 1985, that Blyleven, a 6-foot-3 right-hander, would wear under his Minnesota baseball cap a full, thick, rich red beard.

Tonight, much of the nation, along with the Saint Looey Cardinal hitters, will get a good look at the Blyleven whiskers, and bristling heater and hook, since he is the starting pitcher here in Game 2 of the World Series.

"When I came back to the Twins," said Blyleven, sitting at his locker recently in the Twins clubhouse, "they asked me to shave my beard off. They still had this policy about facial hair."

Clean-shaven, he started off pitching poorly. In the 1984 season, with Cleveland, while bearded, he was 19–7.

"I'm superstitious, like a lot of ballplayers," said Blyleven. "When I'm going good, I'll eat the same breakfast before I pitch, and wear the same clothes, and I like to kick the chalk on the foul line when I go to the mound, though I don't do it at the Metrodome because it's artificial turf and the line is painted and if I kicked it I'd break my foot."

And it came to him that the reason he was pitching so miserably was that he wasn't facially furry enough. He mentioned this to a few teammates. "Grow it back!" they said.

In June of last season, after another pokey start, Blyleven told Ray Miller, the manager then, that if he would only be permitted to again cultivate a woolly countenance, he'd not only move mountains, he'd mow down hitters, too.

Miller ruminated on this, stroking his own clean jaw, and then arrived at a judgment: Throw your razor in the garbage.

Blyleven did, and went on to have a winning season, at 17–14. This year, so luxuriantly hairy that birds could nest in his beard. Blyleven, at age thirty-six, was the Twins second-best pitcher. He had a 15–12 regular-season record and, against Detroit in the American League Championship Series, won two games—including the pennant clincher.

When Blyleven was just a fuzzy-faced stripling with the Twins in 1970, he had a lot of talent, and, he recalled, a lot to learn. "I was in awe when I came up to the ball club," he said. "They had Killebrew and Carew and Oliva and Allison and Tovar and Kaat and Jim Perry. All these great veterans. I just tried to keep my mouth shut and watch them."

One player he watched closely, and who watched after him, was Jim Kaat. There was a kinship between the two that went beyond the baseball field, it went back to the tulip fields, of Holland, Both are Dutch, Kaat's family having been from the Netherlands (he was born in Michigan) while the younger pitcher was born Rik Aalbert Blyleven (the name means "happy life") in Zeist, Holland.

Blyleven emigrated with his parents and three brothers when he was two years old in 1953 to Saskatchewan, Canada. ("My dad, who was a plumber's assistant, landed with only $79," said Blyleven.) From there they moved to Garden Grove, California, and the assimilated "Bert" went on to fame and fortune in his version, as he readily acknowledges with appreciation, of the American dream.

But he remembers what it took early on to be a standout in the major leagues. It wasn't just good stuff, but good thinking. He'd sit and talk with fellow pitchers Kaat and Perry "for hours," recalled Blyleven. Perry taught him about making "adjustments" on hitters and moving the ball around on them—something he'd especially appreciate as he aged and lost some smoke.

"One big thing I took from Kaat was the necessity to field your position," he said. "He said you should always realize that the ball might be hit back at you, and to come off the mound in position. At one time, Kaat didn't, and a line drive knocked out his front teeth. From then on, he'd go into the outfield and have a coach hit line drives back at him. That's how it came about that he won so many Gold Gloves."

Blyleven, too, has won a Gold Glove, emblematic of the best fielder at his position in the league.

He also learned the ways of the world in other respects: he was traded from the Twins because he had had a contract dispute with the owner, and was booed by fans. Pittsburgh lost interest in him when his arm became suspect. Indeed, he had surgery to repair muscle tears in his right elbow in 1982 with Cleveland, and valiantly struggled back to regain his form.

Now, as a woolly if not grizzled veteran (and the second-oldest player on the team to Don Baylor), Blyleven helped pitch a young club to a pennant, and, we shall know soon, possibly a world championship.

He has done it looking a little like Bob Feller and a lot like Vincent Van Gogh.

Jim Kaat Proving His Theories About Baseball Are Timeless

April 6, 1981 / St. Petersburg, Florida

While the other St. Louis Cardinal pitchers are in the outfield at Al Lang Stadium, toiling through their daily sprints, Jim Kaat calmly throws in the bullpen. Now, Jim Kaat isn't against running, especially when he's late for a bus, but he doesn't believe in running as a form of conditioning for pitchers.

It's a theory that cuts against traditional baseball thought—one of many such notions held by Kaat. When George Kissell, the Cardinal minor-league coordinator, asked Kaat to speak to the young pitchers in the system, Kaat consented. "But," he said, "you might not like what I tell them."

Jim Kaat is an old maverick. He's also the oldest player in the major leagues in point of service—this will be his 23rd season, tying Early Wynn's record for longevity for big-league pitchers. And at forty-two years old, Kaat is the second oldest player in the game today. "Gaylord Perry's got me by two months," says Kaat, of the Texas Ranger pitcher.

Moreover, if the Cardinals are to contend for the National League pennant, then Kaat, the left-handed relief pitcher and spot starter, may be an important figure.

Whitey Herzog, the Cardinal manager, says, "We're counting on Kitty." It's a lyrical sound for Kaat, considering that several times in his long career he has heard the drums signaling his departure from baseball. Four teams—the Minnesota Twins, Chicago White Sox, Philadelphia Phillies, and New York Yankees—have all profited in varying degrees from his services, and then let him go; they reasoned that he couldn't go on for much longer, and better make room for younger chattel.

It happened for the first time in 1973. Kaat, then thirty-four years old and a 14-year veteran, was suffering with an injured wrist. Kaat believed it was healing properly, but the Twins sold him to the White Sox for the waiver price of $20,000. In the next two seasons he won 21 and 20 games.

He has won 272 games and lost 228 over his career. Last season for the Cardinals he was 8–7, with a 3.81 earned-run average; he pitched six complete games, including a 10-inning 1–0 victory over the Mets, and the club's shortest game of the season, a 6–1 victory over the Phillies (sweet revenge, they had sold him the season before) in one hour thirty-nine minutes.

When he first came up to the majors with the old Washington Senators in 1959, Ike was still President and cars had fins. And Kaat was a freckle-faced twenty-year-old Dutch kid out of Zeeland, Michigan, who might have posed for 7-Up ads. Today, his face has a deeper cast to it, his red hair is darker, but it is apparent that age has not withered him nor custom made stale his many skills.

Standing 6-foot-5, with broad shoulders and erect posture, Kaat has a deceptively supple pitching motion. He has always been more than just a fine pitcher, he has also been a fine athlete. He could hit and he could field; he's been used as a pinch-hitter and has won 16 Gold Gloves. He slugged a home run last season (the 16th of his career, best among active pitchers), and even stole a base.

"It was against the Pirates," he said, smiling, of his steal. "I'm the last guy in the world they figured would go. They held a kangaroo court after the game and fined Steve Nicosia, the catcher, for it.

"I'm not completely against running, you see. If the opportunity presents itself, well, then you've gotta make adjustments." Kaat began adjusting right from the moment he was called up to the big-leagues. In his first game, the last-place Senators threw him to the Yankees. In the pitcher's meeting before the game, he was instructed to keep the ball low and away to Mickey Mantle. "My first pitch to him is low and away. Perfect. And he belts it right out of the ball park.

"I said to myself: 'Man, I throw the ball the way they tell me to and the guy hits a home run; this could be a hard way to earn a living.'"

What he soon learned was that pitchers' meetings are invariably the same: Don't walk anyone and don't give anyone anything good to hit. "So I had to find out for myself what I can do and what I can't do against specific hitters," he recalls. "Each pitcher is different against each hitter.

"But too many people try to make pitching a great science, as if we're brain surgeons. I try to keep it simple: throw strikes, don't get yourself in a hole by being cute, and try to keep the ball away from the sweet part of a hitter's bat—keep him off balance if you can.

"Unless you're a Tom Seaver or Bob Gibson or Sandy Koufax or Steve Carlton, you're not going to blow the ball by anyone. So I want them to hit it, and get my fielders into the game. I pitch pretty fast, I don't dawdle around out there. It helps my pitching because the fielders are on their toes. They don't fall asleep on me.

"When I was younger I threw a lot harder. As I got older and lost some of my velocity, I went more to breaking stuff and off-speed pitches. I think an athlete has to find out what he can't do. Take Pete Rose. You very seldom see him pull the ball foul. He uses the whole diamond. He knows his strength is to spray the ball. One day he hit three home runs and the next day, first time up, he bunts. He didn't want to get trapped into trying to be a power hitter, which he knows he's not.

"The same way I know running isn't the best thing for me. It stiffens me up. Throwing is the best thing for a pitcher—strengthens the legs and keeps your rhythm. I bet I throw on the sidelines more than any other pitcher. At least thirty or forty pitches about every day. I remember as a rookie going to Fenway Park for the first time. When I arrived at the park I heard this crack-crack-crack coming from inside. It turned out to be Ted Williams taking batting practice before anyone else. He said he thought he practiced hitting more than anyone playing. Same with a pitcher. If you pitch you should throw as much as you can without hurting yourself.

"Whitey lets me go at my own pace here. I guess he figures I've earned the right. Either that or just let the cranky old codger alone."

What has been the secret of his longevity? "Enthusiasm, for one," he says. "The game is like a blood condition for me. It got in my blood and I can't get it out. I've worked at broadcasting and being a stockbroker in the offseason, but what I'd like when I'm finished is to stay in the game, maybe as a coach."

How much longer can he go? "I have no idea. I'm doing something I like and I don't think about quitting while I can still be of value to a team. For some reason, people tell us that in your thirties you're not supposed to be playing anymore. Guys have one bad year in their thirties and they think, 'Well, I guess I should pack it in.' I've never subscribed to that theory.

"I've had some tough times. When Danny Ozark was managing the Phillies he treated me like I was through. He even gave a story to a reporter that amounted to my baseball obituary. Something like, 'The knight in armor is finished.' And Calvin Griffith released me because he said I was washed up. It hurt, but I'm competitive. It got my juices going. And I'm not going to allow the system, if that's what you call it, to beat me down."

* * *

Jim Kaat wound up pitching 25 seasons in the major leagues—his last was 1983—winning 283 games, with an ERA of 3.45 and winning a remarkable 16 Gold Gloves, to go along with the 16 home runs he hit. Kaat was voted into the Hall of Fame in December 2021, at age eighty-three.

Part VIII: 1990s—Artistry and Oddity

Jack Morris and John Smoltz: Game 7 Was a Gift from Above

October 28, 1991/Minneapolis, Minnesota

Nothing was happening, nothing, nothing, nothing, nothing but increasing tension. The zeros on the scoreboard last night in the Metrodome were dropping inning after inning after inning, as if a row of hens were working overtime. It appeared that the best and concluding moments of this baseball season—maybe the best of any baseball season—might last forever.

This was the seventh game of the World Series, and, after three, four, five, six, seven innings, nobody could score. People tried: The Minnesota Twins got a runner to third in the third inning; the Atlanta Braves did likewise in the fifth. But nothing happened. The pitchers, Jack Morris of the Twins and John Smoltz of the Braves, were matching sets of excellence, bookends of bravado.

It was preposterous. It couldn't get more dramatic. It did.

In the eighth, both teams loaded the bases with one out, but the Twins turned a double play to end the Braves threat. In the bottom of

337

the inning, the Braves did precisely the same thing to the Twins, behind Mike Stanton, who had replaced Smoltz.

It went into the ninth inning, 0–0. That is, sixteen zeros. Nothing had happened, and it just kept on happening. And into the 10th: zero, of course, to zero. The longest Game 7 with no score in the history of the World Series.

And there it ended. Dan Gladden hit a broken-bat double, and there was a sacrifice bunt and two intentional walks, and then with the bases loaded and a pulled-in outfield, Gene Larkin, a seldom-used infielder, stepped up to pinch-hit. He was facing Alejandro Pena, now on the mound for the Braves. The noisy home crowd of 55,000 was on its feet and creating a snowstorm by waving its white homer hankies. And Larkin responded. He looped a fly ball over the outstretched glove of left fielder Brian Hunter, for a single to score the lone run of the game.

Suddenly it was over. Suddenly the Twins had won. But the Braves did not lose. They just didn't win the World Series, is all.

Sometimes the gods are just. Sometimes even they, taking time from their flutes and lyres and various dalliances, will determine that we, too, down below, could use a bit more pleasure, especially in these times of gloomy national recession and despairing world affairs and the football season. And so they, along with Kirby Puckett, in the guise of a mere mortal, conspired to give us one more game of baseball.

Not just any game, of course, but a Seventh Game of the World Series. And not just any World Series, either. But one that has gone from the dramatic to the melodramatic, from suspenseful theater to the old Saturday afternoon serial thriller.

Four of the first six games between the Braves and the Twins had been decided by one run, and three had been determined only in the home half of the final inning, to break up a tie game—one concluding in the ninth inning and one in the 12th, with plays at the plate, and, on Saturday night, in the 11th, with Puckett's game-ending home run.

But we needed this game, Game 7, and that's the simple truth. It was only fitting and proper. It was all so unlikely, all so upside-down, but this seems to restore the cosmic balance: Two teams that finished last in their divisions the year before win the pennants. Each team knowing in its heart that it cannot lose, that the fates have ordained that this is their season.

Each team understanding that it has come this far, that it has done it by coming from behind not only during the season, but in game after game, and thus overcoming all the odds fashioned by Las Vegas and Olympus.

Each team has had its improbable heroes: Mark Lemke, brought in for defensive purposes, hits a trio of triples, and is prominent in winning Games 3, 4 and 5; Scott Leius, who was only iffy on making the team in spring training, homers to win Game 2; and Jerry Willard, who had left baseball for a season a few years ago because he was going nowhere, is called in to pinch-hit and hits a sacrifice fly to win Game 4. And finally Larkin.

It just had to come down to the wire, to a photo finish.

The Twins went up two games to none, and then the Braves came back to take a 3–2 lead, and then the Twins tied it up, three games each.

The dream season would end on a dream: Game 7 of the World Series. "Every kid has dreamed about this," said Jack Morris on Saturday night. "When I was a kid, my brother and I used to play whiffle ball and I pretended that I was Bob Gibson and he was Mickey Mantle."

But since this is real life, we know that the gods can be cruel, and, using us for their sport, may turn dreams into nightmares.

Ask Charlie Liebrandt, who got knocked out of Game 1, and then in Game 6 was brought back in relief to start the home half of the 11th inning. He faced one batter, Mr. Puckett, and threw a total of four pitches. Two were balls and two were strikes, including the last, which ended up in the left-center field bleachers.

After the game, a large group of reporters gathered around Charlie Liebrandt's locker. After a long period in the trainer's room and the shower, with most of his teammates gone, Liebrandt, lean, grim, a cup of beer in his hand, and his eyes looking only straight ahead, parted the crowd around his locker. "Nothing tonight, guys," he said to the newsy assemblage.

There was nothing tonight, guys.

Except, of course, for the memory, and the dream, and the nightmare.

And there was the tingling anticipation that all this set up: Game 7. It had to be. And better than anyone could have imagined.

As the scoreboard, in its way, had been reminding us: Oh, oh, oh yes.

Greg Maddux: Modern Art of Mastery On the Mound

June 23, 1998

Greg Maddux is an artist," Joe Torre, the Yankee manager, has said. "Every time you swing at one of his pitches, it's a ball, and when you don't, it's a strike."

Indeed, Maddux, the Atlanta Braves right-hander, permits so little activity on the bases that each game he pitches could be titled "Still Life."

Not last night, however. The canvas got a little crowded for him at Yankee Stadium, in the first game of a series that has been billed as a possible preview of the World Series. Maddux allowed nine hits and three runs before departing after six innings with a 4–3 lead, and he learned from the showers that the Yankees had won, 6–4, with a no-decision for him.

It was less than one of his routine masterpieces—even Picasso had the occasional bungle—but when Maddux had to be dazzling, he was. In the sixth inning, with two runners on base and one out in a 3–3 game, he struck out Scott Brosius and forced Joe Girardi to bounce weakly to the mound.

Maddux then left the game, having been plagued by a stiff neck he had awakened with and which troubled him so much that he almost didn't start. "It was killing him," Braves Manager Bobby Cox said.

Maddux won the Cy Young Award four straight years (1992–95) and is the leading pitcher in the National League again, with a 10–2 record—he has won eight in a row—and a 1.62 earned run average. And he has achieved his mastery so effortlessly that it's mystifying.

Mark Grace, the Chicago Cubs first baseman, observed that Maddux pitches "like he's in a rocking chair." Like Grandma Moses?

"I know absolutely nothing about art," Maddux said last weekend. "If there was an art handicap like there is a golf handicap, I would be a 50."

What, then, is the esthetic secret to his success, which is certain to land him in the Hall of Fame? Now in his 13th major-league season, Maddux has nearly twice as many victories, 194, as losses, 110, and his strikeout-to-walk ratio is also remarkable; last year, he gave up just 20 walks while striking out 177 batters. Last night, he whiffed four and walked none.

There is nothing outwardly noteworthy about perhaps the best pitcher of our time. He has the demeanor of a bookkeeper. He is thirty-two years old, stands 6-feet tall and weighs 175 pounds. He wears glasses off the field, has a physique that would not draw attention at the beach, rarely shows emotion and frustrates batters to such a degree that they nearly weep.

Some pitchers throw the ball at nearly 100 miles an hour, some have wicked breaking balls. Maddux has neither. "I saw Sandy Koufax and I saw Nolan Ryan," he said, "and I knew I couldn't pitch like those guys. I wasn't going to overpower anybody."

His fastball is generally clocked in the mid- to upper eighties, and he uses breaking balls sparingly. "I found that velocity can be misleading," he said. "I rely on location of my fastball and on changeups. If you stand by a highway and watch cars go by, you can't really tell which one is going eighty miles an hour and which is going ninety. And if you throw real hard every pitch, hitters will eventually time them."

Maddux learned from other masters of the mound. His classroom was the dugout. When he studied Mario Soto, he discerned that one could win with, basically, two pitches. "Soto was able to pitch effectively with just a fastball and a changeup," Maddux said. "Which is what I do—though his fastball was better than mine. You locate your fastball, and you keep your changeup down. If that doesn't work, you'll be backing up third and home all day."

Unlike many in sports who analyze and parse and dissect and deconstruct the commonplace components of running, jumping, and hurling, Maddux wants no part of it. "You do something well in sports, it gets magnified," he said. "I just throw a baseball for a living."

His consistency, his professionalism, and his understanding of hitters and of his own abilities, however, belie such a casual approach.

"I try to keep it simple," he said. "At the same time, I try not to be too smart. The fewest amount of pitches you throw a hitter, the greater your chances of getting him out."

Then a crucial element of success for Maddux is that less is more. "In art," Henry James wrote, "economy is always beauty." Not in the eye of every beholder. For batters who must swing at pitches on their fists, or at their knees, or in the crevices of the strike zone where they are least likely to do damage, it is ugly. A tapper here, a pop fly there, a lunge for strike three. Ask Brosius or Girardi, among others. Modern art, one could almost hear a batter mutter. It stinks.

342

No False Modesty For Henderson

May 6, 1991

Rickey Henley Henderson became the Tarzan in all of us, standing triumphantly at third base and beating his gums instead of his chest.

He had just broken the career base-stealing record, and he was not lost for words. He crowed about it right on the spot, right in front of the crowd of 36,139 fans at Oakland-Alameda County Stadium, and before television cameras that would take his sentiments to millions more later on the evening news.

Most of us attempt a little more dignity when the spotlight focuses on us for achievement. We bow, we shuffle our feet, emit an "Aw shucks," and then depart the stage. The moment we're behind the curtain, we leap nine feet in the air. "I did it, suckers!" we shout. "I damn well did it!"

In a game at Oakland last Wednesday, Henderson of the A's had just stolen the 939th base of his major-league career, a record, and the game was stopped and he was congratulated, and in his brief acceptance speech, he pronounced that "Lou Brock is the symbol of great base stealing, but today I'm the greatest of all time."

It was less than gracious, but it was a fact. He was now, in his 13th major-league season, at the pinnacle of baseball base thievery. Of course, fact does not always excuse the expression of such. You don't generally walk up to an ugly person on the street and say, "My, you're an ugly person." And it seemed inappropriate to boast in front of Lou Brock, whose record Rickey broke and who was intentionally on hand to participate in the celebration.

Yet there was some strange charm in Henderson's statement, some poignancy, too, and absolutely some history.

343

Boasting and gloating have a long and tortuous background. And did Henderson say any more than *Veni, vidi, vici*?" Rickey came, Rickey saw, Rickey conquered. And Rickey, like Caesar, said so.

Boasting exists in our fairy tales: "I'll huff and I'll puff and I'll blow your house down." And it was part of everyday speech on the American frontier: "Get out of town by sundown or I'll blow your brains out."

And though a more modest-appearing ethic has often enveloped the sports hero in our culture (didn't pride goeth before the fall?), we've had exceptions, and the swagger in our sweaty stars is becoming increasingly more common.

Once Jack Johnson grinned as he knocked out opponents. Once Dizzy Dean, after his brother and teammate, Daffy, pitched a no-hitter in the second game of a doubleheader, while he had given up a few hits in winning the first game, said, "If I had known Paul was going to pitch a no-hitter, why, I'd have thrown one, too."

And before Super Bowl III, Joe Namath stated, "I guarantee we'll win," when his New York Jets of the stripling American Football League were 19-point underdogs to the Baltimore Colts of the big-daddy National Football League. Namath, though, wasn't so much boasting for himself as he was trying to boost the stock, and the morale, of his team. Many thought it was just the case of a man whistling as he walked through a dark cemetery. But when it was over, and his pledge fulfilled, Namath, in eyes raccooned with lampblack, ran off the field with his right index finger raised: We're A-No. 1, like I told ya.

And there was Muhammad Ali, who told the world that he floated like a butterfly and stung like a bee, and stated his invincibility with "They all must fall/In the round I call," and, as a harbinger to Henderson, allowed that "I am the greatest."

In retrospect, much of Ali's theatrics are considered charming, but many in his time saw Ali as little more than a bigmouthed vulgarian.

Essentially, though, Ali did his dance with a humor that Henderson has not yet mastered, or even attempted.

And much of what Ali did was designed to fill up the house on fight night. He learned, as he has admitted, from the perfumed grappler Gorgeous George, a master of staging and ticket hustling.

There was another point to Ali's act, a much deeper motive, conscious or otherwise. It carried a sociological wallop. Ali came along in the 1960s and became a kind of symbol for the black revolution in America.

"Black is beautiful" was a byword in their communities. In churches and meeting halls, black children were taught to say, and to sing, "I am somebody." And to believe it.

No more shufflin'. No more grovelin'. I stand up and I proclaim: "I am somebody. I am beautiful. I hold my head high."

And that's exactly what Ali did. Today he is one of the most beloved figures in the country. When he was introduced in the ring before the recent Foreman-Holyfield heavyweight title fight in Atlantic City, he drew the longest and warmest applause.

And when the ring announcer said, "And the three-time heavyweight champ-een of the world. . . ." Smiling but subdued, now suffering from Parkinson's syndrome, and with one hand holding the top ring rope, Ali extended four fingers with his other hand at his waist, subtly correcting the announcer, showing that he had won the title four times. And even if that fourth title was only the North American Boxing Federation title, the gesture of Ali's was, well, beautiful. Still.

Rickey Henderson standing at third base gave no hint that he had anything of more worldly, historical, or sociological significance on his mind than pure, unadulterated Rickey Henderson. But he had come a long way, farther even than his sixteen miles' worth of stolen bases. He was Basic Man, Candid Man, Triumphant Man. Oh, man.

Kirby Puckett Is a Rich Man

October 14, 1991

If ever a man deserves a trophy, it is Kirby Puckett, the center fielder of the Minnesota Twins, who is built like a keg of dynamite and periodically explodes like one. He got his trophy yesterday as the most valuable player in the American League Championship Series. He hit a home run in the first inning, went 3-for-5 and drove in the lead runs twice in his team's 8–5 victory over the Toronto Blue Jays in the fifth and deciding game of the playoff. The victory sent the Twins into the World Series.

But that is the least of it, the least of why Kirby Puckett, who stands 5-foot-8 and weighs 216 pounds, deserves a trophy. He got the trophy officially yesterday because he wound up hitting .429 for the series, hit an important home run in Game 4, and drove in six runs in the five games.

Dr. Bobby Brown, president of the American League, in presenting Puckett with the trophy after the game, said that he had seen Puckett play in spring-training games and seen him in regular-season games and in playoff and World Series games, and that Puckett always played the same way. "Hard," said Brown.

But even that pales as reasons that Kirby Puckett deserves a trophy. Kirby Puckett deserves a trophy for being Kirby Puckett.

In the off season of 1989, after a sixth year in the major leagues and a .339 batting average that year, Kirby Puckett, then age twenty-eight, was given a contract of $9 million for three years to play baseball. It was the highest salary ever awarded a baseball player. One year later, with baseball owners scraping gold from mines and delivering it in wheelbarrows to their players, Kirby Puckett's became 40th on the list of players' salaries.

Unlike numerous other players who saw their high salaries swiftly topped, Kirby Puckett never whined, never complained, never beat his fists at the door of the front office and railed, "Where's mine?"

"When you grow up the way I grew up, in the ghetto in Chicago, in the Robert Taylor projects on the South Side, you appreciate that $3 million a year is a lot of money," he said in the midst of a crush of reporters in the raucous, moist, celebratory clubhouse after the game. "I felt that if the club ever wanted to pay me more, I'd be happy to take it. But I signed the contract, and I feel I should live up to it. Hey, I once thought that if ever in my wildest dreams I'd made $50,000—for my whole life—that I'd be rich."

He said he was the baby of nine children living in a three-room apartment on the fourteenth floor of a sixteenth-story project building.

"And a lot of times the elevator didn't work," he said. And not only did he have to climb the stairs, but so did his father, a postal worker, and his mother, who tried to take care of the home and family. They did their job well enough that young Puckett stayed out of trouble.

"They taught us responsibility," he said. "To take care of ourselves. And being the youngest, my brothers and sisters saw to it that I stayed out of trouble, too. So with all that, I just always somehow had my head screwed on right."

He said his biggest problem as a boy was breaking windows by hitting baseballs. "My mother told me to stop busting up the glass," he said, "but I didn't. I'm kinda hardheaded."

He said he knew he could play baseball well from the time he was five years old. "And all I wanted was a chance," he said. "That's all anybody needs."

He got that chance, getting first a baseball scholarship from high school to Bradley University, and later being drafted by the Twins in the winter of 1982.

He says it is no big deal that he plays hard all the time, as Brown noted. "You only work five hours a day in baseball, including batting practice and the game," said Puckett. "That's not so much that you can't give everything you have in that time."

Puckett said that often he's not necessarily thrilled to have to carry the burden of a role model just because he's a ballplayer, but that he understands that little kids look up to him. "I never asked for it, but it comes with the territory," he said. "There are a lot of times that I want to be like everyone else, but you can't have it both ways."

In the third inning yesterday, Puckett had an unusual at bat: he struck out on a wild pitch thrown by knuckleballer Tom Candiotti. "I'm a pretty aggressive swinger," Puckett said. And he managed to reach first base. He was later asked if he still has a lot of little boy in him, because he plays with such enthusiasm. "When you have a child, as I do, the little kid in you is gone," he said. Puckett and his wife, Tonya, adopted a girl last winter. "You play like a man because it's your business."

He was asked, then, why is it he always goes to spring training two weeks early?

"Because," he said, "the early bird catches the worm."

And he smiled, as his black mustache and goatee foamed white from the champagne that his appreciative and frolicsome teammates had just poured over his head.

It was another trophy of sorts for Kirby Puckett, who deserves a trophy.

Ivan Rodríguez's Wedding Was Set for Home Plate, Until...

June 22, 1991

It was going to be one of those glorious little baseball weddings, with the ballplayer and his betrothed walking under a canopy of bats held aloft by teammates from the pitcher's mound to home plate, and there, with a priest instead of an umpire, they would take their marriage vows.

All this was scheduled to take place for Ivan "Pudge" Rodríguez, nineteen, and Maribel Rivera, eighteen, childhood sweethearts, Thursday night in Tulsa, Oklahoma, between games of a doubleheader between the home team, the Drillers, for whom Rodríguez was the regular catcher, and the Shreveport Captains, of the Class AA Texas League.

The wedding ceremony at the ball park never took place.

On Wednesday evening, after a dress rehearsal in the infield that afternoon, Maribel was back home in the apartment she shared with a girlfriend when she heard the news.

Maribel, whose rented wedding gown was hanging in the closet, was cooking dinner for her scheduled father-in-law, Jose Rodríguez Sr., and her scheduled brother-in-law, Jose Jr., both of whom had recently arrived for the wedding from their home in Vega Baja, Puerto Rico. They were listening to the Tulsa game when they heard:

"The Texas Rangers have just taken the contract of the Drillers Ivan Rodríguez. He has been called up. . . ."

The major leagues! Ivan's dream! And, Maribel assumed, no wedding ceremony.

"We were expecting it would happen any day," said Maribel yesterday by telephone, "but I was praying that it would happen after the wedding. I started to cry; tears started coming."

Then, she said, "I picked up the keys to the car and headed for the ball park."

The tears, however, were not from despair, but from joy. And she went to the stadium, not to keep Ivan and his chest protector in Tulsa, but to congratulate him, and share his triumph.

"I was happy," she said, "he had made it. It was where he wanted to go."

The Rangers general manager, Tom Grieve, who may be a hard businessman, now displayed a heart like Cupid's. He offered Ivan a chance to get married as planned and meet the Rangers yesterday in Chicago, where they were playing the White Sox, or fly immediately to Chicago for the Thursday game.

"I want to get up there as soon as possible," said Ivan. But there would be a wedding, in the Tulsa courthouse, on Thursday at 8:30 in the morning.

Instead of her wedding dress, Maribel wore a blouse and shorts, and Ivan wore casual clothes instead of his baseball suit. "We didn't have time for much else," said Maribel, "we had to throw all our stuff into suitcases right away because we had an 11 o'clock flight to Chicago."

Everything had seemed to happen so fast. Maribel remembers when she met Ivan, several years ago in Vega Baja, and she didn't like him at first.

"Too quiet," she said. But soon that changed.

"He started bugging me to go out with him," she said. "Too noisy." But when her grandmother died, "Ivan was there every minute, and I knew what his true feelings for me were."

Ivan was signed by the Rangers when he was seventeen and played his first professional season with Class A Gastonia last year, batting only .238. But the Rangers saw great potential in the 5-foot-9, 165-pound backstop, and moved him up to Tulsa, where he was hitting .274 when he got the call. Over the winter, Ivan proposed to Maribel, and she moved to Tulsa.

"Sometimes he would get down on himself," recalled Maribel. "He'd say, 'If I keep messing up I'll never make the big leagues.' I told him: 'Think positive. Just be yourself. That's all they want.' And he was strong."

They flew into Chicago and arrived at the downtown hotel in late afternoon.

"And the Rangers took off with him," said Maribel. "I didn't know how to get to the ball park, so I stayed in the room."

And, what with the double celebration of his baseball promotion and tying the knot, the two hadn't gone to bed until 5:30 that morning, so she took a nap. Ivan had to work.

The Rangers put Ivan into the starting lineup at Comiskey Park. Maribel watched the game on television. "He got two men out at second base, and he got a hit, with two RBIs," she said. In fact, Ivan, batting ninth for Texas, knocked in his runs in a dramatic ninth-inning, five-run comeback, as the Rangers won, 7–3.

"Did you see me?" asked Ivan excitedly, as he came through the door of their hotel room.

"Yes," she said, "I did."

"I did great," he said.

Maribel didn't reply. "I just went and gave him a hug," she said.

Ken Griffey Jr. Isn't Counting Homers (So He Says)

August 17, 1998/Chicago, Illinois

The clouds were a murky gray and so low on Saturday afternoon here that they looked like the ceiling of the Kingdome when George Kenneth Griffey Jr., the once and forever wunderkind of the Seattle Mariners, hit his 42d homer of the season in Comiskey Park.

Griffey leaned into a first-inning pitch from Jaime Navarro of the White Sox and smacked it into the left-field seats for an opposite-field home run, thus brightening ever so much baseball's most dramatic story this season: the pursuit of the single-season home run record.

Yesterday, he went hitless in four at-bats, but to seasoned Junior-watchers, that Saturday smite may have served notice that the slugger within has awakened. The home run was Griffey's first in August—his last blast was on July 30—and finally moved him up a notch toward the season leaders, the increasingly irritable Mark "Get Off My Blue Suede Shoes"

McGwire and the ebullient Sammy "Embraceable You" Sosa, both at 47 and the still quite distant Roger Maris, the champ at 61 homers.

Watching this from his particular vantage point was Frank Thomas, the White Sox first baseman. "Not going to happen," he said. "The record won't be broken this year, I don't think. Now is the time of year when it gets harder and harder to hit home runs. It gets closer to playoff time, teams are in the hunt, and every game means something.

"Pitchers stop pitching to the big bats. Not going to let one of those guys beat them. And then the hitters start feeling the pressure—they're aware everyone's aware of it. And September is the toughest month of all. A lot different than the first five months of the season. Happens every year."

In the other locker room, Griffey was taking the position he has taken regularly, that he's not really a home run hitter—he did hit 56 last season, his most valuable player year—but a hitter like his dad, Ken Griffey Sr., who played for the Reds and Yankees, among other teams, and batted .296 in his career.

"Dad hit the ball on the ground and into the holes and the gaps and ran; that's how I see myself," said Junior, who in his 10th season has 336 home runs, compared with the 152 his father hit in 19 seasons.

Griffey said he doesn't check the daily charts about the homer chase. "No," he said, "I don't care about Roger Maris's record."

This places him squarely in a minority of virtually one among baseball fans and operatives.

"I just want to help my team win, and play in a World Series," he said. "When you're growing up, you're not dreaming of breaking the home run record. You're dreaming of playing in a World Series."

Someone in Mariners management who asked not to be identified said Griffey was "not as interested in breaking the home run record as some people might think; more interested in it than he says."

The Mariners are out of playoff contention, but one of the few points of interest left in their season is Griffey's hits—and home runs.

(After a fallow period in early summer when he was down to .284, he has raised his batting average to .291, closing in on his lifetime average of .302.)

Griffey, of course, is aware that fans are as deeply interested in the home-run pursuit as he says he isn't. When he hit his home run against the White Sox, the enemy crowd of 21,537 gave him a standing ovation. When he is walked on the road, as often happens when McGwire and Sosa are walked on the road, the hometown fans boo their own pitcher.

"What those fans want," said Jamie Moyer, a Seattle pitcher, who has heard the boos and laughed at the seeming contradiction of them, "is history in the making."

"It can happen," said Frank Thomas, hedging his bet. "Junior's been in a little funk in recent days, but he can come out of it and hit 20 homers in September. Sosa hit 20 in June, didn't he? And McGwire and Sosa can do the same. You never know. Happens every year."

Griffey says he would rather not talk about the homer chase, is tired of it. He would rather talk about his two children, his four-year-old son, Trey—"Trey meaning three. I thought naming him the Third was a little stuffy"—and daughter Taryn, age two.

"I don't come home and talk about my job with them," he said. "My dad didn't do that with me, either. He just wanted to know how we were doing, how school was, did I dissect the frog, that kind of thing. I never knew if he went 0-for-4 or 4-for-4."

He said Taryn loves basketball. "She can dribble the ball," he said proudly. "And when I say she can't play but has to do something else, she pouts and throws a lip at me."

Trey loves a lot of sports, Griffey said, but enjoys baseball a lot. "And he knows when I got a hit or not because I'm standing on a base."

Does he know when Dad hits a home run?

"Oh sure," Griffey said, "because the fireworks go off in the Kingdome. He's a smart kid."

Trey, out of the corner of his eye, also just might be checking out the home run race on a regular basis, like, despite assertions to the contrary, certain other members of his immediate family.

* * *

Griffey finished the season with 56 homers, highest in the American League, while McGwire led the majors with 70, four ahead of Sosa's mark. Griffey hit 630 home runs over his 22-year career, seventh highest in major-league baseball history. McGwire and Sosa were later accused of use of steroids that season and in others, while Griffey Jr. was believed to have never used performance-enhancing drugs.

Roberto Alomar Has Shed His Baggage

December 19, 2001

"Robert Alomar comes to the Mets with some baggage," it was mentioned to Steve Phillips at a news conference yesterday at Shea Stadium. "Did you have any concerns about it before making the trade?"

Phillips, the general manager of the Mets, appeared surprised at the question. "What baggage?" he asked.

"The spitting incident in particular," came the reply.

"Wasn't concerned about it even a little bit," Phillips said about the team's new second baseman. "He's redeemed himself tenfold. And not only are John Hirschbeck and Robbie friendly—they're friends."

It was on September 27, 1996, when Hirschbeck, the home-plate umpire, called a third strike on Alomar, then with the Baltimore Orioles. Alomar argued, Hirschbeck said something Alomar didn't like, and Alomar spit in Hirschbeck's face. It caused a national sensation. Alomar was then a nine-year veteran, a seven-time All-Star, and one who had a fairly low personal profile. A quiet, gentle-looking young man (then twenty-eight) from Ponce, Puerto Rico. Suddenly he was an editorial subject for so many of the evils that plagued society, from the arrogance of big-time athletes to a general breakdown of respect for authority.

After the incident, Alomar first tried to explain his actions—"I just lost my head in the heat of battle, and I'm sorry about it"—then sought to explain how he felt that Hirschbeck had instigated it with a remark.

Alomar said: "He had a problem with his family when his son died. I know that's something real tough in life, but after that he just changed, personality-wise. He just got real bitter."

John Drew Hirschbeck died in 1993 of adrenoleukodystrophy (ALD), a rare brain disease, when he was just eight years old.

The next day, upon learning of Alomar's remarks, an incensed Hirschbeck threatened to kill him. Hirschbeck burst into the Orioles clubhouse—Alomar was not there—and had to be restrained by another umpire.

Alomar was given only a five-game suspension for the incident. At the time, it seemed to be something he would never live down. To many, Alomar seemed distraught at the avalanche of criticism and anger directed at him. He could hardly go anywhere without someone mentioning it. He received abuse from fans in every opponent's ballpark.

"My low point?" he said, repeating the question yesterday. "It was when people thought I had not done something out of the ordinary. That I was a bad person. That's when I need friends, people who love you."

Some thought it might destroy him. The next season he batted .333 and again made the American League All-Star team, which he has every year since. Last season—he went to the Cleveland Indians as a free agent after the 1998 season—he hit .336, his career high, and again led major league second basemen in fielding. He is the career leader in fielding percentage for second basemen, at .987, and many consider Alomar, who will be thirty-four in February, the best all-around second baseman ever and a sure bet for the Hall of Fame.

The ugly occurrence didn't destroy him. There are times when one infamous moment has the potential to wreck a career. It was wondered whether Scottie Pippen would ever live down his refusal to re-enter a Chicago Bulls playoff game in the final seconds. The Knicks Latrell Sprewell has prevailed after choking his coach. Texas Rangers infielder Lenny Randle was stigmatized after he punched his manager, Frank Lucchesi, in spring training in 1977. Soon after, he was traded to the Mets and was booed at first, but he won acceptance, had a good year, and then faded away.

For more than two years after their incident, Alomar and Hirschbeck didn't speak. "I wanted to say something to him, but I didn't know how he would react," Alomar said yesterday. "Then John spoke to me." It was in May 1999. Hirschbeck had been told by a mutual friend that Alomar was a nice guy. "Hey, Robbie," Hirschbeck said on the field, "how you doin'?" Alomar responded with warmth and gratitude.

Since then, Alomar has contributed more than $50,000 for ALD research. And he contributes memorabilia for auctions for the charity arranged by Hirschbeck.

"I give shirts, gloves, shoes, everything I have for it," Alomar said. Essentially, Alomar gives Hirschbeck the shirt off his back. Hirschbeck's son Michael also has the disease and his two daughters, Erin and Megan, are carriers. "If they can ever find a cure for the disease," Alomar said, "it would be the happiest day of my life, and John's."

Alomar, neatly attired in a gray turtleneck and a dark sport jacket, said he had gotten to know Hirschbeck. "He's a great guy," Alomar said. "I feel like we're lifetime friends."

Last week, Hirschbeck was asked about Alomar. "I think he's a good person," Hirschbeck said. "We all make mistakes in life."

And then the talk with the new second baseman at Shea happily turned to dreams of a new season, another new beginning.

Part IX: 2000s—A Look Back and a Look to the Future

So Many Hits, So Much Time for Derek Jeter

August 30, 1999

It was a beautiful, butterscotch day, Yankee Stadium was bathed in sunlight and Derek Jeter, who seems to move in perpetual sunshine, was at bat. Jeter cocked his bat in his customary stance, the bat held in such a high, unorthodox manner that it appears he is sprouting an antenna from his helmet. It was the third inning, runners on first and third, none out and the Yankees were behind, 2–0, to Seattle pitcher Paul Abbott. Abbott, a right-hander, threw, and Jeter, a right-handed hitter, whipped the bat around with the speed of a mongoose attacking a lizard, and lined a single to right field, the 762nd base hit of his major league career.

The myriad statistics that baseball elicits can give one a headache, but a particular number that Jeter is fashioning is remarkable. It places him in a category with the greatest hitters in baseball history.

With his two singles yesterday in the Yankees 11–5 victory over the Mariners, he has more hits in the first four full years of his career, 751 (he had 12 in 1995), than hitters like Ted Williams (749 in his first four seasons), Cal Ripken (745), Lou Gehrig (736), Ty Cobb (729), Pete Rose (723), and Henry Aaron (718) had. If Derek Sanderson Jeter continues at his present, league-leading pace of hits (175)—he is batting .348, third in the American League to Nomar Garciaparra's .350 and Bernie Williams's .349—Jeter projects to 220 hits this season and 796 hits for his first four full years. He will have passed Stan Musial (792) and Joe DiMaggio (791).

"If," said Jeter, seated at his locker before yesterday's game, "man, if's a big word. Baseball's a game of failure. Obviously you fail more than you succeed."

His track record as well as his persona portray anything but the concept of failure. At age twenty-five, he appears the most level-headed of athletes. He is approachable and, as Yankee management has learned, coachable. "He's not one of these young guys who thinks he's got it all figured out," Yankee coach Jose Cardenal said.

In the other clubhouse, Jamie Moyer, a Seattle pitcher, said Jeter had made "huge adjustments at the plate."

"When he first came up," said Moyer, "it was obvious he had talent, but he also had some glaring holes. For one thing, you could pitch him up and in, get him out on his front foot—that is, get him to shift onto his front foot before he swung. You did that with change of speed, and it took a lot of sting out of his bat."

But, added Moyer, Jeter adapted. "That hole no longer exists."

It doesn't exist because Jeter spends good chunks of his time at his craft. While his reputation of dating stars like Mariah Carey may be earned, it has not proved a debilitating distraction to his occupational chores.

Over last winter, he regularly appeared on the Yankees Tampa spring-training grounds to work on driving inside pitches to left field, instead of fighting them off and slicing them to right. He didn't find this kind of diligence extraordinary. "I live in Tampa," he said, with a shrug. "I work on my game all the time."

Don Zimmer, the Yankees dugout coach, who has been in professional baseball for 51 years, said that unlike some superb hitters, like Rose and Wade Boggs, Jeter hits with power, and to all fields. "How do you think he hits balls over the right-field fence—tapping them?" Zimmer said. "He's got a big swing, and for him to have so many hits is phenomenal."

Jeter is also a good-size shortstop, at 6-foot-3, 195 pounds, bigger and with greater range and richer than Johnny Pesky, whom Zimmer remembers as having a terrific major league start. Pesky was a Red Sox shortstop in the 1940s, and had 779 hits in his first four seasons. Pesky got 208 hits in his second season with Boston, in 1946, and batted .335. He dropped slightly in 1947, getting 207 hits with a .324 batting average.

"But they made him take a cut in pay after that season," Zimmer said. "He was a coach for me when I managed the Red Sox, and Johnny told me he's never forgotten that he went from something like $7,000 a year to $6,000."

Jeter, to underscore a difference in eras, went from $750,000 in his third year to $5 million this year, after arbitration. But he says there are no hard feelings about that between him and George Steinbrenner, the team's principal owner. "But he gets upset when Michigan beats Ohio State in football," said Jeter, who is from Michigan while Steinbrenner is from Ohio, "and I do get on him about that."

Jeter, who grew up a Yankee fan in Kalamazoo, said that his favorite player was Dave Winfield, who was not one of Steinbrenner's favorites. "I thought Winfield was the greatest all-round athlete there was," Jeter said. And as far as Winfield's being "Mr. May," as Steinbrenner had disparaged him, Jeter said, "He must have got a lot of hits in May then, to get 3,000 for his career."

As for his career numbers, Jeter said: "I just want to be consistent and play as long as I'm having fun. I hope to have a lot of great years left. After all, I'm still the youngest guy on this team."

Looking around the clubhouse of the defending World Series champion Yankees, it turned out he was right. Only twenty-five. Just a babe. Which gives rise to yet another agreeable, if plump, historical baseball image.

A Final Salute—and Fireworks—as Ripken Bows Out

October 7, 2001/Baltimore, Maryland

The Baltimore Orioles clubhouse in Camden Yards the other day, Cal Ripken was asked if he would have preferred being a basketball player. Silly question, meant to be a little joke.

There was a pause. Ripken was actually mulling over the question. It is known that Ripken loves basketball. He has a full-court gym in his home in Reisterstown, Maryland, and, at 6-foot-5 and a rock-solid 220 pounds and with a closely shaved head that resembles the coiffure of Michael Jordan, is known to be a good player in the games in which he invites college and sometimes pro players to participate in the off-season.

"Well," he said, "I think I chose the right game for me."

If there is a record for greatest understatement, that observation would rank high. This weekend, the end of baseball's regular season, was the culmination, the celebration, the grand finale and farewell of one of the most remarkable careers in sports.

Tonight at Camden Yards, the Orioles played their last game of the season. First there was a forty-five-minute tribute to their longtime star and beloved local hero—he was born in Havre de Grace, Maryland. The groundskeepers even contributed their bit of homage, mowing a huge No. 8 in the center-field grass, signifying Ripken's uniform number.

All this for a man who transformed, to a large degree, the concept of shortstop, proving that a big man could be nimble enough to play a demanding position that was usually the province of shorter, springier water bugs. He broke numerous fielding and hitting records. And he broke a mark for endurance that combined skill, strict adherence to conditioning, intelligence and the will to play through injuries.

In the process, the national attention lavished on him for his pursuit and then his bettering of Lou Gehrig's record for consecutive games is credited with helping to bring baseball out of the malaise it had suffered after the players' strike of 1994.

When Ripken broke Gehrig's mark of 2,130 consecutive games on September 6, 1995—Ripken's streak began on May 30, 1982, and ended at 2,632 games, on September 20, 1998, nearly 17 seasons without missing a game—it made him a national sports figure like few other athletes before or since.

On June 19, Ripken, forty-one years old and playing in his 21st year in the major leagues, all with the same team, announced that he would retire from baseball at season's end.

From that point forward, a cheering farewell tour took place in the major league towns the Orioles visited, a tour capped, perhaps, with the 2001 All-Star Game, his 19th. Ripken was named an American League All-Star as an honor for career achievement, his statistics this season hardly meriting his inclusion on the team. No matter. He homered—Ripken has a history of responding in dramatic situations—and was named the game's Most Valuable Player, becoming the oldest player to claim the award and the only player to win it twice for the American League.

Ripken's final game, filled with sentiment, hardly lived up to his career achievements. He went 0-for-3, lining out to the wall in left in his first at-bat, then popping out to short. In his last at-bat as an Oriole, tipping his cap to a standing ovation before stepping in to bat, he flied out to center field. The Red Sox beat the Orioles, 5–1.

"I've been thinking these last few days about what I'm going to miss, and I think most of all it will be what went on outside the white lines of the playing field, away from the playing field," Ripken said Friday. "Sure, I'll miss the competition, the tension of the games, but I think it'll be the journey, the sitting around in the stadium, on the buses, the horseplay in the locker room, the camaraderie—the people—that I think I'll miss most of all."

Did he believe, as some do, that his longevity record obscured his other significant accomplishments, from two league most valuable player awards to leading the league in fielding percentage four times, in assists seven times and double plays eight times? How about his 3,183 lifetime hits, 1,695 runs batted in, and 431 homers?

"I never felt it obscured anything," he said. "The people who know the game know what I've done on the field beyond playing often. I just tried to play the game, and play it well."

David Cone, the starting Red Sox pitcher in Ripken's last game, said: "He's such a class act. Cal should be the model for all professional athletes. He stays in incredible shape—you'd have to be to play all those games—and he's such a consistent performer, which you'd have to be to post up those numbers for 21 years. He's never had a season in which his numbers were glaringly different. And even at the end, he was still the toughest out for me in the lineup."

And this despite Ripken's .239 batting average, a career low. Not everyone was impressed with Ripken's consecutive-game streak. Bobby Bonds, a coach with the Giants, called it "idiotic." He said everybody needed a rest, and that it had to hurt the Orioles at times for Ripken to continue his streak when he was ailing and a more able body was available. Ripken replied: "People are entitled to their opinion. But their opinion doesn't always make it a fact."

To the accusation that Ripken was selfish in pursuit of Gehrig's record, to the exclusion of team considerations, Gene Lamont, a Red Sox coach who managed against Ripken when they were both in the minor leagues in the late 1970s and then when Lamont managed the Chicago White Sox, said: "If he's selfish, everybody's selfish, because every player who got that close would have wanted to break the record that everybody said would never be broken. I know that when I was managing against him, I was hoping he'd take a day off."

Ripken's streak nearly ended a handful of times, when he sprained an ankle or a knee, but he continued playing. On August 2, 1997, in Game 2,423, he considered leaving with lower back pain but stayed in the lineup and singled in his next at-bat and homered the following day.

The streak endured through Ripken's move from third base to shortstop and back. In 1982 Earl Weaver, then managing the Orioles, believed that Ripken the third baseman could be an excellent shortstop and moved him there. It was also in early '82 that Ripken ran into the most difficult period of his career.

"I went into an early slump and thought every day that I'd be sent back to Class AAA," Ripken said. "But Earl showed the patience to let me grind it out, which is what I've done my whole career, grind it out."

Davey Johnson convinced Ripken before the 1997 season to move back to third. Ripken bridled at first, but eventually agreed to the change. Some teammates expressed displeasure when, on the road, Ripken would stay at a different hotel, to avoid crowds.

Other teammates, like Ripken's good friend, outfielder Brady Anderson, would note that if those guys did what Ripken did, they could establish some rules for themselves, too.

"I never played carefully to avoid injury, but I never dove for a foul ball two rows deep in the stands, either," he said. "I played for today, not for tomorrow, and whatever came around was part of the game."

He said he would now devote his energies to a baseball complex being built for youth in Aberdeen, Maryland. For many, the memory of Ripken the player will not be forgotten, particularly the passion with which he played. He said he got that from his father, the late Cal Sr., a coach and, for a period in the late 1980s, Cal Jr.'s manager with the Orioles.

"My dad not only taught me the value of hard work, that when you work hard good things happen," Ripken said, "but he taught me to enjoy what I was doing. He exposed me to the joy of the game. In the end, baseball for me was fun."

Last night's career-ending final inning found Ripken in the on-deck circle. There were two outs and a man on second and the crowd was chanting, "We want Cal." It was up to Brady Anderson to get on base, but on a 3-and-2 count against reliever Ugueth Urbina, Anderson struck out.

With most of the fans still in the ballpark, still cheering, Ripken made a tour around the park chauffeured in a red convertible. His teammates and the Red Sox players stood in front of their dugouts and watched. Then Ripken came to shortstop, where a microphone had been set up.

For minutes, he couldn't speak, he was so emotionally caught up in the moment. When he gathered himself, he thanked the fans for "sharing your love of the game with me." He said he had lived "a dream" playing for his hometown team and he hoped that "I had made a difference."

He left his particular stage for the last time, to a thunder of fireworks and applause.

Piazza Will Be Catching Games, Not His Breath

February 16, 2006, Phoenix, Arizona

In what looked at first glance like a small airplane hangar festooned with netting, the not-quite-ancient catcher stepped into the enclosed batting cage to begin his first day of spring training in the San Diego Padres complex. He had traded in, involuntarily, as it happened, his Mets blue and orange of the previous eight seasons for the Padres blue and yellow.

In his short-sleeve batting jersey, baggy basketball-like shorts and sneakers, he took his familiar wide-legged stance with his blond bat, a 33-ounce, 34 1/2-inch Mike Piazza model.

While relatively old by baseball standards at thirty-seven, Piazza still has no gray in his full head of dark hair and still swings with the authority of a man who has a lifetime .311 batting average and has bashed 397 home runs, more than Carlton Fisk, more than Yogi Berra or Johnny Bench, more than any catcher in big-league history.

"Oh, jeez," said Dave Magadan, the Padres batting coach, sitting beside the batting cage, as Piazza cracked one of the first pitches from another coach, Tony Muser. "Loud." The ball hit the top of the screen and dropped, nearly hitting Muser.

"Heads up, Muse!" Magadan cried.

"Need a hard hat," Muser said, laughing and bending to pick up another ball from the nearby bucket.

Piazza arrived in camp weighing 230 pounds—"230 ripped pounds," he joked—which is a little bit over his playing weight. But he looked fit. And he will need to be because the job he really wanted for 2006—designated hitter with an American League team with an occasional game behind the plate—never materialized. Instead, he will serve as the Padres No. 1 catcher, blocking pitches in the dirt and bracing for collisions with runners far more than he originally envisioned. Easy street will have to wait.

All of which seemed fine with Kevin Towers, the Padres general manager. "Mike's been one of our nemeses all these years," Towers said. "I hated seeing him come up against us in the late innings when the game was on the line. And the thing I've especially always liked about Mike is that he plays hard. He always runs hard, runs everything out, even if he didn't run well. And he probably didn't throw with the great catchers in the game, but he's a good handler of pitchers.

"He's caught some Hall of Fame pitchers—Tommy Glavine and Pedro Martínez, for two—and he's still got power. He also brings a pedigree and a swagger to our team, something I think we lacked."

Bruce Bochy, the Padres manager, and a former catcher himself, said he was excited about Piazza working with some of San Diego's good young pitchers, like Jake Peavy and Chris Young.

For the Mets, however, Piazza's minuses did not outweigh his pluses. At the end of a seven-year, $91 million contract, they let him go. His work behind the plate was hurting them, it was felt, and he seemed, as he got older, to be more prone to injury. His production as a hitter was nowhere near what it was in his best seasons in New York.

Still, it was somewhat surprising that Piazza got no takers in the AL. "Things have changed in what teams want with DH's," he said. "They want players who can also play a certain amount in the field, too. And I guess I wasn't fitting the bill with them."

So he will catch. Bochy said he did not know in how many games Piazza will be putting on the gear, but he thought it would be a substantial number. "We'll rest Mike when he needs it," said Bochy, who has Doug Mirabelli, recently obtained from Boston, as a capable backup.

"Sure, there's wear and tear on the body, that's to be expected, but my knees are good," Piazza said. "Got all my cartilages. And as a catcher, I've been blessed with that."

Piazza has been named to 12 All-Star teams and caught some of the best pitchers in those contests. He recalled catching Greg Maddux in one of those games, with the slugger Juan Gonzalez striding into the batter's box.

"We got a great count on him, and then we jammed him," Piazza said. "Maddux said at the end of the inning, 'That was awesome. You called the right pitch at the right time.' Nice to hear."

It is all part of a Hall of Fame résumé, but Piazza acknowledged that in some ways he will feel like a rookie this spring, playing with a new team.

"There's always pressure to prove yourself," he said. "I still have to perform. And I think I will. I think I can help this club."

Piazza hit for about fifteen minutes in the batting cage. He emerged with sweat on his brow. How did he feel? "I'm still in one piece," he said with a smile.

Magadan said: "He looked great. He's dangerous."

Pedro Martínez Is Not Playing Favorites

May 3, 2005

"What, you think this is some kind of conspiracy, guys?" Willie Randolph, the Mets manager, said with an upraised brow.

Randolph was sitting in his leather swivel chair behind his desk yesterday in the Shea Stadium clubhouse, replying to a question posed before last night's game against the Phillies.

The question concerned the oddity that the starting catcher, Mike Piazza, would be taking a rest for the third straight start by Pedro Martínez.

Ramón Castro would catch Martínez again, for the fourth time in his last five starts.

"It was a long weekend and we're playing tonight, and we got in at three, four in the morning," Randolph said of Mets trip home after their 6–3 victory over the Nationals in Washington on Sunday night.

"Mike was a little banged up. I didn't get to bed until a quarter of five. Glad I'm not playing today," Randolph said smiling. "I can just sit back and use my brain."

367

And was part of that brain adhering to a request by Martínez to pitch to Castro?

"If there was a conspiracy, or something to it, we'd tell you," Piazza said at his locker. "There isn't anything to it. I'm feeling good, just a little sore. Got in late last night. Need some treatment on my back."

"Look, if I was twenty-five, I'd be catching him tonight," the thirty-six-year-old Piazza added. "I was lying on a couch in the clubhouse when Willie came by."

Piazza said Randolph had asked him how he was feeling, and Piazza said he told him he felt a little beat up.

"If I'm not 100 percent ready, it's not fair to catch Pedro or anyone else," Piazza said. "And it wouldn't matter to me if Martínez wanted Castro to catch him. It's about team, about long-term, and about winning. I know I'll catch him in the future."

Some pitchers like certain catchers to catch them, even if that catcher is not regularly a starter. The Cubs Greg Maddux has been said to request such a catcher, though he has denied it. Some pitchers say that some catchers are closer connected to their rhythms on the mound, to their thinking, the way a good jockey is in tune to a particular horse, or a good spouse anticipates the right moment to utter those sweet nothings.

Not all catchers agree. "It's a bunch of malarkey that a pitcher like Pedro needs a special catcher," said Fran Healy, a Mets television announcer and a former big-league catcher. "Any major league catcher can catch a great pitcher, like Pedro. You tell me that any catcher really made a difference when Seaver was pitching, or Koufax, or Marichal? I don't think so."

There had been speculation that there was bad blood between Piazza and Martínez stemming from the days when they came up in the Dodgers organization, though both have denied it.

In a 1998 interleague game, however, when Martínez was with Boston, he hit Piazza with a fastball and broke his hand. But when Martínez

368

came to spring training with the Mets, he joked with Piazza in a gesture of friendship.

Martínez, who came to the Mets in the off-season as a free agent from the Red Sox—and seems certain to depart with his Hall of Fame credentials intact—pitched the opening game for the Mets in Cincinnati, with Piazza behind the plate. He had said that he does not have any problems with Piazza's catching, although he said he would have to do the job of keeping the runners from stealing, since Piazza does not have the best throwing arm.

After a rocky first inning in the opener, Martínez settled down and pitched beautifully, although he did not get the decision. "I'm a happy camper," Martínez said.

Castro, twenty-nine, caught Martínez in his second start, a two-hitter in which he allowed one run, as the Mets won their first game of the season, after an 0–5 start.

In his next game, his first start at Shea Stadium, Martínez pitched to Piazza. He pitched well, but he had three wild pitches—a career high—with two of them setting up a run and another producing a run.

Those wild pitches may have cost Martínez a victory, and they definitely fueled speculation over whether Castro could have caught those balls that Piazza was unable to block.

Castro caught the next two games that Martínez started. In the first, Martínez beat Florida, 10–1, allowing only three hits in seven innings. In the second, last Tuesday, with Piazza said to be resting, Martínez gave up four runs in seven innings, getting his first loss of the season, after two victories and two no-decisions.

"No pitcher has come to me and asked for a special catcher," Randolph said yesterday in another attempt to put the conspiracy theory to rest. "Pedro told you guys, he's comfortable with Mike."

And, to be sure, quite cozy with Castro as well. Last night Martínez, with Castro the backstop, pitched seven fine innings, giving up one run on four hits with two walks and six strikeouts. He left the game for a pinch-hitter in the bottom of the seventh, and the Mets went on to beat the Phillies, 5–1, with Martínez getting his third victory of the season. So ended the receivers' riddle.

Randy Johnson: Something Old, Something New

April 30, 2002

Randy Johnson, all flamingo-long legs and with the wingspan of a clothesline, has been having about as fine a start to a baseball season as he, or any pitcher—from "Old Hoss" Radbourn to Three-Finger Brown to Sandy Koufax—can possibly have. The 6-foot-10 Johnson, who completed last season by winning Games 6 and 7 of the World Series, has started this one for the Arizona Diamondbacks with six straight victories, striking out an average of 10-plus batters and allowing a little more than a run per contest.

This is his 15th major league season, and he has dominated for some time; in his last five seasons, he has compiled records of 20–4, 19–11, 17–9, 19–7, and 21–6. He strikes out batters so often and with such emphasis that batters feel as though his pitches are whipped by gale force. And he seems to be getting better, at age thirty-eight, as his three straight Cy Young Awards as a Diamondback may attest (he also won one with Seattle in 1995). The Mets will face him this week in a three-game series that begins in Arizona tonight. The Yankees, who could not touch Johnson last October and November, will get another crack at him in June.

The notion that he is getting even bigger to batters appears only a mirage, however. He stands on the mound, peering down for the sign, as though he is standing on an orange crate. His baseball cap is pulled down to shadow in a menacing way his narrowed eyes. His blond mustache and the wisp of hair on his chin might look comical, if the rest of the portrait were not so fearsome. With his 372 strikeouts last season, he accomplished something no other pitcher—not Nolan Ryan or Walter Johnson or even Iron Man McGinnity—has achieved, striking out 300 or more batters in four consecutive seasons.

In the postseason last year, he was 5–1, including a 3–0 record in the World Series, in which he won Games 2 and 6 as a starter and Game 7 as the reliever, when he rescued Curt Schilling in the eighth inning and emerged as the winning pitcher. Until last season, he had been 2–5 in division series play—winning the two games against the Yankees in 1995, including one as a reliever in the deciding Game 5, then losing five straight from 1997–99—and was 0–1 in championship series play.

"I think he's a lot more at peace with himself," Diamondbacks Manager Bob Brenly said. "Last year's postseason success got the monkey off his back. And he got the World Series ring. That eliminated any doubts that this guy wasn't a big-game pitcher. Like all great athletes, he was his own worst critic, and I have to believe that he felt he had something to prove.

"And I'll tell you this: You'll not get a tougher competitor than Randy. He's the hardest pitcher I've ever known to try to take out of a ballgame. A week ago, against Colorado, we were well ahead of the Rockies and I wanted to take him out after seven innings. I told him, 'It'll save you some pitches, and we have some guys in the pen that could use the work.' But the Rockies had been chirping at him from the bench, trying to upset his concentration, and it just pumped him up. He said, 'No, I will finish this game.' I said, 'OK, Randy, OK.'

"The last batter in the ninth inning was Todd Helton, one of the best hitters in the National League. He smoked him—the last pitches were a 100-mile-an-hour fastball, another at 100, a slider at 90 and a fastball to strike Helton out at 99. And this after having thrown around

115 pitches in the game. I wasn't sure my eyes were seeing what they were seeing." Johnson finished with a two-hitter and 17 strikeouts.

So what's going on this season, to make this one seem even better than those that came before? When a reporter repeated some of Brenly's remarks recently to Johnson, seated in a chair in front of his locker in the Arizona clubhouse, he nodded in thought.

"The reason for my success this season?" Johnson said. "I took anger-management classes over the winter."

He had?

"But you can't use it," he said.

Why not?

"Strictly personal."

But what's to hide? A lot of people, he was told, take anger-management courses—even some newspaper editors.

"I can understand that," he said, and laughed. "You can't use it, though, because it's not true."

So it was a joke, but in a way it wasn't, too.

"The difference between the bench jockeying that went on by the Rockies in that game—it might have upset me when I was younger," he said. "I didn't know how to control my emotions on the mound. I remember when I was with Seattle, and Tony La Russa, then the manager of the A's, used to get on me. I'm sure he's a nice man, but he was smart. I'd get so mad that I'd lose focus. He would get me so furious, I'd lose my rhythm on the mound and lose concentration on the hitter. How can the mind be in two places at one time?

"But over the years, I've harnessed anger. I've been able to utilize it to my advantage. Sure, I heard the Rockies, but I was able to set my mind to think only about the batter. What I had to do to get him out."

He said he was learning this more or less by the seat of his pants in the Montreal and Seattle organizations, and became more of a thinking pitcher as the years went by. In particular, he credits Tom House, the longtime Texas Rangers pitching coach, and Ryan for helping him.

"I talked a lot with House," Johnson said, "but I didn't talk much with Nolan, I just observed him—the way he went about his job, his dedication to work habits when he wasn't pitching and his intense focus when he was.

"Nolan and I are both power pitchers, and for much of the early part of my career I went to the max on every pitch, and on every hitter. I saw that Nolan not only paced himself better—especially in the early innings when a power pitcher is trying to get his flow together—but he looked to spot pitches. He hit the inside and outside corners, he worked the eye level of batters—moving the pitches up and down—and he eased up on some pitches and then turned it up a notch on others. In that way, he either slowed up the hitter's bat or speeded it up, so that you offset the hitter's timing. And you can have a little bit in reserve, as I did against Colorado. That's all part of the art of pitching."

Another essential element to his success was the mechanics of his pitching motion. He spent all or part of five years in the minor leagues before getting a shot with Montreal in 1989, then was traded to the Mariners when the Expos thought he would never gain the control needed to win in the big leagues.

"I was all arms and legs and while my elevation was an advantage, I did not have great body control," he said. "I was throwing and falling too far to third base, my arm wasn't coming around at the right angle for greatest effectiveness. In time, this was corrected. But it certainly took time. Not all of it came easy."

As for the "monkey" off his back, he said that he has had good games in previous postseasons, like when he was with Houston and lost, 2–1, to San Diego in the playoffs. He has also been hit hard in some postseason games, as well.

"I think for the most part he had pitched in tough luck," Diamond-backs first baseman Mark Grace said. "And last season we scored runs for him. He never needs a lot of runs to win, just a few."

Johnson said: "I don't think I have to make any excuses for my performances over the years. It's not like I felt I was under enormous pressure. Pressure comes away from the playing field, when fathers, for example, have to put food on the table for their families. I didn't feel that kind of pressure in baseball. I use the word 'challenges.' Sometimes you meet the challenge, sometimes you don't. And then you try again tomorrow. Or next year."

Frank Thomas: "The Big Hurt" Feeling Pained by His Contract

February 26, 2001

Frank Thomas of the Chicago White Sox feels cheated, underpaid, taken advantage of, and maybe he should. After all, the slugger is earning only $9.927 million a year through 2006—$60 million in round numbers. Maybe he was justified in arriving in spring training camp in Tucson last week and then abruptly walking out in a fit of pique. He's been gone for five days now.

Maybe he read the ditty by Damon Runyon titled, "The Old Guy's Lament." Though it was written around 1920, it may still have resonance some eighty years later. The story poem is in the voice of an old baseball player, down on his luck, who now takes tickets at a ballpark turnstile. He goes unappreciated and virtually unrecognized, but, he says, "I was once known as Murderous McGarr!"

It ends with a characterization of the new generation of ballplayers:
Half of 'em nothin' but boneheads,

374

And the other half worse than that;
Look up my monicker, Mister,
And see what I done with my bat!
But think of the dough that they're grabbin',
Guys that can't hit a balloon—
I can see where my parents were crazy
By havin' me born too soon!

You can hardly blame Ruthless Thomas if, like Murderous McGarr, he has a beef with his parents for, as it were, a preconception.

When he signed his last contract extension in 1997, at close to $75 million for seven years, Alex Rodriguez and Derek Jeter, for two, were only then emerging as stars. This season, A-Rod and Jeter signed ten-year contracts for $252 million and $189 million, respectively.

There were other gargantuan contracts, such as the zillions paid Pedro Martínez and Manny Ramirez. As each of them was inked, Ruthless Thomas felt his gorge rise. One can just imagine him in his mansion in Chicago, wetting the tip of his pencil and figuring out the cost-of-living increase that he was not under contract for—and, when done, the steam curling from his ears.

When he signed his previous contract extension—his $2 million in endorsements was not included, of course—he was the sixth-highest-salaried player in baseball. Not now.

"To be fifty or sixty on the pay scale doesn't sit well in my stomach," he told ESPN Radio a few days ago. "I signed a contract, but no, I'm not happy with it anymore because baseball is a business just like any other job. There are A players, B players, and C players. I've been an A player for a long time. I'm probably the one who is furthest out from all those guys who have done what I have done in this game."

Ruthless Thomas had a fine season in 2000, as what has to be considered a part-time player. He is a designated hitter. The reason he is a designated hitter is that he is a butcher at first base, the position he played, or tried to play, for several years. But as a hitter, well, he may identify with another quatrain from Runyon:

You talk of your Ruth, and your Meusel,
And Kelly—don't make me smile!
Them guys hit 'em a furlong
Where I used to hit 'em a mile!

Thomas said last season was the best of his career. He hit .328 with career highs of 43 home runs and 143 runs batted in. But he finished 32 points behind Jason Giambi of the Oakland A's in the voting for Most Valuable Player in the American League. He had also been left off the AL All-Star team.

He was Ruthless Thomas until the playoffs when he became Toothless Thomas. He went 0-for-9 as Seattle swept the series in three games.

"I'd go 0-for-9 in the season, and nobody would notice," he said. "But it happens in the playoffs and it gets highlighted."

It gets highlighted because the money players are expected to perform in money situations. As for going hitless at points during the season and not getting noticed, that is not true.

The nickname that he is best known by is the "Big Hurt." One day a few seasons back, one of the top White Sox executives who contributes to the salary that Thomas now deems inadequate, watched as Thomas struck out, again.

"The Big Hurt," said the executive, "hasn't hurt anybody in two months—except us."

Why did Thomas sign a guaranteed contract for such a long term? Was he doped? Was there a pistol to his temple? Did he succumb to the pleadings of the White Sox owner Jerry Reinsdorf, on bended knee, to take the deal? No, no, and no. The reason was security. As Thomas himself said, baseball is a business. And he figured he had a sweet deal. And he understood that if the Big Hurt got so hurt he couldn't play, he'd still be paid. Like Jayson Williams of the Nets, who sustained a career-ending injury last year, and still will receive the $60 million remaining on his six-year $86 million contract.

When Thomas, meanwhile, was having subpar years, he never suggested, nor was requested, to return even a paltry million or so from his contract.

What if Ruthless Thomas does get the contract extension he seeks? In two or three years, he might be back again to No. 50 or 60 on the big league pay scale. What if Reinsdorf's pockets are finally empty? What then?

Rob a bank? Or, like Murderous McGarr, work the turnstiles? Who could blame him?

Mariano Rivera and the Snow

February 22, 1993

Steve Howe was telling Mariano Rivera, a young Panamanian pitcher, about his spring trainings in high school in Clarkton, Michigan.

"We'd go out to play in March and April and have to sweep the snow off the base paths," the veteran relief pitcher said.

Rivera looked at Howe. "It snows in Michigan?" he asked.

* * *

Rivera went on to pitch 19 seasons in the major leagues, was a 13-time All-Star, is the career leader in saves with 652 (called "The Sandman" for putting rival hitters' bats to sleep) and in 2019 was elected in his first year of eligibility to the Baseball Hall of Fame and was the first player ever elected unanimously by the Baseball Writers Association of America.

Don Sutton: A Dream That Wasn't So Dumb

January 7, 1998

His hair whiter and longer than when he pitched during those 23 years in the major leagues, his face looking somewhat lined and tired—after all, it had been a long trip, 324 career victories and an emergency airplane stopover in Washington on his way from Atlanta to New York yesterday morning—Don Sutton sat at a dais in the front of a large room in a midtown Manhattan hotel. This was for a news conference called in his honor. And if his face appeared to be drawn from the journey—journeys, as it were—his eyes were aglow. After all, the day before he had been told that, in his fifth year on the ballot, at age fifty-two, he had been elected to the Baseball Hall of Fame.

He said much of what might be expected, how this was a thrill, that this was what he had dreamed about since he began pitching in the sixth grade in Clio, Alabama—"Imagine, the son of a south Alabama sharecropper, what a stupid dream to want to go to the Hall of Fame"— and what he had aimed for when he broke in with the Dodgers in 1966.

Even when he went to Cooperstown for the first time to film a commercial a few years ago, he was moved. "Just to visit with the ghosts of some of baseball's greats was awe inspiring," he said.

When he spoke about those who he wished could now share this honor—his mother, his first manager, Walter Alston, a sixth-grade teacher who taught him how to pitch ("and I was pitching that same way in the last game I ever played in, in 1988")—he even grew misty eyed.

There were several baseball questions from reporters, then someone asked: "Last year at this time, Don, you missed being inducted into the Hall of Fame by just nine votes. And at the time, you said, 'The vote didn't mean a thing. With no offense to the Hall of Fame or anyone who holds a key to it, it just wasn't that big a deal.' Is that accurate?"

378

Sutton looked hard at the questioner.

"Yes," he said, straightforward. "But it must be put into context. My wife, Mary, and I had just had a two-pound daughter born to us sixteen weeks early. The most important thing in the world for us then was the health of our baby. It didn't matter to me then if every ballot for the Hall of Fame came up zeros for me. Election to the Hall of Fame was just a byproduct of my job. Baseball was only a part of my life. It wasn't my life. And Jackie was fighting for her life. Doctors had given her one chance in a hundred to live."

He smiled. "She made it," he said, his voice softening. "She's as stubborn as her mother."

The mood shifted, as did the questions. How did he feel breaking in with the Dodgers on a staff with Don Drysdale and Sandy Koufax? "Let me tell you what it was like," he said. "Drysdale would pitch on Friday and knock down six batters and hit three and win, 2–0. Koufax would pitch on Saturday and give up one hit, a broken-bat single, and win, 1–0. And then I took the mound, and I was facing nine angry men who wanted to get even. It was scary."

But not so terrifying that he didn't have a great deal of confidence, pitching in a style he termed crafty.

"I admired Whitey Ford, who didn't have a great fastball but knew how to get batters out," he said.

The toughest hitter he ever faced?

"Clemente," Sutton said, referring to another Hall of Famer, Roberto Clemente. "His strike zone was anywhere between the foul lines— he could hit a knockdown pitch for a double."

Some had questioned Sutton's credentials for the Hall of Fame, though he was the only eligible pitcher with 300 or more victories not in the Hall of Fame. But only once was he a 20-game winner (though he won at least 15 games 11 other times); he was named to only four All-Star teams, and in 23 years he led his pitching staff in victories only four times.

He had two particular arguments for this, both persuasive.

One was, "Longevity counts for something." And when Alston autographed the manager's autobiography, he wrote: "To Don Sutton: When it's on the line I want you to have the ball." Sutton said, "When the guy you work for says something like that, I think it's important."

He spoke about Jackie again. When she was born, he said, she was so small you could hold her in your hand, about the size of an eyeglass case. Now she is sixteen and a half pounds and twenty-nine inches. She is home and still oxygen dependent, but he hopes not for long.

"She's healthy and a real delight," he said brightly. "You'd love her."

Hall of Famers with the Flip Side of Greatness

June 8, 1983

Gaylord Perry, the Seattle pitcher, recently moved into fourth place on the career list of major league losses—he now has 258. The man with the damp delivery is in highly select company.

The leader, with 313, is none other than Denton True "Cy" Young, for whom the most revered pitching award in baseball is named. Of equally sainted memory is the pitcher who leads the American League in losses, Walter Johnson, with 279.

Perry, like Young and Johnson, has certainly had some good days—310 career victories—to go with his bad ones, but these players, among several others of the game's best, have suffered the agony of misfortune.

Young won 511 games, of course, which is also a record. Fine, but he allowed a record 7,078 hits in his 23-year career. He set another record of spreading that number of hits while pitching for teams in both leagues. So that left the field open for Johnson to set the American League record, giving up 4,920 hits, and the fabled Grover Cleveland Alexander in the National, with 4,868.

And you ask why there were so many .300 hitters in the early years? Some say that Johnson was the greatest pitcher ever. And well he might be. But he also hit 204 batters, a major-league record for barbarous pitching, and is tied for the record for most wild pitches, 156. Why, the Big Train once threw three wild pitches in an inning. He still shares the American League record for that piece of business. Young, Johnson, and Alexander aren't the only Hall of Famers to fall on their immortal countenances. Early Wynn, for example, walked 1,775 batters in his career. The players, if not the fans, were forced to stay late when Early pitched.

But for bases on balls in one season, the record belongs to Rapid Robert Feller, whose rapid ball missed the plate so often in 1938 that he walked 208 batters.

Robin Roberts had better control, unfortunately. He holds the record for most home runs allowed in a season, 46. Warren Spahn, meanwhile, holds the National League record for most home runs allowed in a career, 434. But let us leave the great pitchers and move on to other positions and other lugubrious stars. Thumbing through Seymour Siwoff's *The Book of Baseball Records* we begin to mumble in our beards, "Say it ain't so, Joe, and Cy and Ty." Ty Cobb? Well, he was a legendary baserunner. For no one, until Rickey Henderson last season, had been caught stealing as many times in one season as Tyrus Raymond Cobb was in 1915—38 times. Cobb stole 96 bases that season, and Henderson stole 130 in 1982 while being nabbed 42 times.

Babe Ruth shattered records everywhere he went—and he still holds the record, for example, for leading the majors the most seasons in strikeouts, four. His career mark of 1,306 strikeouts lasted until another Hall of Famer, Mickey Mantle, came along to break it. It is now held by the breezy Reginald Martinez Jackson.

Sluggers are like that, though. The record for leading a league in strikeouts for most consecutive seasons, seven, is held by Old Double X, Jimmie Foxx ("X" for wipeout). And no one struck out more times in a five-game World Series (eight) than the esteemed Rogers Hornsby, until Duke Snider, another Hall of Famer, came along to tie him. In All-Star play, Roberto Clemente once fanned four times in a game, a record.

Some heroes don't have to strike out to look nonviolent with a bat. For example, the record for grounding into double plays in a World Series is seven. Joe DiMaggio, of all folks, did that. And for grounding into double plays the most times in one Series game? Three, by Willie Mays.

In the field, some Hall of Famers have had a miserable time of it. George Sisler and Cap Anson are tied with four others for leading the American League in errors at first base the most seasons, five.

At second, Eddie Collins has the modern career record for most errors in a league, 448. And Nap Lajoie is tied for most bobbles in a game, five.

Now, Pie Traynor is generally considered the greatest of all third basemen. On some days, though, Pie was kind of flat. In fact, he made more errors, 324, than any other third baseman in the history of the National League.

Honus Wagner, bow-legged and with a beatific smile, is often ranked with Ruth and Cobb. Like Ruth and Cobb, Wagner had some malodorous days. More than some. He holds the National League career record for most errors by a shortstop, 676. And another Hall of Famer has an equally calamitous mark—Luke Appling holds the record for leading the American League in errors for most seasons, five. It wasn't enough for Cobb to be a disaster on the base paths; opposing batsmen struck balls to this ill-starred outfielder with devilish glee. It is no coincidence, then, that Cobb should hold the career record for most outfield errors, 271.

His play was apparently infectious, for a teammate and fellow Hall of Famer, Harry Heilmann, is tied for the record of most errors by an outfielder in one inning, three.

As for the fielding of immortal pitchers, well, Spahn, who does hold the record for most years leading the league in participating in double plays, five, also is tied for the record of leading the majors in errors for most seasons, five.

And how did the immortal pitchers hit? Pitchers generally aren't supposed to be able to hit well, of course, but Sandy Koufax underdid it. He broke strikeout records as a pitcher, but he also set the record for having been struck out the most consecutive times, 12.

At times, as the evidence shows, even the greatest among us aren't great, or even very good. Somehow, though, that's heartening.

Part X: The Leadership Branches

Marvin Miller, the Nonpareil Bargainer

February 15, 1999

One day in the late 1970s, Bowie Kuhn, then the commissioner of baseball, invited Marvin Miller, then the executive director of the Major League Players Association, to lunch for the first and only time. At one point Kuhn said to Miller, his adversary of more than ten years: "Look, Marvin, you've beaten the owners at every turn. And now the owners need a victory."

Miller, as he recently recalled, couldn't believe his ears. "Bowie," asked Miller, "are you suggesting I throw the game?"

Miller did not, and the owners continued their losing streak. The owners lost at every turn, as Kuhn said, because one man had on his side the insight, the foresight, the experience, the courage and the style—unruffled, unflappable, undeterred—as well as the United States Constitution and labor law. Miller led the players, often at dramatic junctures, out of virtual subservience and into the democratic system of America.

A man of medium height, with a mustache and a quiet, patient demeanor, Miller took over in 1966 as executive director of a loosely organized group of ballplayers, with assets of a file cabinet and about $5,400. He shaped them into what many believe is the most successful union not just in sports, but in the history of American labor.

Not only did he work to raise the level of earnings—the average salary of a major leaguer when he began was $19,000 a year; it is now $1.4 million—but he helped improve playing conditions, from padded outfield walls and better-defined warning tracks to safer locker rooms. He even helped improve play, according to Henry Aaron, allowing players more financial freedom to remain in better shape during the off season instead of having to work at jobs like insurance salesman (Aaron) or sporting goods salesman (Andy Pafko).

He was also instrumental in improving scheduling, such as negating night games on get-away days. And he gave players the freedom that other American workers had—his cataclysmic battle for free agency ended the reserve clause, which had prevented players from bargaining for their services on the open market. As a result, a greater number of teams won pennants than ever before, attendance figures broke records season after season, and the value of teams increased (the Yankees were purchased for $10 million in 1973 and today are worth $600 million or more).

Along the way, he also took one of the poorest benefit plans and built it into one of the best.

Jim Bunning, now a United States senator and a Baseball Hall of Famer who, along with Robin Roberts and Harvey Kuenn, led a players' committee to hire someone to lead their meager union, once said, "The two proudest things I take out of baseball were the perfect game I pitched and being part of the selection group that chose Marvin Miller as executive director."

Aaron, the home run champion and now senior vice president of the Atlanta Braves, once said, "Marvin Miller is as important to the history of baseball as Jackie Robinson."

And Roberts, the Hall of Fame pitcher, said: "I don't know of any-one who changed the game more than Marvin Miller. His legacy is that, through his work, ballplayers for the first time attained dignity from owners. He changed a monopoly into a more realistic setup. He deserves to be in the Hall of Fame."

Two weeks from today, on March 2, the Veterans Committee of the Baseball Hall of Fame in Cooperstown, New York, will gather and vote on the inclusion of new members in their shrine. One of the lead-ing candidates is Orlando Cepeda, the fine first baseman whose best slugging years were with the Giants and Cardinals. His recently pub-lished autobiography, *Baby Bull*, written with Herb Fagen, ably pre-sents the case for Cepeda, who was once imprisoned for ten months in Puerto Rico for possession of marijuana. Cepeda's baseball accom-plishments should merit him selection to the Hall of Fame, just as Miller's do.

But in his way, Miller, who was born in the Bronx in 1917 and who retired in 1985 and lives in Manhattan, is as controversial a choice as Cepeda. Miller is still resented by owners, but shouldn't be. Owners, who feared a thinning of their substantial pocketbooks, had presented him as an ogre from the moment he took his position. He was painted by them as one among "union goons" for his work as chief economist and negotiator for the United Steelworkers.

Kuhn declared on the witness stand in a courtroom that free agency would "ruin" baseball.

When Miller once went to a spring-training camp to talk with play-ers in an outfield meeting—they were refused use of the locker room—the Astros manager, Leo Durocher, fungoed baseballs in an attempt to hit Miller.

But virtually by himself, one decent man, with knowledge and the mission to do the best job possible, beat the owners with their teams of lawyers and press agents, time after time after time.

And despite the overwhelming resistance, he helped improve both the game and the lives of players—and, as it turned out, the lives of the owners, as well. And not just in baseball, but, eventually, in all team sports in this country.

The Veterans Committee would distinguish itself and do what is right and unequivocally just by voting Marvin Miller into the Baseball Hall of Fame.

* * *

Ten years after the above column was written, Marvin Miller was elected by the Veterans Committee to the Hall of Fame in 2019, seven years after his death.

Joe Torre Knows Victory Isn't Everything

October 28, 2003

It was sometime earlier in the season, and I was walking down the runway at Yankee Stadium extending from the Yankees locker room to the dugout. A large-printed sign had been hung overhead about midway through. It read, "There is No Substitute for Victory."

You notice these so-called inspiration signs in locker rooms and perhaps even board rooms, but rarely do you pay attention to them. I had probably seen the sign numerous times but simply paid no attention to it, as I imagine the Yankees hadn't. Except, that is, for one Yankee in particular.

"Oh, that was put up at the direction of George," said Joe Torre, the Yankees manager, when the sign was mentioned to him. George, to be sure, is George Steinbrenner, the principal owner, who hovers over the team like a bloated black cloud. "He likes those kinds of things."

Torre gave no indication of the effectiveness of such a motto of encouragement, just objectively stated the origin of its presence.

But I wondered about the essence of "There is No Substitute for Victory." I said to Torre, "What about inner peace?"

I was only half-joking, thinking that no one could really take the sign totally seriously, it being so lacking in perspective, unless, surely, you were in a combat, or fighting for your survival in some similar fashion. But baseball, that game of ball and stick with the participants wearing knickers? (In fact, the quotation comes from General Douglas MacArthur, who said, "In war, there is no substitute for victory." Steinbrenner just left out the first part.)

"Inner peace?" Torre said. "Absolutely."

Torre's face went from almost bemusement at the sign to one of dead seriousness.

He began talking of his childhood, in Brooklyn, with a father who was abusive to him, to his siblings and especially to his mother. "I remember coming home in the evening and seeing his car parked in front of our house, and not wanting to go in," Torre said. "Sometimes I didn't."

He said that experience motivated him to start, with his wife, Ali, the Joe Torre Safe at Home Foundation, which will raise money to educate the public about abuse in families.

So parental love may be, for Joe Torre, more important than victory. Human consideration may be, for Joe Torre, more important than victory. Helping those who need help may also be, for Joe Torre, more important than victory.

Which isn't to say that victory isn't important to Joe Torre. Ask any of his players and they'll tell you that few hate losing as much as Joe Torre, and few want to win as much as Joe Torre. It's just that, unlike Steinbrenner, apparently, Torre doesn't issue dire statements that, for example, there will be hellfire to pay just because a team goes to Game 6 of the World Series and loses to the Marlins. Steinbrenner wasn't as preposterous after this year's Series loss as he was in 1981 when he "apologized" to the people of New York after the Dodgers beat the Yankees.

He has now promised changes, and some are surely needed. But every team seeks to make changes. The Marlins will make changes. For everything, so we've been told, there is a season. Life marches on, and so forth.

Torre has been hugely successful as manager of the Yankees. The fact that his team has now lost two World Series in the last three seasons hardly negates the fact that he's won four World Series and six pennants in his eight years as Yankees manager.

A lot of teams haven't been in any World Series in that time. One, for example, hasn't played in the season finale in fifty-seven years—oops, fifty-eight, counting this year.

Why has Torre been so extraordinarily successful managing the Yankees?

Because, say people close to the team, he gets the best out of the players. He does that by not being confrontational—unlike, oh, a certain owner. He never embarrasses a player in public. And, in most instances, he remains calm—intense, yes; thoughtful, yes; but also calm. The players pick up on this. They trust him, and trust his actions and reactions. They are more relaxed, while remaining competitive. Tight players fail.

When Torre was away from his home as a youth, he was more relaxed. He was a talented athlete and understood the importance of staying away from unnecessarily imposed pressure. There are numerous reasons why a ballplayer makes it to the major leagues, and Joe Torre obviously fulfilled some of them and had a terrific playing career.

He had modest success as a manager with the Mets, Braves, and Cardinals before taking over the Yankees. But his managerial reign has been the longest consecutive tenure by far in the mercurial, impulsive Steinbrenner era.

It seems apparent that Torre understands what bullying is, coming from the kind of home that he did, and so, as an adult, he knows how to deal with it. Don Zimmer, Torre's bench coach, quit Sunday because he said he had become fed up with Steinbrenner, that Steinbrenner didn't treat him "as a human being."

Torre said the other day that he planned to stay on because "it's still electric for me to get into the dugout and you are still excited."

"As long as that happens, I don't think I can walk away from it," he added. "The players make it worthwhile."

There wasn't anything about victory at any cost. It was about the game, and about the people. It was Joe Torre, who as a boy learned about perspective the hard way, seeing things for what they are.

Earl Weaver's Mind Keeps Whirring

September 23, 1982/Baltimore, Maryland

Smoke curls from behind the manager's desk in Memorial Stadium, and there are little hums and grumbles and coughs, all associated with the workings of the machine that is Earl Weaver's mind.

It is midafternoon on a recent day in the close American League Eastern Division race. At his desk in the manager's office at Memorial Stadium, the Orioles field leader fills out his lineup card for that night. His team is in second place, two games off the lead with two weeks left in the season.

He is thinking mightily. However, the smoke comes not from his ears, as could be supposed, but from the cigarette he puffs, and the sounds derive not from the mental gears but from his conversing with himself. "I oughta play him in," Weaver mumbles. "But maybe I oughta play the other guy."

His baseball cap is back on his head, his brow is creased, his right hand, holding a red pen, is poised. Even though Weaver has announced his retirement after this season, he seems to cogitate as arduously as ever.

He checks over a statistics sheet, rubs his chin and then writes into the fifth spot, "Lowenstein, left field," instead of Roenicke, or Dwyer, for Ayala. He has considered how each hits the Detroit pitcher, Wilcox, and how they hit other right-handers.

Standing beside the desk, watching and waiting for Weaver to conclude is Rex Barney, the former pitcher who now is the Orioles public address announcer and a part-time broadcaster. Barney will take the card to the opposing manager, and bring the other team's card back.

Weaver is in his 15th season as the Baltimore manager; he is third on the career list for winning percentage for managers, and first among active managers, and currently has brought his team back from eight and a half games off the pace. But he is still capable of mistakes, and Barney checks against them.

Barney has deep respect for the whirrings of Weaver's brain, but on occasion he questions the sage, such as when Weaver inserted two second basemen into the lineup. "Uh, hum," Barney said. "Are you sure this is what you want, Earl?"

Barney says Weaver sometimes forgets because he is concentrating so fiercely. No one, Weaver notes, is perfect. He cites other examples of his own fallibility, such as one time, thinking two steps ahead, he went to the mound and told his pitcher to walk the next batter to set up a double-play situation.

"But Skip," the pitcher said, "the bases are loaded already." "Hmm," Weaver said, and rescinded his order. Weaver, it is apparent, is open to reason. In fact, he is dedicated to the logic of statistics. "I rarely go by instinct," he said. "I don't go to a race track and bet on a horse by its name or number. I go by past performance. Even if it's a two-year-old maiden, I try to get a time somewhere."

But now his mind was not on maidens, but on the rest of the batting order, and it went quickly. "This is the easy part, making out the lineup," said Weaver, handing the card to Barney, who found it in order and departed. "The making of the team," continued Weaver, "really comes when the season begins, a year ago September, when the team holds organizational meetings, and you have to decide which positions you need help at.

"Then in spring training you try to put it together. Early in the season, you try to solve the problems which will probably make the difference at the end of the season."

The secret of Weaver's success, Barney says, is his masterful way of using each of his 25 players to get the most out of their ability. Despite his reliance on statistics and experience, Weaver puts stock in superstition. He will use, for example, the same red pen until the team loses, then switch to blue or green or black, hoping one of those contains another winning streak.

Barney says: "He becomes violent when we're winning and his pen runs out of ink." Weaver now goes to his locker and puts on a pair of baseball shoes. There are five other pairs on the floor. A visitor, interested in the intellectual processes of Weaver, asked why he chose those particular shoes to wear this night. "Because," said Weaver, after a moment, "they fit."

Sparky Anderson: Compassion Mixed with Foresight

July 31, 1982

It was late April when Sparky Anderson, the manager of the Detroit Tigers, received a phone call from Mike Ivie, asking for a job.

Managers often get calls like this from players trying to hang on, but this one was different. Anderson said yes, he'd like to take a look at him in the batting cage. Ivie, in Houston, asked when Anderson would like to see him in Detroit.

"When can you come?" asked Anderson.

"This afternoon," said Ivie. Anderson laughed softly, and, not wishing to add pressure to Ivie, said, "No rush, come up in a couple of days." Ivie had just been given his unconditional release from the Houston Astros. Yet he was only twenty-nine years old, a time when he should be in his prime. His overall batting average for nine years in the major leagues was .274. Better than respectable.

Anderson had remembered Ivie when both were in the National League, Anderson as manager of Cincinnati, and Ivie with San Diego and San Francisco. He remembered when Ivie first came up to the major leagues in 1971, and how impressed he was with his talent.

He was, Anderson recalled, a perfect baseball specimen—a 6-foot-4, 215-pound catcher-first baseman with a sweet, powerful swing. Anderson, once explaining Ivie's hitting, pointed to the left-field stands and said, "He can get there real quick."

And Anderson liked Ivie personally. He called him "Michael," and sometimes they'd chat on the field, and once he had dinner with Ivie and his wife. He was a gentleman, Anderson would recall, and he truly cared about being a good baseball player.

In some ways, perhaps, Ivie cared too much. He went through a series of publicized emotional problems. Sometimes he would sit in front of his locker, very tense before a game; sometimes he would tell the manager he just couldn't perform up to his own expectations. Odd things happened. He couldn't throw the ball back to the pitcher when he was catching, and at first base he lost all confidence in his fielding. This was a man with excellent hands and an outstanding arm.

The Padres, unable to harness his great talent after five years, traded him to San Francisco. More problems. He didn't want to catch anymore. He was criticized by some members of the press as a spoiled brat. He went on the disabled list: mental fatigue, he called his problem.

He was sinking in San Francisco and, in April 1981, the Giants traded him to Houston. In Houston, he played just 19 games, and he spent four and a half months on the disabled list. Again, it was listed as mental fatigue.

Later, Ivie would admit that he suffered from a deep fear of failure, that he had put such pressure on himself to succeed that he couldn't perform.

Yet, now married and the father of two boys, he continued to love the game he had played ever since he was a six-year-old in Decatur, Georgia, and where he developed into a star. In 1970, he was the No. 1 draft pick in the nation. He played in a major league game when he was nineteen years old.

When the Astros released him, it seemed that his career might be over, sadly cut short.

But when Anderson saw Ivie swing the bat, he liked what he saw in him as much as he ever did. As for possible emotional problems with Ivie, Anderson said he was unconcerned. "I've never heard of Mike Ivie hurting anyone, doing anything wrong to anyone," said Anderson. "And if he says he's scared, or fears failure, let me tell you, he's not a special case. This is a tough business, and all of us are scared to various degrees.

"I've seen guys so scared they're shaking. I've gone to guys in pressure situations to pinch-hit, and they said they couldn't. I've had guys come to me and ask me to take 'em out of ball games. I've seen a pitcher's hand swell up when he was told he's going to pitch a big game the next day."

So far this season, Ivie, playing only as a designated hitter, has had some outstanding moments—his home run beat Texas, 2–1, and he hit two homers in another game—and going into last night's game against

Toronto, he had the respectable total of 12 home runs in 203 times at bat, but his batting average was only .222.

He says that it's a matter of getting used to American League pitchers, who throw more breaking balls than National League pitchers. "Ted Simmons, who was a great hitter with the Cardinals," said Ivie, "had to make the same kind of difficult adjustment when he was traded to Milwaukee."

Anderson believes that, because Ivie has been out so much the last two years, he has lost some of his batting rhythm. "But he will get it back," said Anderson. "He's been honest with himself, and that's the most important step."

"And if I don't come back the way I hope?" said Ivie. "Then I'll have said, 'OK, you had a good career. You did something a lot of guys want to do and never can. Be a big league ballplayer.' After everything, it's still a dream come true, isn't it?"

Whitey Herzog: The White Rat Is Fiddling

October 20, 1987/Minneapolis, Minnesota

Earlier this season, Whitey Herzog, the St. Louis Cardinals manager, told a story about being called to the office of Augie Busch, the octogenarian owner of the Cardinals.

"Whitey," he recalled Busch saying, "I want to give you a lifetime contract."

"I looked at him and said, 'Mr. Busch, whose lifetime?'"

Herzog settled for an extension of his contract to 1990.

In the two most recent games, however, the first two of the World Series, Herzog hasn't had to do very much to fulfill the terms of his contract. And though his job hardly appears to be in jeopardy, the position of his team in the Series does.

On successive nights in the howling of the Metrodome, the Cardinals suffered cruel and unusual punishment at the hands of the Minnesota Twins. In the fourth inning the Twins exploded for seven and six runs, respectively, and did so with the zealous encouragement of 55,000 fans waving the Twins new secret weapon, the sinister Homer Hanky, and swaying and chanting, "My Baby Loves to Hanky-Panky."

And while the Twins burned, all Whitey could do was fiddle with the pen in his back pocket.

"And after that," Herzog said, "the horses were out of the barn." That is, the games were no longer a contest. The first was 10–1, the second, 8–4—though it was 8–1 before the Cardinals could muster even a little offense in the later innings.

But Herzog could try something. He argued that Bert Blyleven, the Twins slick hurler, was "quick-pitching," or balking, with men on base.

At one point, Herzog ran onto the field and would remember this repartee:

"He ain't comin' to no stop," Herzog hollered to the umpires. "He's stoppin'," said one. "Where's he stoppin'? Show me."

"He's doing what he's done all season," said Ken Kaiser, the third-base umpire, an American Leaguer.

"Just 'cause he's been doin' it all year don't make it right, does it?"

"Got Ozzie on," Herzog said later, "he can't run. Got Curt on, he can't."

Herzog referred to the firm of Smith and Ford, and the inability because of the alleged "quick-pitch" for his speedy operatives to tear around the ersatz turf. But blaming the sound whippings by the Twins on a quick-pitch is, as was once remarked, like blaming the Johnstown flood on a leaky toilet.

Herzog certainly knows better. He is a manager with extensive experience, including leading his troops to victory in the 1982 World Series and being their field commander when they lost in the 1985 Series.

In the latter, the Cards won the first two games against Kansas City before succumbing to the Royals pitching and their own excuse-making and umpire-complaints and an overall dyspeptic disposition.

After the second game, in his small office in the Metrodome made even more cramped by the crush of reporters, Herzog replied to a question about how the Royals were two down, like the Cardinals, and came back to win.

"Two things mean nothing in baseball: last year and yesterday," he said.

Herzog, who enjoys the nickname The White Rat, sat at a desk, still wearing his red baseball jacket, and ate his dinner from a pair of paper plates, periodically stabbing with a plastic fork at some fried shrimp, macaroni, corn niblets, and a salad, washing it down with two cans of light beer.

"They're a hot ball club right now," he continued, "but if they're so good, how come they only won 85 games in the season—and won only nine games on the road after the All-Star break?"

With the Series now moving to St. Louis for three games, starting tonight, he is hoping familiarity will breed runs.

"And good pitching," he said. "We haven't had a well-pitched game yet." He was hoping that John Tudor, his left-handed ace, would be his answer tonight.

Is there anything he'll be saying to his team before the third game.

"What am I going to say?" he replied sharply. "This ain't football."

Well, he was asked, isn't baseball supposed to be a "mental game?"

"I don't know. I'm not that smart."

What did he know about Les Straker, the Twins starter?

"Know he's right-handed, and know he's got a good arm."

Why was it the fourth inning in each game that the explosion came?

"They go around once in the batting order," he said, "and then maybe they think they can hit a guy."

He rose from his desk, the plates nearly clean, and tossed them in the garbage can behind him. He moved to a locker and removed his uniform and shimmied out of the girdle-like rubber belt he wears to try to glamorize his midriff.

An older man from a small radio station, microphone in hand, came up behind Herzog and softly wondered if he might ask a question.

Herzog ignored him, and spoke to someone else.

The man, despite his age, was obviously a novice, and uncomfortable. Herzog seemed to pick that up immediately. The man summoned the courage to pose a question to the manager. "That quick-pitch you spoke about," he said, "who does it affect more, the batter or the base-runner?"

"I don't answer stupid questions like that," said Herzog. "Who does it affect?"

Herzog got up and grabbed a towel for the shower. "Who do you think it affects?" he said.

Herzog brushed past the small white-haired man. "Thank you," the man said, disconcerted. "Thank you."

"What kind of question is that?" said Herzog, loudly, to no one in particular. And he was gone from the room.

So was the older man with the microphone.

Tommy Lasorda's Recipes for Winning and for Minestra E Fagioli

May 15, 1988

Food, insists Tommy Lasorda, the well-fed manager of the Los Angeles Dodgers, is the only weakness he has not been able to conquer. He recalls taking a pack of cigarettes from his pocket, staring at it, deciding he was stronger than the cigarettes and throwing the pack away, never to smoke again. He quit drinking in a similar manner. However, he also recalls the time he stared at a clam on a plate and demanded to know, "Who's stronger, you or me?" The clam stared back, according to Mr. Lasorda, "and right then I knew I had met my match."

Tommy Lasorda's enthusiasm for food is renowned. Once Steve Garvey, the former Dodgers first baseman, had a uniform made with the name "Lasorda" replaced with "Lasagna." Another time some of his players, trying to embarrass him into dieting, had T-shirts printed with "Do Not Feed the Manager" in English, Spanish, French, Italian, and Japanese.

The 5-foot-9 Lasorda, who has admitted to weighing "a light 202 pounds," learned the joys of eating while growing up during the Depression in Norristown, Pennsylvania, with his Italian immigrant father, mother and four brothers.

"Times were tough," said Mr. Lasorda, "so we had to be imaginative." His most vivid memory of that time was of the meals his mother prepared. Perhaps his favorite was minestra e fagioli, or "greens and beans," as the family called it, which had its genesis in the fields and roadsides near the house. Preparation began when a family member went out to pick "dandy-lions," recalled Mr. Lasorda. "My mother, who was a fabulous cook, cut up the greens and added beans and sliced pepperoni and garlic and olive oil and stirred it all up. It was a tremendous meal. And we all learned to cook it."

The boys learned to cook many more dishes besides. They caught on so well they now own a restaurant in Exton, Pennsylvania, and Mr. Lasorda is a partner in two California restaurants. Although he doesn't have time for much cooking, the manager makes an exception when all the brothers get together to make a family favorite, such as minestra e fagioli.

One of the secrets to the success of the dish, according to Mr. Lasorda, is the preparation of the pepperoni: "You slice it thin, then cut each slice in half, so you're not eating big chunks. That really makes it."

There is only one major difference between the way the dish was originally made by his mother and the way Mr. Lasorda, lad of the Depression, currently prepares it. That is, Tommy Lasorda no longer need go into the fields—the outfield, the infield, or any other field—to gather dandelions. He now walks into a market and picks out some escarole. It's one of the perks of regularly collecting a baseball check.

Tommy Lasorda's Minestra E Fagioli
(A Casserole of Beans and Pepperoni)

Time: About one hour, plus overnight soaking.
Yield: Six servings.

Ingredients
- 1 pound cannellini dried beans or 2 19-ounce cans cannellini, drained
- 4 heads escarole, about 3 pounds, washed (or the same weight of Swiss chard, dandelion greens, or endives)
- ¼ cup olive oil
- 5 cloves garlic, finely chopped
- ¼ pound pepperoni, thinly sliced and halved
- A pinch of fresh parsley
- A pinch of oregano
- Salt and freshly ground pepper to taste.

Preparation
1. Soak the dried beans in water overnight. Drain.
2. Blanch the escarole in lightly salted boiling water for three minutes. Drain and chop coarsely.

3. Heat the olive oil in a heavy pot over medium heat and sauté the garlic until golden. Add the pepperoni, parsley, and oregano, and sauté for one minute.

4. Add the beans, the escarole, and three-quarters cup of water. (If using canned beans, add the beans to the pot 10 minutes before the end of the cooking time.) Season with salt and pepper. Cover and cook over medium heat for 30 minutes, stirring occasionally. Add one or more tablespoons of water during the cooking, if necessary.

Leo Durocher: "The Lip"

July 1, 1970

"About six months ago," said Leo Durocher (who perhaps is not the best source for this information), "I quit reading the sports pages. I got tired reading fiction."

The Chicago Cubs manager sat with feet upon his desk in the visitors' clubhouse at Shea Stadium and cracked a wry smile at his remark.

He is speaking to the press now, a reversal from last season. Then he cut off communications with the news media, except for his own pregame and post-game radio shows, when his stratagems and the servings of his pitchers began to be hit hard. The Cubs fell from an 8 1/2-game lead in the National League's Eastern Division to a second-place finish, eight games behind the New York Mets.

He was now telling of a time several years ago when he managed the New York Giants and had said a similar thing, that he was not reading the sports pages.

"One writer was knockin' my brains out every day," he recalled. "I felt like killing him. But another writer gave me some advice on how to handle this guy, and I took it.

"After every game, this guy who was knockin' my brains out came into my office and I answered all his questions with a smile.

"After about ten days, he says to me, 'Leo, how come you're being so nice to me, what with the way I've been knockin your brains out?' And I said, 'Oh, really? Gee, pal, I haven't been reading your stuff.' That really got him. He wrote beautiful stuff about me after that."

If it is true that Durocher has not been reading sports sections for six months, then he did not read that *Look* magazine piece in March which was titled, "How Durocher Blew the Pennant." In it, he was called "the most unprincipled man in sports."

"Naw, I didn't read it," he said. "But a lot of my friends told me what was in it. A lot of guys write things about me and I never see 'em. I wouldn't know 'em if I tripped over 'em. But this guy who wrote it (William Barry Furlong) they tell me he's got buck teeth and dirty fingernails. You gotta hate this guy right away. Right? I mean, buck teeth and dirty fingernails."

What, then, are Durocher's reading habits, now? "I read everything except the sports pages," he said. "Like the *Chicago Tribune*, it comes in sections. I get the paper and dump the sports section into the waste basket.

"It reminds me of Mr. Stoneham (Horace Stoneham owns the San Francisco Giants). Jimmy Powers used to cut Mr. Stoneham's throat every day in a New York paper. So Mr. Stoneham had his secretary cut out Powers's column and drop it into the wastebasket and then put the paper on his desk.

"Most people read sports for relaxation, to get away from the world events. Me, I do the opposite."

Durocher then asked about the article in the recent *Look* magazine by Jim Bouton. "I saw a story in the paper about it with pictures of Mickey [Mantle], Whitey [Ford], and Ralph [Houk]," he said. "Bouton gave it to 'em pretty good. Now why would he do something like that?

How much could he have gotten for it? Five thousand dollars maybe. Did he need the money? I could understand it if his wife and kids were starving . . ."

He was asked what he was doing reading the sports section?

"It was on my desk, turned right to that page, when I came in. I couldn't help see it," he said.

Then he told another story, which he considered humorous, about a sports writer who had obviously been tippling and staggered into Durocher's office in Chicago last year.

The sports writer asked Durocher if he could do him a favor. Durocher said yes. The guy wanted to borrow money, and Durocher reached into his pocket. (Durocher, ethically, did not mention the amount.)

"The next day, the guy knocks my brains out," said Durocher. "That's not so bad—if he also drops my money on my desk. But I never saw him again."

How did Durocher know the sports writer slammed him, since he no longer reads the sports section?

"I got friends who told me," he replied.

Walter Alston: The Methuselah of Managers

July 10, 1974

Walter Alston, legs crossed, leathery face creased, leisurely smoking a cigarette, sat recently in the Dodgers dugout where he has sat for the last twenty years, incredibly, imperturbably.

He came out of nowhere—well, if you consider Darrtown, Ohio (pop. scarce), nowhere—to manage in Brooklyn, which, in baseball in 1954, was indeed somewhere.

Virtually every year for about the next decade or so, after, Alston was supposed to be fired. Every year he wasn't.

The Dodgers are now into their third major change-over in personnel in the last twenty years. First there was the team of Robinson, Erskine, Hodges, Newcombe, Campanella. Then came the Koufax, Drysdale, Roseboro, Gilliam years. Now there is Cey and Ferguson and Buckner and others who are only beginning to dent the headlines. They are fighting the Giants for top spot in the National League West.

Alston sits and works his quiet wonders. He has managed four World Champions and six pennant winners, In between he has also masterminded two seventh-place finishes and one eighth-place.

He now is third on the all-time list for having managed one team most consecutive years. Only Connie Mack (50 years) and John McGraw (31) are ahead of him; but they had a small edge: they owned their ball clubs.

Alston is at the mercy of Walter O'Malley, chairman of the board of the Dodgers,

Every year Alston gets a one-year contract, just one year. In a profession that is notorious for its insecurity, in which managers rarely last more than three seasons with one club, signing a one year contract is a funereal thing to do.

Alston says now that none of this bothered him too terrifically: "I've always felt that if they don't want me, then I don't want to be here."

Although there have been mentions in news reports that he might retire, he gives no hint of this. He says that managing keeps him young, at sixty-one.

An acquaintance walked by in the dugout. "The team gets younger but the manager gets older," the man said to Alston, lamely being light.

"Not hardly," said Alston. He said later that he enjoys working with young ballplayers and that he'd just as soon everybody left him alone so he could do that.

The young ballplayers he has now, he acknowledges, "excited" a lot of people this spring. "But actually when you look at it. we just had one very good month." he said. "Who expected Lopes to hit .350, Crawford to be batting .400, Cey to be way over .300. Ferguson to lead the league in RBIs?

"We always expect our pitching to be good, and our defense has been better than we thought. But"—now he looks at you with light blue straight ungalvanized eyes—"we'll see. Too early to tell."

He is a large, powerful looking man, in a peaceable. small-town manner. But he can get excitable. His most famous eruption was when he saw roommates Sandy Koufax and Larry Sherry coming in after curfew, rush to their room and slam their door. Alston hammered the door open with his fists.

He also enjoys a gag. Last winter he bought a motor bike and gave Dodger coach Tommy Lasorda a ride on it when the latter visited Alston in Darrtown.

"Tom held on behind me and I drove through the little old tractor back roads," said Alston. "I got up to forty miles an hour, then fifty, and I started pouring the coal on. Tom was holding tighter and tighter. All of a sudden I pretended I got dirt in my eyes, I brushed one hand over my eyes." Alston had his head thrown back and was laughing. "and Tom hollered., 'Skip. Skip. will we make it?'"

Alston, though, was in control. Perhaps that is his managerial secret, too. He says that all managers push about the same buttons. "Not much difference between one and the other in strategy," said Alston. "You manage with the material you have. You have sluggers, you go for the big inning. If you have hit-and-run men, you play for one run. erwise, it's handling men and getting the best out of them."

Recently, Casey Stengel. one of only three men to win more world championships than Alston and once a regular World Series adversary of Alston's, was asked about Alston.

Stengel gave a typically cogent explanation of Alston's merits, but one must listen closely:

"You know he has a smart owner because he keeps the seats clean. If you wear a clean dress it'll stay clean when you sit down. He runs a public park and he's not going to be arrested for being neat about it.

"And you know he's kept Alston ever since he got him.

"So that's number two on how you know how smart the owner is."

Eddie Mathews: A Different Sort of Skipper

August 14, 1973/Atlanta, Georgia

"I'm not a good manager," said Eddie Mathews, manager of the Atlanta Braves. "But I'm not a bad manager either. I'm learning on the job." He was being either frank or humble. Whichever, it was both stunning and refreshing.

Managers rarely bespeak such sacrilege. They are offered up a position of this magnitude because they are, of course, the closest thing to infallibility this side of the Tiber River.

And when they make a decision that is—well, not wrong—but is thwarted from sheer luck by the other team, then these paragons run onto the field and hop and flap and kick up dirt around the surprised umpire. an innocent bystander.

To the starkly naked eye, Eddie Mathews has none of those devious bones in his body. His eyes are not shifty. though he does have a slight twitch, which may be his way of suppressing the common managerial disease of shiftiness.

This is Mathews's first full year as a manager, after having taken over for Luman Harris on August 7. 1972. The Braves were in fourth place then, and finished there, 25 games out of first. This season, the Braves are playing at nearly the same miserable .450 pace and, on August 7, 1973, were 19 1/2 games out of first place.

It is Mathews's fault for being here in the first place. He retired from baseball after a fine playing career. He tried selling municipal bonds for two years. But things were going slowly. "You have to wait around for results," Mathews said, "where in baseball you're used to things happening bang-bang. Hit a homer or strike out."

So he returned, in 1970, "to the womb," as he called it. He came back to the Braves as a coach, then succeeded, if you will, to the imperial hot seat. But, unlike some deities, he suffers.

An example: One of his outstanding young players did not run out a ground ball. "The world saw it." says Mathews. Which means, the player was booed by the fans.

"The question is, 'What do you do?'" asked Mathews recently. "Do you bench him? Pull him out of the game; Chew him out in front of the players? Chew him out man-to-man? If you do talk to him man-to-man. should it be after the game. during the game. or the next day. or the next week?

"I decided to talk to him the next day. I mean, you don't want to talk to him right after the game because if you win, that's throwing a wet towel on it. If you lose, that's kicking him lower.

"So I called him in to my office the next day. Now. if that doesn't work, I'll have to try something else."

"If that doesn't work . . ." What kind of language is that for a man who is hired to know all the answers! Maybe. though, this quirky characteristic is a favorable harbinger for Mathews, even in managing, though most of his peers would surely consider it a handicap.

Mathews's mind is opening to new knowledge. He seeks self-improvement instead of reassurances of sainthood. These are some of the things he is learning:

He is discovering the peculiarities of pitchers. Pitchers, it is commonly felt in baseball, are not simply odd, they are simply not human.

"You have to watch the expressions on their faces to know when they are tiring." said Mathews. "Is he breathing deeper than usual when he returns to the dugout? Some relievers are better for some reason when the team is behind, others are better when they're ahead.

"Then you have to know about injuries. A lot of guys try to play when they shouldn't.

"Very little of managing is when to hit-and-run, when to steal, that kind of thing. Most managers are about the same in those skills. Managers don't win too many games but they can lose a lot by not knowing their players well enough."

The work is new and exhausting for the forty-two-year-old Mathews. Some days the team is dragging, and needs a team of oxen to get a runner to first base.

How does he motivate a losing team in the dog days of August? "I can only tell them that the cream rises to the top and that if you can play all out in bad times, you will play that way in good times."

These mental gyrations take their toll, particularly when it goes on day after day. "There was one period when we played forty straight days." said Mathews. "This has to be the toughest game mentally. I laughed when I read that George Allen said his Redskins were flat for the Super Bowl—after they had two full weeks to prepare for one game."

Mathews says he has no trouble sleeping nights. "I get so tired playing everybody's position," he said, "that I'm completely exhausted."

Obviously. Mathews has had no time to read the collection of managers' stories compiled by Jim Bouton, the title of which is *I Managed Good, But Boy Did They Play Bad.*

* * *

Eddie Mathews had been elected to the Baseball Hall of Fame as a player in 1978, one of the great home-run hitters of all-time, becoming only the seventh major leaguer to hit more than 500 home runs (512).

Bill Veeck: A Pied Piper

January 4, 1986

Some will remember how Bill Veeck threw a post-leg-amputation party for himself—he was not about to wallow in self-pity—and danced the night away on his new wooden limb. That was in 1946, more than a year after he was injured. He had been a marine on Guadalcanal during World War II when an antiaircraft gun recoiled into his leg, and the leg became infected.

Others in recent years will remember—who can forget?—that wrinkled old face with that bright, boyish look in his eyes. And you had to remember his laugh, a deep, hoarse, genuinely delighted laugh, with head thrown back and stein of beer gripped solidly.

Others will remember him as the greatest hustler since Jack Falstaff. And perhaps it was no coincidence that when he was the owner of the Chicago White Sox he named the press quarters "The Bard's Room." He understood that it couldn't hurt business to con the reporters some, too.

Bill Veeck will be remembered by many as the guy who brought midgets and orchids to baseball, or exploding scoreboards to the ball field, and signed the first black to play in the American League, Larry Doby, and put old Satchel Paige into a big-league uniform. And he'll be remembered by some as the guy who never wore a tie but who made starchy baseball owners so tight around the collar they got bug-eyed.

And some will remember how much he loved baseball. And some will remember how much he loved people. And some will remember

410

both. "The most beautiful thing in the world," he once said, "is a ball park filled with people."

I have my own memories of William Louis Veeck Jr., who died Thursday of a heart attack at age seventy-one. I remember him covering the Philadelphia-Baltimore World Series in 1983 for the *Chicago Tribune*. And in the outdoor press box in Philadelphia I noticed him at game's end set up his turquoise portable typewriter and begin to hit the keys. He had been forced for financial reasons to sell the White Sox three years before, but his heart was still in the game—it always would be—and now he would write about it. On deadline. He was no phony. This former big-league baseball owner wrote his own stuff. I remember reading one of his pieces afterward and enjoying it very much. He knew the game, had original insights and stuck the adverbs and adjectives in all the right places.

I remember the first time I heard Veeck speak. It was in a hotel in Chicago in 1959—the first year that he ran the White Sox. He had placed billboards all around the city proclaiming, "We will bring a pennant to Chicago." I remember that the hall in the hotel was filled. Veeck at the lectern fidgeted and he seemed to list because of his leg, but he spoke without notes and told stories—old stories, but fresh to my then-fresh ears—about how poorly the Browns in St. Louis drew: One day he asked someone to come to a Browns game. The person said, "What time does it start?" Veeck replied, "What time's convenient?"

The crowd loved him. So did the rest of the city. True to his word, he brought a pennant to Chicago that very first year, and set another attendance record. He made Comiskey Park—often a dreary joint—a swell place for a few hours' entertainment. He not only cleaned up the old park, and had it painted, he even installed washrooms and an outdoor shower for the people in the bleachers.

For the nearly fifty years that Comiskey Park had been in existence, those who had been treated as the underclass in the bleachers had simply been inconvenienced. Veeck cared enough about them—and his promotion—to do something about it. One of the people he brought with him to Chicago was Hank Greenberg, the Hall of Fame ballplayer who became Veeck's general manager there. Greenberg was also his assistant when Veeck owned the Cleveland Indians in the middle 1940s. Greenberg lives in Beverly Hills, and on the morning when it was learned that Veeck had died, I called him.

"I've lost a great friend and great partner—he was the most unusual man I ever met," Greenberg said. His voice was a little shaky. As we spoke, there were moments when Greenberg stopped to gather himself.

"Bill brought baseball into the twentieth century," he continued. "He sold baseball not just on the field, but off the field. Before Bill, baseball was just win or lose. But he made it fun to be at the ball park. Even if it was a lousy game that day, a lady could go home with an orchid he had handed out. Of course, he always wanted to win, and knew he'd draw more if he did.

"I remember the 1948 season in Cleveland when we set the attendance record of the major leagues with 2.6 million. I'd look out the window of the stadium and see these great crowds of people coming over the bridge and heading for the ball park. I told Bill, 'You're like the Pied Piper.'

"Bill wasn't just a guy trying to make a buck by running promotions. He really enjoyed people enjoying themselves. He was color-blind and race-blind and religion-blind. I first met him in 1947 and he talked to me about the Indians—I mean the ones in Oklahoma and Texas—and how unfairly they had been treated.

I never knew from such things. This was so far advanced for me. I was a guy who was concerned with base hits and how to win a ball game. It opened up my eyes. "When he brought Satchel Paige into baseball, a lot of people said he was making a mockery of the game, because Satchel was forty-eight or something. Remember, this was a day when a ballplayer was really old at thirty-two or thirty-three. Well, Satch was 6 and 1 for us down the stretch and we won the pennant."

Though Veeck was out of baseball for the last six years, he couldn't stay away, and was frequently seen in the bleachers in Wrigley Field. Greenberg recalled: "The last time we talked was on Monday when I called him in the hospital. Bill said, 'You know, I think I can get the Cleveland club.' I said, 'You're crazy. Why don't you go someplace where you have a chance to make some money? Why don't you go into the stock market, or some other business. With your talents you can make a lot of money at anything.'

"He said, 'Wouldn't it be great, Hank, to get the old gang together again?'

"He was hopeless. I said, 'You still want to sell peanuts at the ball park, don't you?'

"'Yeah,' he said, 'I do.'"

The Many Poses of Bowie Kuhn

August 7, 1983

Bowie Kuhn's resignation as commissioner of baseball on Wednesday was strange. It was strange because he had already been dismissed. His term did not expire until August 12, but he was hoping to get reinstated. When that became clearly hopeless, he resigned, as he called it. That's not resigning. That's simply making a virtue of necessity.

It was a pose but Kuhn, as commissioner, was accustomed to poses.

He was official greeter, official image and official personage for baseball. And at 6-foot-5, as well tailored as a mannequin, he carried that out with stately, if sometimes farcical, grace.

He once sat in a freezing postseason game—a postponement would have made the television people unhappy, which would have made the owners unhappy—without an overcoat. He wore only a suit, as if the television cameras alone could keep him warm. It was only a pose. Later it was learned that he was wearing thermal underwear.

"Will you buy an overcoat, now that you're no longer commissioner?" Kuhn was asked.

"Well," he said, smiling, "I may take it out of mothballs."

He posed also as commissioner for all baseball, which meant the players as well as the owners. What he was, in fact, was simply witness for management.

Whenever the players and management went to the mat, or the artificial carpet, as the case might be, Kuhn was a witness called by management. Of course. He was hired by management, paid by management, and ultimately, when enough of them felt he no longer served their purpose, he was dismissed by management. He was their employee.

When, for example, there were arbitration hearings concerning the free agency of the pitchers Andy Messersmith and Dave McNally in 1975, Kuhn was witness for management. The pitchers contended that the reserve clause, which bound a player to a team forever or until the team decided that forever had arrived, was unfair and illegal. They contended that it held down wages.

Kuhn took the stand. It was a typical performance:

"The reserve system . . . is necessary to protect not only the integrity of the game, but the economic viability of the game. . . .

"And what I see, looking as best as I can, looking into the future, is the loss of clubs. Some of our clubs would not be able to survive it. There would be the loss of employment, the elimination of any possibility that in the near term we could expand into cities that have much wanted baseball, and where baseball should be; the loss of minor leagues, if not all of them, most of them, and not inconceivably, the loss of a major league."

414

A better witness than that is hard to find. But the owners lost. Free agency was instituted in 1976. And the opposite of everything Kuhn predicted turned out to happen.

Anybody can be wrong, of course. But to be so dead wrong on the major issue of his reign is another matter.

"At no time," said Marvin Miller, then executive director of the Major League Baseball Players Association, "was there put forth by the owners or Bowie Kuhn the slightest modification of the reserve clause— not a comma, not a concept, not a thought."

And Kuhn's uncompromising position, his siding with the hadliners among the owners, would result in his least finest hour, the midseason players' strike of 1981, in which poses counted for nothing. Kuhn virtually vanished.

The strike was an action taken by the players because, among other reasons, they contended that the owners were conspiring to, in effect, nullify free agency.

Kuhn says he worked behind the scenes and did all that was "humanly possible" to settle matters. He may have, but the players' association wasn't particularly aware of it.

Among the owners, the commissioner wasn't allowed to function any more than as a figurehead, with as much voice as the Queen Mother had about the deployment of battleships to the Falkland Islands.

But not one issue does a commissionership make. There was more than just labor relations. Kuhn was allowed to approve player transactions, discipline owners, players and team personnel.

He did this with inconsistency, and, in some cases, with an eye to politics—that is, to the retention of his job and his annual salary of a quarter of a million dollars.

When Ted Turner, owner of the Atlanta Braves, didn't want Henry Aaron, who was about to tie Babe Ruth's home-run record, to play the season-opening game in Cincinnati, but wait to return home to Atlanta, Kuhn stepped in. No, the integrity of the game demands that Aaron play in Cincinnati. He was right.

But when his job was on the line in 1976, he was more practical. One of the teams opposed to him was the Yankees. George Steinbrenner, the owner, had been suspended by Kuhn for two years because he had been convicted of a felony—conspiring to provide illegal campaign funds for the reelection of President Nixon. Eventually, the Yankees changed their vote to support Kuhn as commissioner. "That was due," Kuhn said Wednesday, "to certain blandishments." Whatever that meant, the fact is that Steinbrenner's suspension by Kuhn was shortened from two years to fifteen months.

Kuhn personally is a charming man, a decent man, a man with an unexpected sense of humor. He was perhaps as good a commissioner as his employers would allow, but the commissioner's tether is short.

Among the accomplishments during his tenure, he cites the continuing integrity of the game, and no major scandals. Fine, but there were no major scandals under his four predecessors, either.

Meawhile, Kuhn says that in the fourteen and a half years of his stewardship, attendance in baseball has risen. But there is also a greater population to see more teams with more games than ever before.

He cites attendance records of last year and this year. He cites the recent billion-dollar television contract with the networks that he helped negotiate. Yet all this has come about after modification of the reserve clause, and the coming of free agency, which he so vigorously opposed.

Baseball's popularity continues in America. It does so perhaps not in spite of Kuhn, but hardly because of him.

Where Did Happy Chandler Stand on Jackie Robinson?

June 29, 1991

Did Happy Chandler take unwarranted historical bows? Is the legend of Chandler as being instrumental in Jackie Robinson's breaking the major league color barrier in 1947 based on fact, or self-glorification well after the fact?

A. B. (Happy) Chandler, the commissioner of baseball from 1945 to 1951, and a former Governor of Kentucky and United States Senator, died on June 15, at the age of ninety-two. Stories soon appeared about his contribution to that important event in sports and American history.

And part of Chandler's acceptance speech at the Hall of Fame in 1982 was duly repeated: "I figured that someday I'd have to meet my Maker and He'd ask me why I didn't let that boy play. I was afraid that if I told him it was because he was black, that wouldn't have been sufficient. I told Rickey to bring him on."

A curious posture for a man with this history: the year after Robinson joined the Dodgers, Chandler embraced the Dixiecrats, a segregationist party led by Strom Thurmond; and in 1968 Chandler was eager to be George Wallace's running mate on his third-party ticket.

So what, meanwhile, did Chandler do in the Robinson saga?

"As far as I know, not a thing," said Ralph Kiner, who was with the Pittsburgh Pirates in 1947, and active in player-management affairs.

"It was all Branch Rickey that got Robinson into organized baseball," said Frank Slocum, who worked in the National League office at the time. "Whatever Chandler did was forced on him."

As commissioner, Chandler had to approve all player contracts. Might he have voided Robinson's? "Maybe," said Harold Rosenthal, who covered the Dodgers for the *New York Herald Tribune* in 1947, "he could have invoked the 'best interests of baseball' clause, which gives baseball commissioners sweeping powers." Rosenthal once asked Rickey what would have happened if Chandler had tried to stop him. Rickey said, "If he doesn't approve that contract I have him in Brooklyn Federal court in forty-eight hours."

It is not certain what the Dodger president would have had him in Federal court about (there was, though, a state fair-employment law), but Chandler, an adept politician, was aware that the baseball owners, his employers, wished to stay clear of the courts to maintain their anti-trust exemption.

A stark roadblock for Robinson would also have been contrary to the specious pose held by baseball that it did not embrace Jim Crow but that blacks simply weren't good enough to get major league contracts. Judge Landis, Chandler's predecessor, maintained that stance.

Most accounts of Chandler's death mentioned an owners vote on whether to approve Robinson, which was 15–1 against, with only Rickey casting a yea. There was never a mention of Chandler, who presided at the meeting, speaking out. But Chandler told of a meeting he subsequently had with Rickey in which Rickey asked for his support. Chandler said he gave it.

"I found no evidence that such a meeting between Chandler and Rickey ever took place, except for Chandler saying it did," said Jules Tygiel, author of *Baseball's Great Experiment: Jackie Robinson and His Legacy*. "From my research, Rickey never mentioned it, and Chandler never said a word about it during the time Rickey was alive. I think that Chandler played a neutral role in the Robinson story. He didn't say no. But it was not the role that he later portrayed himself as playing."

Chandler did take some active steps, however. He warned the Louisville Colonels when Robinson and his Montreal team played in Louisville in the Little World Series in 1946 that the commissioner's office would not tolerate any racial protest. And he chastised Ben Chapman, the Phillies manager, for his on-field racial abuse of Robinson in 1947.

"From what I know," said Clyde Sukeforth, now eighty-nine, by telephone from his home in Maine, "Chandler was in favor of Robinson from the very beginning. Mr. Rickey had no problem there at all."

Sukeforth was then a Dodger coach, and a trusted scout for Rickey, and the only other witness to the historic meeting in which Rickey informed Robinson that he wanted him not for the Brooklyn Brown Dodgers, a black team, but for the parent Brooklyn Dodgers.

Whatever the diverse pulls in Chandler—the politician who understood that the time had come, the patriot, the Southerner, the self-aggrandizer, the God-fearing petitioner—he did not try to stop Rickey and Robinson. Others, like Landis, had upheld the racial barriers. Chandler stood aside. While that doesn't exactly pass for being a catalyst, it does, in this case, make it legacy enough.

Part XI: In the Writers' Wing of the Hall

Ring Lardner: Literary Trail Blazer

May 5, 1971

"What did you hit last year?" Carey ast him.

"I had malaria most of the season," says Ike. "I wound up with .356."

"Where would I have to go to get malaria?" says Carey, but Ike didn't wise up . . .

—From the short story "Alibi Ike" by Ring Lardner

It may be true that, as literary critic Gilbert Seldes once said, "Baseball has never recovered" from what Ring Lardner did to its heroes. Lardner's influence may be taken a step further: Baseball-writing specifically and sports-writing in general have never recovered. A not uncommon occurrence is for a sports editor to wince at a cub's florid copy and demand to know, "How come everybody tries to be Ring Lardner? Write if straight."

Neither the editor nor the cub may ever have read Ring Lardner, and therein lies some of the problem. Lardner's humor, bitter satire, and precise ear for the language of the dugout made him one of the finest sports columnists and, eventually, one of America's best humorists and short story writers. He set a journalistic standard for excellence, though not necessarily for style, since his was unique and so personal.

What brings up the discussion of Ring Lardner is the project underway in his home town, Niles, Michigan. Sometime in early summer a historical marker will be placed at the house at 519 Bond Street where he was born. Lardner died in 1933, and only now and due largely to the fundraising efforts of Bob Calvert, *Niles Daily Star* sports editor, is the town formally memorializing "its most talented literary prodigy," as Calvert wrote.

The name Lardner was most recently in national news when Ring Jr. won an Academy Award for his screenplay, *M*A*S*H*, which contained the kind of black humor that made his father's work unforgettable.

Lardner Pere, whose *Chicago Tribune* sports columns once inspired such 'local high school journalism students as Ernest Hemingway and James T. Farrell to imitate his style, continues to be read. Lardner is still taught in college literature courses. Anthologies continue to reprint such short stories as "The Love Nest," "Haircut," "Champion," and "The Golden Honeymoon." Scribner's reports that *The Ring Lardner Reader* and *You Know Me Al* (probably his best work, a fictionalized series of letters from a brash bush-league pitcher) still sell well.

For the sportswriters, Lardner's name tops the legend—they like to pull out at the slightest dangle of a modifier. The legend is that a preponderance of sportswriters have gone on to literary triumphs. But Nunnally Johnson wanted to know, "After Lardner, Heywood Broun, John Kieran, Westbrook Pegler, Damon Runyon, Paul Gallico, Quentin Reynolds, and Bob Considine, who is there?" Johnson added that sports writing in general was filled with "bad writing, grammar school humor, foolish styles, threadbare phrases, spurious enthusiasm, and heavy-footed comedy . . . nauseating sentimentality and' agonized slang . . . [and] above all, breeziness, breeziness, breeziness!"

Lardner was controlled and meticulous in his writing. For example, he noted that, "We say somethin' and nothin', but we say anything and everything. There appears to be somethin' about the 'y' near the middle of both these words that impels us to acknowledge the 'g' on the end of them."

He was also able to capture through his acute baseball reporting a deep insight into America. Wrote Virginia Woolf, an English lady who knew nothing about baseball: "It is no coincidence that the best of Mr. Lardner's stories are about games, for one may guess that Mr. Lardner's interest in games has solved one of the most difficult problems of the American writer; it has given him a clue, a centre, a meeting place for the divers activities of people whom a vast continent isolates, whom no tradition controls. Games give him what society gives his English brother."

It is a fine thing for Niles, Michigan, to memorialize Lardner's birthplace. It is a yet finer thing to read the guy's stuff.

Red Smith: None Better

January 16, 1982

Red Smith, a Pulitzer Prize–winning sports columnist for the *New York Times* and one of the nation's most admired sports commentators, died at Stamford (Connecticut) Hospital yesterday of heart failure after a brief illness. He was seventy-six years old and lived in New Canaan.

The last column in Mr. Smith's fifty-five-year career, "Writing Less—and Better?" appeared Monday and told of his plans to cut back his writing from four to three columns a week.

In the column, he recalled years past when he had written seven columns a week and added: "Between those jousts with the mother tongue, there was always a fight or football match or ball game or horse race that had to be covered after the column was done. I loved it."

In the college textbook *A Quarto of Modern Literature*, between an essay by Winston Churchill and a short story by Dylan Thomas, there is an example of spot-news reporting by Red Smith. It is a column on a heavyweight fight between Joe Louis and Rocky Marciano, written on deadline. It is the only piece of journalism in the anthology, and the only sports story.

To the legion of Red Smith fans, it was not surprising that one of his stories would be included among the works of the finest contemporary writers. For them, Red Smith was virtually without peer in his profession.

When he won the Pulitzer Prize for distinguished commentary, in 1976, Mr. Smith became only the second sports columnist ever to be honored with that award. Arthur Daley of the *Times* was the first, in 1956. The Pulitzer committee cited Mr. Smith's work for being "unique in the erudition, the literary quality, the vitality and the freshness of viewpoint."

He received innumerable awards and several honorary degrees, including one from his alma mater, Notre Dame, from which he graduated in 1927. He was pleased by the attention, but not necessarily impressed. He found trying to master his craft too challenging for that.

"Writing is easy," he once said. "I just open a vein and bleed." But he loved it, he admitted. And he had great respect for the "mother tongue." His knowledge of the language was so widely respected that he was on the board as a consultant for several dictionaries and encyclopedias.

He was as self-effacing as he was esteemed. In *Strawberries in the Wintertime*, the last of his five collections of columns, published in 1974, he wrote in the foreword, "Finding a title for such a mixed bag can be a problem. I considered using a catchier title like *War and Peace, Wuthering Heights*, or *The Holy Bible*, but they struck me as dated."

Instead, the title he used, he wrote, "happens to be the title of a piece about Willie Mays and it captures, I think, some of the flavor of the sportswriter's existence, which is what the late Bill Corum was talking about when he said, 'I don't want to be a millionaire, I just want to live like one.'" Few newspapermen, even of the stature of Red Smith, live like millionaires. But some find their work fulfilling. Mr. Smith, apparently, was one. Sport is often considered less than important, but Mr. Smith believed that his job was significant.

"Sports is not really a play world," he said. "I think it's the real world. The people we're writing about in professional sports, they're suffering and living and dying and loving and trying to make their way through life just as the bricklayers and politicians are.

"This may sound defensive—I don't think it is—but I'm aware that games are a part of every culture we know anything about. And often taken seriously. It's no accident that of all the monuments left of the Greco-Roman culture, the biggest is the ballpark, the Colosseum, the Yankee Stadium of ancient times. The man who reports on these games contributes his small bit to the record of his time."

But Mr. Smith wrote with a light touch and a wryness that put the games and the people involved into perspective. Covering a college football game, for example, he quoted, tongue in cheek, a program hawker: "Get your programs, folks—the names, numbers, and salaries of all the players."

Praise for Mr. Smith through the years sometimes came from unlikely sources. The short-story writer Shirley Jackson, who knew almost nothing about sports, reviewed his book, *Out of the Red*, and said that reading the book "has been, actually, an educational experience unlike almost anything I have known since first looking into Chapman's Homer."

And Ernest Hemingway, in his novel *Across the River and Into the Trees*, described one of his characters starting to read the *New York Herald Tribune*: "He was reading Red Smith, and he liked him very much."

When the *Herald Tribune* advertised Mr. Smith's columns on subway posters, they used Beau Jack, the former boxing champion, for a testimonial. Mr. Smith was delighted by it. "Everyone knew," he said, "that Beau Jack was a functional illiterate."

A small man—he stood 5-foot-7—with a florid face, Mr. Smith once described himself as "a seedy amateur with watery eyes behind glittering glasses, a receding chin, a hole in his frowzy haircut." In his later years, his once bright red hair had turned white. But he retained a youthfulness.

"I know I've grown more liberal as I've grown older," he said. "I seem to be finding this a much less pretty world than when I was younger, and I feel things should be done about it and that sports are a part of the world."

In a sense, Mr. Smith became the conscience of the sports world. In recent years he wrote bitterly of the owners of professional sports teams in their labor-management relations. He wrote the headlines for his columns, and he entitled one on employer-employee relationships in baseball, "Lively Times in the Slave Trade." He frequently criticized the International Olympic Committee, accusing it of trying to impress nineteenth-century ideas on a twentieth-century world.

He was the first columnist to propose publicly that the United States boycott the 1980 Olympic Games in Moscow because of Soviet intervention in Afghanistan. The idea appeared in his column of January 4, 1980, and President Carter formally proposed a boycott on January 20. Mostly because of the boycott, only 81 of the 147 eligible nations participated in the Moscow Olympics.

Walter Wellesley ("I hate the name") Smith was born September 25, 1905, in Green Bay, Wisconsin. He was the second of three children born to Walter Philip and Ida Richardson Smith. His father operated a wholesale produce and retail grocery business.

When Mr. Smith was growing up, he hiked through woods, fished, built lean-tos and enjoyed the outdoors as he would all his life. He was never very athletic, but he did become an avid fisherman, and often enjoyed writing disparagingly about his efforts in that pastime. He said he had caught his casting line in trees all the way from the Andes to Finland.

At home in Green Bay, he also read the classics that were stored in a credenza in the family's living room. And influenced by an older friend who was studying journalism at Notre Dame, Mr. Smith decided to matriculate at the same school and major in the same subject.

He edited the school yearbook, *The Dome*, and briefly participated in track. He said his most notable achievement in college was not quite finishing in a mile race, the only one he ever ran.

He was, though, determined to be a newspaperman. And upon graduation in 1927, he recalled that "I wrote letters to about 100 news-papers asking for a job. I got back one reply. That was from the *New York Times*. And it said no." Writing for the *Times* would come much later for Mr. Smith. Meanwhile, he caught on with the *Milwaukee Sentinel* after sending the city editor a letter of "arrant flattery." The pay was $25 a week.

He covered stories ranging from murders to society news. One year later he took a job for $40 a week with the *St. Louis Star*, as a copy editor. "I hated the routine," he said, "but I've got to credit that job with teaching me about writing. The horrible examples that came over my desk daily shocked me into doing a little better."

A few months later the managing editor fired most of the *Star's* sports staff. Mr. Smith was asked to shift to sports. "All I knew about sports was what the average fan knew," he said, "but I was the most dispensable copyreader."

His first assignment was a night football game, and he wrote his story from the viewpoint of a glowworm that envied the brightness of the stadium floodlights. "It was cute," said Smith, "but people seemed to like it." From then on, his editors knew he was special.

In 1936, he joined the *Philadelphia Record* as a sportswriter and columnist, and in 1945 he began a column full time for the *New York Herald Tribune*. His column was syndicated in ninety newspapers. In 1954, when Grantland Rice died, Mr. Smith became the most widely syndicated sports columnist.

When the *Herald Tribune* became part of the new *World Journal Tribune* in 1966, Mr. Smith became sports columnist for the new newspaper. When the publication ceased the next year, his syndicated column survived. His column in the New York area was picked up by the *Long Island Press* and, oddly, *Women's Wear Daily* in a column titled, "Sportif." In 1971, Mr. Smith was hired by the *New York Times* and joined Arthur Daley and Dave Anderson as sports columnists.

Mr. Smith recalled when he was hired. "There was a lot of electricity around our house," he said. "I felt like I was back playing the Palace." Without a large New York daily for an outlet, said his wife, Phyllis, "Red had been more unhappy than he either knew or admitted."

He was sixty-six years old when he joined the *Times*. "Within the *Times* family," said A. M. Rosenthal, executive editor of the newspaper, "we always felt that bringing Red to our staff, even at an age when most men contemplate retirement, allowed us to fulfill a very special trust for sports. He embodied the spirit, vigor, and youth of sports. We remember him with affection and pride as a wonderful writer and a wonderful man."

Mr. Smith's three or four columns a week were syndicated by the *New York Times* News Service to 275 newspapers in the United States and 225 in about thirty foreign nations.

His work remained outstanding, and he continued to grow as a writer. For one thing, he worked to simplify his style, and he looked harder at his prose. "I have tried to become simpler, straighter and purer in my language," he said. "I look at some of the stuff I wrote in past years, and I say, 'Gee, I should have cooled it a little more.'"

He continued to believe that his responsibility as a sportswriter was "to add to the joy of the reader interested in the games and to capture the grace and drama and beauty and humor."

He avoided the cliches and flowery approach that many sportswriters had adopted, and he tried to cover games and people with the accuracy and insights of a good reporter. He preferred covering sports like baseball, football, boxing, and horse playing ("not horse racing," he emphasized), and disdained what he called "back and forth" sports like basketball and hockey.

He combined his unusual style of a sports columnist with the style of a news-side analyst when he covered several political conventions. But in 1968, at the Chicago Democratic Convention, he was moved deeply.

"In the past," he wrote at one point, "it seemed to make sense for a sportswriter on sabbatical from the playpen to attend the quadrennial hawg killings where Presidential candidates are chosen, to observe and report upon the politicians at play. After all, national conventions are games of a sort, and sports offer few spectacles richer in low comedy . . . It is sadly different this week in the police state which Richard "The Lion-Hearted" Daley has made of the city he rules. There is no room for laughter in this city of fear."

His serious view of subjects would increase. In earlier days, he was, by his estimation, guilty of "Godding up" the players. And some commentators on the sports world criticized him for giving the Sports Establishment's high-handed treatment of athletes a kind of sanction. He would begin to change.

Mr. Smith was a warm, generous man who was as witty and insightful in person as he was in print. To young writers, he was unfailingly helpful. He would answer letters seeking his advice. To one college student who sent Mr. Smith his school newspaper columns, he wrote back:

"When I was a cub in Milwaukee I had a city editor who'd stroll over and read across a guy's shoulder when he was writing a lead. Sometimes he would approve, sometimes he'd say gently, 'Try again,' and walk away.

"My best advice is, try again. And then again. If you're for this racket, and not many really are, then you've got an eternity of sweat and tears ahead. I don't mean just you; I mean anybody." And then he proceeded to make specific and pertinent suggestions.

He felt dearly about his friends, and eulogized many in his columns. One of his closest friends was Grantland Rice. "He wrote of men he loved and deeds he admired," wrote Mr. Smith "and never knew how much bigger he was than his finest hero."

Mr. Smith's books included such collections of his columns as *Out of the Red*, *Views of Sports*, and *The Best of Red Smith*. In 1933, he married Catherine Cody of St. Louis.

They had two children—Terence, now editor of the Washington Talk page of the *New York Times*, and Catherine Halloran of Grafton, Wisconsin.

His wife died in 1967. In 1968 he married Phyllis Warner Weiss. They lived in New Canaan and in Martha's Vineyard, Massachusetts. In addition to his wife, son, and daughter, Mr. Smith is survived by five step-children, John Kimball Weiss of Brandamore, Pennsylvania, Karen Weiss Ghent of New York, Robin Weiss of Old Town, Maine, Peter

Weiss of West Berne, New York, and Jenifer Weiss of Washington; six grandchildren and two great-grandchildren.

Jerome Holtzman: They Had Ice Cream Every Friday

August 11, 1990

Jerry Holtzman—Jerome Holtzman to the readers of his baseball column in the *Chicago Tribune*—grew up, like many of us, in a house with kids. Unlike the homes of many of us, the house contained 300 kids, about 150 boys and 150 girls. It was on the West Side of Chicago, and called the Marks Nathan Jewish Orphan Home.

Jerry went to live there when he was ten years old, with his younger brother and sister, after his father died, in 1936, and his mother, in those dark Depression days, was unable to properly look after her children.

The mind builds its own castles, and its own dungeons, and an orphanage during the Depression conjures the life of Oliver Twist and gruel and water, and stinging raps on the ear. "I thought it was terrific," Holtzman said recently. "The building was about a half-block square, and there was a ball field beside it, and we had ice cream every Friday night. My wife, Marilyn, says there has to be something wrong with someone who liked an orphanage."

There was pain, certainly, in separation from his family home, but Jerry Holtzman learned somewhere that you try to make the best of a situation, and you do not look back in anger or sorrow or bitterness.

So Jerry Holtzman, now sixty-four, stocky, with a shock of wavy gray hair, eyebrows furry as caterpillars, wearing suspenders and smoking a cigar not quite as long as his arm, has made his way, one of the brightest, most respected men in his profession. So good, in fact, that last Monday in Cooperstown, New York, he was inducted into the writers' wing of the Baseball Hall of Fame.

Once, Holtzman walked over to a ballplayer with a surly reputation and introduced himself. "I'm not talkin' to the press today," said the ballplayer.

"No problem," said Holtzman, lighting his cigar. "Maybe I'll catch you next year. Or the year after that."

Several years ago, Holtzman discovered a way he hoped he could augment his sportswriter's salary. He bought the rights to ten of the finest sports books, bound them handsomely and reissued them in a set. "I took a bath on it," Holtzman recalled.

Nonetheless, behind a batting cage in Shea Stadium one evening, he was introduced to Nelson Doubleday, who then owned Doubleday & Company. "It's nice to meet a fellow publisher," Holtzman said.

In his remarks at the induction ceremony in Cooperstown, as the ballplayers Jim Palmer and Joe Morgan sat nearby waiting to receive their induction plaques, Holtzman thanked first his wife for her support, and his family, including his three daughters and his son. One of his children wasn't there, however.

"We lost Catherine Ellen six months ago, to cancer, three days before her thirty-seventh birthday," said Holtzman. "A day or two before she died, she said to me, 'I'm sorry I won't be with you in Cooperstown, Dad.' She was a much-loved person and an avid baseball fan. I taught her how to keep score when she was a freshman in high school, and she learned to keep an almost perfect scorecard."

It was with still heavy heart that he recalled that, and yet Jerry Holtzman wished to share with those in the modest-sized but packed Cooperstown Central High School auditorium—the ceremonies had been moved indoors because of the pelting rain—the memories of this much-loved person, and something that she loved.

It is like Holtzman himself, a man who hums when he types, who shares with his readers his love of baseball, and of sportswriting. Holtzman said he grew up not with dreams of becoming a baseball player, as many youngsters did, but of becoming a baseball writer.

He worked on his high school paper and, he said, discovered he had "a modest flair for writing."

He joined the *Chicago Times* in 1943 as a copy boy, immediately after "graduating" at seventeen from the orphanage. "They gave me a suit and $10," he said. He spent two years in the Marines, returned to the newspaper in 1946, covered high school sports for eleven years, and then in 1957 became a local baseball writer for the *Chicago Sun-Times*, and moved, nine years ago, to the *Tribune* as its national baseball columnist.

In 1974, Holtzman recorded and edited the sportswriting classic *No Cheering in the Press Box*, a warm and provocative collection of interviews with veteran sportswriters.

"I remember Jimmy Cannon telling me, 'A sportswriter is entombed in a prolonged boyhood,' because we're always writing about youth, the athletes," said Holtzman. "But I also remember Shirley Povich saying that when he was young, all the players were heroes, but it seemed he matured overnight, and stopped writing about the roar of the crowd. I know what he meant."

Another who is also in the baseball writers' wing at Cooperstown discussed the coming honor with Holtzman. "It'll change your life," the man said.

This concerned Holtzman. "I don't want my life to change," he said. "I like it the way it is."

Shirley Povich Dies at 92; *Washington Post*'s Longtime Sports Columnist

June 7, 1998

Shirley Povich's sports column ran in the *Washington Post* on Friday, which was not unusual, since his columns have appeared in the *Post* for seventy-four years, or since he began working there in 1924, at age nineteen. Mr. Povich's column Friday, headlined "Recent Baseball Feats Require Footnotes," was literary yet earthy, opinionated yet generous, topical yet filled with historical perspective, and a pleasure to read, none of which was unusual.

What was different was that it was his last. Shirley Povich died of a heart attack Thursday night at his home in Washington. He was ninety-two.

"While he retired 'officially' in 1974," an editor's note that preceded Friday's article said, "He continued to write columns for the newspaper." There were more than 15,000 of them over seven decades.

In the final column, which he wrote on Wednesday, Mr. Povich questioned, among other things, whether Mark McGwire, the hulking, slugging first baseman for the St. Louis Cardinals who has hit 414 career home runs, is a greater home run hitter than Babe Ruth. That seems a growing sentiment, but it was not a popular one with Mr. Povich, who covered Ruth and his exploits. "To judge McGwire a better home run hitter than Ruth at a moment when McGwire is exactly 300 home runs short of the Babe's career output is, well, a stretch," he wrote.

And he underscored the opinion about Ruth with a first-hand anecdote that almost no one but Mr. Povich could have provided: "Walter Johnson once said when asked to compare the Babe's swats with those hammer blows of Lou Gehrig and Jimmie Foxx and Hank Greenberg:

'Lemme say this, those balls Ruth hit got smaller quicker than anybody else's.'"

Mr. Povich, 5-foot-8, trim and always neatly attired, was widely admired by generations and was considered one of the country's best sports columnists. "If it hadn't been for his friend Red Smith," Jerome Holtzman, the *Chicago Tribune* sports columnist said, "Shirley would have been regarded as the best sports columnist in the country."

In his unobtrusive manner, and with a quiet New England way of speaking that this Maine native never lost, Mr. Povich was also considered one of the finest gentlemen in the sometimes inelegant world of sports. He was known, read, and enjoyed by a wide range of people—including presidents, starting with Calvin Coolidge.

In the 1930s, the *Washington Post* was the fourth paper in circulation in a five-paper town. Katherine Graham, whose father, Eugene Meyer, bought the *Post* in 1933, became the publisher herself years later. She once claimed that Mr. Povich, then writing his "This Morning" column six days a week, "was responsible for one-third of our readership."

Mr. Povich, like many fine newspaper columnists, was on the side of the underdog. He regularly took the owner of the Washington Redskins, George Preston Marshall, to task for not hiring a black player.

On one occasion Mr. Povich wrote: "Jim Brown, born ineligible to play for the Redskins, integrated their end zone three times yesterday."

Marshall finally did hire a black player, Bobby Mitchell, in 1962.

Mr. Povich and his wife, the former Ethyl Friedman, whom he met on a blind date in 1930, were married for the last sixty-six years. He is survived by his wife and three children: David, a lawyer in Washington; Maury, the television talk show host, and the youngest, and Lynn, a

435

managing editor with MSNBC. "It was a very male family, as you might expect, but being the only girl, Dad really tried not to leave me out of things," Lynn Povich said.

Mr. Povich won numerous prizes for his writing, from the Grantland Rice Award to election to the writers' wing of the Baseball Hall of Fame. He was cited for outstanding service as a World War II war correspondent with the Marines in the Pacific in 1945.

Surely, the strangest acknowledgment he received was when he found himself listed in the initial volume of *Who's Who in American Women* in 1958. The editors had lifted a paragraph on him from *Who's Who in America*, although it plainly said he was married to Ethyl.

"The next year," he recalled with amusement, "they dropped me, like they used to do in the New York Social Register if you had married a stripper—the snobs."

The name Shirley for a boy was not uncommon in Maine. He was born on July 15, 1905, in Bar Harbor to parents who were Orthodox Jewish immigrants from Lithuania. His father later owned a furniture store in Bar Harbor. Mr. Povich was the eighth of ten children and was named for a grandmother, Sarah, or "Shirley," as it was loosely translated into Yiddish.

As a youth, he got a summer job caddying at a country club that catered to wealthy vacationers who owned mansions in Bar Harbor. Edward B. McLean, then the *Post*'s publisher, suggested that Mr. Povich, seventeen, come to Washington where there would be two jobs for him, one as caddie on McLean's personal golf course at $20 a week and the other as a copy boy at the paper at $12 a week.

Mr. Povich, who had never been on a train, had never been out of Maine and had never owned a pair of long pants, accepted. His first task was to carry the bag of McLean's friend, Warren G. Harding, President of the United States.

At the *Post*, Mr. Povich rose first to police reporter and then to a position in the sports department, all while studying law at Georgetown University. His first byline came on August 5, 1924, above a report on the Washington Senators. In 1926, at age twenty-one, he was named sports editor, the youngest sports editor of a metropolitan daily in the nation.

And he went on from there, covering events as diverse as the famed Jack Dempsey-Gene Tunney "long count" heavyweight championship fight in 1927 to the Olympics to Ruth's "called shot" in the 1932 World Series. ("He didn't really call the shot," Mr. Povich said of Ruth. "He was pointing at the pitcher, Charley Root, for quick-pitching him, and he was calling him names.")

At ninety-one, he attended a Washington Bullets game. He was never enamored with basketball, and wrote, "They don't shoot baskets anymore, they stuff them, like taxidermists."

Mr. Povich said the following to Holtzman, in the book *No Cheering in the Press Box*:

"Despite the fact that I was a precocious young sports editor, I would describe myself as a late bloomer. Maturity came late to me. I was about 30 when I discovered I wasn't a clear thinker. I was a hero worshiper, a romanticist, highly sentimental and entirely impractical. I was constantly overwriting, often attempting to make the event and the game more exciting and dramatic than it was."

In his 1969 autobiography, *All These Mornings*, Mr. Povich described how he suffered two fractured vertebrae on Okinawa in World War II. He was taken off a ship that was headed for combat and was transferred, despite his reluctance, to a hospital in Pearl Harbor. Many who went ahead on the ship, including the legendary war correspondent Ernie Pyle, were killed.

"I was leading a charmed life," Mr. Povich wrote, "for reasons unknown to anyone before or since."

A Formidable Foursome: Grantland Rice, Damon Runyon, Dick Young, Jim Murray

Grantland Rice: A "Gee Whiz" Writer

January 2, 2000

Rice was generally considered the best-known sportswriter of his generation. He read widely and brought a certain literate quality to sports writing that hadn't quite been there before. He began writing for the *Nashville News* in 1901, after graduation from Vanderbilt. He later wrote for the *New York Mail* and *New York Tribune*. In 1930 he began his popular syndicated sports column, "The Spotlight." Of the two so-called schools of sports writing in the early part of the century—the skeptical "Aw Nuts" writers versus the more romantic "Gee Whiz" writers—Rice was clearly in the latter group.

He wrote perhaps the most famous opening paragraph in sportswriting history. It appeared on October 19, 1924, as a lead to his report on the Notre Dame-Army football game, won by Notre Dame, and which starred the Fighting Irish backfield: "Outlined against a blue-gray October sky, the Four Horsemen rode again. In dramatic lore they are known as Famine, Pestilence, Destruction, and Death. These are only aliases. Their real names are Stuhldreher, Miller, Crowley, and Layden."

Damon Runyon: The Ultimate "Runyonesque"

He began writing for newspapers when he was twelve years old. He worked for newspapers in Pueblo, Colorado, Colorado Springs, Denver, San Francisco, and became one of the country's star reporters—and sports columnists—with the *New York American*. He covered wars, murder trials, and World Series with equal distinction. Like Lardner,

438

it is Runyon's short stories that enlarged his fame. His "Runyonesque" characters live on in the musical *Guys and Dolls* adapted from his short stories.

From the lead in a column from the 1930 Kentucky Derby:
"Say, have they turned the pages
Back to the past once more?
Back to the racin' ages
An' a Derby out of the yore?
Say, don't tell me I'm daffy,
Ain't that the same ol' grin?
Why it's that handy
Guy named Sande,
Bootin' a winner in!"

Dick Young: The First Sports Writer in the Clubhouse

He revolutionized sports coverage when, as a beat reporter for the *New York Daily News* assigned to the Brooklyn Dodgers in the early 1940s, he began to go into the clubhouse after games to find out what the players had seen and thought during the game. Before this, reporters in the press box wrote solely what the reporters had seen and thought during a game.

In 1957, Young began writing his column, "Young Ideas," after the team owner, Walter O'Malley, decided to move the Dodgers to Los Angeles. In 1982 he moved on to the *New York Post*. Writing with wit and a hard-hitting, direct style, he was frequently in verbal battles with an assortment of sports figures throughout his years as a columnist. The following is from a 1957 column:

"This is called an obit, which is short for obituary. An obit tells of a person who has died, how he lived, and of those who live after him. This is the obit on the Brooklyn Dodgers.

439

"Preliminary diagnosis indicates that the cause of death was an acute case of greed, followed by severe political implications. . . . and, now, Walter O'Malley leaves Brooklyn a rich man and a despised man."

Jim Murray: We Laughed, We Cried

Murray, who won a Pulitzer Prize in 1990, began his career as a reporter for the *New Haven Register*. He moved on to write for the *Los Angeles Examiner, Time* magazine, and *Sports Illustrated*, before joining the *Los Angeles Times* as a sports columnist in 1961. He soon became widely syndicated, and was highly praised for his acerbic wit (and, not surprisingly, highly denounced by some of the subjects of his wit). But, like all good writers, he could also touch a sensitive chord.

From a column in 1979, in which he tells of the loss from an operation of his "good eye"—the other eye had seen only a hazy world—and now admitted that he was virtually blind: "I'd like to see Sugar Ray Robinson or Muhammad Ali giving a recital, a ballet, not a fight. Also, to be sure, I'd like to see a sky full of stars, moonlight on the water, and yes, the tips of a royal flush speaking out as I fan out a poker hand, and, yes, a straight two-foot putt.

"Come to think of it, I'm lucky. I saw all of those things. I see them yet."

Roger Angell: "Summer Habits"

May 31, 1981

For Roger Angell, a writer for the *New Yorker* magazine, baseball would be missed (if a threatened strike indeed occurred).

"It's part of my summer habits—and maybe my winter habits, too," he said. "I suppose I'd get along all right without it, but I'd rather not.

There is a continuity with baseball—and there'd be a feeling of loss with it, like, there goes something else in our lives."

One of the qualities that Angell likes best about baseball has been its relative stability. He wrote: "Within the ball park, time moves differently, marked by no clock except the events of the game. This is the unique, unchangeable feature of baseball and perhaps explains why this sport, for all the enormous changes it has undergone in the past decade or two, remains somehow rustic, unviolent and introspective. Baseball's time is seamless and invisible, a bubble within which players move at exactly the same pace and rhythms as all their predecessors."

Part XII: A Quintet of Sportscasters

Ralph Kiner's "Amazin'" Interview with Casey Stengel

Ralph Kiner, then with the Pittsburgh Pirates, won or shared the National League home-run title each of his first seven seasons in the major leagues, 1946-1952. He hit a total of 369 in his 10-year big-league career (shortened by a back injury). Upon his retirement in 1956, his ratio of 7.1 home runs per 100 at-bats was second only to Babe Ruth, and he was elected to the Hall of Fame in 1975. Following his playing career, Kiner became a New York Mets broadcaster. Following is his first day on that job as the 1962 season began.

It is a fairly oft-told, but forever beguiling tale, more or less, of the first *Kiner's Korner*, the postgame interview program with Ralph Kiner that became iconic for New York Mets fans, and emblematic. It came about half an hour after the new-born Mets first home game ever, on April 13, 1962, in which the team lost 4–3 to the Pittsburgh Pirates.

"It was a horrible place to work, cramped and dingy, in a room in the basement of the ball park," recalled Kiner, in the spring of 2012, by phone from his home in Palm Beach, Florida. "Casey was my very first guest." The irrepressible Stengel was, of course, the manager of the Mets, which he called, "The Amazin's," but Amazin' how, was left to the imagination of the listener. (At one point in the season Stengel took note of his embryonic and hapless team, which went on to lose 120 games out of 160, for a major-league record of ineptitude. "We have to learn to stay out of triple plays," he said. And famously, he was supposed to have asked, in exasperation, "Can't anybody here play this game?")

"The show was going fairly well, but I hadn't done TV before and wasn't sure how to end the interview with Casey, who was a non-stop talker," continued Kiner. "So when I was getting waves to cut from my director, I said, 'Well, Casey, thanks for coming on....' Casey was experienced enough in interviews to know that it was over. He said something about, 'Glad to be here,' got up and the lavaliere, the little microphone, was still clipped to his uniform, and he walked away, and pulled the whole damn set down."

* * *

From *Summers at Shea* by Ira Berkow, published by Triumph Books, 2013

Harry Caray: Nearly a Part of the Playing Field

May 20, 1987/Chicago, Illinois

For nearly two months, the faithful at Wrigley Field rose for the seventh-inning stretch and turned west to an empty window in the broadcasting booth and sang, "Take Me Out to the Ball Game." At Wrigley Field, the baseball pious often sway to the tune.

For the last several years, a tradition had been built with Harry Caray, the Cubs broadcaster. He had leaned out of that window, holding a long silver microphone like a baton, and urged the congregation, "Now let's hear yah! Ah-one, ah-two, ah-three, Take me out to the ball game, take me out with the crowd...."

But for almost two months there was no Harry Caray in that window. The fans had no lead but a recording of Caray crooning that baseball staple.

Caray, at age seventy, had suffered a stroke in February. But today, for the first time since his illness, he was back, being cheered like mad, and warbling as of old.

"No," he said earlier, "I didn't practice singing. I don't wanna get on key."

Caray had returned from his home in Palm Springs, California, to Wrigley Field to work a game. "The new Harry Caray," as he described himself. He had lost forty-one pounds during his illness and rehabilitation, and ate less and drank a great deal less, and went from 229 pounds to 188.

His doctor told him he had to stay that way. No more late-night drinking bouts, he said, no more late-night eating binges. The self-proclaimed Mayor of Rush Street, a center for Chicago night life, will spend more time resting. Oh, perhaps there will be nights when a bus driver as in days of yore will stop the bus in the middle of the street, ask Caray to board, and then Caray will go through shaking hands with the passengers and exit in the rear.

But Caray, the broadcaster of the people, will surely one day again be out in the bleachers on afternoons for a few innings, calling the game from among the fans, his gravelly voice competing against the wind in the microphone, as he tries to snatch his flying papers and notes.

Though his girth has shrunk, his hair is still white, his glasses thick, his laugh ready, his effervescence fresh, his salesmanship sharp. He is still selling his product—baseball and the Cubs—and still selling himself, as he has done for the last forty-four years, as a broadcaster for the Cardinals, A's, White Sox, and, from 1982, the Cubs.

He was a nationally known figure even before the station on which he now broadcasts the Cubs, WGN, became a superstation, and so is regularly watched and listened to in most of the states of the union, and Russia. (Caray once got a letter in broken English from a Russian who had devised some kind of satellite dish.) Stepping onto the playing field a few hours before the game, Caray breathed deeply. "It looks beautiful," he said. "The green grass, the ivy-colored walls—it's baseball the way it's meant to be played."

A vendor called out, "We missed ya, Harry, the whole town missed ya."

Indeed, there were billboards on the expressways here that stated the prevailing sentiment: "Hurry Back, Harry."

"It's strange," Caray said, "but all through my career I've been criticized for wishing people a speedy recovery, or saying hello to this one or that. Well, now I was at the other end. I couldn't move my leg, I couldn't move my arm, I couldn't control my speech. And then I got boxes of mail, expressions of love in letters and flowers from people I didn't know, and it breathed a little more hope into me."

There had been a threat of rain, but the sun was shining for Caray, and for the expected near-full house of some 35,000 for senior citizen's day, and for the special senior citizen in the broadcasting booth.

"How ya doin', Ryno?" said Caray, as the announcer came into the clubhouse.

"Good," said Ryne Sandberg, "but heck with how I'm doin', how you doin?'"

Caray tapped Rick Sutcliffe on the back. Sutcliffe looked up, took off his earphones and stood up, with a slightly moist look in his eyes.

"I'll be as nervous as you are today," said the pitcher.

"I was hoping to just slip quietly into the booth and go to work," said Caray, "but, gee, there's been so much hype."

"Holy cow!" said Billy Williams, the batting coach, upon spying Caray. "We got everybody now." "I'm half the man I used to be," said

Caray, patting his flatter stomach. "Looks great," said Williams. On the air, Caray told his sidekick, the former pitcher Steve Stone, that, in his absence, "you really did me proud." Stone had helped a battery of celebrities, from the comedian Bill Murray to the columnists George Will and Mike Royko, who filled in for Caray.

"Just keeping the seat warm, waiting for today," Stone told Caray.

After the Reds came to bat in the first half inning, Stone said, "There's a special phone call for you."

"Hello, Harry, this is Ronald Reagan." The president was calling to wish Caray well. "I'm a little familiar with Wrigley Field," said the former sportscaster. "I broadcast a lot of ball games there." Sharing the Booth

Caray recalled the time when Reagan shared the booth with him in St. Louis when Reagan played Grover Cleveland Alexander in the movie *The Winning Team*.

The president said he remembered, and said, "Well, I know you've got to get back to the ball game, but I just wanted to say, even though there were a lot of big-name celebrities substituting for you, there's nothing like the real thing."

"Thank you, Mr. President, and bye-bye." "Bye-bye." Then Caray, in his familiar modulated excitement, said, "In all the excitement, Bobby Dernier is on first after having beat out a bunt!"

Someone walked past a television monitor and asked, "Does it sound like Harry?"

"Just like him," came the reply. "Just like him." THE VOICE OF THE CUBS "Harry Caray from Wrigley Field inviting you to stay tuned." * * * "Holy Cow!" -No, he says, Phil Rizzuto was not the first to use this phrase. ("If he was, then he must have whispered it to his second baseman, Gerry Priddy.") * * * "He POPPED it up!"—Derisively. * * * "There's Andres

Galarraga. Spelled backwards it's A-G-A-R-R-A-L-A-G."—He has a knack and propensity for spelling names backward at the drop of a syllable. * * * "The pendulum of percentages swings to the home team."—When the home team comes to bat in the bottom of the ninth inning with the game tied. * * * "Jo-DEE, Jo-DEE Davis."—To the tune of Da-VEE, Da-VEE Crockett. * * * "Too big to be a man, too small to be a horse."— On a large player, like Dave Parker. * * * "Cubs win, Cubs Win, CUBS WIN."—On those special days, victory, at the last out, invariably comes in triplicate."

Tony Kubek on Don Mattingly: No Ring, No Matter

November 21, 1995

Once upon a time there was actually a winning Yankee tradition, with the Yankees going about their winning ways confidently and quietly. Now they don't win, and, led by their eggbeater owner, go about it noisily and chaotically.

Don Mattingly, however, is probably the best day-to-day Yankee— or, if current speculation is correct, the best former Yankee—who has never won a championship or played in a World Series. He is in the Yankee tradition of champions.

Mattingly, at thirty-four and with a chronic back problem, has given signals that he will retire from baseball. If so, baseball will be the poorer for it.

"Donny's one of those people in the game who takes pride in what's important in the game," said Tony Kubek, the former championship Yankee shortstop, and the former Yankee broadcaster, from his home in Menasha, Wisconsin.

"It reminds me of when I first had a tryout with the Yankees, and Frankie Crosetti, the old shortstop who was then a Yankee coach, said to me, 'Kid, you heard about Ruth and Gehrig and DiMaggio and all the legends about how sluggers won championships for the Yankees. Don't you believe it.'"

"He said: 'It has always been good defense that won. It's the defense that makes the play in a close ball game that wins. Don't ever forget that.'"

Kubek recalled how he would stop during infield practice and watch Mattingly at first base. Kubek would marvel at Mattingly's intensity—the trademark lampblack under the eyes giving him a look of racoon concentration, the bill of his cap pulled low, the bushy mustache, a scraggle of hair about the ears, the blousing of his pinstriped pants drawn about the ankles—and how he worked on things obvious and subtle that could make the difference in games.

One example: Observing Mattingly diligently practice the 3-6-3 double play—that is, first baseman to shortstop to first baseman. "And no one turned it better than Mattingly," said Kubek. "He was quick to get off the throw to short, and then quick to get back to cover the base. A lot of first baseman don't get back to the bag fast, so the pitcher has to cover, and it's hard for a shortstop to hit the moving target. You see a lot of balls wind up in the first-base dugout. Just that play could make the difference in a game, and has."

Jack Brickhouse and the Confessions of a One-Time Little Leaguer

July 3, 1989

One morning not long ago I drove by a small ball park on the far North Side of Chicago, empty now except for the sprinklers whirring, and the shadows under the warm morning sun.

It is a lovely, miniature, blue park with light poles and a turnstile and, neatly painted bleachers and an electric scoreboard in center field and, in left field, a tall chain fence with a scraggly vegetation crawling up it, an apparent attempt to imitate the ivy on Wrigley Field, another ball park in town.

"We tried to grow vines," said a groundskeeper named Bob, who emerged from a shed when I stopped to walk around, a sort of sentimental journey for me. "But," he added, "the rabbits kept eating the seed."

The park is called Thillens Stadium, and it was here that a softball player named Bill Skowron smashed home runs in an industrial league. A few years later he was booming baseballs for home runs in Yankee Stadium.

It was here that the four-man King and his Court beat nine-man teams; and where the famous Bloomer Girls, a women's softball team, played (with their stars, the sisters Frieda and Olympia Savona); and where donkey baseball was tried—with hitting and catching and running the bases all done on donkeys—but had to be scrapped because so many players fell off the animals, breaking assorted legs and arms and collarbones.

And it was here that I played Little League baseball, more or less.

Reading that this summer is the fiftieth anniversary of the Little League, founded in Williamsport, Pennsylvania, by Carl Stotz, I am filled with mixed emotions.

On one hand, I experience a certain pleasant reverie of the days when I donned a Little League uniform in Thillens Stadium and sallied forth.

But I also recall some of those days with mortification.

I can sympathize with those college athletes today caught between the whirlpool of establishment riches and the rocks of penniless purity. At the age of twelve, I was trapped in just such a pickle.

It was 1952, and I lived on the West Side of Chicago. My friends and I played stick ball and stoop ball and Kick the Can and Red Rover and Knuckles, a card game that sometimes concluded with blood literally dripping on the table. Mostly, though, we played baseball and softball.

We played in winter wearing gloves and galoshes. We played in spring and summer and fall, from dewy morning to sultry afternoon to breezy evening. We played in the alleys, where we swept away the droppings of peddlers' horses; and in the streets, shouting at motorists ("Hey, mister, this ain't no boulevard"); and in the parks, where a hit might bounce off a tree in short left field or off an old lady carrying packages across the cardboard second base. Such carefree times. Then disaster struck.

One day, I visited my cousin on the alien North Side. At a park near his home, a Little League team that played at Thillens Stadium was practicing. The team was called the Indians. I saw them wearing uniforms. Real ones. I mean, they were woolen, smaller versions of the actual Cleveland Indians white home uniform, made from the local Wilson Sporting Goods Company that made the major-league uniforms. They were dazzling. Not the typical gray Little League uniform with the script, Federmeyer's Pharmacy, taking up the whole front of the shirt.

Now, Little League was a new thing in 1952. There was none in my neighborhood. The Thillens Little League was, as I recollect, the only one in the city.

This Little League was so highly professional, it was on local television. And Jack Brickhouse—*the* Jack Brickhouse—who announced the Cubs and White Sox games on TV, announced the Thillens Little League games, too.

A position was open on the Indians because one of the players was going off to summer camp. I tried out and made the team.

I was filled with excitement as I returned to the West Side. But my pals greeted the news with disdain. First, I'd be playing on the North

451

Side—"where all the fruits are." Second, I was a "phony" because I'd be wearing an actual *uniform*. Third, I'd be a fruity phony if I wore those Little League spikes, which were actually rubber and not steel.

All this added up to an ultimatum. Play in our games or in that punk Little League. Why not both? I insisted. "No!" Hard-core purity versus establishment opulence.

What a decision! But the gaudy riches of a faraway land called irresistibly.

I would not dare to wear my marvelous uniform through the streets of the West Side. I slunk along the shadows to the Pulaski Road bus, my uniform in a bag under my arm.

My friends learned when my games were. They came and sat in the stands and made unpleasant noises, including telling people I was fourteen years old.

My embarrassment, probably, was enough of a salve to their envy, since I returned to the neighborhood games. But my worst moment was yet to come. One evening in a televised game at Thillens, I struck out. I uttered some ungentle words to myself as I dragged my bat to the dugout. Yes, they were expletives I had learned on the West Side streets. I didn't realize the TV camera caught my entire monologue. And I had no idea that Jack Brickhouse was taking up my case. "That's OK, young fella, you'll get 'em the next time. Happens to all of us." Or something along those lines as they had later been repeated to me. I adored Jack Brickhouse ever since.

Earlier in the day, I had asked my parents to watch the game at home. Even though I was less than the star of the game—I did happen to hit a double—I thought she'd be bursting with pride that I was a TV celebrity. I fully expected to be showered with praise from her.

As I walked in the door, my mother met me and cried, "That's what they teach you on the North Side, such language?"

The chicken had come home to roost.

Joe Garagiola: When Old Ballplayers Are in Need of Help

January 21, 1998

"Gentlemen," or "Dear Sir," the letters begin, and then the stories of needy people pour out: one must have a prostate operation but can't afford it, another has a wife who needs a double mastectomy and hip replacement, another is on the verge of suicide. And there are phone calls: "Joe, this is embarrassing because I don't like to ask for help, but"— and then one after the other tell their improbable stories, improbable because most of them were major league ballplayers, American heroes or icons, basking in glory for a game, for a season, for a decade.

Joe Garagiola, known widely as a funny man, and the author, in fact, of the long-ago book *Baseball is a Funny Game*, listens. "We'll do what we can," he says. "We'll try to help."

And Garagiola begins the process of coming to the rescue of these people, who have discovered that life may not be such a funny game. In an age of multimillion-dollar contracts, it seems hard to imagine that stars of the past are reduced to this state. But some never made a great deal of money, or lost what they had.

Garagiola, the onetime major league baseball catcher, sportscaster who was elected to the broadcasters wing of the Baseball Hall of Fame in 1991, and star of the *Today* show, is, more to the point now, the former president and still the guiding light of the Baseball Assistance Team, or BAT, an organization devoted to helping people once associated with professional baseball who are down on their luck.

Last night, BAT held its seventh annual awards dinner in a midtown Manhattan hotel and, as usual, former ballplayers like Joe DiMaggio and Ted Williams and Bob Gibson and even the relatively reclusive Sandy Koufax attended. They were present because they believe in the cause—which

453

has raised several million over the last eleven years for the unfortunate former players and their families—and they were present because of the persuasion and urging of Garagiola. Baldish, garrulous, still a sometime quipster ("I went through life as the 'player to be named later'") Garagiola unabashedly uses his celebrity, his wit, his compassion to do good. He is Sister Brown of the Salvation Army, but wearing a baseball cap.

I remember one afternoon during spring training two years ago at Al Lang Field in St. Petersburg, Florida, Garagiola was accompanied by a man whose face was badly deformed on one side. He had gone through numerous operations for cancer. The man was Bill Tuttle, a standout center fielder for the Detroit Tigers in the 1950s. Tuttle had reluctantly come to BAT and Garagiola when the cost for the operations mounted, operations that were needed because of the cancer that had developed from his years of chewing tobacco.

The dangers of chewing, a long-time habit of ballplayers, was an issue of grave importance to Garagiola, and he was going from spring-training camp to spring-training camp to speak with players as a group in each clubhouse, with Tuttle and Tuttle's wife relating their heart-breaking tale. "C'mon, you guys are invited, too," he said to reporters. "Everyone should know about this."

There was no profit in this for Garagiola, other than for, and again, this seems the only proper term, his heart and soul.

Garagiola won't give names of those who have sought help unless the player consents, as did Bernie Carbo, the onetime Red Sox out-fielder, who got hooked on alcohol and drugs. "I look back and I get chills," Carbo once said. "I see a grave at the bottom of a hill with a skeleton in it reaching out and that skeleton is me saying, 'Come back, come back.'" Carbo came to BAT. He said it saved his life.

One pitcher, whom Garagiola had played against, wrote: "My legs are in the making. I went for a fitting and for the first time since July I walked and what a thrill that was."

454

Another thank-you letter arrived after BAT had sent a check to cover expenses for the funeral of a man's wife. "He was a tough Yankee first baseman," Garagiola said. "He thought everybody had forgotten him."

"My pride and self-confidence have completely disappeared," wrote a onetime catcher, whom BAT soon assisted. "I stay in the house almost every day—usually in my pajamas."

Another who needed help, said Garagiola, played in a World Series in the 1970s and finished his career in 1987.

"Those who we help," said Garagiola, "are not all old-timers. They are getting younger."

Part XIII: A Few Who Knocked at the Hall Door, But Have Been Denied Entry

The Universe and the Case of Pete Rose

July 6, 1989

It was not a dark and stormy night, it was a dark and somewhat overcast night, but the rings of Saturn came in remarkably clear anyway through the lens of a large, powerful telescope on Long Island.

The man who owned the telescope, which had been set on a platform on the beach beside his home, had invited friends over to observe close up the latest goings-on in the solar system.

The lights from the house had been turned off, and no lights were on near the telescope, the better, to quote the wolf from Little Red Riding Hood, to see you, my dear. That is, Saturn, and a red giant star, which came in yellowish, and various nebulae.

In the dark, as each person one at a time leaned down and squinted into the viewer and *oohed* and *aahed* or said, "I can't quite make it out," someone turned to another and, nearly stepping on his toes in the black night, said, "What do you think is going to happen to Pete Rose?"

Precisely. In cosmic settings come cosmic questions. Thus we attempt to unravel the riddles of the universe.

Still, after nearly four months of virtually daily headlines and news reports, the Rose case remains intriguing to the country.

Could he have been that dumb or that arrogant or that addicted, to gamble on baseball and the Reds?

Will the commissioner be allowed by the courts to make a ruling?

If it were anyone other than a star of this magnitude—a Rose giant, in effect—would he have captured so many headlines, been the cynosure of so many cameras, have dominated so many conversations?

"It's all a tempest in a teapot," said a woman at a July 4th picnic. "I'm tired of it."

"I guess," someone else said, "the problem is that we have so few heroes, that nobody wants to lose another one."

Whether it ought to be or not, we've made heroes of our sports stars, and none more so, and for a longer period, than baseball players.

Baseball, from the turn of the century, was marketed as the National Game. It was the first national sports event that made an impact in the newspapers—before there was any kind of professional football or tennis or basketball or hockey or golf. It was the first to have regularly announced games on radio. It was the first to have cards produced with the likenesses of the ballplayers on them, so that kids could carry around images of their heroes in their pockets.

A paper entitled "An Examination of Professional Baseball Players as Heroes and Role Models" by two University of North Dakota professors, Monty E. Nielsen, and George Schubert, was presented at the Baseball Hall of Fame in Cooperstown last month. It quotes Governor Mario M. Cuomo of New York describing the game's significance:

"Baseball, more than any other sport, is a uniquely American tradition that binds generation to generation, unlike any other ritual in society. It's a Little Leaguers' game that major leaguers play extraordinarily well, a game that excites us throughout adulthood. The crack of the bat and the scent of horsehide on leather bring back our memories that have been washed away with the sweat and tears of summers long gone . . . even as the setting sun pushes the shadows past home plate."

Elsewhere in the paper, a writer named Richard Crepeau notes some characteristics admired in the American culture that are depicted in professional baseball:

"Morality, truth, justice, opportunity, the self-made man; Horatio Algerism, competition, individualism and team play, initiative, hard work, relentless effort and hustle; instant and automatic action, self-independence, never-give-up-the-ship; respect to proper authority, self-confidence, fair-mindedness, quick judgment and self-control; it is all important that the game be clean; and good sportsmanship."

Pete Rose, who embodied all of these traits; Pete Rose, who played in more winning games than any other major leaguer dead or alive; Pete Rose, who grew up in an area along the Ohio in which the residents are sometimes called River Rats, and then only a few miles away hit the hit that broke Ty Cobb's hallowed career record; Pete Rose, who only a few years ago reached the absolute apex of national popularity by being on the cover of a Wheaties box, this Pete Rose is now involved in a scandal with charges that he tampered with, or might have jeopardized, this game, this dream, this thing that so many of his countrymen look to as one of the few constants of integrity, of childhood and adulthood, of nationhood, of, well, of universehood, too.

Maybe that's why Rose, like Saturn, remains ever present in our cosmos.

The Signed Confession of Shoeless Joe Jackson

June 24, 1989

In the current movie *Field of Dreams*, Shoeless Joe Jackson and seven teammates of the Chicago White Sox—the historically besmirched Black Sox—who were banned from baseball for allegedly throwing the 1919 World Series to the Cincinnati Reds, are sentimentalized and glorified.

"Is this heaven?" one of them asks, when a ball field is erected and they emerge from what might be assumed is a place down below to play ball forever in the friendly confines of an Iowa cornfield.

"Shoeless Joe batted .375 in the Series, hit the only home run and didn't make an error," someone says in the film. "How could he have thrown the Series?"

Of course, it's possible. It's possible to not hit in the clutch, or to miss a sign, or a cutoff man, or to short-leg a fly ball in left field, with none of this embossed in the box score.

Beyond this, in this year of the fiftieth anniversary of the Baseball Hall of Fame in Cooperstown, the Senate in South Carolina, Jackson's home state, on Monday passed a unanimous resolution asking organized baseball to exonerate him, with hopes of his one day being elected to the Hall of Fame, since his career batting average of .356 is third highest in baseball history.

Jackson through the years maintained his innocence, until his death in 1951. But at three p.m. on September 28, 1920, Jackson was called as a witness to the grand jury of Cook County investigating the scandal. The transcript was recorded in a signed confession, and then swiftly disappeared because, it is believed, of a cynical deal cut between the White Sox owner, Charles A. Comiskey, and the gambler Arnold Rothstein. The lack of hard evidence helped Jackson and his teammates to be found not guilty in court.

Three years later, when Jackson sued Comiskey and baseball to be reinstated—Commissioner Landis had banned him despite the court's decision—the confession mysteriously resurfaced, and Jackson lost the suit.

Recently, the confession reappeared in an exhibition about the scandal at the Chicago Historical Society. Jackson's testimony is conflicting and compelling. Following are excerpts:

Q. (by assistant state's attorney Hartley L. Replogle): Did anybody pay you any money to help throw that Series in favor of Cincinnati?

A. They did.

Q. How much did they pay you?

A. They promised me $20,000 and paid me 5.

Q. (Did Mrs. Jackson) know that you got $5,000 for helping throw these games?

A. She did . . . yes.

Q. What did she say about it?

A. She said she thought it was an awful thing to do.

Q. That was after the fourth game?

A. I believe it was, yes.

(Jackson said that Lefty Williams, the Chicago pitcher, was the intermediary between him and the gamblers.)

Q. When did he promise the $20,000?

A. It was to be paid after each game.

(But Jackson got only $5,000, thrown onto his hotel bed by Williams after the fourth game. Jackson was asked what he said to Williams.)

A. I asked him what the hell had come off here.

Q. What did he say?

A. He said [Chick] Gandil (the Chicago first baseman, and player ringleader) said we all got a screw . . . that we got double-crossed. I don't think Gandil was crossed as much as he crossed us.

461

Q. At the end of the first game you didn't get any money, did you?

A. No, I did not, no, sir.

Q. What did you do then?

A. I asked Gandil what is the trouble? He says, "Everything is all right." He had it.

Q. Then you went ahead and threw the second game, thinking you would get it then, is that right?

A. We went ahead and threw the second game.

After the third game I says, "Somebody is getting a nice little jazz, everybody is crossed." He said, "Well, Abe Attell and Bill Burns had crossed him." Attell and Burns were gamblers in the conspiracy.

(Then Jackson was asked about the fourth game of the Series.)

Q. Did you see any fake plays?

A. Only the wildness of [Eddie] Cicotte (Chicago pitcher).

Q. Did you make any intentional errors yourself that day?

A. No sir, not during the whole series.

Q. Did you bat to win?

A. Yes.

Q. And run the bases to win?

A. Yes, sir.

Q. And field the balls at the outfield to win?

A. I did. . . . I tried to win all the games.

Q. Weren't you very much peeved that you only got $5,000 and you expected to get 20?

A. No, I was ashamed of myself.

Q. Where did you put the $5,000 (that Williams gave him)?

A. I put it in my pocket.

Q. What did Mrs. Jackson say about it?

A. She felt awful bad about it, cried about it a while.

Q. Had you ever played crooked baseball before this?

A. No, sir, I never had.

Q. You think now Williams may have crossed you, too?

A. Well, dealing with crooks, you know, you get crooked every way. This is my first experience and last.

Barry Bonds Blocks Out Controversy and Focuses on Hitting

March 24, 2006/Scottsdale, Arizona

On this spring morning splashed with sunshine, Barry Bonds, in uniform but hatless, shaved head aglow, emerged from the dugout and onto the sparkling grass at Scottsdale Stadium. Like a true hitter, he immediately sized up the situation.

"Wind's blowing in," he said, checking the flapping flags in center field. "I might have to swing harder."

He smiled. It was, and was not, a little joke. Then he walked to the batting cage under the right-field stands to commence his daily labors.

Amid all the devastating distractions going on in the life of Barry Bonds, it may be surprising to learn that, this spring, at forty-one, he is once again thriving at the plate. He has 10 hits, including four home runs, in his first 16 at-bats for the San Francisco Giants. That translates into a .625 batting average for a player with a surgically repaired right knee and a reputation that has taken still another battering, this time from a new book that links him ever tighter to the use of steroids.

"I try to stay real," Bonds said Friday, when he was asked about his surprising start. He was sitting in his familiar leather chair in the corner of the Giants clubhouse here, and he was asked what he meant by the word *real.*

"It means staying focused, in good times and bad," he said. "It means doing what you've learned to do in this business all your life. It means when you get in the batter's box that it's just you and the pitcher and the ball. Your mind is clear for the job at hand.

"It means that you don't give up," he went on, in a conversation that was limited to baseball. "You take what comes and you deal with it. It's like you hit a line drive right at the second baseman. You're out. That's real. But you also did your job. Some guys might throw up their hands and bemoan what happened. That's turning a positive into a negative. I've learned not to do that."

Bonds is a seven-time National League Most Valuable Player, the holder of the single-season home run record of 73, and, with 708 career home runs, in striking distance of Babe Ruth's mark of 714 homers and Henry Aaron's record of 755. But beyond this, he is a symbol, more or less, of an often-reviled generation of suspected steroid users.

On Friday, the capacity crowd of some 12,000 at the Giants home ballpark in Arizona seemed generally unconcerned with Bonds's continuing problems. Nearly 800 miles away, in San Francisco, lawyers representing Bonds failed in an effort to obtain a temporary restraining order against the new book, *Game of Shadows*.

Here, people cheered him when he came to bat, with only a smattering of boos mixed in. And on a day when he lined softly to second, lined a single to center, walked and flied to left, no other batter received such lavish attention.

"I've been mechanically right," Bonds said of his at-bats. "Everything has been perfect. But it's only temporary."

Still, it was something for him to savor, a reminder of the skills Bonds always possessed before everything became tainted by steroids. Others still notice those skills, too.

"I see the guy do things that other people can't," said Giants catcher Mike Matheny, a player who used to scheme against Bonds when he caught for the Cardinals. "I don't care what you're taking—and I'm not saying he is, or has, taken anything. But he has that amazing discipline at the plate, how quick and short and compact his swing is."

Bonds had several arthroscopic operations on his right knee last season and did not play until September; he hit five home runs in 14 games. He wears a large brace on the knee and does little running now. Yet in the very first inning Friday, he moved easily in left field to chase down two fly balls.

"I feel good," he said. "I feel I'll be ready to go." For how long? "I'll know by July, by the All-Star break, how much more, if any more, I can go on."

Bonds was asked if the ball indeed looked like a grapefruit to him, that he is seeing it so well.

"No," he said. "The ball never changes size."

Matheny disagreed. "He has to see the ball differently," he said. "I've heard about Ted Williams seeing the ball so well. In my time, I thought Paul Molitor did, too. And everyone in the major leagues has gone through periods of seeing the ball great. I know I have. But those periods don't last very long. With Barry, it's every at-bat."

Willie Upshaw, one of the Giants hitting coaches, said: "His wrist work, his hips, his hands, even his feet work in perfect unison. Everything in your body is fighting for control when you swing. You drive off the back foot into the front foot. And your front foot has to be planted solid. If you have that, you don't lose bat speed, no matter your age. Barry has that."

And, in a season in which many difficulties may still await Bonds, on and off the field, he also has a philosophy that he says he will attempt to live by.

"What you can't do is take failure to heart," he said. "There's going to be a lot of failure. No one bats 1.000. Or even .500. You have to think, next time, I'll get 'em."

Curt Schilling: Improving as a Pitcher, Improving as a Person

September 5, 2001

Curt Schilling did not quite wince when the phrase sports hero was mentioned in the same sentence as his name, but he did shake his head. People should not take this hero thing seriously, he cautioned. The adulation, the attention, the headlines of being a star pitcher in the major leagues are part of the trappings of his trade, not an insight into his soul.

Schilling, the Arizona Diamondbacks veteran right-hander, the only pitcher in the major leagues to win 19 games this season, and second only in strikeouts in the big leagues to his teammate, Randy Johnson, was saying recently that, yes, "I might be stronger on the pitching mound than, say, the guy delivering mail to your home, but I might be weaker than him in other ways."

"Nothing about my life separates me from anybody on earth," Schilling said, sitting in the visitor's dugout in Veterans Stadium in Philadelphia before a game recently. "You can't equate the ability to strike out people with being nonhuman."

Schilling, thirty-four, and in his 14th season in the major leagues, speaks from experience. Three times his pitching shoulder gave out on him, but three times his career was saved by modern medical procedures, and, to be sure, a powerful will to rehabilitate and return.

This spring, Schilling's wife, Shonda, was diagnosed with melanoma, a skin cancer. After four months of painful surgeries and various procedures, the disease is in remission, but must be looked after guardedly and protected from the sun. Three years ago, Schilling had a cancer fright of his own. He was told that if he continued to chew tobacco he might be a candidate for cancer. He had been aware of how some former players had had half their faces removed after operations because of the aftereffects of chewing tobacco, and how some died early deaths.

A year and a half ago, on a golf course, someone offered him a pinch of tobacco, saying it wouldn't hurt.

"And I took it like a fool, and I got hooked again," said Schilling, a plug of chewing tobacco in his right cheek. "I tried to quit twice this year, but failed. Shonda hates it. And the possible consequences scare me, absolutely. Especially when you have a wife and three kids."

His children are Gehrig, six, Grant, four, and Gabriella, one and a half. "And I bawled like a baby when my first kid was born," he said, "like a lot of fathers, I guess."

Curtis Montague Schilling is 6-foot-4 and is listed at 231 pounds. His body is not svelte, perhaps because his diet includes potato chips in the clubhouse, but he has proved to be an extraordinary athlete. He has been a National League All-Star four times, and was initially scheduled to start this year's game against the American League. In 1993, he helped pitch the Phillies to the World Series, where he won one game and lost another. He has twice tied for the league lead in games started, has twice led in complete games and twice in strikeouts, with 319 and 300.

He was traded last year in July from the Phillies to the Diamondbacks, after having shoulder surgery in the off-season. He was 6–6 with the Phillies before the trade, and 5-6 with Arizona the rest of the year. Since the beginning of this season he has been sensational, teaming with Johnson to fashion the most prodigious one-two pitching punch in baseball, and one of the best in years, drawing comparisons by some to the Sandy Koufax-Don Drysdale Dodgers of the 1960s.

Schilling and Johnson are two of the strongest candidates for the Cy Young Award, emblematic of the NL's best pitcher of the year. "We have a friendly rivalry about it, and joke about it some," Schilling said.

"But I can't do what I do every fifth day and wonder out on the mound who's going to win the Cy Young."

So, he says, he dismisses those thoughts while pitching. "I'm not sure two pitchers on the same team have ever ended up 1-2 in the balloting," he said. "That would be great. But the important thing is for the team to win, then we've accomplished our goals."

Going into last night's games, the Diamondbacks led the NL. West by two and a half games over second-place San Francisco. Johnson is 18–6, with a 2.31 earned run average and 326 strikeouts. Schilling is 19–6, with a 2.91 ERA and 245 strikeouts. Schilling is also tied for the major league lead in complete games, with six, and while he has previously won 17, 16, and 15 games (twice) in a season, this is the first time he has won as many as 19. He will try to become the first 20-game winner in the major leagues this season when he pitches against the Giants tonight.

Is he pitching better than ever? Mark Grace thinks so, and so does Matt Williams. Larry Bowa doubts it. Grace, the Arizona first baseman, and Williams, the team's third baseman, had both faced Schilling as opponents in past years. Bowa was his manager with the Phillies in 2000. "When he came back from surgery last season, he was throwing more curveballs, developing that pitch, because he couldn't throw quite as hard as he had before," Williams said. "It made him a more complete pitcher, combining finesse, now, with power."

Grace said: "I think there's a little more intensity about him. Maybe it comes from his personal life in recent times, his ability to concentrate under adversity. And maybe it has something to do with watching Randy Johnson, getting a lift from him and competing with him."

Bowa said Schilling remains one of the best prepared pitchers he has ever known—he logs every pitch to every batter in every game on a computer, and then studies that—and is also "one of the great competitors."

"He'll still call up John Vukovich, one of our coaches, and ask how we pitch to a batter he's unfamiliar with," Bowa said. "And we help, especially against teams from the East," where the Phillies play.

"Curt's still dominating," Bowa added. "He doesn't feel there's any batter he can't get out—whether you hit 60 homers or bat .400. That's a competitor."

Schilling thinks this may not be the best season he has ever had—he might not reach the 319 strikeouts he had in 1997, or the 2.35 ERA he posted in 1992—but it might be the most consistent. He believes his curveball is better—sharper—than ever, which gives him another pitch to go with his once-again mid-nineties fastball, slider, and split-finger. And Johnson has indeed been an influence on him.

"Randy has one gear—intense," Schilling said. "In close games I'd concentrate so hard I'd have a headache after the game. But when I was six, seven runs ahead, I might experiment with pitches. Randy doesn't. He's still bearing down with his best stuff. I do that now, and I think that kind of focus has made me a better pitcher."

It was difficult, certainly, to be working in spring training last March when his wife learned she had cancer. "But it's my job, it's something I had to do," he said. "People ask me if it's made me a better pitcher, giving me a perspective maybe I hadn't had. No, not at all. Shonda and I have been very active with trying to help in the fight against Lou Gehrig's disease. Try putting yourself in their shoes. Being around those people, that has given us all the perspective we've needed.

"But then something like Shonda's illness hits home. You think it can't happen to you, and then it does. No, her battle hasn't made me a better pitcher, but it's made me a better person, I hope, and a better husband and father. It made me appreciate more than ever what kind of person Shonda has been, how for six months of the year she's raised three young children—the loneliness, the anger, the frustrations—while

I'm away playing baseball. That hasn't been easy. I marvel at how strong she is, and how she's dealt with all of this."

Shonda Schilling has said that her illness may have temporarily "dampened my spirits, but it hadn't tested my faith." And she has taken an active role in melanoma awareness.

It's acknowledged that a certain portion of the nation looks for its heroes on its playing fields, but not Schilling. The star pitcher has discovered that his hero is the woman with whom he shares his life.

* * *

The 2001 season ended with Schilling leading the National League in wins with 22 (and six losses), an ERA of .298 and 293 strikeouts, compared to Johnson's 21 wins (and six losses) and led the league with an ERA of 2.49 and 372 strikeouts. Johnson won the Cy Young Award with 156 votes to the second-place finisher Schilling's 98 votes.

Alex Rodriguez Would Add, Not Subtract

November 18, 2000

In an attempt to improve their team, the Mets management entertained the signing of a high-priced free agent. This free-agent's agent was asking for a salary greater—millions greater, in fact—than any other player on the team, a team that had some pretty high-priced players to begin with. The free agent's agent also wanted certain special considerations to go along with the millions. Such as throwing in a luxury box in the deal. And his own suite in hotels on the road. This was almost laughable.

Some observers said the Mets shouldn't do it, that such special treatment would be disruptive in the clubhouse. There are, after all, professional jealousies in the clubhouse, and egos as big as Yellowstone National Park.

No, we aren't talking here about Alex Rodriguez, the current major free agent in the news, but Mike Piazza.

And, if memory serves, the Mets and Piazza made it to the World Series, and lost four games by a total of five runs. Some jealousies. Some disruption.

Piazza came to the Mets in 1998 and received a contract for $91 million for seven years, or $13 million a year. The second-highest-paid player on the Mets was pitcher Al Leiter, who was making $32 million for four years, or $8 million a year.

Now the Mets have expressed interest in obtaining Rodriguez, the Seattle shortstop, who, at the tender age of twenty-five, may be the best all-around player in baseball.

Rodriguez's agent, Scott Boras, was seeking a deal in the neighborhood of $200 million-plus for 10 years. Plus a bunch of perquisites, like office space in Shea Stadium for an A-Rod marketing team (which he'd pay for). Boras asked whether the Mets were going to build a new stadium, what the state of the minor league system was and whether the Mets would have more billboards around town for Rodriguez than there would be for the Yankees shortstop, Derek Jeter.

Too much, said Steve Phillips, the Mets general manager. If we acquiesced to these demands, it would be divisive in the clubhouse.

"It's true that some players might wonder why a guy would need a marketing office, and some of the other things," Leiter said yesterday from his home in Fort Lauderdale, Florida. "Some guys might get upset."

But if Rodriguez added significantly to the Mets, would his contract still cause problems?

"You mean if A-Rod drove in big runs and made great plays in the field and we won, would that cause problems in the clubhouse?"

Yes.

"No," Leiter said.

Phillips has his reasons for having withdrawn from the Rodriguez bidding, but none seem so convincing in light of the possibility of his getting a wonderful shortstop, especially when the Mets are shaky at that position.

I'm not one to count other people's money, and my bank account probably wouldn't allow me to pay $200 million for someone to chase a baseball. But I'm not the Mets, and they seem able to afford it. After all, money seemed not to be the major sticking point.

Maybe it's all posturing and negotiating. This is how it's often done. And then comes a meeting of the minds, the millions, the limos.

Part of a manager's job is to bring reason and cohesion to a club-house, regardless of the circumstances. Leo Durocher, for example, dealt firmly with the Dodger players in spring training in 1947, some of whom had signed a petition not to play with Jackie Robinson.

"Take your petition and shove it," Durocher said. "You oughta know that Robinson's a great player, and he's going to make all of us a lot of money."

Turned out to be true, of course. And with Rodriguez's ability, the Mets players could thicken their wallets. Not only would they have a better chance to make the World Series again, but this time possibly take home the winner's share (better than $300,000, about $100,000 more than the loser's share).

Rodriguez also has a reputation for being a good guy in the club-house, a hard-working athlete without exaggerated views of himself.

As for seeking more billboards than Jeter—which, I guess, like office space, would not be a deal breaker—I recall when Bill Russell was offered $100,000, the same as Wilt Chamberlain, but insisted on $100,001. No Celtic complained.

Phillips said yesterday that the Mets pursuit of Alex Rodriguez was history.

"It's a decision I think is right for the organization," he said. "We're not going to look back on it."

He may indeed look back on it ruefully come next October, and Octobers after that.

(Excerpt from "Only Language He Needs to Know is That of Baseball" July 24, 2006)

* * *

Rodriguez retired after the 2016 season having played 22 years for Seattle, Texas, and the Yankees. He was a three-time MVP, batted .295 lifetime, with 696 home runs (fourth at the time of his retirement) and 2,086 RBIs (third at the time of his retirement). He admitted to steroid use between 2001 and 2003, and said it was to overcome pain from a hip injury. He was eventually given a 162-game suspension, which kept him out of the entire 2014 season.

* * *

Kenji Johjima, the Seattle Mariners Japanese catcher, trying to communicate in his accented English not only speaks to his teammates, but he also sometimes talks to an opponent. An example of this occurred in a Yankees game last week.

When Alex Rodriguez (now the Yankee third baseman) went to the plate, Johjima greeted him with "Hello," then added something else in English.

"I didn't quite get what he was saying," Rodriguez said. "And then he pointed. I thought he was messing with me. So I looked over to Jerry Meals."

Meals was the home-plate umpire.

"Jerry told me, 'He says your fly is open,'" Rodriguez said.

And it was. The zipper was broken. As soon as he could, Rodriguez changed his pants.

Johjima shrugged when the incident was related to him.

"I was just trying to be helpful," he said. "I asked him if that was part of his batting routine. And we both laughed."

Credits

All columns and feature stories in this book written between 1967 and 1977 appeared first in the Newspaper Enterprise Association syndicate and are reissued with permission of NEA. All columns and feature stories written between 1981 and 2020 appeared first in the *New York Times*, and are reissued with permission from the *New York Times*. Other articles that were not written for NEA or the *Times* are given credit where they appear in the context of that particular piece.

Acknowledgments

I've had the great pleasure of working with a number of creative, multitalented, and sensitive book editors over my many years in the publishing world, but none were more creative, more multitalented, more sensitive and a complete pleasure to deal with than the editor of this book, Jason Katzman. And it was Jason who early on saw the possibilities in *Baseball's Best Ever*, and then edited it with a fine, firm head, hand, and heart.

And a bow to the sports editors both at Newspaper Enterprise Assn. and the *New York Times* who were instrumental in much of the work that appears in this book but first had to pass muster with them.

First among equals is Murray Olderman at NEA (based in New York), who hired me in 1967 from the *Minneapolis Tribune*. It was the esteemed sportscaster Beano Cook who said, "Working for Murray Olderman is like going to Yale." Murray, besides holding three college degrees including Phi Beta Kappa from Stanford, and fluent in several languages—as an Army first lieutenant at the end of World War II in Europe he was assigned to interrogate German military prisoners—he was not only an award-winning writer but also a nationally recognized sports cartoonist.

Joe Vecchione hired me at the *New York Times* and, as at NEA, gave me, with much appreciation, considerable rein to roam the sports world, first as a reporter and feature writer and then as a columnist.

A special appreciation to Sandy Padwe, then the deputy sports editor, who recommended me to Joe.

It was a pleasure and honor to work alongside the terrific stable of "Sports of the Times" columnists over my twenty-six years at the *Times*: Dave Anderson, Harvey Araton, Bob Lipsyte, Bill Rhoden, Selena Roberts, Red Smith, and George Vecsey.

Following Joe as sports editor was Neil Amdur, highly creative and with a vast knowledge of sports, under whom I continued on the path that Joe had established, and who recommended me for senior writer at the *Times*. Neil also made a great difference in my life when he suggested to executive editor Joe Lelyveld that I join the team that would produce the series "How Race Is Lived in America." I wrote the 8,000-word story that began on the front page of a Sunday edition—the lone sports-related article in the fifteen-part series—about the white quarterback, Marcus Jacoby, at the historically black Southern University and subsequently shared in the 2001 Pulitzer Prize for national reporting that was awarded to the *Times* for the series.

Other editors at the two organizations that I worked for and whose invisible but invaluable input are in the collected pieces in this volume include the *Times*, deputy sports editors at various times Sandy Bailey, Bill Brink, Lawrie Mifflin, Arthur Pincus, and Rich Rosenbush. Other truly significant editors on the desks at both organizations were Jill Agostino, Harold Claasen, Bob Cochnar, Alan Finder, Joyce Gabriel, Ernestine Guglielmo, David Hendin, Geoge Kaplan, Hana Umlauf Lane, John Lane, Ralph Novak, and Mike Sisak. And a squeeze to Dolly, who one day some years ago said yes to my proposal of marriage. I've never had a better day.

—